Nirvana
FAQ

Series Editor: Robert Rodriguez

Nirvana FAQ

All That's Left to Know About the Most Important Band of the 1990s

John D. Luerssen

Backbeat Books

An Imprint of Hal Leonard Corporation

Published in 2014 by Backbeat Books
An Imprint of Hal Leonard Corporation
7777 West Bluemound Road
Milwaukee, WI 53213

Trade Book Division Editorial Offices
33 Plymouth St., Montclair, NJ 07042

The FAQ series was conceived by Robert Rodriguez and developed with Stuart Shea.

Printed in the United States of America

Book design by Snow Creative Services

Library of Congress Cataloging-in-Publication Data

Luerssen, John D., author.
    Nirvana FAQ : all that's left to know about the most important band of the 1990s
/ John D. Luerssen.
        pages cm
    Includes bibliographical references and index.
    ISBN 978-1-61713-450-0
1. Nirvana (Musical group) 2. Rock musicians–United States–Biography. I. Title. II.
Title: Nirvana frequently asked questions.
    ML421.N57L84 2014
    782.42166092'2–dc23
    [B]
                                                                                            2014003409

www.backbeatbooks.com

For Heidi, Meredith, Hayley, and Jack

Contents

Foreword
Another Curt

When people suggest to me that my band and my songs had some kind of significant influence over Kurt Cobain and Nirvana, I have to wonder. I really just think Kurt liked my music. I can't imagine the Meat Puppets really having that big of an impact. I mean, I'm influenced by people, too. Everybody who plays music is. And none of us are that fuckin' original, really. It's just you have that voice or talent or whatever.

I never heard a lot of the Meat Puppets sound in Nirvana's music, but I always thought some of the songwriting was really clever. The tunes were a little bit traditional, but there was always a little bit of a spin on them that made them distinctly Kurt's own. That's something that I've kind of always been a proponent of, while—of course—being cautious not to be entirely derivative.

Honestly, I think I'm pretty minor. I think Kurt had plenty of motivations. He was probably really into Kiss and the Beatles, and we all know he loved the Melvins. And I always heard a lot of Black Flag. So it makes sense to me that he supposedly sent his early demos to SST Records.

Most people who are familiar with the Meat Puppets know that we were influenced by the Grateful Dead. We weren't a jam band in the classic sense, but their music spoke to us. Even when my brother Cris and I were playing hardcore punk music, we loved the Grateful Dead. So, if Nirvana was as influenced by us as some say, then they were indirectly influenced by the Dead—the ultimate hippie band.

The Meat Puppets stuff that Nirvana covered on *MTV Unplugged* was pretty much just a kind of folk music anyway. The guys at SST—Chuck Dukowski and Greg Ginn, who were in Black Flag—listened to the Dead when they were younger. We were on SST Records at the time, and I can remember when they started getting into it again. It began to influence Black Flag toward the end, and later, when Greg was doing Gone, he was way into jamming.

We did a bunch of tours with Black Flag, but that tour in 1984 when they released *My War* was the longest. At that point, they would go see the Dead whenever they could. Henry Rollins would, too. I know for a fact that Henry loved 'em.

Moving ahead to the summer of 1993, Nirvana's management at Gold Mountain—which was also our management—got in touch with us and asked us to go out on tour with them. They were about to put out *In Utero*. And that's how we met them. I hadn't known them at all before then, but I liked what they were doing.

The follow-up to *Nevermind* was a hectic period for them. Nirvana had moved into arenas, kind of against their will. We had played some larger places by then, mostly opening for people and doing festivals, and we were comfortable playing those kinds of venues. They were good guys. Kurt and Dave and Krist were all really easy to get along with, and we kind of became pals. It was a lot of fun.

It's always nice to have people that you admire be into your songs. And I thought it was a really cool idea to put different bands like ours and the Boredoms—a cool Japanese punk band—with a comedian like Bobcat Goldthwait. I really respected how Nirvana took matters into their own hands and just did what they wanted to do.

Novoselic was probably the most accessible and the most affable right off the bat. He and I became good buddies. Years later, we worked together in a band called Eyes Adrift. During the tour, we'd hang out in each other's hotel rooms or go get coffee and chat. We weren't big museum guys or anything. Besides, it was a bus tour—you're getting hauled around, and you're either at the hotel or at the venue.

I watched Nirvana play every night. I remember at one Halloween show—in Ohio, I think—they played in costume. Kurt was dressed as Barney the Dinosaur, Pat Smear was Slash, Grohl was a mummy, and Krist pretended to be someone famous—Ted Danson, maybe.

I can't remember if we jammed onstage. Maybe we did, but I don't remember it. I think I would remember that. That would have been killer. I jammed with the Foo Fighters one time after Kurt was gone, and that was fun. Eddie Vedder was out touring with the Foo Fighters and Mike Watt. Eddie and I had played together on "Big Train" [a song from Watt's 1995 solo album *Ball Hog or Tugboat*], so we did that as a jam. I don't remember doing a jam with Nirvana on that tour, but it might have happened.

Midway through the *In Utero* tour, Kurt told me that they were going to go up to New York to do an episode of *MTV Unplugged*. He told me that Nirvana wanted to cover three of our songs—"Plateau," "Oh Me," and "Lake of Fire"— but they were having trouble figuring out how to play them exactly. That was the kind of lead-in to Kurt asking my brother Cris and I, "Would you guys want to come and play the guitars?" And we were like, "OK!"

Even though we were honored to be a part of it, the whole thing was pretty grassroots. Those guys were really unpretentious and still sort of befuddled by their huge fame. That kind of success does sort of create a "gods" effect, but they were really easygoing. For what they wanted to do, it made sense, and up until then, I hadn't really paid that much attention to what *Unplugged* was, but we always liked playing acoustically, so we thought it was a great idea.

I've heard it suggested that the songs of mine Kurt picked to play were selected because they were a challenge for him to sing. I don't really know about that, because I just have those two registers I can sing in: I can sing in my normal talking voice or I can sing like Alfalfa from *The Little Rascals*. Back on *Meat Puppets II*, which was where those songs came from, I was kind of using my Alfalfa voice. I was kind of pitchy, and I really hadn't a clue about proper vocals. It was kind of a weird-ass record for the time. With that said, Kurt didn't just pull it off—he did an amazing job. He actually tagged the notes and had a "lost boy" sort of warble going on.

I remember we practiced for about a week or so up in New Jersey at a rented space in Weehawken. We were in there every day for quite a bit of time. But it wasn't like we would go over and over the stuff. They would play their songs, and then we would do our little bit. It was never really that "together" until we did *Unplugged*.

The overall vibe was similar to how the Meat Puppets have always operated. They were like, "We know these songs and it will work out." And once the cameras were rolling, that was a real show. It wasn't like a bunch of takes—we played straight through. And it was pretty amazing. Our band had done some television, like Conan O'Brien, but nothing like that.

During rehearsals, we jammed on Lynyrd Skynrd's "Sweet Home Alabama." There was never any plan to put it in the show—it was just for fun. I know Novoselic loves the Rolling Stones. That's probably his favorite band. And they were all into classic rock to a degree.

In March 1994, we were supposed to tour again with Nirvana in Europe. We flew to Germany to find out the shows were canceled. Kurt had overdosed. It sounded pretty bad.

There was such a weird feeling during *Unplugged*. It wasn't morbid, but it was definitely like black flowers and, "Wow, where do we go from here?" There was so much pathos in the delivery of those tunes. As amazing as it was, I was concerned. There were obviously some issues there. And then, when that happened to Kurt, I was like, "Oh no. That's no good." They were in Rome, and we were supposed to hook up with them in Prague a couple days later. It was more than just being like, "Bummer. We don't get to do these shows." It was more like, "Shit. Man, this is worrisome."

When Kurt died, it was rotten. It just took the wind out of me. I didn't have any words for it, and people kept asking me about it. Later that summer, it felt bittersweet when we went out for three months with Stone Temple Pilots. It was fun. I was glad to be doing shows and trying to think positive thoughts and tend to our own little hit, "Backwater."

A number of years later, with my own band in limbo, I started doing some solo shows just for fun. I was up in Seattle, and Krist came out to see me. He asked me if I wanted to start a band. We got into it for real, and we had Bud Gaugh from Sublime playing the drums. We all got together down here in Austin and went into the studio to start jamming on some songs I had. We came up with the record really quickly, and we dug it and liked each other a lot, but at the time, Krist really wanted to be in politics and was fed up with the music business in general. I talked him into doing an album on an indie label. We had offers on a bunch of different major labels, but we just didn't want to go through the scrutiny again in the light of Nirvana and Sublime, who had dealt with their own tragedy following the death of Bradley Nowell. So we did it on an indie, which was going back a few steps. We toured the United States and had a tour set up in Europe, but Krist decided he didn't want to do it after all, and that was that.

Not long ago, the Meat Puppets did some shows with Soundgarden, and I know Novoselic was talking about coming out to see our show at the Gorge. I know he and Kim Thayil are still close. But we didn't connect, and we haven't talked in a while.

When I look back on our affiliation with Nirvana's tours and *MTV Unplugged* album, I still feel like it's a blessing. It was a totally beautiful experience. I've never had any bad feelings about it at all. It was an amazing time and an amazing experience. Things like that don't happen very often, and people definitely dwell on it. For me, it's such a small part of who I am and what I've done. I just got caught up in something that got very big.

Curt Kirkwood of the Meat Puppets
As told to the author
September 7, 2012

Acknowledgments

T his book would not be possible without the support of my loving wife, Heidi Luerssen, and our great kids, Meredith, Hayley, and Jack. None of them particularly love Nirvana, but the fact that they have tolerance of my musical tastes is always appreciated.

Curt Kirkwood provided a great foreword. And, of course, this book would not be necessary without the musical revolution Nirvana ushered in back in 1991.

Special thanks go out to John Cerullo, Robert Rodriguez, Bernadette Malavarca, Wes Seeley, Mary Vandenberg, Jaime Nelson, Dave and Pinky Luerssen, Liz Luerssen, David and Caitlin Everett, Ann and John Crowther, Jane, Theo, and Luke Crowther, Marie Garner, Dick, Harriet, and Jay Mercer, George Mercer, Tom Jardim and Karen Fountain, Ken and Beth Hoerle, Dennis McLaughlin and Yvette Scola, Rob and Anastasia Harrison, Scott and Noreen Singer, Stan and Marci Bandelli, Kim and Rob Hinderliter, Tasneem Carey, Louis Cowell, Michelle Weintraub, Joanne and Stu Turner, Jose and Donna Rios, Marc McCabe, Jim and Monica Gildea, Doug and Dawn Heintz, Bill Cort, Jennifer Luerssen and Andrew Tavis, James, Jamie, and Andrew Luerssen, Doug and Karen Luka, Dave Urbano, Angelo Deodato, Jeffrey Schneider, Dan Yemin, Nick Catania, John Kieltyka, Chrissy Bradley, Ben Forgash, Kevin Houlihan, Tim Dodd and everyone at WCBS-TV, Paul Cavalconte, Tim Glynn, Mary Glynn Fisher, Bill Garbarini, Mary Jane and Ray Aklonis, Jason Karian, Mike McGonigal, Melissa Olund, Bill Crandall, Lauren Musacchio, Lauren Taitz and Mike Spinella and everyone at *Rolling Stone* and Wenner Media.

Introduction
Bring Your Friends

Before hearing Nirvana, I had always veered toward punk, post-punk, and the contagious, poppier side of alternative rock. My favorite albums were *Never Mind the Bollocks, Here's the Sex Pistols, London Calling* by the Clash, *Armed Forces* by Elvis Costello & the Attractions, and the Replacements' *Pleased to Meet Me.*

In the summer of 1989, my favorite bands were the Stone Roses and the Pixies. With the latter group, I had liked *Surfer Rosa*'s unique hooks and raw production, but the sheen of *Doolittle*—which dropped that spring—had me at hello.

I was pulling new records to needle-drop at my college radio station on the campus of West Chester University that fall when I first uncovered *Bleach*. I'd like to say that everything changed instantly for me, but it didn't.

Nirvana's first album was unlike most of the records serviced to college radio at the time. It was much cruder than, say, Sonic Youth's artful *Daydream Nation*, less sophisticated than Fugazi's first two EPs, and not nearly as immediate as Dinosaur Jr.'s "Freak Scene." I liked "Floyd the Barber," though, and began playing it during my air shifts. I soon identified "About a Girl" as being equally radio-worthy. But, honestly, the record didn't captivate me all that much, and within a month or two, I lost interest.

A year and a half later, I was working as an intern at Advanced Alternative Media, an independent music-promotion and artist-management outfit in Manhattan. Although I had already graduated, I had delusions that an unpaid internship at such a place might land me a job at a record label. While that plan failed, I remember hearing one of the staffers read aloud from *CMJ New Music Report* that Nirvana had just signed to Geffen for a large sum. "You mean the band that does 'Floyd the Barber'?" I asked. Affirmative nods came back my way. "Huh," I thought.

I didn't give the band another thought until September 1991, when I went to the mail slot on the front porch of my parents' house. As a sporadic music writer back then, I had managed to convince a number of record-label publicists to keep sending me review copies of their latest releases. Waiting for me among a bunch of other new releases that day was a package from DGC that included promotional copies of an album by an L.A. band the Nymphs and *Nevermind*. Without haste, I put the Nirvana CD into the player and—with my windows wide open—shared it with the rest of our neighbors on Arlington Avenue.

I knew little about the band, but I remember being completely blown away by the music. As I read the group's bio and looked at the promotional photo of them sitting around some industrial yard, I was mesmerized. "Smells Like Teen Spirit" was instantly amazing, while "In Bloom," "Lithium," "Drain You," and "On a Plain" were nearly as great. From that point on, I was—like the millions of music fans who would hear *Nevermind* in the months that followed—a fan. A couple of decades later—after all the hullabaloo and tragedy—I'm pleased to reveal that hasn't changed.

John D. Luerssen

Nirvana
FAQ

Maybe Just Happy

Kurt Cobain's Childhood

Cobain Is Born

Kurt Donald Cobain was born on February 20, 1967, at Community Hospital in Aberdeen, Washington. Kurt was the first child born to Don, a twenty-one-year-old mechanic, and his nineteen-year-old high-school sweetheart Wendy.

Born with dark hair and a dark complexion, Kurt weighed seven pounds, seven and a half ounces at birth. By six months, his hair had turned completely blond; his complexion would become fair, and his eyes would become a striking blue.

Kurt's Ancestry

Donald Cobain's family, which hailed from Montesano, Washington, was of French, Scottish, and Irish descent. They could trace their lineage back to Skey Townland in County Tyrone, Ireland. Originally named Cobane, his Irish ancestors hailed from Inishatieve, a village near Pomeroy. They immigrated to Cornwall, Ontario, around 1875 before relocating to Grays Harbor County.

Wendy's family, the Fradenburgs, settled in nearby Cosmopolis and had German, Irish, and English ancestry. Her Uncle Delbert was the clan's first musical success. He was a respected Irish tenor who appeared in the 1930 motion picture *King of Jazz*.

Happy in Hoquiam

The Cobains initially set up home at 2830½ Aberdeen Avenue in nearby Hoquiam. The tiny rear house wasn't far from Derrell Thompson's Chevron station at 726 Simpson Avenue, where Donald—with his flattop hairstyle and black-framed glasses—earned his living working on cars.

Wendy Elizabeth Fradenburg—who was nicknamed "Breeze" as a teen—was an attractive blonde who became pregnant with Kurt just three weeks after her spring 1966 high-school graduation. Although Wendy had conceived her son out of wedlock, Don made an honest woman of her when the two young lovers eloped to Coeur d'Alene, Idaho, in his father Leland's car. They were married on July 31 of that year.

When they brought Kurt home in late February, Don and Wendy came to the realization that they needed a larger house. They didn't need to look far. For an extra five dollars a month, the Cobain family moved into the front house at 2830 Aberdeen Avenue proper.

The extra expense was a concern for Don, who stepped up to head mechanic at the Chevron station in 1968. For his efforts, Don earned a meager $6,000 that year, but while lack of money was a constant strain on the young couple, their son was always beautifully dressed.

Kurt was an extremely happy baby who grew into a fascinating toddler; a wonderful, optimistic child. "He got up every day with such joy that there was another day to be had," his mother told *Rolling Stone* in April 1992.

Toddler Tapes

The Fradenburg family was quite musical. Wendy's older brother Chuck played in a local band called the Beachcombers—who once released a popular local single, "Purple Peanuts" backed by "The Wheelie"—and her younger sister Mari played guitar. When the family came together, they would sing songs together.

When Kurt was a toddler, his family would participate in family jam sessions, some which led to recordings of him singing songs like the Beatles' classic "Hey Jude" and "(Theme from) *The Monkees.*" Portions of these recordings can be heard in the 1998 Nick Broomfield documentary *Kurt & Courtney*.

"He would do anything. You could just say, 'Hey Kurt, sing this!' and he would sing it," Mari Earl told *Goldmine* in 1997. Aunt Mari was also the first to put a guitar in her charismatic young nephew's hands when Kurt was aged two. As a lefty, he turned it around and began to pluck at it. It was the start of a musical bond that would last for much of his life.

Kurt's interest in music and his outgoing personality came together when he was as a toddler. He would sing to people at random when his mother took him out shopping in downtown Aberdeen. In the 1993 book *Come as You Are*, Cobain described himself to writer Michael Azerrad as "an extremely happy child" who spent a lot of time singing and screaming.

By the time he turned four, Kurt would sit at the piano and make up songs, including one about going to the park and getting candy. These impromptu creations were so instinctual and appealing that they frequently left his Aunt Mari stunned.

Boddah

Shortly after his second birthday, Kurt began to talk about a make-believe friend he named "Boddah." When Kurt got into any sort of trouble, he would blame his misdeeds on his imaginary pal.

Things got to the point that as a preschooler Kurt expected his mother to set a place for Boddah during meals. At one point, Kurt was accused of bothering the neighbor's cat, but he, of course, blamed it on his made-up friend.

Before long, Wendy had had enough of "Boddah." She expressed her frustration to Kurt's uncle Clark, who was on his way back to serve in Vietnam, and who asked his nephew if he could bring Boddah with him to keep from being lonely. It was at this time that Kurt—surprised by his uncle's request—turned to Wendy and whispered that Boddah wasn't real.

Aberdeen

The Cobains bought their own home in Aberdeen—the largest city in Grays Harbor County—in September 1969 for $7,950. Located midway between the Wishkah River and "Think of Me" Hill—named for a cigar brand that had advertised in the area decades earlier—the 1,000-square-foot, three-bedroom structure, which was built in 1923, stood at 1210 East First Street.

The modest two-story, three-bedroom home was set in a working-class part of Aberdeen eventually dubbed "felony flats" by locals. In January 1992, Cobain would describe his own family as "lower-middle-class" in an interview with *BAM*. Kurt portrayed the neighborhood as "white trash posing as middle class." But back then, before his thoughts soured on the house where he had spent the bulk of his early life, it was home.

Kim

The timing of the Cobains' house purchase was ideal, considering Wendy became pregnant with her second child in the fall of 1969. In the summer of 1970, Kurt welcomed a younger sister, Kimberly. She strongly resembled her older brother, with the same stunning blue eyes and light blonde hair.

When Don and Wendy brought Kim home from the hospital, Kurt was determined to carry his baby sister into the house. "He loved her so much," his father told Charles R. Cross in *Heavier Than Heaven*.

One Smart Kid

Kurt's intelligence was obvious to his parents early on. "It kind of scared me because he had perceptions like I've never seen a small child have," his mother told *Rolling Stone* in 1992.

At just three and a half, Kurt knew a lot about the Vietnam War, having learned about it from the evening news. He would absorb the information while he sat in front of the television, drawing in his coloring book.

"He had life figured out really young," Wendy continued. "He knew life wasn't always fair."

Robert Gray Elementary

Kurt began attending Robert Gray Elementary in September 1972. The school was just three blocks from the house on East First Street.

On his first day of school, the five-and-a-half-year-old was accompanied by his mother, but soon he would be making the journey to kindergarten on his own. Clutching his metal Snoopy lunchbox, and with a wide smile, Kurt was outgoing and bright. While most of his classmates were too afraid to have their picture taken with a bear cub another student had brought in for show-and-tell, Cobain was only too happy to pose for a photograph.

In first grade, Kurt Cobain was a happy, inquisitive student with a Snoopy lunchbox. When a bear cub was brought in for show-and-tell, he was one of the few children brave enough to pose with the animal.
Leland Cobain

A Budding Artist

Kurt already loved to draw, and his knack for art flourished in kindergarten, where he created paintings and sketches and worked with modeling clay. At this young age, he could render high-quality drawings of characters as diverse as Aquaman, the Creature from the Black Lagoon, and Mickey Mouse.

He loved to receive art supplies as gifts, and his parents, grandparents, uncles, and aunts were glad to help foster his creativity. Kurt continued to draw cartoon images like Snoopy and Disney characters such as Pluto. He displayed his finest work on his parents' refrigerator or on his bedroom walls.

"He was a sweet little boy," Cobain's kindergarten-room mother Barbara Mallow told the Aberdeen *Daily World* in 1994. "He was so talented artistically, and it was amazing what he could draw at such a young age. He drew all the time."

Iris and Leland

Kurt's paternal grandparents played a prominent role in his early life. His grandmother Iris Cobain adored her grandson, and he loved her just as much.

Iris nurtured Kurt's interest in art. She was an avid collector of the Norman Rockwell plates produced by the Franklin Mint of images originally taken from the *Saturday Evening Post*. Kurt's grandmother depicted her favorite Rockwell images in needlepoint. A print of his legendary Thanksgiving painting "Freedom from Want" hung on the wall in her Montesano trailer.

Iris had a tough life, having grown up poor after her father died at work at the Rayonier Pulp Mill, where he was asphyxiated by poisonous fumes. She was courted by Leland Cobain, who also struggled with the loss of his father as a teenager. Leland's dad was a county sheriff who was killed when his gun accidentally discharged.

Not long after, Leland enlisted in the Marines and was sent to Guadalcanal. However, his issues with alcohol and anger management affected his career in the Armed Forces, which came to an end after he beat up an officer. He was sent for a psychiatric evaluation and ultimately discharged.

When Leland returned to civilian life, he married Iris and they started a family. While their sons Donald, Gary, and James were born healthy, tragedy struck with their third child, Michael, who was born severely mentally retarded and died in an institution at age six. Leland—who had landed a job as an asphalt roller—relied on the bottle as a coping mechanism, but he was a violent drunk.

Most Fridays—his payday—Leland would come home after work intoxicated and take it out on his dependents. "He used to beat my mom," Don Cobain told Cross. "He'd beat me. He beat my grandma, and he beat Grandma's boyfriend. But that's the way it was in those days."

Leland, who had gone virtually deaf from his years of loud roadwork, had mellowed drastically by the time his grandchildren were in the picture. He was still grumpy and prone to using foul language, but that was usually the extent of his rage. He taught Kurt woodworking and marveled at his young grandson's ability to draw pictures of characters like Goofy and Donald Duck on command. "Even when he was a little kid, he could draw a picture of Mickey Mouse that looked perfect," Leland told *Melody Maker* scribe Everett True in November 1991.

The Fradenburgs

Wendy's mother Margaret Dawson "Peggy" Irving was a lifelong resident of Grays Harbor. Born in Aberdeen in 1924 to James Irving and Ada Dawson, who migrated from Britain around the turn of the twentieth century, she was raised in the family's country home in Wishkah Valley, where she attended McDermoth School and Weatherwax High School in Aberdeen.

When she was just ten, she witnessed her father stab himself in the abdomen in front of his family. The suicide attempt landed him in a Washington mental facility, where he died two months later after ripping open his stab wounds.

She went on to marry Charles T. Fradenburg, five years her senior. They eventually settled in Cosmopolis, where they raised seven children. At one point during World War II, Peggy and her sister Irene shared a home in Aberdeen while their husbands were overseas. Upon his return, Charles drove a road grader for the county, while Peggy—whose hobbies included gardening and poetry, plus dressmaking and upholstery work—raised Wendy and siblings Judy, Janis, Mari, Lisa, Chuck, and Patrick.

Despite the gruesome events of her childhood, which haunted her at times, Peggy lived a full life. She loved the singer Johnny Mathis, and especially cherished her summers with her family at Kalaloch, a resort community inside Olympic National Park alongside the Pacific Ocean. However, Charles' death from a heart attack in 1979, aged just 61, and the loss of her son Patrick in 1991, were tough blows on her and the family.

"Seasons in the Sun"

As his art progressed, Kurt's interest in music also continued to grow. His parents sought to nurture this fascination and bought him a Mickey Mouse drum set. Yet as much as he loved the kid-size kit and burned up hours at home each week mastering it, he was far more enthralled with Uncle Chuck's real drums and Aunt Mari's real electric guitar.

Kurt's developed a fixation with the pop records of the day, including "Season in the Sun," the 1974 mid-tempo chart-topper smash by Terry Jacks. The song—originally titled "Le Moribund" or "The Dying Man"—was first performed in 1961, in French, by Belgian performer Jacques Brel. Canadian Terry Jacks sold three million copies of the single in the United States alone. Nirvana, of course, covered the song, although it wasn't officially released until the 2004 boxed set *With the Lights Out*.

Speaking of boxed sets, the Cobain family had their own four LP collection of 1970s hits by Ronco, a company that rivaled K-tel Records at the time in issuing compilation albums of hit singles that were marketed through television advertising. Released in 1973, the set included tracks like Jim Croce's "Time in a Bottle," Johnny Nash's "I Can See Clearly Now," and the Looking Glass' beloved one-hit wonder "Brandy," among others.

"We grew up on power ballads," Kurt told *Melody Maker*'s Ann Scanlon in September 1991. "We grew up on AM radio, and AM radio is nothing more than melodic bullshit—the Carpenters, Tony Orlando & Dawn, stuff like that."

Yesterday and Today

Six-year-old Kurt was intrigued by his aunt and uncle's album collections as well as their grown-up instruments. But one such disc—a highly collectible pressing of the Beatles' *Yesterday and Today*—freaked out the vulnerable first grader.

The "butcher cover"—which featured the smiling Fab Four dressed in white smocks and covered with pieces of meat and decapitated baby dolls—was recalled due to widespread negative reaction after its release in June 1966. While most of the 750,000 copies of the pressing with the macabre Robert Whitaker cover—which was intended to be a commentary on the Vietnam War—were withdrawn and replaced, some survived to become valuable pieces of rock history.

Understandably, Kurt ran toward Mari clutching the LP with a frightened expression.

Financial Strain

Eight years in, Don and Wendy Cobain's shotgun marriage began to show signs of distress. Each felt underappreciated, and outside of their love for their children they had less and less in common. Money was always tight, but it got tighter in 1974, when Don switched jobs, leaving the service station behind for an office job in the logging industry at Mayr Brothers.

Don had taken a step back with the hope of moving forward, but he was only earning a base salary of $164.00 a week at a time when the US was in a recession brought on by the previous year's stock market crash and oil crisis. The timber industry did, however, provide for overtime (which never seemed to go far enough), but more work meant more stress, which led to arguments at home.

Tensions over money meant that Don would often rely on Iris and Leland to help make ends meet. But he made paying them back a priority and, in turn, Kurt's grandparents always kept a $20 bill handy in case their son and daughter-in-law needed groceries.

Strict Dad

Don's severe parenting style continued to bother Wendy as Kurt grew older. In her mind, kids would be kids, and there were effective ways to make your point without getting physical. Her specialties were sarcasm and criticism.

Because Don had been raised by the stern hand of Leland, he was of the view that being struck was simply a part of childhood. As much as Don had struggled himself with this kind of punishment as a child, when Kurt picked on his little sister or stepped out of line in any number of ways, his father served up spankings.

Another part of Don's regular routine was to poke Kurt hard. If it was more emotionally hurtful than anything else, his father's need to dominate his son soon began to have a devastating effect.

By the time he reached grade-school age, Kurt had grown afraid of his dad and started hiding out in his bedroom closet as a way to steer clear of him and the ever-increasing troubles at home. He began secretly acting out, throwing empty 7 Up cans stuffed with stones at passing police cars while hiding in the bushes.

Sibling Rivalry

As they grew older, Kurt and Kim had a pretty normal brother-sister relationship. They played together as much as they fought. The crux of their rivalry stemmed from the fact that Kurt got the bulk of the attention from his parents and grandparents. Such imbalances would make any sister—or brother, for that matter—envious.

Kurt might have been able to draw characters like Mickey Mouse and Donald Duck, but Kim learned how to mimic their voices, to the amusement of her older brother and their parents. Wendy spoke on a number of occasions of her dream that one day her offspring would land jobs at Disneyland, with Kurt drawing the characters for his sister's voiceovers.

Disneyland

Speaking of Disneyland, in March 1975, Kurt's belated eighth birthday present from Iris and Leland was a special trip to the massive park and resort in Anaheim, California. His grandparents—who were vacationing in Arizona that winter—flew him from Seattle to Yuma. Despite his age, Kurt took the airplane ride alone, meeting the elder Cobains at the airport. From there, the trio traveled by car for a two-day visit to Southern California.

Aside from seeing Mickey, Goofy, and Pluto up close and taking several turns on the Pirates of the Caribbean ride, Kurt was also taken by his grandparents to the Knotts Berry Farm amusement park and Universal Studios in Hollywood.

Broken Arm

In addition to Don's parents, Kurt and Kim's aunts and uncles often helped with babysitting. Three of Wendy's sisters lived within walking distance of the Cobains, and Gary, Don's little brother, even looked after the kids on occasion. But that stopped after Kurt—who had boundless energy—broke his right arm while roughhousing with Gary. Thankfully, his limb healed perfectly.

Ritalin

Kurt's nonstop energy caused his parents and his second-grade teacher some concern. When Wendy consulted his pediatrician, it was determined that Red Dye Number Two food coloring might have been to blame for Kurt's hyperactivity, so red M&M's were off the table for the youngster. (Two years later, in 1976, the food coloring was pulled from the market after being linked with cancer.)

When the elimination of Red Dye Number Two didn't work, Kurt's sugar intake was reduced, but that caused only a minor reduction in his energy levels. The restless child was prescribed Ritalin for a period of time, although he was never formally diagnosed with attention deficit hyperactivity disorder.

The prescription drug was later linked to addictive behavior in adulthood. Tests showed that children who used Ritalin in childhood could be susceptible to illegal drug use and abuse in later life. Years later, Kurt would explain to his wife, Courtney Love, that his desire for hard drugs had been fostered by his use of Ritalin as a boy.

Bonding over Baseball

Don Cobain was a sports enthusiast and an original fan of the short-lived Seattle Pilots baseball team who taught his son the intricacies of baseball at a young age. As a first grader, Kurt was introduced to T-ball, the initial stage of Little League, with his dad acting as his team's coach.

Young Kurt—who was quick to back the Seattle Mariners when they launched their franchise at the Kingdome in April 1977—was eager to please his dad. Although he didn't always exhibit signs that he loved the sport like his father did, he relished the time they spent together, and continued to play America's pastime well for a number of years.

For Don—who had never been as close with his own father as he would have liked—these shared activities filled a void in his own life. For Kurt it was a chance—at least initially—for some recognition from his peers, and some extended family at a time when he was emotionally fragile. In July of '77, he and his team were featured in the Aberdeen *Daily World* after they won first place in the town's Timber League.

Birthday Sounds

Aunt Mari continued to feed Kurt's desire for music, and in 1974 she gave him a blue Hawaiian slide guitar and toy amplifier for his seventh birthday. She also gave Kurt three of his very own Beatles albums when he turned eight.

Writing about the gifts in one of his notebooks in 1991, Kurt, then 24, praised his aunt. "I am forever grateful knowing that my musical development would have probably gone into a hole if I had to soak up one more year of the Carpenters and Olivia Newton-John," he wrote, in an entry later published in the 2002 volume *Journals*. He also conveyed the disappointment he felt in 1976 when he found out that the Beatles had broken up six years earlier.

Daredevil

As a third-grader, Cobain began to envision life as a stuntman—something he says was inspired by the success of Evel Kneivel. "I took all my bedding and pillows out of our house, and put it on the deck, and got up on top of the roof, and would jump off [on my bike]," Cobain told Australia's Triple J radio. He also relayed a story of how he once took a thin piece of metal and duct-taped it to his chest before putting firecrackers on it and lighting them on fire.

The Divorce

Midway through 1974, Don and Wendy Cobain's marriage began to show signs of trouble. Throughout 1975, things became increasingly strained. Just days after Kurt's ninth birthday, Wendy told Don that she wanted a divorce.

Don struggled with the fact that his marriage had come to an end. For months he told Kurt and Kim that he and Wendy were separating, and he prayed for reconciliation. Because of this, Don rented a room by the week in Hoquiam, beginning on March 1, 1976, with the hope that his family would be whole once again.

It was not to be. Don was served with divorce papers later that month. He avoided reading the documents, let alone signing them. Finally, on July 9, Donald Cobain was held in default for failing to respond to his wife's petitions.

A divorce settlement went through that month, just after America's Bicentennial, with Wendy keeping her prized 1968 Camaro. She also kept possession of the home and custody of the kids. Don held onto his 1965 Ford pickup and was given a $6,500 lien against their home in Aberdeen, which would be payable whenever the home was sold or Wendy remarried. He was ordered to pay $300 a month in child support ($150 per child). He would also be required to pay for medical and dental expenses, and was granted what the courts called "reasonable visitation."

The divorce devastated Kurt, who turned inward. Noticeable shifts in his personality became evident. In June of '76, the once happy and upbeat Kurt purportedly took to his bedroom wall to express his sadness, frustration, and overall pain. "I hate Mom, I hate Dad," he wrote. "Dad hates Mom, Mom hates Dad. It simply makes you want to be so sad."

"It just destroyed his life," his mother would admit to *Rolling Stone* in 1992. "I think he was ashamed . . . He just held everything [in]." In that interview, Wendy believed that her son, then twenty-five, was still suffering from the impact of his parents' breakup.

"He was a happy-go-lucky kid," Kurt's uncle, Jim Cobain, told the *Daily World* in May 1994. "And then he changed from the divorce. He became kind of introverted and into himself."

Perhaps Kurt put it best in an interview with Jon Savage for *Howl* in 1993. "I couldn't face some of my friends at school anymore, because I desperately wanted to have the classic, you know, typical family," he explained. "Mother, father. I wanted that security, so I resented my parents for quite a few years because of that."

Stomach Problems

Like many young children of divorce, Kurt believed that he was—at least in part—to blame for the dissolution of his parents' marriage. Of course, this wasn't the case, but the torment and sorrow he felt from their split caused him to internalize his feelings, which soon affected him physically and resulted in a stomach condition.

Kurt was hospitalized at one point in 1976. At first it was believed that he wasn't eating enough, which led the doctors to give him barium and X-ray his stomach to test for cancer and ulcers.

Malnutrition was evident, but the stress from his home life is what kept him from eating. Off and on, anxiety would plague Cobain. And, as is well documented, he would suffer from stomachaches for the rest of his life.

Living with Don

In the hope of diverting some of her son's attention away from the pain he was feeling, Wendy allowed Kurt to keep a black kitten that he had found wandering around the neighborhood. The nine-year-old Kurt loved his pet, and spent much of the summer of 1976 looking after the animal, which he named "Puff."

In August, Kurt asked to live with his dad, and Wendy, seeing how her son had been affected by the divorce, agreed. At the time, Don was staying temporarily with his parents in their double-wide trailer in Montesano, but that fall, the Cobain men rented a trailer of their own, across the street from Leland and Iris.

In doing so, Kurt left his cat behind, but he would see the animal often as he visited with his mother. Unfortunately, without Cobain around to regularly look after Puff, the cat eventually ran away.

Fitting In

Kurt also began attending Beacon Elementary School in Montesano that year. To his teacher, Sheryl Nelson, he seemed like a sweet but confused little boy. "He had put up a wall," she explained to the *Daily World*. "He didn't get nasty or loud. He sort of turned off." Kurt would lose himself in his drawings, but his artwork was one of the ways he made an impression on his peers.

Much to his surprise, the blond-haired, blue-eyed fourth-grader found a popularity that he hadn't experienced in Aberdeen. This status gave him a much-needed confidence, which was bolstered by the fact that he had his grandmother's undivided attention while she looked after him each afternoon until Don got off work. From there, he and Don would spend hours together involved in sports.

Don's guilt over the split with Wendy resulted in him spoiling his little buddy. He gave his son a Yamaha Enduro-80 mini-bike, which only upped the boy's coolness factor in the neighborhood. Kurt began to bury much of the anguish he felt about the divorce deep inside. Outwardly, he was all smiles.

By fifth grade, Kurt's good looks, intelligence, and unmistakable mini-bike defined him as one of the coolest kids in "Monte." Many of the girls were attracted to him. Among the fifteen or so kids who would hang out together, Kurt was king.

Turning On

By the time he was ten, Kurt enjoyed visiting his aunt Mari, who had begun to allow him to try out her music equipment. She kept her guitars and amplifier and other assorted musical equipment in her dining room, when she wasn't setting up for gigs, because it allowed her to rehearse.

"He started asking if he could turn on the equipment, play my guitar, and sit behind the microphone," she later told Gillian Gaar. "I don't have any vivid memory of what he sounded like, but I remember him being very careful not to damage the equipment. He respected it."

Columbia House

Aside from the Beatles records he already treasured, and the Top 40 radio he continued to absorb throughout fourth grade, Kurt's musical curiosity grew. Like many boys his age, he began delving into the top hard-rock acts of the era.

A friend had talked Don into subscribing to the Columbia House Record and Tape Club in the fall of '76. As records showed up at the trailer every few weeks, Kurt was exposed to the likes of Led Zeppelin, Kiss, and Black Sabbath, and amassed a sizable album collection by 1977.

The Promise

In October 1977, Don Cobain began dating. Kurt had been finally feeling secure again under his dad's roof, but now Don's activities made him uncomfortable. He feared losing Don to another woman, and went so far as to make his father promise he wouldn't remarry. Don gave his son his word, and vowed they would always be together.

Two months later, however, Don met Jenny Westby, a divorcee with two children of her own. They began dating, and outings with the children were planned. Kurt liked Westby and got along well with her children. Mindy was a year behind Kurt in school, while James was just five at the time.

Don and Jenny were married in 1978, and the two families became one, with all five of them residing in the trailer Don had rented a year and a half earlier. At first, Kurt adored his stepmother, but he soon began to struggle with feelings of guilt. He wondered if he was betraying his own mom, Wendy—who he would regularly visit on weekends—by getting too close to Jenny.

Kurt lashed out at his dad for remarrying, which became a recurring topic as he withdrew. He began to take aim at his stepsister, mimicking her and saying hurtful things about her unfortunate overbite.

Fleet Street

Don Cobain thought that things might improve if the family had more space, and if Kurt had his own room. And when Jenny learned she was pregnant in the spring of '78, there was little choice but to find a bigger home.

Don was right. Perhaps it was the change of scenery, but as the family moved into an actual house at 413 Fleet Street South in Montesano, the emotional environment was much better for all concerned.

In addition to the privacy of own bedroom, Kurt was elated to have a baby brother after Chad Cobain was born in January 1979. Turning twelve, Kurt wandered the streets of small town Montesano without supervision. He could vanish for hours, exploring the town from top to bottom, either on foot or, more likely, on his bicycle.

Visitation Aggravation

As much as Kurt tried to have a normal life, the agonies of divorce were evident whenever his parents tried to get together to plot out their visitation schedules. Holiday schedules were difficult to orchestrate, with both sides disagreeing about when and where Kurt and Kim should be shuttled.

There was almost always bad blood whenever Don and Wendy spoke. As a result, Kurt loathed returning to Aberdeen. Things became so heated that after one fight over child support, Wendy—who had since began working as a clerk at Pearson's, a department store in Aberdeen—insisted that Kim would no longer be allowed to go on camping trips with her father and his new stepfamily.

Being Frank

While Don settled into a comfortable second marriage, Wendy began a lengthy, tumultuous relationship with a longshoreman named Frank Franich. It wasn't long before Kurt, now a fifth-grader, developed a serious dislike of his mom's boyfriend, who had moved into her home in Aberdeen.

Cobain viewed Franich as a bad influence on his mother, who started drinking heavily and often. Wendy was already opinionated, and alcohol only intensified this trait. That, coupled with Frank's intolerant mindset and violent tendencies, regularly resulted in some devastating outcomes. It got so bad at one point that Franich broke Wendy's arm. Unfortunately, Kim, who lived with them and was most exposed to the dysfunction, saw the whole tragic thing unfold. But despite concerns from her side of the family that things would only get worse, Wendy stayed with Frank upon her discharge from the hospital.

Wendy refused to press charges, and she and Frank made up. As bad as their fighting was, Franich made a good living, and he helped her make ends meet. Of course, the fighting continued, and it broke Kurt's heart to see his mother on the receiving end of Franich's abuse. Much to the disappointment of both of her children, Wendy and Frank would stay together for four or five years.

Hurting Kurt

By the time Kurt was in sixth grade, he had become an attitudinal pubescent. He mouthed off to his parents and their respective significant others and began to act out in other ways—even bullying another boy at school to the point where his behavior was confronted.

At the urging of school officials, Kurt's parents sought professional help for their son. But when his parents disdain for one another kept them from being in the same room with Kurt for family counseling, the therapist was quick to suggest that the boy needed to be in the sole custody of either his mother or his father.

Don and Jenny stepped up and agreed to raise Kurt together, while despite efforts to gain legal custody, Wendy and her ex-husband struggled to come to terms. Finally, on June 18, 1979, Donald was granted legal guardianship over his son.

Cobain playing drums as an eighth-grader in the Montesano Junior-Senior High School band.

MHS Yearbook, 1981

Playing in the Band

Kurt entered Montesano Junior High School as a seventh grader in the fall of 1979. Although he knew that playing in the school band was unhip, he loved music, and he was secretly thrilled to play the drums. He mastered the snare and bass drum, learning '60s hits like the Champs' Latin-flavored "Tequila" and the Kingsmen's "Louie Louie"—songs that by then had morphed into marching-band favorites.

Meatball of the Month

Pictures of Cobain in his school yearbook depicted a handsome twelve-year-old in the attire of the day—jeans, Lacoste rugby shirts, and Nike sneakers. Kurt's popularity continued at this stage, and he was even featured in the MJHS weekly student newspaper, the *Puppy Press*. For the Halloween 1979 edition, Kurt drew a picture of a trick-or-treat bulldog for the paper.

Inside the mimeographed publication, his profile—under the banner "Meatball of the Month"—revealed that Kurt was a big fan of Meatloaf at the time. His favorite song was "Don't Bring Me Down," the contagious smash by the Electric Light Orchestra. He also disclosed he was a fan of the TV show *Taxi* and Burt Reynolds' movies. His ultimate meal was pizza with Coca-Cola.

Wrestling for Kanno

Although Kurt was smaller than a lot of his schoolmates, he was scrappy and full of energy, which he used to his advantage when he joined the MJHS wrestling squad that winter. A delighted Don religiously attended every match to root for his son.

But there was an underlying reason why Kurt chose to participate in the team sport. The coach was his art teacher, Kenichi Kanno, a man who saw Cobain's artistic potential and encouraged him creatively as much as he did athletically. Kurt was motivated by his teacher's interest in his artistic side, and with Kenichi looking on, he tried his hardest when he got on the mat.

Not Just a Normal Kid

Kurt may have been a little moodier and more artistic than his peers in seventh and eighth grade, but he seemed pretty normal to those who played ball games with him in the neighborhood after school and on the weekends. Mike Lunceford, who played Little League baseball with Cobain, told the *Daily World* in 1994 that Kurt seemed "kind of reserved," adding, "It seems like he had a normal amount of friends."

Another Montesano classmate, Scott Cokely, explained to the Aberdeen newspaper that Kurt was picked on occasionally because he was small. Despite being kind of quiet, Cokely remembered that Cobain "had a sense of humor, too," and was often sarcastic.

While one friend, John Herzog, told the newspaper that he remembered Kurt as "just a normal kid," others saw him differently. At this age, Cobain became aware that he was different than a lot of his classmates. As Cokely recalled, "I felt that, too. You're not a jock, and you're not a scholar."

Kurt would eventually figure out why he had started to alienate himself from certain kids at school. "I obviously didn't relate to them," Kurt told *BAM*'s Jerry McCulley in January 1992, "because they didn't appreciate anything artistic or cultural."

Drawing Vaginas

Kurt's artistic focus throughout seventh grade kept him from focusing intently on his studies. He would sit in class and doodle detailed pictures of guitars, cars, and other objects. Once he mastered these things, he moved on to his own imaginative drawings of Satan.

Kurt also began to craft his own cartoonish pornography, which he proudly showed off to his classmates. Speaking to Charles Cross, fellow student Bill Burghardt remembered Kurt drawing "a totally realistic picture of a vagina. I asked him, 'What's that?' and he laughed."

Like most boys his age, Kurt had become interested in photos of naked women, and now—after sharing copies of *Playboy* and *Penthouse* with friends—had taken his interest to the next logical level.

Scoliosis Scare

In the spring of 1980, the Montesano Junior High nurse called to report that Kurt was at risk for scoliosis. Although Don and Jenny arranged for a doctor's evaluation, which determined he didn't in fact have curvature of the spine, Wendy misunderstood the physician's evaluation on the basis of information communicated to her through her son. Looking at the length of his arms in comparison to the rest of his torso, she wasn't convinced.

Evidently Kurt wasn't either, as he would later tell Jon Savage in 1993 that he had been diagnosed with "minor scoliosis in junior high," and that he still suffered from it. Despite having, as he put it, "back pain all the time," he insisted that it "really adds pain to [Nirvana's] music. It really does. I'm kind of grateful for it."

TV Junkie

Despite the objections of his father and stepmother, Kurt watched innumerable hours of television, including everything from cartoons and syndicated reruns of 1960s and '70s shows to NBC's *Saturday Night Live*. When his parents tried to restrict his viewing hours, Kurt would protest until they gave in. When that didn't work, he'd walk the block to his good friend Rod Marsh's house to get his fill.

Life with Don and Jenny

If Jenny tried her hardest to treat Kurt like one of her own, her stepson didn't always see it that way. He complained to friends—and to grandparents Leland and Iris—about her rigidity, especially the restrictions she placed on how much Pepsi he could drink, and the fact that his father always sided with her. Don Cobain later admitted this to Charles Cross, explaining that he worried about how his son's difficult personality might affect his marriage. Things were getting to the point where his son's behavior was jeopardizing his relationship with Jenny, and Don didn't want to lose her.

As troublesome as Kurt could be, he loved his baby half-brother Chad. He had a love-hate relationship with Mindy, and he even stuck up for his step-brother. When James, who was the batboy on one of Kurt's baseball teams, was hit by another boy, Kurt stood up to the bully. James looked up to Kurt and was influenced by his fondness for movies like the 1977 blockbuster *Close Encounters of the Third Kind*.

Writing Songs

Kurt first attempted writing his own songs—specifically lyrics and melody—soon after he turned thirteen. Although he didn't have his own proper guitar at this stage, just an awkward wooden Hawaiian lap guitar of his dad's, he would formulate ideas. When he got to his aunt Mari's dining room, he would plug in, and his own tunes came to life.

Bands like Blondie and Devo were high on the charts, and it soon became apparent to Cobain that his musical ideas could be just as valid as those that made it to the market. He read about groups like the Clash and Ramones in *Creem* magazine, and although he hadn't heard much of their music yet, he was curious about punk because it seemed to be more about attitude than technique.

As for his lyrics, Cobain told *Howl* in 1993 that, even at this early stage, he never took them very seriously. Even then, he said, he wasn't looking to tell stories in his poems, telling the publication, "It's always been abstract."

Kurt also had a strong curiosity about what made instruments work. Around this time, when his father's guitar amplifier stopped functioning, Cobain took it apart to see if he could fix it. Such skills would come in handy as his interest in music grew.

Kurt's Claymation

Alongside his drawings, Kurt had a strong interest in other visual arts. By the time he was in eighth grade, he began to make his own "Claymation" shorts on a Super-8 camera Don had obtained. He made a movie that showed aliens—clay figures Kurt had sculpted—landing in his Montesano backyard. When he showed it to his stepbrother, telling him that their house had been invaded by extrater-restrials, nine-year-old James believed him.

Suicidal Tendencies

In 1979, Kurt's great-uncle Burle Cobain committed suicide. The sixty-six-year-old shot himself in the stomach and then in the head with a .38 pistol. His younger brother Leland discovered the body.

Two years later, Kurt spoke nonchalantly to his friend John Fields as the two fourteen-year-olds walked home from school about how he planned to commit suicide someday. "I'm going to be a superstar musician, kill myself, and go out in a flame of glory," Kurt told Fields. Cobain's adolescent friend recounted the story in *Heavier Than Heaven*, adding that he told Kurt not to say such things.

"I want to be rich and famous and kill myself like Jimi Hendrix," Kurt told John. At the time, both kids were unaware that the iconic performer behind such classics as "Purple Haze" and "Hey Joe" had died not from suicide but from an accidental overdose of sleeping pills on September 18, 1970.

According to various reports, Kurt had shared the same plan with several other friends in Montesano during their eighth-grade school year. Cobain told Rod Marsh that he had "suicide genes," citing the death of Burle and the aforementioned tragic events surrounding the suicide attempt of Wendy's maternal grandfather.

Suicide had been at the forefront of Cobain's mind that year after he, Marsh, and Bill Burghardt found the latter's older brother hanging from a tree outside an elementary school as they walked to school. Stunned at their discovery, the boys stared at the hanging corpse for approximately thirty minutes, until the authorities eventually cleared them from the scene.

Getting High

By the fall of 1980, Cobain began smoking pot, first at parties alongside another regular vice, alcohol, which could be found in any parent's unlocked liquor cabinet. Kurt rang in New Year's Eve 1981 with his friend Trevor Briggs, eventually throwing up after smoking too much marijuana.

The experience hardly discouraged him from smoking pot. The drug was easily accessible in Monte, and it was inexpensive. Marijuana gave Kurt an escape from what he felt was a mundane suburban existence, so he began smoking it regularly with friends. He also experimented with LSD.

By the time eighth grade was nearly over, Cobain was smoking marijuana more frequently. When the next school year got underway, he began cutting class to get high—or, on days when he didn't have art class, skipping school altogether.

Football, Track, and Wrestling

Despite his affinity for weed and his smaller frame, Kurt was still feeling a need for social acceptance when his freshman year at Montesano High School got underway. He even tried out for the football team late that August, and although he made the first cut, he dropped out after two weeks because he felt overwhelmed by the physical demands.

Cobain went on to join the track team, where he ran the 200-yard dash and threw the discus. Despite the fact he was a natural athlete who excelled in these areas, he began to lose interest, missing a noticeable number of practices as he began to forgo school responsibilities and extra-curricular activities in favor of his own artistic pursuits and increased recreational drug use.

Kurt continued to wrestle on the varsity squad of the Montesano Bulldogs, but his small size and growing disinterest meant that he was no longer the important contributor he had been during his time at MJHS. Just the same, his affiliation with these activities, coupled with his good looks, meant that he was still fairly well liked, even if he was less and less interested in popularity.

"I was accepted by cool people because the cheerleaders thought I was cute," Cobain told *Spin* in January 1992. "The jocks knew the jock-girls thought I was cute. I just chose not to hang around with them."

Kurt's Wrestling Story

In *Come as You Are*, Cobain relayed a story regarding the last days of his wrestling career that may or may not have been embellished, explaining how he had taken to the Bulldogs wrestling mat in one of the lower weight categories during the team's 1982 championship match. With his father cheering on the squad—which had an impressive record of twelve wins and three losses that season—Kurt said he decided to intentionally lose just to make a point. When the referee's whistle blew, he claimed, he had looked at Don—with whom he was increasingly at odds—and "instantly clammed up."

"I put my arms together and let the guy pin me," he boasted. He even insisted that during this entire defiant act, he allowed himself to be pinned a staggering four times in a row, until his dad stormed out of the gymnasium.

Later, in interviews with Charles Cross, Don—as well as other schoolmates from the era—would deny Kurt's account. Perhaps parts of the story—such as being pinned four consecutive times—were an exaggeration, but Leland Cobain would later remember in *Heavier Than Heaven* how his son had complained about the match. "That little shit just laid there," Don supposedly carped. "He wouldn't fight back."

Down to the Basement

About a month ahead of his fourteenth birthday, Cobain moved into the cellar of Don and Jenny's house. His father had renovated a basement bedroom on Fleet Street so that his teenage son could have more space to play his records, which included albums by Boston, Elton John, and Journey.

Although he enjoyed the privacy, friends from this era told Charles Cross that in some respects Kurt felt banished to the basement. Things with his dad and stepmom became tense as their son stopped participating in family activities.

Cobain was also lazy, and he routinely defied most authority. He was unwilling to perform his assigned chores and, for the most part, stopped communicating with the family except when absolutely necessary.

Overbearing Parents

Kurt's shift away from sports and conformity toward art and music didn't sit well with Don or Jenny, and although Wendy was supportive of her son's interest in art, her role in Kurt's life had diminished by this point.

Cobain opened up about the subject to *Kerrang!* in November 1993, during the *In Utero* tour. "That overbearing influence stuff is probably the only thing I resent about my parents," he said. "They tried to tried to mold me; they were convinced I was gonna be a bum because I wasn't interested in all the normal things kids are into. And that was probably the most damaging thing that happened to me while I was growing up."

Stoned in School

Cobain was happy to push the envelope. Once, in the ninth grade, he asked his friend Darrin Neathery if he wanted to go outside of the school and smoke some pot with him. "We walked right outside in front of the school behind this big Rhododendron bush," Neathery recalled in the documentary *Nirvana: The Untold Story*. "It was probably about the stupidest thing to do, and of course he gets away with it. It was ballsy. He was anti-authority."

First Electric Guitars

Chuck Fradenburg gave his nephew a choice on his fourteenth birthday: he would either buy Kurt a bicycle or an electric guitar. It was a no brainer for Kurt, who spent much of his time doodling rock stars in his notebooks. He chose a second-hand guitar from Rosevear's Music Center at 211 E. Wishkah Street in Aberdeen.

At first, Kurt wasn't quite sure how to string the used Lindell—a Japanese-made brand from the 1960s—which had been repainted and given a silver pickguard. He sought the help of his aunt, who helped him to string it over the phone. Mari reminded him that, as a lefty, Kurt would need to turn the instrument over in order to string it.

Although the guitar frequently became inoperable, Cobain taught himself to repair his unique-looking sunburst-red axe. It quickly became a part of who he was. Kurt brought it to school to show it off, and for a while he carried it with him wherever he went.

Warren Mason

Warren Mason played alongside drummer Chuck Fradenburg in the blues band Fat Chance. Because Chuck's home was also home to the weekly Fat Chance rehearsals, Kurt began attending the sessions.

Responding to Chuck's pleas—and under the influence of the marijuana, beer, and Jack Daniel's that were always in supply—Mason agreed to give Cobain guitar lessons. Kurt would pay Warren $10 an hour to teach him, under the condition that Cobain upgrade his guitar. The Lindell would need to be replaced, and Mason found him a used Ibanez for $125.

"He could already spray notes around like Jimmy Page," Mason told Christopher Sandford in his 2004 book *Kurt Cobain.*

"You could see his eyes get excited when he watched the band," Mason told the *Daily World* in 1994. Kurt was a quiet, attentive student who conquered his goal of learning Led Zeppelin's classic "Stairway to Heaven" and soon got to be a pretty good guitarist. He also learned AC/DC's "Back in Black."

Unfortunately, the rehearsals lasted just three months before Kurt's mother put an end to them after deeming his eighth-grade report card unacceptable. Wendy punished Kurt by taking from him one of the things he most loved to do.

Kurt Commits Bloody Suicide

By the time he was fifteen, Cobain had enlisted his stepbrother James to help him make a new film he called *Kurt Commits Bloody Suicide.* Young James shot the footage of Kurt simulating the act of killing himself by pretending to cut his wrists with the edges of a soda can.

Kurt utilized fake blood and other special effects to create the movie. When Don and Jenny saw the film, eerie as it was, they were more concerned about Kurt than ever.

"There was something wrong . . . something unbalanced," Jenny told Cross. The film aside, she was also disturbed by the way horrific subjects like murder and rape seemed barely to faze him.

These films did have a positive effect on James, however. Cobain's stepbrother went on to become a professional filmmaker, writing and directing independent movies like 2005's *Film Geek*, 2008's *The Auteur*, and 2011's *Rid of Me.*

Living with Iris and Leland

By March 1982, Kurt had decided that, although he wanted to remain in Monte, he could no longer live with Don and Jenny. He moved into his grandparents' trailer on the outskirts of town and took the bus to school.

It was during this time that Kurt found himself becoming close again with Iris, who was always supportive of her grandson's interests. He even related better to Leland, with whom he partnered on making a dollhouse for Iris' birthday. Even so, during his time under his grandparent's care, Kurt found himself more alone than ever.

Living with Uncle Jim

After Cobain wrapped up ninth grade, he left Montesano behind and moved in with his uncle Jim in South Aberdeen. It was a short-lived but generally positive experience for Kurt, who spent the summer with his rock music–loving, pot-smoking uncle.

Jim was only two years younger than his brother Don, but he was a very different spirit. Uncle Jim had a really nice stereo system and a ton of records by everyone from the Grateful Dead and Led Zeppelin to the Beatles. He was happy to play the stereo loud, which the fifteen-year-old Kurt loved.

During his time with Jim, his wife, and their baby daughter, Kurt worked successfully on salvaging and restoring a guitar amplifier. Unfortunately, due to the cramped living quarters, he was soon passed on to a different uncle.

Uncle Chuck

For a few weeks, Kurt couch-surfed from one Fradenburg family member to another, until he landed with his uncle Chuck, with whom he'd remain for the third quarter of 1982. It was Chuck who had given Kurt the tools to rock the previous year when he bought his nephew the Lindell guitar and helped arrange for him to get lessons, while also inviting him to hang out and show his musical stuff at band rehearsals.

But when Wendy realized it wasn't the best environment for Kurt, she pulled the plug on the arrangement, and in October '82, Kurt wound up moving home to Aberdeen to live with his mother—who had finally split for good from boyfriend Frank Franich—and his younger sister Kim.

Teenage Angst

Cobain's Teen Years

Weatherwax Outsider

Moving back in with Wendy meant transferring to Aberdeen's Weatherwax High. With a student population that tripled Montesano's, Kurt was an outsider—mostly by choice. He kept to himself, uninterested in trying to infiltrate the teenage cliques.

Although he liked getting high, Kurt didn't care for the associations with stupidity that came with being a stoner. He'd already done the "jock" and "preppy" things when he was younger. Unlike most kids his age, Kurt was all about his art and his guitar.

"I felt more and more alienated—I couldn't find friends I was compatible with at all," Cobain told *Rolling Stone* in April '92. "Everyone was eventually going to become a logger, and I knew I wanted to do something different. I wanted to be some kind of artist."

Years later, he would reveal in interviews how he used to get beaten up at Weatherwax by Aberdeen's metal-head rednecks. Kurt stuck out as a nonconformist as his sophomore year unfolded. But that's not to say that he had no friends at all. He still visited with family in Montesano most weekends, and kept connected with many of his friends there.

"Kurt was like an agate in a field of stones," Larry Smith, his uncle by marriage, wrote to the fan site Mexican Seafood in 1998. "He stood out like a sore thumb because of his singular and unique self-preservation tactics. This got him into much trouble during his teenage years. He was obviously disdained (and feared) by the 'redneck elite.'"

Cartoon Critical

Kurt's drawing abilities offered him an outlet to vent about the parental figures that left him disappointed. In one series of panels about "Jimmy, the Prairie Belt Sausage Boy," the title character takes verbal abuse from his dad, who—according to a description of the cartoon in *Heavier Than Heaven*—calls Jimmy a "lousy little creep" and scolds him for failing to live by his father's American values.

Other versions of "Jimmy" show a mother working diligently to please her man. Clearly a shot at his stepmother, the character tackles her list of errands—including pottery class, the PTA meeting, a beef stroganoff dinner, and more—before satisfying her man. "Yes, yes, mmm honey, it feels good in the ass," Cobain wrote. "Mmm, I love you."

Boingo and Beyond

By Christmas 1982, Cobain was already moving toward more artistic music. He asked for, and was given, *Nothing to Fear*, the second studio LP by Southern California new-wave band Oingo Boingo, which boasted the minor hit "Wild Sex (in the Working Class)."

Aunt Mari also bought him the album *Tadpoles*, a compilation of songs by the Bonzo Dog Doo-Dah Band from the UK television show *Do Not Adjust Your Set*, on which they were the house band. Kurt became obsessed with one song on the record, a novelty number known as "Hunting Tigers Out in Indiah," which he learned to play on guitar. He also sought out the soundtrack album to the television show *H. R. Pufnstuf*, which he had admired as a kid.

Organized Confusion

With his aunt's encouragement, Kurt made his first known demo tape of original material during a visit to her home in Seattle over Christmas 1982. He had brought with him his electric guitar, and—using her four-track recorder—he took his first step toward a future as a recording artist. He borrowed Mari's electric bass and improvised percussion by playing out beats on his mother's empty pink Samsonite suitcase. Recognizing his aunt's generosity and encouragement, Kurt was always respectful of her and extremely careful with her equipment.

Kurt called the project Organized Confusion. His aunt told *Goldmine* that his songs were very repetitious. "Most of what I remember about the songs was a lot of distortion on guitar," she explained. As for Kurt's voice, she remembered it sounding "like he was mumbling under a big fluffy comforter, with some passionate screams once in a while."

Although Kurt might ask for technical help when he got stuck with a particular approach, he was pretty secretive when it came to the final output. At that stage, Mari recalled, Cobain was guarded because "he didn't really like someone just poking fun at it." As a songwriter in her own right, she understood that, and she never pried.

There's Only One Way to Rock

Despite his increased interest in eccentric rock, Cobain was still into the mainstream sounds blasting out of Seattle's KISW-FM studios. The station's antenna may have been 109 miles away, but kids in Aberdeen could pick up the signal on clear nights. Playing the likes of Rush, Tom Petty, John Cougar, the Police, and Genesis during Kurt's sophomore year, the station gave him an opportunity to hear many of the latest commercial records of the day.

The station also regularly played Sammy Hagar, who was riding high with top rock tracks like "There's Only One Way to Rock," "Your Love Is Driving Me Crazy"—a #13 US pop hit—and the title cut from his 1982 album *Three Lock Box*.

Kurt and his friend Darrin Neathery traveled with Neathery's sister to the Seattle Center Coliseum on March 29, 1983, to see "The Red Rocker" and opening act Quarterflash, a Portland band (and Geffen labelmates of Hagar's) best known for their 1981 US #3 hit "Harden My Heart" who were currently plugging new album *Take Another Picture*.

Neathery later claimed he and Cobain consumed a six-pack of Schmidt beer in the backseat of a car en route to the show. Kurt himself remembered how he wound up wetting his pants because they were stuck in traffic and he couldn't get to a bathroom.

Cobain also divulged to journalist Everett True that he got so stoned inside the venue that he managed to set himself on fire with a Bic lighter. "I looked down and butane had spilt out everywhere and my shirt was on fire," he chuckled.

At some point during the night, Kurt bought a Hagar T-shirt at the merchandise table, which he wore to Weatherwax and around Aberdeen in the days and weeks after the concert. Within a few short months, however, Kurt would publicly abandon his appreciation of commercial rock 'n' roll.

Pee Chee

Steve Shillinger befriended Kurt in high school after he discovered Cobain was a Motörhead fan. It was there on his Pee Chee notebook, on which Kurt had drawn the band's logo in addition to a picture of the group's front man Lemmy Kilminster flipping off a Ronald McDonald statue.

"I said, 'Hey. That's awesome,'" Shillinger explained in the documentary *Nirvana: The Untold Story*. "From then on we hung out."

Maiden Voyage

For years, Cobain would tell friends and acquaintances that the first concert he ever attended was a 1984 Seattle show by American hardcore icons Black Flag. Perhaps he was embarrassed by the truth. In April 1993, Kurt came clean about his having attended an Iron Maiden concert in a large venue in the summer of 1983, but he made no mention of the Hagar show whatsoever—or the "butt rock," as he called it, that he admitted he had once loved.

"The only major arena-rock concert I went to was on the Fourth of July," he told journalist Everett True, referring to a date on the UK metal band's *World*

Piece tour. "People were shooting bottle rockets and throwing M-80s into the crowd all night."

To clarify, the Maiden gig—also at the Seattle Center Coliseum—actually took place on June 28, 1983. Kurt also traveled to the Tacoma Dome that summer to see a show by metal stalwarts Judas Priest.

Meeting the Melvins

One day in the summer of 1983, Cobain was hanging around outside the Thriftway in Montesano, doing nothing in particular, when an employee by the name of Roger "Buzz" Osborne came up to him. Buzz, the store's box-boy, gave Kurt a flyer promoting a concert to be held in the parking lot the following day.

On first impression, Buzz resembled singer Russell Hitchcock, the short, puffy-haired half of the Australian soft-rock duo Air Supply—at least according to how Kurt would later describe him. Cobain perused the handbill, which was plugging a free, live concert called the Them Festival that would feature Osborne's own band, the Melvins, who were named after one of his co-workers in the store.

The Melvins—at the time comprised of Buzz on guitar and vocals, bassist Matt Lukin, and drummer Mike Dillard—had initially seemed to fit in among the area's flannel-clad loggers, playing stoner-rock staples by Cream and Jimi Hendrix in their earliest rehearsals. But by the time they rocked the rear lot of the Thriftway, they had pretty much morphed into a hardcore punk band.

Unlike anything that had ever been seen or heard in the area, the Melvins played fast, loud, energetic rock 'n' roll. It was exhilarating to Cobain, looser, quicker, and far less technical than the Iron Maiden songs like "Run to the Hills" and "Flight of Icarus" that he had been listening to at the time.

"This was what I was looking for," he wrote in his journal about the Melvins sound. As his friends and acquaintances shouted for Def Leppard songs and stood bored and indifferent in the audience, Kurt was both entranced by the band and disgusted with his company. Suddenly he had an epiphany. As he wrote in his notebook, "I found my special purpose."

Discovering Punk

After the show, sixteen-year-old Kurt went up to Osborne, who was three years older than him, and praised the Melvins' set. He told Buzz of his own interest in music, and it wasn't long before Buzz started acting as a musical mentor to him.

"I was instantly a punk rocker," Kurt explained to *Option* in January 1992. "I asked Buzz to make me that compilation tape of punk-rock songs and got a spike haircut."

Osborne happily lent Kurt his punk records and made him mixtapes of tracks by bands like Black Flag. He also shared a book about the Sex Pistols with Kurt and lent him back issues of *Creem*. Cobain became the band's silent tag-along, devouring it all.

"It was really revolutionary to me," he told *M.E.A.T.*'s Karen Bliss in September '91. "Being exposed to music that was completely different from what I was used to before was really exciting."

Never Mind the Bollocks

The first Clash record Kurt ever heard was *Sandinista!*, the iconic British band's iffy 1980 three-LP set, which he discovered in his fourteenth year. Its convoluted experimentalism gave him a skewed opinion of punk, and he later explained how it had turned him off so badly that it kept him from getting into punk until Osborne opened his eyes to the genre.

In Cobain's opinion, *Sandinista!* was "terrible." To be fair, it lacked the immediacy of the band's first three essential studio albums. Had he first heard those, he might have thought differently of "The Only Band that Matters" and the rebellious genre in general.

When Osborne shared with him the Sex Pistols' 1977 album *Never Mind the Bollocks*, Kurt was amazed. Writing in his journal, he called the sensational, controversial foursome "a million more times important than the Clash" and heralded their one-and-only official album for having "the best production of any rock record I've ever heard. It's totally in-you-face and compressed." He identified most with the band's mouthy-but-sensitive front man Johnny Rotten, and concluded, "All the hype was totally deserved."

The Cling-Ons

If the majority of people in Montesano and Aberdeen didn't quite get what the Melvins were doing in the middle of 1983, there was still a group of a dozen or so teenage kids in the area who sought something harder and heavier than the pristinely produced metal bands that were selling out US arenas at the time.

Punk rock had an attitude and a level of sophistication and exclusivity that was missing from metal. And, upon hearing it, Kurt liked how it wasn't afraid to embrace melody. Although the Melvins were ridiculed by most of the flannel-clad kids around Grays Harbor, the band had a small pack of loyal followers, of which Cobain was one.

The "Cling-Ons," as Buzz named them, came to the band's occasional shows as well as their practices, which by 1984 were being held in a room at the rear of new drummer Dale Crover's house at 609 W. Second Street in Aberdeen. The rehearsals were a place for camaraderie among the area's teenage misfits, including Greg Hokanson (who Buzz called "Cokenson") and Kurt's friend Jesse Reed (nicknamed "Black Reed" for his fondness of Black Flag) from Weatherwax.

Cobain had received his driving license on his sixteenth birthday, which made him a good candidate to roadie for the band. With Kurt behind the wheel of the "Mel-van," as it was known, he and the other core Cling-Ons happily schlepped gear before and after shows.

It helped that Cobain had known bassist Matt Lukin—who was three years ahead of Kurt at MHS—from baseball and wrestling, and that Buzz and Dale liked him. And with Crover's practice space being just a half-mile from Wendy's home, Kurt rarely missed a rehearsal. By his own count in 1992, Kurt had witnessed over 200 Melvins practices. As he thought about getting his own band started, he studied Osborne's group carefully, making mental notes along the way.

Public Image

One of the first indications of Cobain's musical shift came when he began to spike his hair (which he had cut shorter) at the front. At the same time, he was reticent to cut it too short, resulting in a coif that was a cross between Billy Idol and Rod Stewart. In his journal, he called it "the first bi-level haircut in Montesano history."

Kurt also started wearing punk-rock T-shirts, ensuring those in his Aberdeen and Montesano neighborhoods knew he was different. In advertising his interest in underground bands, wearing the shirts also served as a means of sparking conversation with any kindred spirits or curious classmates.

Wendy's Unorthodox Mothering

Although Kurt was back in Wendy's full-time care, their relationship was tumultuous. As much as he loved his mom, they argued incessantly, and she regularly put him in an uncomfortable position.

At just thirty-five, Wendy was an attractive young mom who still had the body for the bikini she wore while sunbathing in her Aberdeen backyard. Kurt's friends gawked at her, and she was well liked by them all—especially after she agreed to buy them alcohol. On at least two known occasions, Wendy bought beer and tequila for sleepovers.

Wendy also had questionable judgment when it came to men. In one instance, she dated a twenty-two-year-old. Kurt suspected that his mom's new boyfriend was only interested in her on a physical level, and although she upheld the belief that there might be more to it, he chastised his mother until the relationship ran its course.

Despite these challenges, as an adult, Kurt would look back on his mother's commitment to him with gratitude. "My mother was a fantastic, attentive, and compassionate mother throughout my childhood, until I started becoming incorrigible and rebellious," he told *Kerrang!* in 1993. "She was eighteen when she had me, and she did a really great job. I appreciate it every day."

The Outsiders

Kurt first found himself drawn to reading after discovering the work of S. E. Hinton in junior high. Her tales of teenage struggles and alienation, told in books like *The Outsiders*, *Rumble Fish*, and *Tex*, spoke to him.

"I skipped school a lot, especially during high school, junior high, and the only place to go during the day was the library," Kurt told Jon Savage in 1993. When he was in school, he used reading as a means to avoid people. If they thought he was deep into his book, they left him alone.

Bob Hunter

If Cobain made few positive impressions at Weatherwax, he found the creative support he longed for in the school's art teacher, Bob Hunter. Hunter was quick to identify Kurt's talent and, in turn, the sixteen-year-old looked forward to his back-to-back midday art classes.

Cobain's lunch period was anchored by Hunter's basic and commercial art classes. Kurt responded well to the loose classroom setting, where kids were allowed to listen to rock music while they worked. Cobain took most of his assignments seriously, and became one of Hunter's most capable students.

In the teacher's estimation, Kurt could have gone on to be a professional artist, had he applied himself. "I saw him as the type who could have been a professional painter in New York, L.A., or Chicago," Hunter told the Associated Press in April 2004. "But even then I don't think I appreciated how sensitive he was. When I look at his lyrics now, I can see more of what went into his art."

At the time, Kurt was building toward a career as a commercial artist, and with the encouragement of his mother and Hunter—who entered his work into contests—the plan was for him to attend art school. Of course, his life took a different path.

Shock and Awe

Kurt's artwork was not without humor. In one caricature, he drew pop star Michael Jackson with one gloved hand in the air and the other on his crotch. When Hunter told him it wouldn't be appropriate to display the image in school, Kurt drew an unflattering picture of President Ronald Reagan instead.

His artwork also had a penchant to shock, as evidenced by one mind-blowing rendering of a sperm turning into an embryo. "I find it amazing that someone that age could go and do that," Hunter told *Daily World* writer Claude Iosso in May 1994. "It was totally different from anything anyone else was doing for that assignment. There's a lot more going on in this person's head."

Fellow students began talking about Kurt after he created the work for an assignment about metamorphosis in 1984. Some thought he was peculiar; a few others thought he was a visionary. Either way, his originality was undeniable.

In My Room

Despite his artistic abilities, Cobain spent most of his time in his bedroom, playing guitar. "I wasn't thriving socially," he told the University of Washington newspaper the *Daily* in May 1989. "At the time, I thought I was inventing a new sound that would change the whole outlook of music."

Aside from The Cling-Ons, with whom he spent a fair amount of time, there were fewer and fewer people with whom he could identify at Weatherwax. "In Aberdeen, I hated my best friends with a passion, because they were idiots," he continued. "A lot of that hatred is still leaking through."

First Kisses

Aside from his musical awakening, Cobain's sixteenth summer marked his first intimate encounter with a girl. Kurt had a thing for Andrea Vance, the sister of his Monte buddy Darrin Neathery. In turn, she was drawn to Cobain's eyes and his bright white smile, not to mention his soft, dirty-blond hair. One day he stopped by her babysitting job.

Cobain took things slow at first, sitting close to Andrea on the couch while watching *The Brady Bunch* and playing Rock 'Em, Sock 'Em Robots with the kids she was looking after. He came back the next day, and they smooched. For the next few days, he would stop by the house, and he and Andrea would make out. But it didn't go any further. Kurt kept his hormones under control.

Suicidal Thoughts

Kurt gave serious consideration to committing suicide in the summer of 1983. He was unhappy about the way his life was shaping up, displeased with his discordant relationship with Wendy, and unsatisfied by marijuana's inability to help him escape his problems. Although he enjoyed being destructive—he admitted to stealing alcohol and breaking store windows—he was in a deep depression.

"I decided within the next month that I'll not sit on my roof and think about jumping, but I'll actually kill myself," he explained in his private notebooks, later published as *Journals*. "And I wasn't going out of this world without actually knowing what it is like to get laid." Although he didn't follow through on his suicide plan, Kurt's fixation on losing his virginity took him to a very dark place.

Molestation Accusation

Sixteen-year-old Kurt Cobain's mind was obviously not right when he and two friends—Trevor Briggs and John Fields—followed a developmentally disabled eighteen-year-old girl home from school. Their original plan—as it had been on previous occasions that year—was to get her to let them into her house so that they could steal her parents' liquor.

For Trevor and John, that plan was left unchanged. Kurt, however, had other ideas this time about the girl he would describe in his journal as "half-retarded." She offered him Twinkies, and after he ate them, he sat on her lap. He touched her breasts and asked her to have sex with him. She agreed, and undressed before him in her bedroom. He wasn't sure of what to do, and asked her if she had ever had sex before. She revealed that she had done so, mostly with her cousin.

As badly as he wanted to lose his virginity, Kurt started to become sickened by his own behavior as he took advantage of the girl during what he called his "first sexual encounter."

"I tried to fuck her, but I didn't know how," he confessed in his notebook, elaborating on how "her vagina smelled" from either sweat or poor hygiene. "I got grossed out very heavily . . . so I left."

Kurt was so ashamed and embarrassed about the incident that he didn't attend school for an entire week. When he finally returned, he was given a full day of in-school suspension as punishment for his truancy. As he sat outside the principal's office, the girl's father came in looking for a yearbook with which to identify the individual who had messed with his daughter.

Cobain wasn't immediately identified—he had been absent on the day year-book pictures were taken—but the girl soon gave her father his name. Worried he'd be branded a "retard fucker" around town, and deeply depressed about his actions, Kurt began planning his own suicide.

Suicide Tracks

Cobain may have been a distraught sixteen-year-old, but he had clearly thought long and hard about taking his own life. Now, his plan seemed foolproof.

One night, soon after he had been identified for his transgression, he got drunk and stoned and walked down to some nearby train tracks. Placing a large piece of cement on his chest and legs, he laid on his back with his body stretched across the tracks and waited for the 11:00 p.m. train.

As the train came closer, Cobain prepared to die. But when the train approached and then passed him by, Kurt realized that he had been on the wrong track. His plan had failed.

After a few minutes, he stood up, dusted himself off, and went home. Although it took him some time to process, he eventually took what had happened as some kind of sign he should live.

Interrogated and Released

The following Monday, Kurt began his morning ritual by taking the bus to school. Wendy thought her son was going to class, but instead he disappeared into the woods adjacent to the school to drop acid. He was still feeling ashamed and despondent, and he needed an escape.

One night not long after, Cobain was stopped and interrogated by police as one of the short list of people suspected of molesting the girl. He admitted that he had been intimate with her but explained that they had never actually had intercourse, so, he said, he hadn't done anything that would violate the law.

Kurt explained to detectives that their encounter was consensual; as the girl was over eighteen, and because she was not legally classified as mentally retarded, there was nothing the officials could charge him with.

Kurt Goes Punk

The 1983–84 school year marked a significant shift in Kurt's appearance. He did away with polo shirts, replacing them with his own homemade T-shirts. In addition to paying tribute to the bands he loved, Cobain also designed his own "Organized Confusion" shirt, even though his band of that name never got off the ground.

He grew his hair longer and wore black boots or Chuck Taylor sneakers and a black trench coat. He had his Sony Walkman on at all times, listening to punk mixtapes as he strolled the hallways at Weatherwax, where he was a unique presence to some, and a freak to most others.

When Andrea Vance saw him at a party in Montesano, a number of months after they locked lips, she didn't even recognize him. With his hair dyed dark red, she told Charles Cross, "He didn't look like the same boy."

Jackie Hagara

At the outset of his junior year at Weatherwax, Kurt found himself interested in a girl named Jackie Hagara, who lived two blocks from him. She was also two years younger than him, but because Cobain was so far behind in math, they were in the same freshman math class.

If most girls in the class thought it was peculiar that this older boy was being kept back, Hagara liked his smile and his artistic side. Kurt showed her the pictures he doodled in class; one, of a rock star on a desert island, impressed her, so he rendered a poster-sized drawing of the same image, airbrushed it, and gave it to her as a gift.

Kurt would wait for Jackie at a particular spot in their neighborhood so he could walk to school with her. He eventually worked up the courage to ask her out, only to discover she had a boyfriend. Just the same, she allowed him to hold her hand, and he even kissed her, but it went no further.

The Fat Man

When Cobain wasn't playing his guitar or working on his art, much of his junior year was spent looking for a way to get wasted with his Weatherwax outsider clique, which overlapped with the Cling-Ons and included Jesse Reed, Greg

Hokanson, and the Shillinger brothers, Eric and Steve. When their parents' respective liquor cabinets became insufficient, the enterprising sixteen-year-olds made an arrangement with a questionable adult who would buy them all the beer they could drink in exchange for one quart of cheap malt.

"The Fat Man," as they called him, was an obese alcoholic who lived in an old, deteriorating building called the Morck Hotel with his retarded adult son. According to Reed, the man was in no shape to walk any distance, so they would push him to the grocery store in a shopping cart when they needed beer. First, though, they would have to help the man get dressed. Over time, Kurt began to feel compassion toward the man, and he ended up buying a toaster and a John Denver album for him at the local Goodwill store. When Cobain gave him the gifts for Christmas 1984, the beer-getter was stunned by the generosity and began to cry. From that point on, Kurt was an ace in the eyes of the Fat Man.

Cobain also used the man and his son as inspiration for the short stories, songs, and art he created. He sketched pictures of the Fat Man in his notebooks and dreamed up humorous if not outlandish imaginary escapades for the sad, downtrodden pair.

Kurt vs. Wendy

Wendy's frustration with her son's behavior had reached fever pitch by early 1984, and her criticism of him was matched by his of her. "Wendy was awful to him," Greg Hokanson said in *Heavier Than Heaven*. "He hated her."

The fact that Kurt was typically stoned or drunk when his mother started in on him didn't help. In one instance, Hokanson witnessed his friend tripping on acid while Wendy went off on him.

Wendy was often intoxicated during this era, too, and her judgment was still a major source of irritation to Kurt. Briggs recalled how, on one occasion, when he and some others were partying in Kurt's room, Wendy came upstairs, looking to join them.

This behavior irritated Kurt, and he would mention her inappropriateness in future arguments. Why she couldn't she act like a normal mom, he wondered? Didn't she understand that she had no place in his room, where weathered Iron Maiden posters covered the walls, Black Flag blasted from the boom box, cigarette tar made the walls sticky, and bong water stained the rug?

Pat O'Connor

In February 1984, Kurt's mother became involved with a longshoreman her own age named Pat O'Connor. In another exercise of questionable judgment, she soon allowed Pat—who came with a sordid past—to move into her home.

It wasn't exactly the seventeenth birthday gift Kurt had been hoping for. Neither he nor his sister Kim liked Pat. He was a heavy drinker and all-around chauvinist, but a well-paid one, according to a palimony lawsuit that made the regional news in 1984 and revealed that Pat made $52,000 a year. The ex-girlfriend who had filed the suit alleged that Pat had told her to quit her job at a Washington nuclear power plant, promising he would take care of her—but then, when she did so, he left her for Wendy, whom he married in August that year.

Pawn Star

During one highly charged incident prior to their marriage, Wendy had learned that Pat—who was drunk at the time—had been cheating on her. Kim heard her mother threatening to kill her live-in boyfriend over his infidelity. In a moment of clarity, Wendy asked her daughter to collect all of O'Connor's guns—he had several—and bring them to her in a garbage bag.

As O'Connor came through the door, Wendy told him she wanted to murder him, but she was unsuccessful in her attempts to load one of the weapons. Pat—realizing his girlfriend needed time to cool off—left for the rest of the night. Wendy worried that if she didn't get rid of the guns she might go through with killing him, and she also feared that at some point he could return and shoot her or her children.

That night, Kim and Wendy took the guns to the edge of the Wishkah River, just two blocks from their home. They dropped the bag along the banks, but the weapons were never fully submerged, and were promptly recovered by Kurt.

The next day, as Pat and Wendy made up, Kurt learned that O'Connor thought the guns were long gone. So he did as any resourceful young man might and took them to a pawnshop, putting the money he got for them toward a Fender Deluxe amplifier.

Kurt's Feminist Awakening

Because Kurt spent a lot of time in the company of women during the course of his young life, he had a respect for them that was admirable and not all that common among the redneck loggers of Aberdeen. Perhaps that was why he was so ashamed of himself after his inappropriate sexual behavior with the mentally challenged girl. He realized that his actions were way out of line.

The time he had spent with his mother and sister as a young boy, and later as a teen, coupled with his relationships with Iris and even his experiences with his stepmother and stepsister, meant that Kurt was usually sensitive to a woman's needs and feelings. But Kurt's ability to communicate with the women in his life was seen as a weakness by O'Connor, an obvious sexist and womanizer. Pat called Kurt a "pussy" and told him to act more like a man, and when he failed to see a change in his new stepson's attitude, he started calling him "faggot."

In Pat's eyes, Kurt was peculiar, because he never brought home any girls and rarely talked about them the way *he* did—as sex objects. He taunted Cobain, boasting of how he was getting laid on a regular basis at Kurt's age. Kurt finally had enough of O'Connor's insults and decided he would rise up to the challenge. He returned his focus to Jackie Hagara, with the goal of getting lucky.

Loftin

O'Connor's disapproval was exacerbated by Kurt's friendship with Myer Loftin, an openly homosexual classmate who shared his appreciation for art and Led Zeppelin. According to Christopher Sandford's Cobain biography, Loftin was referred to as "Kurt's fancy-boy" and "buttfucker" by the closed-minded at school, and by the macho community at large.

Cobain enjoyed outraging the status quo by walking arm in arm with Loftin from Weatherwax to Wendy's place. He would also enrage Pat by leering at Myer when his classmate came over for dinner. At school, Kurt told kids in the smoking section that he preferred to wear women's panties.

"I started being proud of the fact I was gay, even though I wasn't," Kurt told *Come as You Are* author Michael Azerrad. "I really enjoyed the conflict."

Just the same, Kurt—who really did prefer women, and had a prized pile of dirty magazines in his room—dropped Loftin like a bad habit one day, revealing he was getting too much static at home for being friends with the town's token young homosexual.

"Get the Fuck Out"

Responding to Pat's challenge, Kurt went out one Sunday evening in April 1984 to a party he knew Jackie Hagara would be attending. He hung around her that evening and let her know that he had strong desires for her. Midway through the night, the friend Jackie had arrived with became extremely drunk, and Kurt suggested they take her back to his house so she could sleep it off. Back at Wendy's, the friend passed out on a guest bed just outside of his bedroom.

Meanwhile, inside Kurt's room, he and Jackie started making out. They took their clothes off, and as their bodies rubbed against each other they fell into his bed. Hagara was clearly looking to initiate sex with Kurt, but before it could happen, Wendy walked in on them.

She had come upstairs to point out to Kurt that there was active lightning in the sky, not expecting to discover him in bed with a girl. As Hagara told Charles Cross, Wendy screamed for him to "Get the fuck out of my house!"

Deep down, Pat—who observed the exchange—was secretly proud of his stepson, but he held his tongue as Cobain and Hagara got dressed, woke her friend, and left. They walked out of the house and into a torrential downpour.

Virginity Lost

With Jackie's friend now coherent, the three of them walked to the other girl's house. Although Kurt still hoped to complete the act of losing his virginity with

Hagara that evening, it was not to be. He was aware that Jackie had a boyfriend who had been incarcerated, and she told him he was being released from jail that night. When the other boy showed up at her friend's place, Cobain pretended to be the other girl's beau.

After Hagara and her boyfriend took off into the night, Kurt wound up hooking up with her friend. And so, although it didn't go as planned, Cobain did lose his virginity that night.

The next day, a Monday, Kurt woke up very early in the girl's parents' house and realized he probably had no place to live. As he slipped out of the door, he felt happy to have finally had intercourse, but realized that the previous night's escapades had put his living arrangements in jeopardy.

Couch-Surfing and Squatting

After attending school that Monday, Kurt went home to Wendy's with Buzz Osborne to see if his mother had calmed down. As she threw into a tirade, however, it became immediately apparent he had crossed her line of what was acceptable. She made it extremely clear that Kurt would no longer be welcome in her house.

"His mom was just freaking out the entire time, telling him what a total fucking loser he was," Osborne explained in *Heavier Than Heaven*. Kurt collected is belongings—four garbage bags full of clothes and other personal items, plus his guitar and amp—and threw them into Osborne's van.

Like any seventeen-year-old kid in his situation, Kurt had no idea what to do next. His friends tried to comfort him, but he was broke, jobless, and flunking the eleventh grade.

At first, Kurt crashed on Dale Crover's porch, keeping warm by sleeping in a large refrigerator box. From there, he figured out he could keep warm by sleeping in apartment buildings with heated common areas. He would arrive late at night with his sleeping bag and be up in the morning before any of the tenants were any wiser.

Cobain spent time with Paul White, another boy who was in a similar predicament. They soon discovered that they could sleep in the waiting room at Grays Harbor Community Hospital. When they weren't sleeping, they would watch television without being hassled, because the hospital staff assumed they were waiting on a family member with a terminal illness. A hungry Kurt turned ever more resourceful, charging his commissary meals to nonexistent room numbers.

One place Cobain did not crash—contrary to popular belief—was under the Young Street Bridge near Wendy's house. Sure, he spent a considerable amount of time hanging out by the banks of the Wishkah, smoking pot and drinking with other kids, but his suggestion to interviewers that he actually lived there have long since been refuted by both his sister Kim and future bandmate Krist Novoselic.

Back to Don and Jenny

After spending much of the spring and summer of 1984 as a transient, Kurt made the difficult decision to move back in with his father and stepmother on Fleet Street in Montesano. Don reached out to his son after hearing that Kurt was sleeping on dusty sofa in a garage near Wendy's place.

Cobain had felt unwanted by his father for most of his teen years, and he harbored a lot of resentment toward Don and Jenny. Still, by August, he was tired of being homeless, and was looking forward to having a place to play his guitar, even though he would continue to have a turbulent relationship with his father. Even so, when Kurt retreated back to his basement room, it was understood that he was only there on a temporary basis.

Guitar Prowess

Kurt spent hours on end playing his guitar and had developed into a capable musician. Playing the instrument was therapeutic, or—as he wrote in his journal—it made him "less manically depressed."

Although he kept up his punk appearance, he absorbed music of all varieties, from the schlock pop of Air Supply to tunes from John Cougar Mellencamp's *Uh-Huh.* "He could play any song after listening to it just once," stepbrother James Cobain explained to Charles Cross.

When the family rented the iconic 1984 heavy-metal parody *This Is Spinal Tap* on video, Cobain and his stepbrother watched it several times in a row. Kurt quickly taught himself songs from the fictitious band's soundtrack album, including "Hell Hole" and "Big Bottom." Members of his family began to realize that—in addition to his art—Kurt had developed into a real talent on the guitar.

Kurt and James also recited memorable lines from the film, including "These go to eleven," a hilarious statement about specially designed Marshall amplifiers by the band's guitarist Nigel Tufnel, played by comedian Christopher Guest.

Navy Blues

As a seventeen-year-old, Kurt had little interest in school and no real desire to work. After trying to be patient—during which time Jenny even found her stepson some lawn-mowing work that he didn't care for—Don gave Kurt an ultimatum: if he didn't work or focus on his studies, he would be joining the armed forces.

Don went so far as to ask a navy recruiter to come to the house on Fleet Street. Cobain listened intently to the man's spiel and told Don he would think about it. After couch-surfing and living like a bum for a good part of the past year, the navy sounded like a place with structure, and one where he could count on a place to sleep and a regular meal.

Kurt talked it over with his friend Jesse Reed, but the negatives—he would have to follow orders, and he wouldn't be free to do as he wanted—outweighed the positives. When the recruiter came back the next night in the hope of having him sign on, Kurt told him he wasn't interested after all.

Point Taken

Kurt's uncle by marriage, Lawrence Smith, had great memories of Kurt during his teenage years. Despite his various struggles with his parents and authority, Jenny Westby's brother called Cobain "truly an amazing person" in a 1998 Internet post.

"I can't even describe what an effect this young man named Kurt had on those around him—even his detractors were at least made to think by his ability to get his point across," Smith explained.

According to Uncle Larry, the teenage Kurt was an articulate individual who could effectively make his thoughts known—"even to a raging redneck"—by tilting his head or changing the tone of his voice.

I Found God

Cobain and Jesse Reed had become inseparable since bonding over punk rock as members of the Cling-Ons. Jesse's girlfriend had broken up with him, and Kurt helped lift him out of his heartbreak. "He became like my brother," Reed told Aberdeen's *Daily World* in 1994. "The guy was so spontaneous and creative, so fresh—he picked me up through a rough time."

Jesse's home life was very different to Kurt's. The Reed family was very close-knit, steered by born-again Christian parents who attended church regularly. Because Kurt and Jesse had become the best of friends in 1984, it seemed only natural that Jesse's parents, Ethel and Dave Reed, might suggest to their son that his troubled friend start joining them for church service.

After all the recent chaos and trouble in his life, Kurt was seeking some inner peace. He started joining the Reeds at the Central Park Baptist Church, located midway between Montesano and Aberdeen, each Sunday.

In October 1984, Cobain was baptized in the church, and he became a born-again Christian. Throughout the fall of 1984, he made it known that he had accepted Jesus Christ into his life.

Life with the Reeds

In September 1984, a month prior to his baptism, Cobain was invited to move into Jesse Reed's parents' house in North River, Washington, a rural community more than ten miles outside of Aberdeen. Dave Reed—a Christian youth counselor who had played in the Beachcombers with Kurt's uncle Chuck for years—called both Don Cobain and Wendy O'Connor to discuss the idea.

Dave felt like he could make a difference by offering Kurt religion and structure. It helped that Jesse's parents had grown to love Kurt after getting to know him quite well during the previous year. With no other ideas left for their misunderstood seventeen-year-old son—plus with the boy's contempt for them—Don and Wendy agreed to let Kurt live with the Reeds.

Dave and Kurt had the run of the second floor of the Reed's massive, 4,000-square-foot home. The boys were in heaven as they played their electric guitars for hours at high volume. Jesse's father had an abundance of equipment and albums collected during his twenty years playing rock 'n' roll.

Every afternoon, after getting off the Aberdeen school bus, Kurt would play guitar for between five and seven hours. "He would just take my amp and play and play and play," Dave Reed told the *Daily World* in 1994. "He was focused like a laser beam."

Pot Sucks

Soon after his religious transformation, Kurt became hypercritical of Jesse for getting high—despite the fact he himself had been smoking pot incessantly only days earlier. In Kurt's eyes, Jesse was a bad Christian.

That fall, Kurt wrote a letter to his aunt Mari about his lifestyle change. "Pot sucks," he wrote, despite citing some of the absurd exaggerations from the 1930s film *Reefer Madness*. He also acknowledged that his own marijuana use had impacted his ability to communicate effectively with his mom, explaining how "for a while there I became almost as lethargic as a moldy piece of cheese."

Need for Weed

If Kurt had turned to religion out of trepidation and uncertainty, it was understandable, but once he felt secure again, by late '84, he had already begun to exhibit contradictory behavior. He continued to attend the Reeds' Baptist church until the end of the year, but he also returned to smoking weed regularly. He was also—as Jesse Reed told Charles Cross—"on an anti-God thing."

Giving Up

By now, Donald Cobain and his son had pretty much severed ties. Most of Don's time was occupied by his new family, and in Kurt's estimation, he had simply become "one of the last things of importance on his [father's] list."

"He just gave up," the Nirvana front man explained in an unattributed audio interview circa 1992. "I just want him to know that I don't have anything against him, but I don't want to talk to him, because I don't have anything to share with him. I'm sure that would probably really upset him, but that's just the way it is."

Black Flag

On September 25, 1984, Buzz Osborne and Matt Lukin took Kurt—plus Jesse Reed and some other Cling-Ons—to his very first punk show at the Mountaineer in Seattle. The bill was headlined by Black Flag, who were already the preeminent US hardcore band. The gig was named the second best of the year by the city's local arts weekly, the *Rocket*.

Lukin—who later became the drummer for Mudhoney—remembered how the event affected Cobain. Kurt, he recalled, was deeply moved by the aggression of slam-dancers in the circle pit, the uniqueness of the band's fans, and the presentation of vocalist Henry Rollins, guitarist Greg Ginn, bassist Kira Roessler and drummer Bill Stevenson.

"He was totally blown away," Lukin told *Rolling Stone* in 1992. But although Kurt came to worship the L.A.-area band, he had no interest in mementos. "I never wanted Henry Rollins' autograph," he told *BAM* in early '92. "I just wanted to talk to him."

3

Memoria

Krist Novoselic's Childhood

Krist Is Born

K rist Anthony Novoselic was born on May 16, 1965, in Compton, California. The firstborn son of Croatian immigrants Krist (originally spelled Krste) and Maria (originally Marija), the future Nirvana bassist and co-founder lived with his parents in an apartment in nearby Gardena, California, for the first few years of his life. When his brother Robert was born in 1968, they relocated to a modest home in San Pedro—the port district of Los Angeles—before eventually moving into a bigger house when his sister Diana was born in 1973.

New Villager

According to Krist, Novoselic is an unusual name among Croatian, Serbo-Croatian, and Slavic people. The literal translation of it is "new villager." His father's family originated from the village of Iz, part of a group of islands off the Adriatic Coast in Dalmatia, not far from the city of Zadar. His mother hailed from the village of Prizlaka, north of Zadar.

Settling in San Pedro

Novoselic Sr. was born in 1935 and left Yugoslavia in the mid-1950s, having trained as a machinist. He was held in Udine, Italy, for six months before officials granted him passage to the United States. However, his release was further delayed due to an influx of Hungarian refugees who were fleeing Soviet control. During this transition, German, Dutch, and Belgian companies came to the camp to recruit new employees. Kristo, as he was now known, signed on to work on a tugboat on the Rhine. For six years, he was based in Köln, Germany.

In the early 1960s, Mr. Novoselic made it to the United States, first settling on the East Coast before traveling to the Los Angeles area, where a new community of Croatians had begun to establish itself. He found work delivering the Sparklets brand of bottled water and soon met Maria, who had just emigrated from Yugoslavia to San Pedro and was working as a hairdresser.

Ironically, Kristo and Maria had never met prior to their respective arrivals in California, but their fathers were both fisherman who had come to know one another through their work at sea. After a short courtship, Kristo and Maria were married in 1964.

Bilingual Boy

In the Novoselic household, English was the family's second language, and Croatian was regularly spoken. When he began attending kindergarten, Krist had to work hard to master English, which ultimately became his primary language.

Novoselic Anglicized his name to "Chris" in an effort to fit in with his American classmates at the Leland Street School in San Pedro, which was just two blocks from his home at 1126 W. 23rd Street. Although he was only five, Novoselic would later vividly remember his kindergarten teacher, Mrs. Boneto, and how she was mourning the loss of her son, who was killed in Vietnam.

Accordion

As a child, Novoselic began taking accordion lessons from a teacher in San Pedro after finding out that his friend Silvio was learning the instrument. Later, when he discovered rock 'n' roll was the music for him, he abandoned the accordion for the guitar and, ultimately, the bass. Although he picked up the instrument infrequently later in life, Krist did play the instrument quite capably during Nirvana's 1993 *MTV Unplugged* session.

Double Trouble

Novoselic's younger brother Robert was born in 1968, and, nearly three years his junior, became a willing accomplice to Krist's pre-teen mayhem. The boys took a liking to vandalism, and would throw eggs at houses and rocks at cars.

In one incident, they slashed the tires of parked car in their California neighborhood. When their father found out about it, he whipped them. "It was action and reaction," Krist later explained to the fan site Novoselic.com. "We were scared of him. But it wasn't like he was an abuser—I don't think he abused us at all. It's not like he would slap us for anything."

AM Radio

As a young boy, Krist listened to a lot of AM radio, which was home to most US Top 40 stations in the 1970s. His father was fond of Volkswagens and would work on his own while his eldest son kept his company. They would listen to the hits of the day in the driveway and, from time to time, at swap meets his father would attend.

Around the time of Krist's tenth birthday, his father acquired a four-track tape deck, the precursor to the eight-track machines that became popular in the mid-1960s. He discovered classic 1960s music like the early Rolling Stones catalog, Chuck Berry, and surf music icon Dick Dale.

Kiss and More

Novoselic's obsession with music took an important turn in 1976 when his father bought an FM tuner. "I started tuning into these FM stations, and I discovered different kinds of bands, like Kiss," Novoselic told John Hughes of the Washington State Legacy Project in 2008.

Before long, posters of the makeup-clad members of Kiss adorned his walls. But as Novoselic wrote in his *Seattle Weekly* column in 2008, the band's early work revealed something equally important: "an unabashed devotion to Beatle pop song-craft." The band's balance of accessibility, heavy guitars, and unorthodox imagery on their eponymous 1974 debut album—highlighted by tunes like "Cold Gin," "Strutter," and "Black Diamond"—hooked Krist and a million other sixth-graders that year.

When Krist entered junior high in the fall of 1977, he left the Top 40 behind for good as he discovered the hard rock that was being transmitted on the Los Angeles–area dial. He quickly became well versed in the work of bands like Aerosmith, Led Zeppelin, and Black Sabbath.

No Sports

Because Krist was very tall—he eventually grew to six-foot-seven—people often assumed he would have a knack for basketball. But although Novoselic played the sport as a youngster in San Pedro, he was never really interested in it (or sports in general) much past grade school.

"I had my moments where I could be OK at [basketball]," the future Nirvana bassist told the Legacy Project, but he never cared enough to stick with it. To this day, he still has minimal interest in athletics. "Usually, [when it's] like the Super Bowl or whatever, the playoffs, I have no idea who the game teams are, who's playing," he explained. "It's just something that is completely off my radar."

4

Take a Look at Who You Are

Moving to Aberdeen

In 1979, Kristo and Maria Novoselic decided to move their family north to Aberdeen, Washington. Kristo had visited friends and family in the area years earlier, when he was a young bachelor just settling in California, and he knew that it was home to like-minded Croatian immigrants—and that it offered affordable housing and job opportunities.

"My parents had some personal issues going on, and they thought that if we moved out of California things would get better," Krist told John Hughes. The family sold their home in California and were able to use the proceeds to buy a bigger, nicer home in Washington State and still have money left over.

To sweeten the deal, the existing homeowner, Pentti Koski, offered Kristo a job in the machine shop at his business, Harbor Machine & Fabrication. The family settled into their new home at 1120 Fairfield Street, across from the Young Street Bridge on top of Think of Me Hill.

Culture Shock

As a product of the Los Angeles suburbs, Novoselic was quick to recognize that he was different. Where others in Aberdeen wore Nike or Adidas sneakers with flared jeans, Krist wore straight-leg Levi's and deck shoes, and his clothes, which were timely in San Pedro, had him pegged as a dork by some at Weatherwax High.

He soon discovered he couldn't stand the bulk of his classmates. They were foreigners to him. "They were assholes," he told Everett True in *Nirvana: The True Story*. "They treated me really badly."

Devo and Zeppelin

Novoselic sought comfort from the stresses of the school day by listening to hard rock and the experimental bands like Devo he had recently discovered. His tastes were a far cry from the other kids in Aberdeen, who were—by and large—still into the Top 40 music in rotation on KGHO.

"There weren't a lot of kids in school that I could relate to with music," Novoselic told John Hughes. "Music was so important to me, and I was just way ahead."

Kids would laugh when he mentioned groups like Aerosmith. "I had these bands that were dear to me, Led Zeppelin and Devo, when everybody else was into Kenny Rogers," Krist told the *NME* in November 1991. "Three years down the road all these people that I considered to be infidels, the unenlightened, were listening to Led Zeppelin. I remember feeling angry that all of those people were grabbing a hold of my sacred cow. But that's the way things go."

Some of that may have had to do with radio reception around Aberdeen, which was far enough away from Seattle that the signal from the city's leading rock station, KISW, was hard to pick up. Luckily for Novoselic, he lived at the eastern end of Aberdeen, and had strong reception, which meant he could continue to have new music in his life.

Feel Lucky, Punk

Novoselic had his first exposure to punk rock music in 1979 via Seattle's KZOK. The station, located at 102.5 FM, had a Sunday night specialty show called *Your Mother Won't Like It*. The show allowed listeners to act as guest DJs, and one night the guest hosts brought in a bunch of punk records by the likes of the Weirdos, the Ramones, the Sex Pistols, the Stooges, and the New York Dolls. Excited by what he heard, Krist stuck a cassette in his tape deck and recorded the broadcast. He loved the music so much and listened to the tape so frequently that he wound up wearing it out.

Highway to Hell

When Novoselic first heard Black Sabbath's "Iron Man," in 1980, he became an instant fan. "That riff was so heavy—even more than Deep Purple's epic 'Smoke on the Water,'" he blogged in 2009. "Sabbath not only played heavy music; as the band's name itself suggests, they alluded to the occult."

Sabbath's dark allure was bolstered by a local televangelist who was using some of the music Krist loved to point out what he saw as an allegiance between hard rock and Satanism. The television preacher touched on AC/DC's classic *Highway to Hell* cover, which showed guitarist Angus Young wearing devil horns, before playing Led Zeppelin's "Stairway to Heaven" backward, claiming it held the hidden message "I love you sweet Satan." Black Sabbath's current album, *Born Again*, was another talking point, which prompted Novoselic to run to the record store the next day.

Although Sabbath front man Ozzy Osborne's debut solo album wouldn't see release until later that year, *Blizzard of Oz* became one of Novoselic's all time hard-rock favorites. Speaking about his love of what became heavy metal, and its dark, demonic imagery, Novoselic further explained, "When I was a teenager, I not only cranked my stereo because I loved to rock out—I wanted to send a message to a world that I thought was insane."

Living in Croatia

Novoselic's parents realized he was unhappy about his new school and—as he put it to Hughes in 2008—"a lot of dysfunctional things that are pretty personal." They thought it might benefit him to spend some time in Yugoslavia.

Krist looked at it as an opportunity. He flew over in the summer of 1980 and, aged fifteen, spent a year living with his father's sister. Living in the urban center of Zadar in a large apartment building was a fun, eye-opening experience that would stay with him his entire life.

That fall, Krist enrolled in a local public school, or what Yugoslavians called "gymnasium," where he was faced with a very demanding course load that included algebra, Marxism, and a history class that focused heavily on his parents' native land. Although the subjects required hours of study, he acclimated quickly, and did well with the structure his curriculum commanded, which was far different than the school environment he was used to in the United States. One of his classes was on civil defense, and on a few occasions, his instructor brought a large machine gun to class and showed the students how to assemble and disassemble it.

Feeling Stiff

Novoselic brought his love of the radio with him overseas, tuning in to the radio broadcasts from Italy that were transmitted across the Adriatic Sea. Perched on the twelfth floor of his aunt's apartment, he discovered music by British bands like Madness and Elvis Costello—part of the Stiff Records stable—that had become popular in the Italian market.

His curiosity piqued, Krist used a shortwave radio to dial in to the BBC, where he uncovered heavy UK rock acts like Deep Purple. He found the Croatian youth invigorating—kids would be drawn either to punk or to classic-rock bands like the Doors, who were experiencing a global cultural resurgence.

He shared this obsession with the close friends he'd made, bringing cassettes of songs he recorded off the radio to parties and small gatherings. Novoselic was happy to share his vast appreciation of rock 'n' roll and his knowledge of its growing subgenres with his Croatian friends.

Back to Aberdeen

When the school year ended, soon after Krist's sixteenth birthday, his parents called him home from Zadar. As much as he had enjoyed his year in Croatia and the new friends he'd made, he missed his family, and he knew he was needed on Think of Me Hill.

Krist's mom was launching her own beauty salon—which became known as Maria's Hair Design—in Aberdeen around this time, while his dad had taken a job on Terminal Island, working extended hours as a machinist for StarKist Tuna. Krist was expected to look after his younger siblings after school and on weekends, and to keep them out of trouble.

Often they hung out with neighborhood kids, but a lot of time was spent in front of the television, as the children watched *Gilligan's Island* and *I Dream of Jeanie* after school and music shows like *American Bandstand* and *Soul Train* on Saturdays. For his help, and for the convenience of his parents, Chris would ultimately be given a car.

No Credit

Novoselic re-entered Weatherwax as a sophomore in the fall of 1981 and soon learned that the school credits he earned in Yugoslavia wouldn't transfer. He would now be a part of Aberdeen's class of 1984.

"I guess they couldn't translate what the credits were," Novoselic explained to Hughes, acknowledging that he was required to pass certain subjects like Washington State History in order to graduate.

Party On

Unfazed by the alteration in his graduation plans, Krist—who had found himself unchallenged by the Weatherwax curriculum—made a strong social transition. With his towering height and endearing smile, he was hard to miss, and he quickly found himself accepted by a group of Aberdeen kids who smoked pot and drank alcohol.

The sixteen-year-old had begun to drink booze in Zadar, and smoking weed seemed like a logical next step as he sought a release from his increasingly dysfunctional home life. Novoselic—who would describe himself as a "maladjusted" teen to Hughes in 2008—used marijuana, beer, and liquor as a means to cope with the stress of his parents' crumbling marriage.

Scorpions Bite

Novoselic's first rock concert was a Scorpions show, held on July 16, 1982, at Seattle's Hec Edmundson Pavilion, part of the German hard-rock band's tour in support of their breakthrough album, *Blackout*. The band, fronted by Klaus Meine, had released the hard-rock hit "No One Like You" that summer. But despite a bill featuring up-and-coming support acts like Iron Maiden—whom Krist preferred to the Scorpions—and Girlschool, Novoselic would describe the gig a decade later as "totally boring."

Novoselic came away from the experience craving a kind of diversity and excitement in rock that wasn't easily accessible in mid-1982. Outside of Rush and the Police, Seattle radio was relying much of the time on the same old Led Zeppelin and Journey tracks. MTV was still in its infancy, and months away from reaching Aberdeen, when Krist turned to the USA Network's late-night show *New Wave Theatre* to uncover music videos by left-of-center bands. The Sunday night specialty shows on Seattle's FM radio stations were his only other options for new music.

Later, Stoners

For a two-year period between 1981 and 1983, getting wasted was of key importance to "Novie," as his buddies on the Aberdeen party circuit would call him. Krist became a heavy drinker, while he developed such a substantial marijuana habit during his tenure with the partiers in Aberdeen that he ultimately had to step away.

By his eighteenth birthday, getting high no longer felt as fun as it had. Part of it was the company—he could no longer relate to the Camaro crowd's awful taste in music, which he dubbed "the slick, canned sounds of mainstream heavy metal," in his 2004 book *Of Grunge and Government*. The "stoner" crowd in Aberdeen was, he wrote, "a counterculture without a mission." And, as he matured, the circuit's soundtrack of Judas Priest and Iron Maiden no longer inspired him. He had outgrown his clique.

Looking back on his time as a teenage recreational drug user in 2008, Krist seemed ashamed. "It wasn't a good idea," he told Hughes of his weed use. "[When] you're a young person and you're smoking pot, you don't realize that there's a toll—there's a price to pay. You could suffer from developmental issues and that will hold you back in a lot of ways."

Plugging In

In his junior year of high school, Novoselic was given an electric guitar as a gift from his mother. The instrument—a cheap Italian model—was purchased at Kathy's Attic, a store on Heron Street in Aberdeen.

Like his future bandmate Kurt, Krist took lessons from Warren Mason, who instructed students on guitar and other instruments out of Rosevear's Music in downtown Aberdeen. Novoselic was a quick learner, with a strong musical understanding dating back to his early accordion lessons, and after just a couple of months he felt able to abandon his training with Mason.

Left to their own devices while their parents worked, Krist and his brother Robert—who had also taken lessons—spent hours plugged into his amplifier. Together, they would work out the parts for classic B. B. King sides.

"I just started picking out songs and I guess I got obsessed with it," he later told the Washington State Legacy Project.

Ooooh! *Barracuda!*

On his eighteenth birthday—and a year later than most kids in Washington State—Novoselic obtained his driver's license. In return for his cooperation in watching over his younger brother and sister while his parents worked (plus his desire to get himself to and from work), Kristo helped his oldest son acquire a used 1967 Plymouth Barracuda.

According to Krist, the sixteen-year-old vehicle was purchased for approximately $600 from a used car lot in Aberdeen in 1983. And if it wasn't the coolest ride in the world for the time, it was at least reliable.

It should be noted that in the decades since Krist drove his 'Cuda, the Plymouths—which were manufactured between 1964 and 1974—have become hotly sought-after restoration projects for classic pony and muscle-car collectors alike.

Hey, Jack Kerouac

In 1983, during a day trip to Seattle's University District, Novoselic walked into a city bookstore and asked if they had any titles by Jack Kerouac. When the store clerk gleefully recommended *The Dharma Bums*, Krist became an instant fan of the beat generation's literary pioneer.

Although Kerouac is best known for his 1957 classic *On the Road*, the bookstore employee's recommendation of *The Dharma Bums* had a geographical significance. Based in part in a Washington State fire-lookout tower, the book finds the protagonist, a Zen hermit named Japhy, exploring his own inner space and savoring every one of life's simple moments.

For Krist, Kerouac's 1958 novel gave him a newfound confidence and became one of the most inspirational books he would ever read. "Reading Kerouac confirmed the sense of independence I have always felt," he wrote in *Of Grunge and Government*. "*The Dharma Bums* is about the journey of life and meaningful connection with people."

Taco Bell

At the outset of his senior year at Weatherwax, Novoselic threw himself into his work as a means to avoid having to hang with his old stoner crowd. He took vocational classes in the evening at Grays Harbor College, working in the school's Comprehensive Employment and Training Act (CETA) program. Soon enough, he started work at the College after class buffing floors for extra money.

Novoselic also landed a regular job working nights at a Taco Bell in Aberdeen, and—after saving money for new stereo speakers and musical equipment—he completely drifted from local social scene. Luckily, he was about to meet some kindred spirits.

Osborne and Lukin

One of Novoselic's Taco Bell co-workers named Bill had been expelled from Aberdeen High School after setting off a pipe bomb at the school. As a result, he was attending Montesano High School, where he befriended Buzz Osborne and Matt Lukin.

Osborne and Lukin would visit their friend at his job, which is where Krist first made their acquaintance. At the time, Buzz and Matt were amused by the big, tall, goofy teen working behind the counter who sang along loudly to the Christmas carols piping through the store's Muzak system.

As Buzz taught the gospel of punk rock to all within an earshot, Novoselic explained that he knew a little about the genre and was interested in artists like Elvis Costello. That was all Osborne needed to hear. They started hanging out, and Krist went to check out some Melvins practices during the time they were still playing with original drummer Mike Dillard.

Osborne gave Krist a compilation tape of the punk and hardcore music he and Lukin loved. Some of it—Black Flag, the Dead Kennedys, the Circle Jerks, MDC, Bad Brains, and Minor Threat—was completely new to him. Much of it was cerebral, if not totally radical. It was an epiphany. Bands like the DKs and MDC were among the few anti-Reagan voices that existed in 1983. Krist was not a fan of the presidential administration of the time, and these bands spoke to him.

"I needed a breath of fresh air and was immediately intrigued," he wrote, in *Of Grunge and Government*, about the bands he learned about from meccas like Los Angeles, San Francisco, and Washington, D.C. "These new sounds were raw and vital."

Meeting Shelli

One day in the fall of 1983, Novoselic—then a senior—was walking the halls of Aberdeen's lone high school when he overheard two younger girls walking ahead of him talking about one of their favorite records: the Sex Pistols' *Never Mind the Bollocks*. Novoselic chimed in with his approval and struck up a conversation with one of the Weatherwax juniors, Shelli Dilly.

Their friendship—steeped in their mutual appreciation of cool music—was propelled by Krist's humorous charm. Dilley would eventually become Novoselic's girlfriend—and, later, his first wife.

Flipping for Flipper

Krist loved punk's message, and its aim to irritate—if not provoke—the status quo. Now, he was good buddies with the punk-rock guru of Grays Harbor. "Buzz was the guy who spread the good news around town, but to only the most deserving," Novoselic told *Option* in January 1992, acknowledging that most of the kids in Aberdeen would dismiss the music he now loved.

Osborne lent Krist a stack of American hardcore records, including *Generic Flipper*, the 1982 debut album by the explosive San Francisco foursome Flipper. Although he didn't get the album on his first or second try, the third time he played it, he lost his mind. "It was a revelation," he explained to the long defunct magazine. "It made me realize it was art. It was valid. It was beautiful." For Novoselic, it became as important to him as Led Zeppelin's *IV* and *Physical Graffiti* or Black Sabbath's *Vol. 4* and *Masters of Reality*.

Thrifty = Nifty

After visiting a Salvation Army store in Grays Harbor in 1983, Novoselic discovered he could score vintage clothing from the 1950s and '60s dirt cheap. His appreciation of vintage items meant that he could find unique shirts for a dollar, and he realized that he could still look cool on a low budget.

For Krist, punk was a state of mind—a means of liberation—so, with his thrift-store threads, he thumbed his nose at the status quo and forged his own unique identity. He didn't subscribe to typical punk fashions and wouldn't be caught dead wearing a studded leather jacket or sporting a Mohawk haircut.

"An alternative vision didn't have to be stuck in the hippy 1960s—it was reborn through punk," he explained in his 2004 book. It was an extension of his belief that—although he was discovering and loving punk—he could still be loyal to the Aerosmith and Led Zeppelin records he had cut his rock 'n' roll teeth on.

Besides, thrift stores were a great place to score old albums, many of them in good condition. Novoselic bought a pristine copy of the three-LP *Woodstock* album for under a dollar, while a British pressing of one of his favorite Beatles records, *Rubber Soul*, was his for 25 cents.

Introducing Dale

By early 1984, Mike Dillard had quit the Melvins due to personal obligations, leaving Osborne and Lukin in need of a drummer. When Buzz asked Novoselic if he had any recommendations, he came up with two names. Krist knew of a drummer in the area named Aaron Burckhard and arranged an introduction. While Osborne and Lukin pondered whether Burckhard would be a good fit, Novoselic introduced them to a second candidate named Dale Crover.

Buzz came to watch the sixteen-year-old Crover perform with one of the two covers bands he played in, and he was impressed. After talking to him for a while, he asked Dale to join the band, and soon enough the powerful young drummer was hosting the Melvins' practices at his parents' home in Aberdeen.

The Crovers were supportive and happy to let the Melvins rehearse in their back room. The noise could be heard from a few blocks away and attracted kids living nearby to come and hang around.

Of course, these porch rehearsals would become an important gathering place for Nirvana's future members, not to mention the Northwest grunge sound. The amphetamine-paced American hardcore sound Osborne had embraced was giving way to a slower, heavier sound. The Melvins were taking audible cues from their heroes in Black Flag, who had made a sonic shift that same year.

Underbite

Kristo and Maria Novoselic ultimately split up, divorcing in 1984, not long after Krist's high-school graduation that June. For the nineteen-year-old, who had been living with the strain of his parents' broken marriage for years, the breakup was as much a relief as it was a sadness.

That summer, Krist underwent surgery to his face to correct an underbite that he would later compare to Jay Leno's. Performed by a Seattle-based plastic surgeon, the procedure was equal parts cosmetic and necessary, as his bottom teeth didn't line up correctly.

For six weeks, Krist's mouth was wired shut, until the swelling subsided. Hours after the surgery, Matt Lukin checked in on his friend. "His head was totally swollen up like a fat oriental baby," he told Michael Azerrad.

While he lived for the time on soft food—including plenty of milkshakes—Novoselic continued to head out to parties all summer, drinking to the point of excess. Although he never actually used them, he was required to carry a pair of wire cutters with him at all times, in case he started choking or needed to throw up.

Meeting Cobain

Novoselic had first been introduced to Kurt Cobain a year or so earlier, after his younger brother Robert brought Kurt home to hang out one day. Krist slowly became aware of Cobain but—because he was two years younger—paid him little mind in the hallways of Weatherwax. They began to notice each other more frequently at Dale Crover's place after the Melvins' practices shifted there.

That first meeting stuck with Cobain, who remembered hearing a loud racket coming from a stereo on the second floor of the Novoselic residence one day in 1983. "Oh, that's my brother Chris," Robert told Kurt when he asked about the noise. "He listens to punk rock."

Not long after his parents' divorce, Krist began turning up at the Central Park Baptist Church. If, at first, it seemed like Novoselic was looking for spiritual guidance, his presence at the church was short-lived. As Dave Reed would later tell Charles Cross, the towering teen seemed like he was there "just for the girls."

One day, after learning that Krist also played guitar, and knowing they already had some musical common ground, Jesse Reed invited Novoselic home to play with him and Cobain. They seemed to hit it off as they jammed, attempting renditions of some hard-rock classics and some original songs Kurt had been writing.

5

I Can Bend It, I Can Shape It, I Can Mold It

Fecal Matter and More

Dropping Out

In early 1985, Kurt Cobain dropped out of Aberdeen High School. He was struggling hard in most subjects, save for art, and when he bothered to show up at school he rarely participated in classes. Guidance counselors and school officials advised him that if he planned on graduating at all, he would need to remain at school for an extra year and buckle down.

At the encouragement of his host family, the Reeds, Kurt agreed to check out an alternative school in Aberdeen named Continuation High in the hope of avoiding dropping out. The school offered one-on-one instruction in an informal setting, but Cobain only lasted a week before quitting altogether. In doing so, he lost out on any chance of an art scholarship—something his old teacher Bob Hunter had led him to believe he might have a shot at. Hunter had entered one of Cobain's art pieces in the 1985 Regional High School Art Show, and it wound up being displayed by the Superintendent of Public Instruction.

Later, even after achieving fame, Kurt was obviously bothered by his failure to graduate. Speaking to *Details* in February 1992, he lied about having graduated, boasting of how he "got a couple of scholarships to art school" but "blew them off." He eventually came clean a year later, telling *Howl* writer Jon Savage, "I quit with only two months to go. I've always copped out of things."

Fingered

That winter, Kurt took a full-time job at the Lamplighter Restaurant in nearby Grayland, which Dave Reed had arranged for him. Cobain worked at the position for several weeks, earning $4.25 per hour washing dishes, helping in the kitchen, and bussing tables.

In March of '85, Kurt cut his finger while washing dishes. After receiving stitches, he decided that he couldn't work in a job where he might risk further injury to his hands. "He told me that if he lost his finger and couldn't play guitar, he'd kill himself," Jesse Reed told Cross.

With no structure in his life, Kurt spent his days in Dave and Ethel's home, hanging with Jesse, who had also started skipping school. They drank and did drugs together while Jesse's parents were out at work.

Wattage in the Cottage

By now, Kurt was becoming more prolific as a songwriter and had begun to write lyrics to match his musical ideas. Titles found in his notebooks at the time included "Samurai Sabotage" and "Wattage in the Cottage." Another song, "Diamond Dave," was about his appreciation of Mr. Reed, while "Ode to Beau" was given a country presentation and told the unfortunate tale of a boy from Weatherwax who had committed suicide.

Eighteen and Life

Cobain's eighteenth birthday was a special one, thanks to Dave and Ethel Reed, who invited the church youth group and its leader, Pastor Lloyd, to their home. In the company of the Reeds, Kurt felt inclusion and love—things that he had long perceived to be absent in his own home.

In a letter to his aunt Mari Earl (then Fradenburg), Kurt mentioned the party and acknowledged that life at Jesse's parents' home was good. Or, as he wrote to her, "It was nice to know people care about ya." He also thanked her for the gifts she had sent from Seattle: the Led Zeppelin biography *Hammer of the Gods* and a book of Norman Rockwell illustrations.

Unfortunately, the Reeds had been nearing the end of their rope since Kurt's finger injury. He had become withdrawn, and he was having a negative effect on Jesse. Over time it became apparent that, by letting Kurt stay with them, they were enabling him to hide away from the world. When Kurt kicked in a window one afternoon after he had forgotten his key, Dave told him he had overstayed his welcome.

Krist and Shelli

By the early spring of 1985, Krist Novoselic was working at Foster Painting Company in Aberdeen, where he began to run into Shelli Dilly. Shelli—who had also been friends with Cobain at Weatherwax—had dropped out in her senior year and was now working full time at a nearby McDonald's.

Just seventeen, Dilly had a strong work ethic and managed to pay for her own apartment across the street from the fire department on Market Street. One day, when she bumped into Krist, she asked him for his number, and they got together, initially as friends. With their common musical interests, they began sharing records and going to shows together. It wasn't long before romance blossomed.

Crover's Porch

By the spring of 1985, Novoselic was regularly attending the Melvins' practices at Dale Crover's parents' back porch on Second Street in Aberdeen. Here, among the kids who hung out on the porch and in the yard, he befriended Cobain.

"There would be the band and there would be other teenagers, and there was this one kid who started hanging out there," Novoselic told John Hughes. "[Kurt] could play guitar, and he was interested in music. He was maladjusted or wasn't interested in the mainstream culture . . . searching for something."

Early Impressions

When Novoselic first came upon Cobain at Dale's place, he was impressed to see that Kurt was able to play guitar, but not in the way that most musicians in Grays Harbor could. Kurt was a lefty, which meant he needed a left-handed axe to play, so there could be no impromptu jamming with the members of the Melvins.

Furthermore, he was unable to play many of the songs most rock guitarists learn early on—Sam the Sham & the Pharaohs' "Wooly Bully" or the Animals' "House of the Rising Sun." Still, Kurt was very creative on the guitar, and when it came to the songs he knew—or those that he had written himself—he exhibited an innovative approach that stayed with his new friend.

Both owed their deep fascination with punk to Osborne, and they were like-minded in their outlook, which put ideology leaps and bounds above imagery. They were also open to certain records and artists from the past.

For Novoselic, most of Cobain's allure was that he was easy to be around. "I actually saw this pretty sweet dude with a nice temperament," Krist explained to Hughes in the Legacy Project. "He was just pretty mellow."

Kurt remembered being drawn to Novoselic soon after he dropped out. "It wasn't too hard to find each other," Cobain told *BAM*'s Jerry McCulley in 1992. "We started going to punk rock shows in Seattle and Tacoma."

Much to Kurt's disappointment, Novoselic had no interest in being in a band at this point, even though he was well aware he could also play guitar.

Food Stamps

In April 1985, Cobain was back on the street, sleeping on his friends' parents' couches or in their garages or crashing in heated apartment building hallways, as he had done in the past. He also began receiving $40 per month in food stamps, which he would later explain he used to buy Jolly Rancher candy and other types of junk food. He would take the change—which was given in cash under a certain denomination—and buy beer.

YMCA

That May, Cobain landed a part-time job working at the YMCA through the Aberdeen Unemployment Office. While he had yet to land a permanent residence, he was happy to be working. He served as a janitor and would occasionally be asked to help with the children's activities or as a lifeguard.

Kurt loved working with young children, and although the position was short-lived, he remembered the experience fondly to *Option* in January 1992. "I do love kids," he explained enthusiastically as he mentioned his half-sister Breanne. "I taught pre-school kids how to swim and did daycare, and I babysat during my teenage years."

Night Janitor

Ironically, Kurt also worked a second part-time job as an evening janitor at Weatherwax High that May, the same month he should have been graduating from the school. He only took the job because, aside from desperately needing money, he knew that none of his former classmates would be able to see him. Only Jesse—who managed to get his diploma—was aware of the job, and he promised to keep it under wraps.

Cobain didn't care much for the position or the idea of working at night, when he should be partying or playing guitar. He quit in July 1985. Word has it that he also tried to land a job cleaning dog kennels for a veterinarian around this time. Sadly, his application was turned down, having seemingly been deemed unqualified to wash down dog mess.

Krist's VW Bug

By May 1985, Novoselic's Barracuda was a distant memory as he shifted toward the Volkswagens that his father knew and loved and took ownership of a VW van. Krist's microbus—a 1968 model that was painted like a zebra—was just the first in a long line of VWs that he would own through the years.

In Novoselic's opinion, vintage Volkswagens were tough, forgiving, and relatively easy to maintain. He has since owned several classic Beetles and a pair of vans, including a restored 1965 model that is significant in that it is as old as he is.

The Pink Apartment

Not long after Kurt was bounced from the Reeds' house, their son, Jesse, opted to follow him, and together they arranged to stay at Jesse's grandparents' house in Aberdeen while they looked to secure a place of their own.

On June 1, the pair took occupancy of a dilapidated studio apartment at 404 N. Michigan Street after Jesse put up the security deposit, with Kurt agreeing to split the $100 monthly rent. The dwelling's interior was painted Pepto-Bismol pink, so it was only fitting that the small studio space was nicknamed "The Pink Apartment" by the duo and all of their friends.

Although the place came with some furnishings, they quickly filled their new home with stolen yard furniture. Kurt also elected to decorate the place in his own unique way, frightening the neighbors by writing "Satan Rules" and "666" in soap on a front window.

Equally disturbing was a blow-up doll that hung from a noose and was visible for all passersby to see. One night, while the roommates were frying on acid, a policeman from the Grays Harbor County Sheriff's Department came to the door. Kurt opened the door in fear the officer might see the headstone crosses he had stolen from the local graveyard and decorated with polka dots.

Furthermore, Cobain had acquired a number of sample cans of Edge Shaving Gel, which were being given away throughout Aberdeen, and which he and Jesse used for huffing. As Steve Shillinger remembered in *Nirvana: The Untold Story*, "We were really, really heavy drinkers and substance abusers from a young age. Kurt made this apparatus to huff isobutene. He declared himself addicted to shaving gel at one point."

As they got high, they smeared the gel all over the walls and the stolen crosses. "We were branded Satan worshippers back home," Kurt told *Melody Maker* in 1989. "Fuck, this girl came knocking on our door looking for a wallet and she goes, 'You know what all the other kids told me in the neighborhood? Don't go there, they worship the Devil.'"

"Maybe it was those desecrated cemetery pieces buried in our front yard," Cobain snickered at the time. "But you didn't have to do anything to be considered extreme [in Aberdeen]. Just take a lot of acid."

Cleaning for Affybud

The apartment that Cobain and Reed had occupied was an utter disaster. The odor of spilled, stale beer and vomit, the piles of garbage, and the mountain of greasy dishes that went untreated for the entire summer of 1985 made clear to Kurt and Jesse that they needed help cleaning up the place.

Whether they were truly incapable or just lazy, Cobain did take the initiative to post a notice in the neighborhood's Polish Club Tavern advertising for help in exchange for marijuana. The flyer—according to Sandford—covertly offered affybud, a strain of marijuana that originates in Afghanistan. It read, "for the pleasure of cleaning for 2 dedicated partyers, payment of all the ab you can toke."

One woman actually considered the offer and dropped by the apartment, only to turn on her heels, dry heaving at the smell of rotting food, soiled underwear, and vomit.

Messing with Jesse

Although Jesse Reed was stronger than his roommate, Kurt had a tendency to try and provoke his good friend, who was as gullible as Cobain was sneaky.

When Kurt suggested that if Jesse let him write something on his forehead, he could reciprocate, his pal agreed. Reed couldn't have expected that Kurt would print "666" on his friend's face in permanent marker, but he should have learned his lesson when Cobain ran away laughing before Jesse could return the favor.

Kurt kept testing Jesse. He talked Reed into getting a Mohawk haircut, promising he would follow his friend in an act of rebellious solidarity. But after his friend Steve Shillinger came over to the apartment with hair clippers to administer the punk hairstyle, Cobain told Reed it looked stupid and went back on his word, making Jesse wonder if that was his intent all along.

Graffiti Police

Kurt's newfound affinity for vandalism matched his artful inclinations when he began spray-painting controversial phrases like "Abort Christ" and "God is Gay" on the sides of cars and on local buildings, including his own workplace—the YMCA—in the summer of 1985. The following day he was assigned the task of scrubbing the graffiti off the side of the structure. Elsewhere, he supposedly vandalized a neighborhood boat by spraying "Boat People Go Home" on its side.

These events led up to another caper in which he inexplicably wrote "Ain't got no how watchamacallit" on the rear wall of the SeaFirst Bank building. For his trouble, he was arrested on the evening of July 23, 1985, with the police report revealing that he had been booked for malicious mischief after Detective Michael Bens' pulled up and caught him in the act of defacing the back of the building. Three other men in Cobain's vicinity—presumably his friends—took off running as he was apprehended.

At the Aberdeen Police Station, Kurt wrote out an apologetic confession of his crime, explaining, "Now I see how silly it was for me to have done this, and I'm sorry that I did." He was fingerprinted, photographed, and released on his own recognizance. Several weeks later, he was ordered to pay a $180 fine and given a thirty-day suspended sentence by a local judge who warned him that, as a legal adult, he would need to stay out of trouble to avoid jail in the future.

My War in Walla Walla

Eleven months after Buzz Osborne and Matt Lukin had first introduced Cobain to the brilliant, dangerous spectacle of Black Flag's live show, the Melvins members traveled with Novoselic to catch the explosive quartet's August 22, 1985, performance in Walla Walla. The six-hour, 334-mile road trip across Washington State from Aberdeen took place in Krist's zebra-striped VW bus and affirmed just how dedicated these young men were to the pursuit of punk music.

The show may have been sparsely attended—there were just a few dozen kids in the Walla Walla Community Center for the gig—but for Novoselic, who was already fascinated with the group's 1984 album *My War* and its just released long-player *Slip It In*, the concert was a spiritual awakening.

By this point, the band's heavy, dark vibe had more in common with Black Sabbath than their hardcore origins, and their music—which was a prototype for grunge if ever there was one—was devoid of boundaries. When he heard poetic front man Henry Rollins thrash the commercial rock music of the day with lines like "Swimming in the mainstream / Is such a lame dream," Novoselic totally identified with his liberating message.

"We know that Grunge is a mix of old school heavy rock and punk," Krist wrote in the March 19, 2010, edition of *Seattle Weekly*. "And that's where *My War* comes in . . . the music was an explicit affront to the mores of the mainstream. They were dangerous."

"Shut the Fuck Up!"

According to biographer Charles R. Cross, late one August night, while Jesse Reed was working at Burger King, Cobain had some of his fellow Cling-Ons come over for some impromptu jamming. This didn't sit well with the obese, mustachioed neighbor on the other side of Kurt's pink wall.

After pounding on the walls proved unsuccessful, the man came to the door to ask them to quiet down. Cobain got smart with the guy and wound up on the receiving end of a couple of hard punches. According to his friend Steve Shillinger, Kurt stopped smiling and doubled over in pain as the neighbor ordered him to "shut the fuck up!" When Jesse heard about what had happened, he couldn't help think that his roommate deserved it.

Kurt Boots Jesse

At the end of the summer of 1985, Reed—who had already announced to Cobain his intentions of enlisting in the navy—came home to find that Cobain had trashed his senior yearbook in mockery of his graduation achievement. He cut out various pictures of his former classmates and glued them to the wall before covering them with red crosses.

This despicable act was the last straw and demanded a confrontation. When Reed challenged Cobain for destroying his personal property, Kurt responded by telling him to get out. Jesse retreated to his grandparents' while Kurt remained in the apartment until October, when he was evicted for failing to pay the rent.

Bigger Than U2

During his final weeks in the apartment, Cobain wrote songs that were as influenced by punk and classic rock as they were U2 and R.E.M., two of his favorite bands at the time. If songs like "Spam" and "The Class of '85"—the latter featuring the lyric "We are all the same / Just flies on a turd"—were inspired by the aforementioned guitar-driven pop bands, he never let on about it to Osborne for fear of ridicule.

He fantasized about forming a band that would be bigger than U2, who had just conquered Live Aid. He conveyed such aspirations to friends like Steve Shillinger. Of course, he still had no one to play with in Aberdeen.

In the Navy?

In the days after his eviction, Kurt once again considered joining the navy, following the path of his estranged best friend Jesse Reed and another pal, Trevor Briggs. Briggs had already enlisted, and told Kurt—who was sleeping in the backseat of an old Volvo that belonged to Greg Hokanson's mom at the time—about the buddy system, which would have placed them in boot camp together.

Cobain seriously considered the navy this time and even went so far as to take the Armed Services Vocational Aptitude test at the recruiting office in Aberdeen. But after enduring the three-hour test—which he passed—he began having second thoughts.

Sleeping in Krist's Van

With nowhere else to go in the early fall of 1985, Cobain occasionally crashed in the back of Novoselic's safari-themed Volkswagen van behind Krist and Shelli's apartment. During the day, when the couple worked, Kurt would hang out at the Aberdeen Timberland Library, reading and sleeping.

Novoselic's generosity was an extension of his growing bond with Kurt, who deeply impressed him with his expressive, compelling drawings. Their mutual appreciation for rock 'n' roll was, of course, the initial link between the two friends. Meanwhile, Shelli gave Cobain a nice stash of blankets and leftover food from her McDonald's job when she could. But as the nights got colder, Kurt realized it might be time to get a job and arrange for his own permanent residence.

The Shillingers'

In October, when the nights started getting colder, Cobain knew he needed a better living arrangement than the backseat of Novoselic's van. He spoke to Steve Shillinger about his predicament, and the two went to Steve's father Lamont—an English teacher at Weatherwax—to see if there might be a place in the family's home for Cobain.

Although the Shillingers' house at 408 W. First Street was already cramped—they had six children of their own—they took Kurt in, and for the next ten months he was again given a place to belong. Grateful to be sleeping on their living-room sofa, Cobain helped around the house, tucking his sleeping back neatly away during the day and doing whatever was asked of him—at first. He appreciated being included with their family during the Thanksgiving and Christmas holidays that year.

Breanne Is Born

Although Cobain's relationship with his mother Wendy had become distant by December 1985, he was thrilled to visit his brand new half-sister Breanne O'Connor at their Aberdeen home on Christmas Day. Cobain would go on to treasure his youngest sibling for the rest of his life. One needs to look no further than the inside booklet of Nirvana's third and final album *In Utero* to see her acknowledged right next to James Osterberg—the birth name of rock icon Iggy Pop!

There is also speculation that Breanne appears in Nirvana's "Heart-Shaped Box" video as the blonde little girl in the Ku Klux Klan outfit. Like her famous older brother, she would later change the spelling of her name to keep people guessing. In some instances she has been referred to as Brianne, and in others—such as when she appeared on MTV's *The Osbournes*—as Brieann.

Illiteracy Will Prevail

By the fall of 1985, Cobain had decided that he wanted to form his own band. He began to rehearse with Melvins drummer Dale Crover on bass and his friend and fellow Cling-On Greg Hokanson on drums. He named the trio Fecal Matter.

Late in the year, after a sparsely attended December gig at the Spot Tavern in Pacific Beach, Washington, Kurt arranged to bring the band to his aunt Mari's in Seattle for a four-track recording session. But with Hokanson absent—he only lasted a few more practices—Crover assumed the drumming duties and bass work on what became the notorious Fecal Matter demo *Illiteracy Will Prevail*.

Cobain arrived at Earl's that December with a notebook full of lyrics and went about recording on a TEAC machine in her music room. "It was loud," Earl told *Goldmine*'s Gillian G. Gaar in February 1997. "They would put down the music tracks first, then he'd put the headphones on, and all you could hear was Kurt Cobain's voice screaming through the house! It was pretty wild." At the time of the session, Earl's husband even joked to her about closing the window so the neighbors wouldn't think they were beating him.

Together, Cobain and Crover tracked titles like "Suicide Samurai," "Downer," "Laminated Effect," "Spank Thru," "Control," "Class of '86," "Blather's Log," "Instramental," "Anorexorcist," "Accusations," "Insurance," "Vaseline," and "Sound of Dentage." There was also a song about the oldest daughter on the

1960s television show *Family Affair* becoming pregnant, which was titled "Buffy's Pregnant," plus an intriguing tune called "Bambi Slaughter" about a troubled teen who sold his parents' wedding rings to the local pawnshop.

Aside from fourteen proper songs, the tape also included a short montage of dialogue from the classic marijuana film *Reefer Madness*, a short rendering of Devo's "Turnaround," and a smattering of Cobain's guitar riffs.

No More Fecal Matter

In January 1986, Cobain tried out a new incarnation of Fecal Matter with original Melvins member Mike Dillard on drums and Buzz Osborne on bass. But when Buzz refused to buy a bass amplifier, Kurt realized his friend was uninterested in playing with him on a permanent basis.

Fecal Matter's second lineup came undone a few weeks later. On February 8, Osborne, Crover, and Lukin recorded the Melvins' debut EP, *Six Songs*, which was released by C/Z Records soon after. The seven-inch EP featured songs like "Easy as It Was," "Now a Limo," and "Grinding Process." It was produced by the label's then co-owner Chris Hanzsek and featured a photo of the band taken by Krist Novoselic.

Super-8

Aside from his musical pursuits, Cobain continued to make Super-8 films with the help of Steve Shillinger. In one thought-provoking silent film seen by biographer Charles Cross, a nineteen-year-old Kurt could be seen wandering through an old abandoned building sporting wraparound sunglasses and a T-shirt advertising KISW-FM, "Seattle's Best Rock."

In another homemade movie, Cobain wore a Mr. T mask to which he attached a vacuum cleaner. In doing so, he made the *A-Team* star appear as if he was snorting a mound of cocaine (actually a large pile of flour).

According to a *Rolling Stone* report from August 2012, Shillinger is apparently still in possession of a number of the old, unreleased home movies that the friends made while Cobain slept on his family's sofa in 1985 and 1986.

Melvins Roadie

The Melvins would usually play gigs on Fridays and Saturdays, and Kurt would happily serve as their roadie—a job he did for no pay and little sleep. For Cobain, the reward was an education, as he learned firsthand about the music business while he fantasized about the day he might have someone else carry his amp and handle his guitars.

The resultant exposure to members of the Olympia and Seattle music scenes was invaluable. When the Melvins had a triumphant gig, it was motivational. When things went wrong—especially on the business end—Kurt made a mental note. He was learning the rock 'n' roll business firsthand while preparing himself to make his own move.

Not only did Cobain move equipment, he occasionally drove the group's 1972 Dodge Sportsman Royal Van (a.k.a. the Mel-van). At one point, in order to quell his boredom during the hours before one of Buzz's shows, Kurt doodled his interpretation of the front cover of Kiss's classic 1974 debut album on the side of the vehicle.

Making Friends

During his travels with the Melvins, Cobain began to spend a few nights a month in Olympia, where Osborne's band played regular gigs at house parties. It was during one such keg party at a house known as the Dude Ranch that Kurt first encountered the likes of Slim Moon and Dylan Carlson, plus a guy named Kurt Flansberg and his girlfriend Tracy Marander, whom he had seen around at a host of punk gigs.

Moon and his pals were music snobs who had always perceived the Melvins entourage to be stupid and creepy. As they walked up the driveway to the party, Cobain—in his grey trench coat—overheard Slim and Dylan having a conversation about Chicago punk band Big Black. As he passed them by, he exclaimed, "I like Big Black!" This was Kurt's way of letting them know he was educated about cool bands and—although he hung with the Melvins—wasn't just one of Buzz Osborne's blind disciples.

Arizona

Novoselic and Dilly left Grays Harbor in March 1986 in search of better jobs. After speaking with friends who had lived and prospered in Phoenix, the young couple relocated to Arizona.

What Krist and Shelli didn't realize, however, was that Arizona was a right-to-work state where better-paying union jobs weren't prevalent. Although they liked the dry heat of the Phoenix area, the opportunities the couple had hoped for weren't there. By the autumn of '86, Novoselic and Dilly were back in Aberdeen, and within six months they wound up renting a place above a garage in Hoquiam.

Skateboard Graffiti

In the spring of 1986, Cobain hatched a business idea that he hoped would make him some money while fueling his passion for art and vandalism: spray-painting skateboards with his own customized graffiti.

Attempting to launch his own enterprise, he hung flyers around Aberdeen and waited for the phone to ring. Only one kid called, with a request was for an exploding head, which Kurt proudly painted on his young client's board. Unfortunately, the kid never paid Cobain his fee, and Kurt gave up on the idea.

Brown Cow/Brown Towel

With the encouragement of Osborne and Crover, Cobain took the stage at a Melvins gig at Olympia's GESCCO (Greater Evergreen Students' Community Cooperation Organization) on May 3, 1986. In the company of twenty onlookers, he recited original poetry titles like "I Like Porn" and "Sky Pup" while Buzz and Dale built an explosive, discordant sound-wall behind him.

Although he wasn't playing guitar, the stage felt like a place where he could be free as he jumped around the stage singing/screaming out his own prose. The trio called themselves Brown Towel, although they were mistakenly billed as "Brown Cow" by the promoter on the flyer for the show, which also featured two other acts, Danger Mouse and Grinder.

After the gig, Cobain mingled with attendees, including the aforementioned Carlson and Moon. The latter was something of a music scenester and musician in his own right who went on to form the Seattle label Kill Rock Stars in 1991.

Kurt's future girlfriend Tracy Marander was also at the show. Cobain had first met her outside of a Seattle punk show at some point in 1985. She had walked up to talk to Buzz Osborne while he and Kurt were sitting in a car drinking at the gig. During the conversation, Cobain was distracted enough not to notice a police officer sneaking up on him. When he failed to put his bottle down, he was arrested for underage drinking.

Jail

Cobain's problems with the law continued that month when he was arrested on May 18 after police officer John Green found him intoxicated on the roof of an abandoned building located at 618 W. Market Street.

Kurt was booked for trespassing and possession of alcohol by a minor at 12:30 a.m. on the night in question. Instead of being released on his own recognizance—which is typical of such infractions—he was instead detained after Aberdeen police discovered that he never paid the $180 fine stemming from his arrest ten months earlier.

Cobain called Mr. Shillinger, pleading with his friend's father to bail him out, but Lamont—a religious man—refused, believing it was time for the nineteen-year-old Kurt to take responsibility for his own misconduct. In an act of kindness, Lamont did visit Kurt the following day and give him a carton of Winston Lights cigarettes, which undoubtedly helped him bide his time during his eight-day incarceration. On May 25, after police took his mug shot, he was released.

According to a 2008 interview with Krist Novoselic, an Aberdeen police dog bit Cobain during one of his altercations with the law, but it is unclear if it was during this bust or his 1985 arrest. Years later, Kurt would fabricate a story of

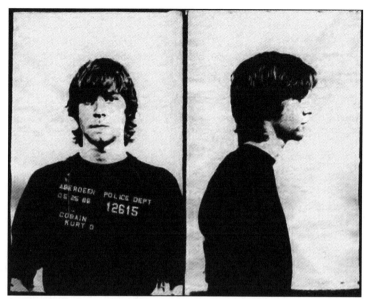

A mug shot taken of Cobain on May 25, 1986, by the Aberdeen Police Department after his arrest for trespassing and being a minor in possession of alcohol.   *Aberdeen Police Department*

how he created hand-drawn pornography for his fellow inmates, trading it for cigarettes. According to his friends, however, he was too scared to speak to anyone else during his incarceration.

Frozen Pizza Punch Out

Things became increasingly heated at the Shillingers' during the summer of 1986. Steve's brother Eric had had enough of Cobain's couch-surfing, and once again it appeared that Kurt had overstayed his welcome.

Matters came to a head one night in August, when they fought over a frozen pizza. The fight got nasty fast, and the Shillinger boy gave Cobain two black eyes. (Eric got one, too, for his trouble.)

Kurt left for good that night and crashed in the Melvins' practice space at Dale Crover's house. The next day, Steve brought his belongings over and made it clear that he wasn't welcome back.

Heroin

Cobain would later tell Michael Azerrad that he had first tried heroin in the summer of '86, having discovered he liked opiates after ingesting several Percodans at some earlier point.He was attracted to the drug's euphoric high and its taboo image. It was thrilling and dangerous.

"It was really scary," he told Azerrad. "I always wanted to do it—I always knew I would."

Others would later dispute Kurt's claims, placing his introduction to the drug several years later, around 1990. By most accounts, in 1986 Kurt was still more likely to be found smoking weed and drinking.

"Spank Thru"

After duplicating a bunch of copies of *Illiteracy Will Prevail* on the Shillinger family stereo, Cobain began circulating his demo tape among friends and peers in and around Aberdeen in the early months of 1986. One of those on the receiving end was Novoselic, who accepted the tape but neglected to give it a fair listen until he returned from Arizona the following fall.

When Novoselic eventually gave the cassette his consideration, he found himself impressed at how good it was. He was especially taken with the song "Spank Thru."

"I heard that song and I go, 'This is a really good song,'" Novoselic remembered to Hughes. "It's a well put-together song. It's got a hook. It's kind of unique. It sounds different."

6

Smile on Your Brother

Kurt and Krist Align

Living with Lukin

Despite the fact he'd always had bad luck living with others, Cobain decided to try again in September 1986 when he and Matt Lukin from the Melvins found a rental home they could afford in Aberdeen. A "shack," by most accounts, the four-room rear-yard residence at 1000½ E. Second Street lacked kitchen appliances and had a sketchy foundation and a leaky roof. But the fact that it was just two blocks from his mother's place was enough reason for Wendy O'Connor to front her son his half of the $400 needed to rent the place.

Wendy and Kurt had grown closer during the previous year, and his half-sister's birth was part of the reason. He loved Breanne, and although he still loathed his stepdad, he was happy to come by and visit with his mom, do his laundry, and have a home-cooked meal when Pat was out of the house.

As with Kurt's previous apartment, the dilapidated state of his new place was exacerbated by the fact that it was a complete and utter mess. His collection of turtles occupied a bathtub in the living room, and their droppings gave off an awful smell. Meanwhile, Lukin—who worked construction—had begun a crude renovation, knocking down an unwelcome wall.

Cobain's friends and Lukin's bandmates came by to party and jam on their collective musical equipment, which they kept in the living room. Much of their free time was spent getting wasted on Schmidt (a cheap beer known for the images of animal scenery on the packaging) and LSD. At one point, Kurt was taking acid five times a week. He lived mostly on Kraft Macaroni and Cheese, although when he was feeling adventurous he would cut up a couple of potatoes and make homemade french fries.

Despite the noise, few if any of the neighbors—some of whom Kurt had befriended—ever complained. According to Charles Cross' biography, Cobain was happy to share his beer with two neighborhood teens born with fetal alcohol syndrome, while an elderly neighbor suffering from senility came over often to listen to Lynyrd Skynyrd's *Greatest Hits*.

The Sellouts

Upon Novoselic's return to Grays Harbor that fall, Cobain once again pitched the idea of forming a band together. Krist had previously resisted the idea, but in his post-Arizona mind-set he agreed to give it a try.

The pair began jamming regularly in Cobain's shack that fall and tried out a variety of different band lineups and configurations. In one incarnation, which lasted for about a month, Kurt played guitar, Krist was on bass, and a local musician named Bob McFadden played drums. In another, Cobain played drums and Krist played guitar with a local bassist name Steve "Instant" Newman during a handful of rehearsals in Novoselic's dad's garage.

The noise tested Kristo's neighbors' patience. "When they started, they used to practice in my garage and the neighbors [would ask], 'Mr. Novoselic, can you tell your kids to [quiet] down?'" Krist's father explained to Dave Rolland of the fan site Novoselic.com. "I got lots of complaints."

The Melvins gave the band the opening slot for a gig at the Pourhouse in Aberdeen, which Krist and Kurt hoped would bring in some quick cash. Performing as the Sellouts, they played a live set consisting of fewer than a half-dozen Creedence Clearwater Revival songs, which they imagined would go over well with the loggers that frequented the establishment. It also helped that some of the earliest songs Kurt ever learned to play—aside from "Stairway to Heaven" and the Cars' "My Best Friend's Girl"—were tunes penned by CCR's John Fogerty.

According to Novoselic, the tavern show "was just kind of something to do to screw around on the side" while they ironed out original material. Unfortunately, the $60 payday from this first gig wasn't enough to keep Cobain from getting into a band-ending fight with Newman.

Steve slugged Kurt with a vacuum, and Cobain responded by clubbing the bassist—who supposedly lost some fingers in a subsequent chainsaw accident—with a two-by-four.

Polynesian Condos

Considering he was such a slob, the notion that Cobain would take a job that entailed cleaning and repairing anything seemed ironic. Yet in order to make ends meet, Kurt did just that by accepting a position at the Polynesian Condominium Resort, located twenty-five miles from Aberdeen in Ocean Shores, in late '86.

Cobain earned $4 an hour as a maintenance man at the sixty-six-room coastal motel, where he would spend his working hours hiding out in empty rooms, sleeping off hangovers, eating any food left behind in the refrigerators, and watching television. When necessary, he would leisurely change light bulbs and handle the occasional overflowing toilet.

Kurt told Dilly about a maid's job that opened up, and soon they were riding the bus to the Polynesian together. In *Heavier Than Heaven*, Shelli marveled at how Cobain did so little for his paycheck. "He wasn't really a maintenance man at all," she said.

Still, he did enough to keep his boss, Betty Kalles—the head of housekeeping—happy. Speaking to *Kurt Cobain* author Christopher Sandford, she called Kurt "a model worker." When he set his hours, Kurt's stipulated that he could only work a Sunday-through-Thursday schedule. He needed to keep his Fridays and Saturdays free to practice music.

When he finally quit the job in the spring of 1987, Kalles said Kurt told her that "the chemicals he was using to wash the windows were making his fingernails soft and he was unable to play guitar." For Cobain, who aspired to be a musician above all else, he couldn't risk additional damage to his playing hands.

Higher and higher

While Cobain worried about the damage to his fingers cleaning agents at Ocean Shores could cause, he showed no sign of slowing down his drug and alcohol use during the winter of 1986–87. He spent most of his money on booze, weed, and acid, and, when he was broke in the days leading up to receiving his paycheck, he'd start huffing aerosol cans.

Getting annihilated on anything and everything he could was his main pursuit outside of playing music with Krist. Working was just a means to get obliterated.

Cobain also began talking to friends about the likelihood that he probably wouldn't live past thirty and again touched on the topic of suicide. Based on the way he was living, it seemed as if he had made up his mind about leaving behind a young corpse.

Stiff Woodies

That fall, when he wasn't working in the warehouse at Sears Roebuck on South Boone Street in Aberdeen or jamming with Kurt, Novoselic was hosting rehearsals for an informal band called the Stiff Woodies. Together, in the vacant room above his mother's Beauty Parlor on South M Street, Krist, Kurt, and an assortment of Melvins members worked out ill-fated songs like "Vaseline and Gasoline."

At Buzz Osborne's suggestion, the group scheduled a gig at the Pourhouse, supporting the Melvins, in late 1986. This led to a live radio session on KAOS-FM. It helped that the short-lived musical collective featured the KAOS Radio DJ Kurt Flansburg, who took the microphone for a version of AC/DC's "Sin City." Elsewhere, Krist provided vocals on an original called "Breakdance Boogie," for which he was backed by Osborne, Cobain, Dale Crover, Mike Dillard, Gary Cole, and Matt Lukin. The final efforts of the session counted a pair of Buzz-sung numbers that included a new tune called "Loose" and the Kiss cover "C'mon and Love Me."

Describing their sound in the January 1992 issue of *Option*, Kurt said that this pre-Nirvana band "sounded exactly like Black Flag. Totally abrasive, fast, punk music."

"There were some Nirvana elements," he continued, "some slow songs, even then. And there was some heavy, Black Sabbath–influenced stuff. I can't deny Black Sabbath or Black Flag."

Around this time, Novoselic, Dillard, and Crover also rehearsed a bunch of Mentors covers, but their renditions of the Seattle metal band's songs (performed as the Meltors) never made it out of the practice room.

Recruiting Burckhard

By early 1987, Cobain and Novoselic decided to get serious about their own band. They began regularly rehearsing at Kurt's shack on Second Street, and by February they had hired Aaron Burckhard, a friend of Krist's who went to community college locally, to round out their trio.

Burckhard was, as Novoselic explained to *Option*, "this stoner guy" whose biggest asset was the fact that he actually had a drum kit. But Aaron's presence helped the band get off the ground.

Burckhard was a full-blown metal-worshipper and product of a broken home who wore a moustache and lived with his mom. He had survived two serious road accidents, including one in which a car caught fire as it rolled over, killing its driver.

During the first quarter of '87, the trio practiced most nights, getting drunk and stoned as they repeatedly rehearsed their set. But when the group began to play out it became more and more apparent that Skid Row, as they were initially known, would be an ill fit for the Aberdeen flannel crowd.

7

She Eats Glue, How About You?

March 1987–March 1988

17 Nussbaum Road

T he band that would become Nirvana got their official public unveiling on Saturday March 7, 1987, when the trio—still operating under the name Skid Row—plugged in at the rural Washington home of Tony Poukkula.

The Raymond keg-party show had been arranged by a neighborhood friend named Ryan Ainger who was trying to give Kurt the courage to play in public with his new group. Acting as their very first manager (albeit without the band's permission), Ainger booked the gig and then, if that wasn't enough, he hauled the trio, their entourage, and their equipment to the party in a van borrowed from his day job as a carpet installer.

The band's set mixed originals like "Aero Zeppelin," "If You Must," "Mexican Seafood," "Pen Cap Chew," "Spank Thru," and "Hairspray Queen" with crowd-pleasing covers of Led Zeppelin's "Heartbreaker" and "How Many More Times." For the Zeppelin numbers, Poukkula joined them on guitar.

More party performances—including one in Aberdeen, where the trio followed a Dale Crover side-project—were to follow that year, but the group was especially fond of the gig in Raymond. According to Cobain's journal, he and Novoselic were extremely intoxicated and began to frighten the party's mullet-sporting attendees, prompting guests to move into the kitchen and away from the band. The spectacle became even grander when they started jumping off tables and through windows.

As the band continued to play a discordant soundtrack that included a lengthy variation on Flipper's "Sex Bomb," Shelli Dilly and Tracy Marander began to perform a mock lesbian scene. Later, Dilly got into a drunken fistfight in the driveway with another woman.

As Kurt told *Option* five years later, he and Krist were "pretending we were rock stars." Novoselic played shoeless and shirtless, with fake blood smeared across his chest and duct-tape across his nipples. Cobain rocked a *Munsters* T-shirt.

"We were totally wigging the rednecks out!" Kurt added. "That was the idea of punk rock in the first place—to abuse your audience. What better audience to have than a redneck audience."

Whisker Biscuit

In advance of their first performance, Cobain pondered a number of band names, including Bat Guana, Designer Drugs, Gut Bomb, Egg Flog, Fish Food, the deliberately misspelled Imcompetent Fools, Poo Poo Box, Pukeaharrea, Puking Worms, and Whisker Biscuit. Other ideas like Bliss, Pen Cap Chew, Throat Oyster, Windowframe, Ying Yang Valvestem, and Ted Ed Fred were also considered before Kurt and Krist decided on a proper name.

Tracy

Over the course of their running into one another at various gigs and parties during the past year and a half, Cobain and Marander's initial flirtation had blossomed into a sexual relationship by early 1987. The attractive, brown-haired, brown-eyed Tracy—who was a year older than Kurt—was all the more appealing to him because she was a veteran of dozens of punk-rock shows.

Kurt was self-conscious about his skinny body during their first intimate moments, and when the full-figured Marander commented on his thin physique, Cobain took it the wrong way and quickly covered himself. At times, due to an apparent lack of self-esteem, he wondered if he truly deserved her.

Tracy was remarkably knowledgeable about music—most notably punk and indie rock—and dressed the part. She was also a photographer who happily documented many Northwest punk shows in the company of her friend Tam Orhmund.

Marander was the kind of warm, supportive female figure Kurt had always wanted in his life. And, in addition to their love of the same kinds of music, they both had pet rats.

Buzz—Off!

In April, Buzz Osborne announced he was dissolving the Melvins and moving to San Francisco. Having already recorded the band's new album, *Gluey Porch Treatments*, at Studio D in Sausalito, Buzz was drawn to the Bay Area's more viable music environment.

Yet the band wasn't really splitting up. Dale Crover went with him, leaving Matt Lukin behind. Within a month of their moving, Lukin received word that the Melvins were playing live shows with replacement bassist Lori "Lorax" Black, the daughter of iconic child star Shirley Temple.

In time, Lukin got over getting booted from the Melvins and went on to join the legendary Seattle band Mudhoney with one-time Green River members Mark Arm and Steve Turner and former Bundle of Hiss drummer Dan Peters.

As for Cobain, the departure of Osborne felt liberating, as Kurt was no longer under the influence of his mentor. Buzz had scoffed at the melodic elements in Kurt's songs, and the Melvins' absence gave Kurt room to evolve as a songwriter and performer.

Lukin—Out!

With the Melvins down in San Francisco, Cobain began to feel freer to speak his mind with Matt Lukin. They began to argue with each other to the point where Kurt took a roll of masking tape and ran it down the center of the shack. He told Lukin to stay on his side and warned him not to cross over. Things quickly came to head when Kurt refused to let Matt or his friends use the bathroom, which was on his side of the room. Tired of Cobain's filth, turtles, and pet rat, Lukin moved out.

Carpet and Carlson

Having quit his maintenance job six weeks earlier, Cobain was completely broke by May 1987. His friend Ryan Ainger would bring Kurt along to help out with his job as a carpet installer when he could. Cobain's work ethic impressed Ainger's bosses, who made it clear that if he wanted a full-time job with the company, it was his.

Kurt resisted the offer, fearing that he might injure his hands with the sharp knives the job required. Still, he stayed on long enough to help his friend Dylan Carlson get some work with the company. The outspoken Carlson—who had some controversial opinions about politics, religion, and social issues—also moved into the shack, and would forge a tight bond with Kurt during the next two months.

White Lace and Strange

Skid Row continued to grow more and more serious in their ambitions into 1987. Practices were forums for Cobain's new songs like "White Lace and Strange" and "Help Me I'm Hungry," while live gigs, like their show at the Community World Theater in Tacoma in April and a subsequent concert at GESCCO in Olympia on May 1, were opportunities to tear the roof off.

The band's main form of transportation to early gigs was Novoselic's trusty Volkswagen bus. By removing some of the backseats, they could make just enough room for their equipment.

Skid Row's live sets, which ran between forty-five minutes and an hour, now included future fan favorites like "Floyd the Barber" and "Downer." The trio also expressed their diverse musical appreciation by bookending their live gigs with covers of Shocking Blue's obscure 1969 single "Love Buzz" and Cher's "Gypsys, Tramps & Thieves."

At the Tacoma show, Kurt, Krist, and Aaron shared the bill with other up-and-coming bands like Nisqually Delta Podunk Nightmare, Soylent Green, and Yellow Snow. The band then acquired their first non-party performance after Tracy urged the CWT's Jim May to book them.

For this concert, Kurt attempted to glam himself up in a silk Hawaiian shirt, flared pants, and four-inch platform shoes. Regardless of the front man's attire, the band sounded amazing and left many attendees—including May and a local musician named John Purkey—stunned and surprised at how well they played.

Meanwhile, the GESCCO gig—which was hastily booked by new Cobain ally Slim Moon, and proved to be the venue's final-ever show—wasn't exactly professional. While Cobain kept his wits about him, Novoselic was apparently so intoxicated that the band very nearly couldn't play.

Slim on Krist

When Everett True interviewed Slim Moon in 2005 for his book, *Nirvana: The True Story*, the Kill Rock Stars label's co-founder described Novoselic during the trio's infancy as "Tall and drunk." Krist had been known to dance on tables at parties—often until they collapsed—and once set off a fire extinguisher at an apartment, making it impossible for others to breathe. As much as he could be difficult and sarcastic, he was equally lovable, which is why he was able to get away with such antics.

KAOS Demo

Despite Krist's drunken state, KAOS radio host John Goodmanson had known Cobain from Melvins shows in Olympia, and he liked what he heard from Skid Row. He arranged for the band to play a ten-song set on the air at midnight on either April 17 or May 6, 1987, depending on which source you believe. Either way, the performance that aired on two overlapping radio programs titled *Out of Order* and *Toy Train Crash Backside Bone Beefcake* is of great historical importance, since a recording of it became the group's first demo.

According to Steve Fisk, who later produced some of Nirvana's *Blew* EP, the band landed the session thanks to Goodmanson and Donna Dresch, members of the local band Danger Mouse who liked what they heard in Olympia and brought the trio up to record "Spank Thru," "Love Buzz," "Floyd the Barber," "Downer," "Mexican Seafood," and "Hairspray Queen."

"There wasn't much banter," Goodmanson told Everett True in 2005. "They were like, 'Are we still on the air?' after every song."

The Name Game

On June 27, 1987, Cobain, Novoselic, and Burckhard played under the name Pen Cap Chew at the Community World Theatre in Tacoma, alongside bands like Hell's Kitchen, Silent Treatment, and Soylent Green. Six weeks later, they played the same venue—a converted adult movie theatre—yet again under the name Bliss.

Other groups on the August 9 bill included Inspector Luv & the Ride Me Babies, Sons of Ishmael, and the Magnet Men, who featured a drummer by the name of Chad Channing. (Future Soundgarden bassist Ben Shepherd was a bandmate of Channing's at the time.)

There is some speculation as to whether Burckhard was still in the band by the time of the August gig. According to Shepherd, Mike Dillard may have been subbed in (using Channing's kit) for this show.

Olympia

After a series of journeys to Olympia, first with the Melvins and now with his own band, Cobain decided that the city was an ideal fit for him. Although it was only an hour away from Grays Harbor, it was a world away from the restrictive hinterland of Aberdeen. Bolstered by an artistic community full of punks, hippies, and students at Evergreen State College, the town was perfect for the twenty-year-old Cobain.

Encouraged by Marander and friends Moon and Carlson, Kurt left Aberdeen behind in June 1987, stuffing all of his belongings—little more than a milk crate full of records, his guitar, and a plastic garbage bag full of clothes—into Tracy's car.

Life on North Pear Street

Together, Cobain and Marander took occupancy of an apartment in a multi-family home at 114½ North Pear Street in Olympia, adjacent to a pizzeria, for which they paid $137 a month. Although Kurt had few acquaintances in the city, his friends Slim and Dylan lived close by.

While Kurt looked unsuccessfully for a job, by July Tracy was working the midnight shift in the cafeteria at airplane manufacturer Boeing in Seattle. She had an hour-plus commute each way, meaning that she was usually gone from ten at night until nine the next day. In her absence, Tracy would leave Cobain a list of chores to do while she was gone.

With their array of pets including Kurt's turtles, multiple cats, a rabbit named Stew, a cockatiel, and a pair of rats, cleaning up after the animals was essential. At first Kurt kept on top of it, but as time went on—in typical Cobain fashion—he grew less and less reliable.

At one point, Goodmanson dropped in on Kurt, hoping to have Nirvana contribute a song to a cassette compilation he was working on with local musician Donna Dresch. When Kurt answered the door in his underwear, with a paintbrush in his hand, the KAOS DJ couldn't help but think—as he would later relay to True—that his acquaintance was taking advantage of Marander.

Stomach Trouble

By mid-1987, Cobain—who was intermittently using prescription drugs like codeine and the painkiller Vicodin—had started to experience stomach pains that would continue to aggravate him for years to come. Speaking to Michael Azerrad in 1993, he explained how his insides hurt when he ate, describing the pain as "burning, nauseous, like the worst stomach flu you can imagine."

When he wasn't playing music or getting loaded on drugs and alcohol, Kurt was noticeably quiet and seemingly depressed. While Tracy worked, Kurt spent time listening to records in many of rock's subgenres, including noisy bands like Big Black and Sonic Youth, vintage hard-rock acts like AC/DC and Led Zeppelin, and indie pop acts like the Vaselines and Olympia's own Beat Happening.

Playing for Free

Cobain relished any opportunity to play during these early months of his career, and like many upstart musicians, he played for free. But even when the opportunity to get paid a meager sum came along, he flat-out refused. His band would not take any money until he was convinced that they were good enough.

Of course non-paying shows were always available. More gigs meant more experience and more exposure for Kurt, Krist, and Aaron as Jim May booked the group to play alongside bands like Lethal Dose, Panic, and Bleeder at the CWT in Tacoma that spring and summer.

REDRUM Redecorating

Cobain's appreciation of the 1979 horror movie *The Shining* carried over into his interior decorating when he painted the bathroom on North Pear Street blood red. According to Marander, he even wrote the word "REDRUM"—"MURDER" spelled backward—on the wall in homage to the film.

Cobain continued to mutilate religious items like crosses and sculptures, as he had done before, and used them as decorative items. He pilfered local cemeteries and painted red tears under the eyes of a stolen Virgin Mary statue, turning it into a unique piece of art.

Kurt also garnished the apartment with his homemade drawings. A defaced Beatles poster showed Paul McCartney with glasses and an Afro, while other rock posters were turned over to serve as canvases for Cobain's own graffiti poems and perverse caricatures. One old Led Zeppelin poster was given a disturbing twenty-line sonnet that listed an array of afflictions including head lice, pneumonia, and gangrene.

Domestic Life

If Kurt was peculiar to some, he was an ideal fit with Tracy—at least at first. She appreciated his offbeat but expressive approach to art and was happy to dote on him in a motherly way. In turn, Cobain cooked meals—including dishes like vanilla chicken and fettuccine Alfredo—for her.

Marander appreciated the gesture and knew that he was making such high-calorie meals in the hope he might gain a little weight—something that was always difficult for him. He loathed the pizzeria next door, but when they could afford it the couple would frequent the nearby Fourth Avenue Tavern. They enjoyed spending time together doing simple things, like taking their clothes to the nearby Laundromat.

Image Conscious

According to Marander, Cobain was bothered by the fact he was so thin, but despite his best efforts to try to gain weight—be it ordering powders from the back of magazines or preparing high-calorie meals—he remained super-skinny. His legs were so skeletal that he would rarely, if ever, wear shorts.

Kurt often dressed in layers, and it was common for him to wear long underwear plus several shirts with jeans. According to Tracy, he would even go so far as to wear one pair of Levi's over another if he was feeling particularly self-conscious.

Quiet Period

By the fall of 1987, Cobain had acquired a job at Lemon's Janitorial Service, where he earned $4.75 an hour cleaning office buildings and industrial facilities around Olympia. It was an ironic job for a man who continued to be a complete slob in his private life.

Kurt took some of the proceeds from this job and bought a used Datsun. As with the other positions he'd held in the past, however, he gave up on it before long.

Around this time, Krist and Shelli settled into a house in Tacoma, a half-hour or so north of Olympia. Novoselic continued to balance his job in the warehouse at Sears with a position as an industrial painter, while his significant other had accepted a position working with Marander in the cafeteria at Boeing.

Burckhard had since announced that he had accepted a job as the assistant manager at the Burger King in Aberdeen, and the requirement for nighttime working hours at the fast food restaurant prompted his resignation from the band. Without a drummer, Novoselic and Cobain's musical bond fell into an unexpected lull. After months of traveling up to Aberdeen by bus for rehearsals, it looked like Kurt's dream had ground to a halt.

In a letter written late in the year, Kurt asked Krist if he wanted to get the band back into action. Krist called Kurt and suggested that they build a rehearsal space in the basement of his Tacoma home. Cobain was elated, and soon, after they'd collected enough scrap wood and old carpet from construction sites, the band's new practice room was ready.

Rocket Drummer

With a replacement for Burckhard needed to get the trio back on track, Cobain placed a classified advertisement in the Seattle music newspaper the *Rocket* in October. It read, "SERIOUS DRUMMER WANTED. Underground attitude, Black Flag, Melvins, Zeppelin, Scratch Acid, Ethel Merman. Versatile as heck. Kurdt 352-0992." As the ad shows, Kurt had also begun playing with the spelling of his name.

Unfortunately, the solicitation yielded no replies, but Cobain and Novoselic continued to work on material and practice together as time allowed. When Dale Crover returned to Aberdeen that December, to visit family, they reconnected with him. Crover was recruited to play with them for rehearsals and a demo session set for the next month.

"Cracker"

Sometime during the month of December, Cobain used a four-track to record several songs including "Cracker," an early version of "Polly." He was inspired to write the song after learning about a disturbing incident that had taken place in Tacoma that June, where a fourteen-year-old girl had been kidnapped, raped, and tortured by a man named Gerald Friend before escaping when her captor stopped at a gas station in the city.

Cobain also recorded demos of "Sad" (which became "Sappy") plus "Clean Up Before She Comes," "Beans," "Bambi Slaughter," and "Spectre." The latter was an early hybrid of future Nirvana songs "Misery Loves Company" and "Seed."

Reciprocal

With Crover in tow, Ted Ed Fred—as the band was now known—began rehearsals on Saturday January 2, 1988, for a planned studio demo. After spending three successive weekends working on material, the group entered Reciprocal Recordings in Seattle on January 23 to record a studio demo.

Cobain was drawn to Reciprocal and its cheap rate of $20 per hour after seeing an ad for the facility in the *Rocket*. Session producer Jack Endino—who would also track local favorites Mudhoney and Soundgarden—was a guitarist in the local outfit Skin Yard and co-owned the facility with Chris Hanszek. If Reciprocal was hardly state-of-the-art—it was cramped, dated, and worn—its vintage equipment worked fine and was actually ideal for the fuzzed-out guitar approaches the band was crafting.

A friend of Novoselic's named Eric Harder carted the band and their gear from Tacoma to the 900-square-foot studio in an old campervan. After the load-in, they got started, blasting through ten songs over the course of a long afternoon.

By the time the session was over, Endino realized Kurt's last name was not "Covain," as he had initially thought, and as he quickly mixed down the demo and transferred it to cassette, the producer marveled at the power of the trio's end-product, which he would give a proper mix later on. The studio recording, which Endino would later name the *Dale Demo*, included—in order—"If You Must," "Downer," "Floyd the Barber," "Paper Cuts," "Spank Thru," "Hairspray Queen," "Aero Zeppelin," "Beeswax," "Mexican Seafood," and an incomplete rendition of "Pen Cap Chew."

Although the latter wound up being cut off near the midway mark when the group's reel-to-reel tape ran out, it would have to do, because Cobain and Novoselic didn't have another $30 to part with for a second reel. The session was tracked between the hours of noon and 6 p.m., and Cobain paid the full $152.44 for the session hours—plus the cost of the first tape reel—using money from his job at Lemon Janitorial. Krist had been between jobs at the time.

Going Pro

On the evening of the session, Kurt, Krist, and Dale listened to the playback of their demo twice as they traveled in Harder's camper to their first gig in five months. Once they arrived in Tacoma, Crover confronted Cobain after learning that he was refusing to take any money for his performances. In Dale's eyes, he should at least get $20 for gas. After all, the shows May was booking into the Community World Theatre were making some money by this point.

Crover fought with his good friend backstage, insisting he needed to get what he deserved. Kurt resisted. When May got word about the fracas—and knowing that he had done well to get Cobain and Novoselic's band for free during shows throughout 1987—the CWT boss offered conciliation and handed Kurt a ten-dollar bill.

It might have been a paltry sum, but it was symbolic, because for the first time they were being paid for playing Cobain's original compositions. After playing the ten songs from their newly minted demo—plus "Annorexorcist," "Erectum," and a set-ending rendition of Led Zeppelin's "Moby Dick"—the band traveled home aware that they were now officially professional musicians.

Radio Shack Hacks

The day after Ted Ed Fred's CWT show, Harder—the proprietor of Aberdeen's Radio Shack—filmed the band miming to the newly cut demo takes of "If You Must" and "Paper Cuts" in the front of his store. Shooting after store hours, Harder incorporated special effects that seemed cheesy and slipshod to Kurt and Krist when they watched the finished VHS tape. Cobain was upset that his trio didn't come off looking more professional. He watched the tape repeatedly, thinking of ways he might improve the band's presence.

Cleaning Up

With his renewed focus on the band, the early months of 1988 marked a period of increased sobriety for Cobain. No longer would he spend his days in a stupor. With his commitments to songwriting, practicing with Krist, and his janitorial job, drugs and alcohol became more of a recreational pursuit.

Cobain even gave up his longstanding cigarette habit for a time, as he knew it took its toll on his vocals. While this was a short-lived lifestyle change, it made others realize just how serious he was about moving his music career forward in the weeks following his twenty-first birthday.

Mustache Man

Dale Crover's position in the band was always temporary, and when he went back to San Francisco to resume working with Buzz Osborne, he suggested a replacement by the name of Dave Foster.

Like Cobain and Novoselic, Foster hailed from Aberdeen. Unlike his new bandmates, he looked like a logger, wearing a mustache, short hair, and acid-wash jeans at a time when all three were decidedly unhip. But Foster could play, which meant Kurt could keep his band in motion.

Driving his dilapidated Datsun from Olympia to Aberdeen, Cobain would pick Foster up en route and together they would travel to their practice space at Krist's in Tacoma.

The band's first show with Foster occurred in March 1988 and was also Kurt and Krist's first live gig in Olympia. Held at the Caddyshack—a house rented to college students located near a golf course—the party performance was a mixed success.

Billed as Bliss—the latest in an endless run of tentative names—the trio sounded strong to attendees, but their image seemed uneven and unrefined to Evergreen's sophisticated collegiate hipsters—a point made clear when a Mohawk-sporting attendee mocked Foster's redneck-like appearance.

Cobain came away from the show embarrassed, and Foster was the reason. He told the drummer he needed to make some changes if they were going to make it. Foster agreed to cut his drum kit down from a twelve-piece metal-style kit to a more primitive six-piece rock 'n' roll setup, but he balked at shaving his mustache.

Naming Nirvana

In the days that followed the Caddyshack gig, Cobain—who was intrigued by Buddhism at the time—came up with the last and final name for the band. Kurt announced the trio's new name to Novoselic and Foster, showing them a hand-drawn flyer for their next show, as Nirvana, at the CWT on March 19.

"Nirvana" is a Buddhist term for a place or state free from pain, worry, and the external world, although Krist's interpretation was a little looser. "Big amplifiers," the bassist explained, when *Melody Maker* asked for him to define the band's name in October 1989. "Not giving a shit and having fun," he continued, with a smirk. "Dreaming . . . Being free from distraction and not being uptight. Jamming, having lots of good shows, being polite, respecting our moms and dads."

First Show as Nirvana

Playing alongside the Vampire Lezbos and Slim Moon's band Lush, Nirvana took the stage for an electrifying set at the Community World Theatre on the third Saturday in March 1988. Cobain steered the band through a sixteen-song set that featured an opening rendition of Shocking Blue's "Love Buzz" and the public debuts of "Blew" and "Big Cheese."

Nirvana mirrored their other recent shows by again winding down their set with a Led Zeppelin–inspired "Moby Dick" jam. When the audience clamored for another number, the trio delivered a second crowd-pleaser to close the performance—a fiery interpretation of Creedence Clearwater Revival's "Bad Moon Rising."

A tattered flyer preserved from the Community World Theater show on March 19, 1988. Featuring drummer Dave Foster, this was first known gig the band performed as Nirvana.   *Author's collection*

8

Can You Feel My Love Buzz?

Nirvana on 45

Demo Blitz

With copies of Nirvana's first studio demo burning a hole in Cobain's hand, he set about sending handwritten letters to record companies that he admired, "shopping" his demo tapes by mailing the unsolicited packages to indie labels like San Francisco's Alternative Tentacles.

SST Records—home to his beloved Black Flag, plus the Meat Puppets, punk favorites the Descendents, and blistering indie trio Dinosaur Jr.—was a primary target. But label-owner and Black Flag co-founder Greg Ginn was underwhelmed by the demo, so he passed.

Chicago's Touch and Go—which gave experimentalist like Big Black, the Butthole Surfers, and the Jesus Lizard an outlet for their releases—was another company Kurt hoped would sign Nirvana. Cobain later claimed he was so persistent that he repeatedly sent customized demo packages to the company's owner, Corey Rusk.

In one letter, he explained that his band would be willing to pay for the bulk of the pressing and recording costs, before desperately pleading for a response. "Do you think you could PLEASE send us a reply of 'fuck off,' or, 'not interested,' so we don't have to waste more money sending more tapes?"

When asked about this by Cobain biographer Charles Cross, no one who worked at the label had any recollection of receiving the packages.

Endino Spreads the Word

After Jack Endino compiled his final mix of Nirvana's Reciprocal Session, he made sure to dub off extra copies to circulate among his connections around Seattle. The move was as much about Endino putting his production wares on display as it was about helping out his recent clients. Of course, if Jack hadn't believed in Nirvana, he never would have done it.

Endino passed a copy to Shirley Carlson, then a DJ on the influential University of Washington radio station KCMU. He also gave a cassette to Dawn Anderson, a contributing writer for the *Rocket* who ran her own fanzine, *Backlash*. A third tape went to Jonathan Poneman, co-owner of the new Seattle indie label Sub Pop.

The reaction was decidedly positive. Carlson began playing "Floyd the Barber," and later "Paper Cuts," on her radio show on 90.3 FM. Anderson contacted the band to express her interest in writing an article about them, and later did. And perhaps most importantly, Poneman asked Endino for Cobain's telephone number.

Central Tavern

Nirvana's first Seattle gig was planned for early April at the city's Central Tavern, hot on the heels of an Olympia party performance at the Witch House in March 1988.

Save for Poneman and his partner Bruce Pavitt—plus Cobain, Novoselic, and Foster's respective girlfriends—the venue was empty. Due to poor turn out, the band played only one complete song—their rendition of "Love Buzz"—before giving up.

"We didn't even play," Cobain remembered to *Option* in January 1992. "We just loaded up our stuff and left."

Sunday Showcase

Despite the failure of the Central Tavern show, Jonathan Poneman and Bruce Pavitt saw and heard something in Nirvana that made them want to give the trio another shot at being on their label. Poneman booked Nirvana a showcase slot as the opening act at his "Sub Pop Sunday" event on a bill featuring Blood Circus.

In advance of the gig, which was scheduled for Sunday, April 24, 1988, at the Vogue in Seattle, Pavitt played Nirvana's demo for his Muzak co-worker Mark Arm. Arm, who had been in the famed Seattle band Green River and now doubled as the front man for new Sub Pop signing Mudhoney, worked alongside Bruce in the tape-duplication department of the elevator-music service company. Pavitt and Poneman both valued Arm's opinion.

Arm—perhaps feeling a bit threatened—dismissed Nirvana as a lower-grade Skin Yard, but that didn't stop him from making sure he was in attendance during the new trio's showcase gig. Meanwhile, word of the show spread among the city's underground population thanks to Carlson, who continued to play songs from the Endino demo in advance of the performance.

Before the gig—which could be seen for a mere $2 cover charge—Cobain's anxiety prompted him to vomit as the group sat in an adjacent parking lot, waiting to play. (Because Foster was under twenty-one, the group remained outside in Novoselic's Volkswagen van until their stage time.)

JULY 3 ∞ the VOGUE

BLOOd CIRCUS

NIRVANA

≈God⋅⋅Country⋙

A Special Sunday show

from denver

the FLUID *

A flyer announcing Nirvana's "Sub Pop Sunday" performance with Blood Circus and the Fluid.   *Author's collection*

That night's turnout was respectable if somewhat small and gave the trio a suitable setting for their hour-long, fourteen-song showcase, but things went wrong when Kurt blew some chords and the P.A. system malfunctioned. Afterward, Cobain expressed his disappointment about the performance and how apprehension had gotten the better of him.

In an unsent letter to Crover, later published in *Journals*, Kurt acknowledged the pressure of the show—their big shot at a record deal—and wrote of how he felt he was being judged. "There was a representative from every Seattle band there just watching," he explained. "We felt like they should have had score cards."

Future Nirvana photographer Charles Peterson was in the audience at the urging of Pavitt and Poneman, who talked the band up as the next big thing. Peterson was so unimpressed he didn't take one single picture of the group that night. "I thought they were atrocious," he told *Goldmine* in 1997. "I just thought, 'This is a joke. This is not going to go anywhere.'"

Cobain was left feeling depressed by the idea that Nirvana had blown their one chance to make a record. "We totally sucked," he told Michael Azerrad in *Come as You Are*. "We fucked it up." With that in mind, no one was more surprised and elated than Kurt when Poneman called to tell him that he and Pavitt wanted to do a record with them.

Sub Pop 101

Sub Pop Records evolved out of Bruce Pavitt's *Subterranean Pop* fanzine, a crude publication that he launched in the early 1980s, while attending Evergreen State College. Designed to help expose the budding American independent record labels of the era that Pavitt admired, the project earned him course credit and accolades from fellow scenesters in Olympia. The 'zine's title quickly morphed into *Sub Pop*, and by 1982 it had evolved into a series of successful compilation cassettes. That same year, the fifth installment of the series—which boasted tracks by underground bands like Jad Fair, the Embarrassment, and Pell Mell— managed to sell an impressive two thousand copies.

By the end of '83, after releasing nine cassettes, Pavitt relocated to Seattle and began writing his "Sub Pop USA" column for the *Rocket*. In 1986, Sub Pop became a bona fide record label with the release of its flagship vinyl compilation *Sub Pop 100*, which featured up-and-comers from the American underground like the Wipers, Scratch Acid, Naked Raygun, and Sonic Youth.

The aforementioned Seattle band Green River—whose members included Mark Arm and future Pearl Jam co-founders Jeff Ament and Stone Gossard— agreed to record their debut EP for Sub Pop in June of '86, but financial woes kept Pavitt from issuing *Dry as a Bone* until July 1987. The label would tout the five-song disc—which was co-produced by Ament and Jack Endino—in local ads as "ultra loose GRUNGE that destroyed the morals of a generation."

That same year, Jonathan Poneman invested a savings bond worth approximately $20,000 in the label and became partners with Pavitt. Poneman was a frustrated musician-turned–KCMU DJ who originally hailed from Toledo, Ohio, and had been introduced to Bruce by a mutual friend, guitarist Kim Thayil.

That July, Poneman and Pavitt released "Hunted Down"/"Nothing to Say," the debut single by Thayil's band Soundgarden. Then, in October, they released the group's debut EP, *Screaming Life*.

Poneman's goal was to make the label synonymous with the Northwest, much as Motown was a representation of Detroit. Focusing on the primal rock sound emerging in their backyard, the company became a full-time pursuit in 1988—right around the time Nirvana came to Poneman's attention. After raising $43,000 that April and legally incorporating as Sub Pop, the company released Mudhoney's legendary debut single "Touch Me I'm Sick" in August, five months after the band had tracked it at Reciprocal with Endino.

While Sub Pop would go on to be credited with the Seattle Sound, Jack Endino definitely deserves equal recognition. Utilizing the same economical work ethic exhibited on Nirvana's Reciprocal demos, Endino would go on to produce a total of seventy-five releases (including singles, EPs, and albums) for the label in just two years, capturing the raw, explosive sound of grunge.

Grunge Defined

In 1981, Arm—using his birth name McLaughlin—wrote to the Seattle fanzine *Desperate Times* about his local band Mr. Epp & the Calculations, describing them as "Pure grunge! Pure noise! Pure shit!"

Years later, as mentioned above, Arm and his friends at Sub Pop would appropriate the term to help define Green River. Long before it became the name of a musical sub-genre of which Nirvana, Soundgarden, and many others would become a part, "grunge" was used to describe acts that played a scuzzy style of guitar rock.

Although the longstanding Mudhoney front man has been acknowledged as the inventor of the term, he denied this in a 2001 interview with the *Stranger*. "The term was already being thrown around in Australia in the mid-'80s to describe bands King Snake Roost, The Scientists, Salamander Jim, and Beasts of Bourbon," he said.

On 45

Not long after the Vogue audition, Poneman met with Cobain and Novoselic (who arrived late and was intoxicated) at the Café Roma in Seattle. But things didn't go quite as Kurt had expected when Jonathan offered to release a single to test the waters.

Cobain had been hoping to land a full album deal with an accompanying single or EP release. He was also disenchanted to learn that Sub Pop wanted to make "Love Buzz," Nirvana's Shocking Blue cover, the A-side of the proposed single, instead of one of his originals.

Despite these frustrations, Cobain and Novoselic recognized they had little choice but to take Sub Pop's offer. At the time, Poneman and Pavitt's label was the only one interested in working with Nirvana. For the time being, a seven-inch single would have to be enough. An agreement was reached for a 45 release that would be produced by Endino, with the recording costs to be picked up by Sub Pop.

Nirvana supported the always-controversial Butthole Surfers at this October 1988 Halloween party, held at Union Station. In later years, the Gibby Haynes–fronted Texas outfit would return the favor, opening some of Nirvana's final shows, including the band's last US gig on January 8, 1994.   *Author's collection*

Love Buzz

Novoselic had discovered Shocking Blue's 1969 track "Love Buzz" after he picked up the Dutch rock group's second album, *At Home*, at a garage sale.

Formed in The Hague in 1967 and steered by main songwriter Robbie van Leeuwen, the band had become best known for their 1970 chart topper "Venus," which appeared on the same album.

When Krist played "Love Buzz" for Cobain, Kurt loved it, and they learned to play it immediately. At early shows, the obscure cover became their calling card, which explains why Sub Pop wanted it as Nirvana's first A-side.

Back with Burckhard, Briefly

While Kurt and Krist were meeting with Poneman, Dave Foster was in the midst of a two-week jail stint on assault charges. Nirvana's drummer had gotten into an altercation with the son of the mayor of Cosmopolis.

In addition to the jail time, Foster was ordered to pay the victim's medical bills and had his driver's license revoked over the incident. During his incarceration, Cobain and Novoselic asked Aaron Burckhard to rejoin the band. For rehearsals at Novoselic's home in Tacoma, Aaron used Foster's drum kit.

Although things returned to normal for a few days, Burckhard wound up getting tossed from the band after he was charged with driving while intoxicated.

Officer Springsteen

Burckhard and Cobain had been drinking together after practice when they ran out of beer. To replenish their stock, Aaron borrowed Kurt's Datsun and went to retrieve more booze. However, the drummer was diverted in his completion of this errand and wound up stopping in at the bar where he was picking up the beer for a few cocktails on his own.

Later, on the way back to meet up with Cobain, Burckhard was pulled over by an African-American police officer named Springsteen. Aaron goofed on the name the cop shared with rock superstar Bruce Springsteen and things got heated. Next, the drunken drummer did the inexcusable and—according to Nirvana historian Everett True—allegedly called the cop "a fucking nigger." As a result, Kurt's car was impounded and Novoselic reluctantly went to bail Aaron out.

Remarkably, it was not this incident that sealed Burckhard's fate but the fact that he was too hungover to make it to practice the next day. Cobain and Novoselic sacked him for good. After their troubles with Burckhard, and Foster's own set of unfortunate circumstances, they decided to find a completely new drummer.

Cobain and Novoselic discretely placed another ad in the *Rocket* in the spring of '88, hoping to find the right kit man. This was done without the knowledge of either Burckhard or Foster.

"DRUMMER WANTED. Play hard, sometimes light, underground, versatile, fast, medium slow, versatile, serious, heavy, versatile, dorky, nirvana, hungry. Kurdt 352-0992." They didn't get a response.

Firing Foster

While Cobain and Novoselic planned to fire Foster, they figured they would wait until they had a proper replacement. They kept Dave in tow for a pair of Olympia shows during the month of May, including a birthday party at The Glass House in Olympia on May 14, and one a week later behind the K Dorm at Evergreen State.

When it came time to notify the drummer, Cobain chickened out. The mustachioed Foster was never officially fired. Kurt wrote a letter announcing his discharge—which can be seen in *Journals*—but he never actually mailed it.

In the unsent note, dated May 29, 1988, Kurt addressed the drummer's failure to make rehearsals. He also called Foster out on his questionable priorities—which put fixing up a racecar over making band practices.

Foster only discovered he had been relieved of his duties in Nirvana after he saw an ad in the *Rocket* for a Seattle show Nirvana had booked to play with the Butthole Surfers and Blood Circus.

Chatting with Channing

Following the aforementioned K Dorm gig on May 21—which saw Nirvana play alongside acts like Herd of Turtles, Lansdat Blister, the Speds, and Telefunken—Krist and Kurt began talking to a drummer they had become acquainted with in recent months. Aware of Chad Channing's drumming abilities, Kurt and Krist relayed how they already had a single deal with Sub Pop. They asked the Tacoma-based, Bainbridge Island–reared kit man if he might like to jam with them, and things gelled.

Although Chad wasn't ever told he was formally hired, he became Nirvana's drummer after he returned for practice after practice above Maria Novoselic's hair salon, where the band was once again rehearsing. Channing was instantly compatible with the band. As Cobain noted in his journal, he and Novoselic could relate to their new drummer—and, like them, he was committed to playing music five nights a week.

Introducing Chad Channing

Chad Douglas Channing was born on January 31, 1967, in Santa Rosa, California, to parents Wayne (a.k.a. Doug) and Burnyce. Channing's family—which also included two sisters, Kyrstie and Joelle—relocated several times during his childhood due to his father's unpredictable career as a radio disc jockey. By the late 1970s, the Channing family had settled in Anacortes, Washington.

As a boy, Chad was very active and excelled at soccer and other sports, but his athletic aspirations were squashed when he was injured in a freak gym accident at age thirteen. Channing fell during a physical-education class and shattered his upper left femur, which resulted in the need for eight surgeries and five years of recovery and physical therapy.

While Chad was moving in and out of hospital beds and body casts during the eighth and ninth grade, he was home-schooled by a tutor but was prone to periods of extreme boredom. To help with this, his parents bought him a candy apple–red electric bass guitar, and before long he was teaching himself to play Van Halen songs.

Realizing that Chad—who was drawn to the likes of Black Sabbath and the Sex Pistols, and everything in between—was a natural musician, his parents encouraged this pursuit and bought him a used, cobalt-blue drum set when his casts came off. The drum pedals helped improve his leg strength, and before long he was jamming with friends and, later, garage bands. Upon Channing's return to school, he joined the band and learned to read music. He also learned to play the guitar.

Unfortunately, Channing's high-school experience was drastically affected by his accident, and the school district's home tutor wasn't enough to keep him from falling two years behind in his studies. Faced with the prospect that he might not graduate until he turned twenty, Chad—who was planning to pursue music over a formal career anyway—decided, with his parents' support, to drop out. At one point, after his parents separated, he took a job working as a sauté chef at a Seafood restaurant in Bainbridge Island.

By the summer of 1985, Channing—already a veteran of a band called Color Me Gone—was playing in Mind Circus, a group that also counted future Soundgarden bassist Ben Shepherd among its members. After stints with assorted lineups of 48 School, the Magnet Men, and Stone Crow, Ben and Chad evolved into Tic-Dolly-Row by 1987.

North for the Northwest

Channing was only five-foot-six, and with his small build and long dark hair, his massive North drum kit looked all the more impressive. The uniquely shaped fiberglass set, which Chad had bought from a large music store in Yakima, Washington, was unlike any other being used by drummers on the Northwest rock scene in 1988.

His new bandmates liked how Chad's kit was as distinct as the music they were creating. They also admired how forceful his playing could be. When they performed live with Channing for the first time at the Vogue over Memorial Day weekend, Nirvana hit the attendees like a ton of bricks.

If Chad was the best fit yet, Cobain and Novoselic still had some molding to do. Channing's timing wasn't perfect, but it was good enough. When he expressed an interest in writing songs and disclosed his heavy pop and progressive-rock influences, however, Nirvana's founders had to made it subtly known that such input was neither necessary nor welcome.

Chad Tours Redneck City

Channing had grown up comfortably in Anacortes, a popular boating destination on Fidalgo Island, and was taken aback when Cobain and Novoselic gave him a tour of Aberdeen one night after rehearsals above the hair salon.

"I thought to myself, 'holy crap.' It was really bad," he said in *Heavier Than Heaven*. He was startled when he saw the neighborhood where Kurt had grown up—which he would call "a slum"—firsthand.

After riding by some of the abandoned buildings Cobain slept in and showing Chad their alma mater, Weatherwax High, they dropped in on their old stomping ground, the Pourhouse Tavern, for a cold one. Looking around the barroom, there were mullets and mustaches and flannel on every stool. Or as Channing put it, "It was redneck city."

Making Sure

Despite the fact that Nirvana had a commitment from the label, Sub Pop's principals still wanted a chance to see the band with Channing in action. Poneman managed to get them on the bill at the Central Tavern on Sunday, June 5, as the opening band.

Although the crowd was sparse and there were P.A. problems, Poneman and Pavitt knew their hunches were correct. Nirvana's session with Endino was booked for the following weekend.

Sub Pop's Money Woes

According to Chad Channing, right before the "Love Buzz" sessions, Sub Pop's own money troubles made the Nirvana camp suspicious about the company they were dealing with. Bruce Pavitt had the audacity to call Cobain in Olympia, looking to borrow $200 to help finance the project.

Although Cobain—who was perpetually broke—laughed off Pavitt's request, it especially bothered Novoselic, Tracy Marander, and Channing. "We were shocked," Chad told Cross.

Tracking "Love Buzz"

Nirvana returned to Reciprocal on June 11, 1988, with producer Jack Endino to record their debut single. Unlike their extremely productive demo session on January 23, this time Nirvana finished tracking only "Love Buzz" during this initial five-hour Saturday-afternoon session. Some of the delay could be blamed on the homemade twenty-second sound montage Kurt wanted to incorporate into the song.

"That was an audio collage of little snippets put together by Kurt at home through skillful use of the pause button on his cassette deck," Endino later explained on his official website. "We spliced it on to the beginning of the tape but the Sub Pop folks made us shorten it." According to Jack, midway through the single mix—which was made on July 16—a noise break culling extra sounds from Cobain's sonic collage was also added.

A second five-hour recording session held on June 30 found the band tracking "Big Cheese"—which became the B-side—"Spank Thru," and "Blandest." Endino ultimately erased the latter song at Kurt's insistence—because, as Jack put it, it was "just not ready yet"—but versions remained on the group's original cassettes from the afternoon.

It turns out Nirvana hadn't properly rehearsed "Blandest" before they attempted to record it, and the studio take was actually the first time Channing ever played it. Although they thought about returning to record the song (a Cobain original) at a later date, it fell by the wayside.

Ironically, the band came looking for it four years later as a possible inclusion on their *Incesticide* compilation, but Endino had to remind Novoselic that the session version was erased from master tapes. It is believed that the bootleg copies of the track that surfaced in the 1990s originated from Nirvana's own rough mix cassettes. According to Jack, a copy was likely stolen at some point from one of the members. Fittingly, the Nirvana camp stole it back and eventually released it on 2004's *With The Lights Out* boxed set.

The Fluid and the Flu

In the midst of their studio work that summer, Nirvana gigged regularly. They played a show with King Krab, Millions of Dead Leninz, and Slim Moon's band Lush for around fifty attendees at the Hal Holmes Community Center in Ellensburg on June 17.

A Sub Pop Sunday gig at the Vogue with the likes of Blood Circus and the Fluid on July 3, which preceded a show with Leaving Trains at the Central Tavern on July 23. The latter concert would later become significant to Nirvana devotees as it was booked by Nikolas Hartshorne, who went on to become the King County Medical Examiner at the time of Cobain's death in 1994.

Elsewhere, the group played with Soundgarden—who had become one of Seattle's best-known bands by this point—at the Capitol Lake Jam in Olympia's Capitol Lake Park on August 20. Nine days later, the band again played the Vogue, this time with local act the Treacherous Jaywalkers. Cobain had the flu, and because of the resulting fatigue he reportedly played much of the gig lying on his back.

Backlash

In September 1988, Nirvana earned its first bona fide write-up when *Backlash* publisher Dawn Anderson ran an interview she titled, "It may be the Devil and it may be the Lord . . . But it sure as hell ain't human."

In the piece, Cobain—who was now spelling his name "Kurdt Kobain"—and Novoselic spoke of the tension they felt before and during their first Sup Pop Sunday performance. They also touched on how they were schooled by the Melvins, although Anderson was quick to stress that Nirvana was anything but a clone band.

Anderson described the trio as "the kind of band that can turn an entire audience into zombie pod people by their sheer heaviness." In doing so, she was paying them a high compliment.

"Love Buzz" Photo Shoot

One afternoon in August 1988, the members of Nirvana—who had all taken the day off from their respective jobs—traveled to Seattle in Novoselic's van to pick up a local photographer named Alice Wheeler, who had been hired by Sub Pop for a mere $25 to shoot the cover of the group's debut single.

Using an infrared lens that gave the pictures a desired "fuzzy" effect, Wheeler shot eight rolls of film that day, according to a 1997 *Goldmine* article by Gillian G. Gaar. The band used a variety of locations around Tacoma, including the foot of the Tacoma Narrows Bridge and at Point Defiance Park's Never Never Land during the session.

Image seemed important to Chad, who sported a beret, shades, and a Germs T-shirt. Meanwhile, Novoselic seemed less concerned about appearing cool and had on a short-sleeve buttoned shirt. Kurt—who never rode a motorcycle past his teen years—wore an old Harley Davidson T-shirt with the motto "Live to Ride."

Buttholes Birthday Party

On the third Saturday in October 1988, Nirvana were hired to play a private birthday party in Bainbridge. The trio played on a backyard skate ramp for a bunch of suburban punk and skateboard kids.

A week later, on October 28, Nirvana opened for a national act for the first time in Seattle, supporting the Butthole Surfers at Union Station. This was a significant show for Cobain, who was a massive fan of the controversial Texas band's music. In *Journals*, Cobain famously lists the group's eponymous 1983 debut EP—which includes songs like "The Shah Sleeps in Lee Harvey's Grave"—among his Top Ten favorite records of all time.

The Butthole Surfers—who at the time had albums with titles like *Cream Corn from the Socket of Davis* and *Locust Abortion Technician* in their canon—would play a further part in Nirvana's history later on.

Smashing

Two days after the Butthole Surfers show, Nirvana played a party at Evergreen State's Dorm K208 in Olympia. During the Halloween-themed gig on October 30, Krist and Kurt made themselves up, putting fake blood on their necks.

Although the set marked the addition of songs like "School," "Mr. Moustache," "Sifting," and "Run, Rabbit, Run!," this show was special for another reason.

Slim Moon's new band Nisqually Delta Podunk Nightmare played before Nirvana, and proved to be a hard act to follow, especially after Slim and his drummer got into a fistfight in the middle of their set. When Cobain took the stage, he felt challenged. He didn't want to be one-upped, so he played with the kind of intensity that captivated the crowd. Midway through "Love Buzz," he trashed his Fender Mustang guitar—the first time he had ever smashed his guitar onstage.

It was all the "Greeners" in attendance could talk about for weeks after the show. Kurt's destructive outburst had cemented the trio's popularity in Olympia. Of course, Cobain's habit of demolishing his instruments would become more and more prevalent as it became more affordable in the months and years that followed.

Singles Club Starter

Nirvana's debut single, "Love Buzz," was released in late November 1988 on Sub Pop Records, replete with a blurred cover picture of Kurt (credited as Kurdt), Krist (listed as Chris), and Chad. Backed with the original "Big Cheese," it was the first release in Sub Pop's Singles Club—which the company had announced the month prior—and the label's twenty-third single release overall.

Nirvana had known they would be the Singles Club test case since August, and it didn't sit well with Kurt. When Poneman told him, Kurt was furious, but because there was no contract between the parties at this stage, there was little he, Krist, or Chad could do.

Although the single was advertised as being limited to 1,000 hand-numbered copies, in actuality 1,200 copies were pressed, according to an invoice prepared by Secord Printing in Redmond, Washington, on November 17, 1988. The fledgling label was billed $248.00 to manufacture the semi-gloss paper sleeves used for the seven-inch, 45 rpm collectible.

With the advent of the Singles Club, Sub Pop's subscribers would pay $35 to receive a limited edition single via mail each month for a year. While the company's intention was to eventually make all of these limited edition releases available only to subscribers, copies of early releases—including Nirvana's first 45—could be purchased individually via mail order for just $3.50.

Given the catalogue number "SP 23," the first 1,000 copies of "Love Buzz" were numbered in red fine-point marker, while the additional 200 had a red line drawn across the space left for the number on the sleeve. One hundred of these were given to the band to sell or distribute in order to help promote the release.

On the A-side, the message "Why don't you trade those guitars for shovels?" appeared near the run out groove. It was a tribute to Kristo Novoselic, who often needled Cobain and his son about their career choices. Meanwhile, both sides were stamped with the words "K-Disc," with black-and-white paper labels on the record.

Collectors are urged to be cautious when pursuing this heavily counterfeited 45, which, in the quarter century since its release, has sold for as much as $2,000.

A flyer from Nirvana's show supporting Vancouver hard-core punk trailblazers D.O.A. at the Underground in Seattle, December 1, 1988.   *Author's collection*

Big Cheese

Some would later hypothesize that Cobain had written the flipside of "Love Buzz" about Sub Pop boss Jonathan Poneman. Although the lead character in the song is named "Mike," this notion seems possible, based on the distrust Kurt had toward Poneman, who was also briefly doubling as Nirvana's manager. Others have argued that the song's hastily written lyrics take a more general look at the pressure that up-and-coming artists feel to appease managers and labels.

A different, more probable interpretation suggests that the song is about a kid in school who is sent to the principal's office after talking back to a teacher. Either way, "Big Cheese" clearly finds Cobain questioning someone who was in a position of authority, or had control over him—or both.

Tam Ohrmund

Just as "Love Buzz" was released in late 1988, Cobain had decided that having his label head double as his manager was a conflict of interest.

His mooted replacement, Tracy's good friend Tam Ohrmund, had no practical experience in managing bands, but what she lacked in know-how she made up for in enthusiasm.

In an effort to lure her into the job, Kurt made her a mixtape of his favorite songs of the moment by bands like AC/DC, the Bay City Rollers, the Velvet Underground, the Knack, Soundgarden, Blondie, and Metallica. Ohrmund accepted the job and put together Nirvana's first press kit, which included photos from the trio's recent K Dorm gig and a biography. At Kurt's suggestion, and since Nirvana had yet to land an album deal, she mailed the packages out to labels like Touch and Go.

Too Good to Ignore

In December 1988, the *Rocket* reviewed Nirvana's debut 45. Writer Grant Alden praised "Love Buzz," planting an important seed about the band that made many sit up and take notice by calling it "one hell of a first effort."

"Nirvana sit sort of at the edge of the current Northwest sound," Alden wrote, adding that they were "Too clean for thrash, too pure for metal, too good to ignore."

Kurt evidently felt the same way—at first at least. Two weeks earlier, after dropping off a copy of the single to KCMU on the day he picked up the singles at Sub Pop's offices, he had stopped at a payphone on the way back to Olympia to request the A-side. When the song finally came on the radio, Marander—who was chauffeuring him that day—watched as a huge smile came over her boyfriend's face.

9

Fill Me In on Your New Vision

Bleach

On the Road for Rehearsals

With Nirvana's practice space located in Aberdeen above Maria Novoselic's salon, and only Krist having regular access to reliable transportation, getting the members of the group together was anything but simple. Novoselic—who had been living at home again that fall after he and Shelli broke up in September 1988—would drive to pick up Cobain in Olympia, then head up to Seattle to scoop up Channing, who traveled into the city by ferry. Back in Aberdeen, they would practice for three hours before Novoselic drove them back.

During these lengthy commutes in Novoselic's van, the band would listen to albums by local bands like Mudhoney and TAD, plus cassettes of the Pixies' *Surfer Rosa*, the Smithereens' *Especially for You*, and the Sugarcubes' *Life's Too Good*. All of this material would influence the sonic direction of Nirvana's upcoming material.

Inking with Sub Pop

The accolades for "Love Buzz" earned Nirvana the right to a proper contract with Sub Pop in late 1988. But in order to move things beyond a handshake agreement with Poneman and Pavitt, Cobain and Novoselic needed a strategy.

Kurt tracked down Donald Passman's book *All You Need to Know About the Music Business* at his local library and read it from cover to cover. He then insisted upon a formal agreement with the label, which seemed anxious for a full album.

To motivate Pavitt, the towering Novoselic supposedly showed up unexpectedly and intoxicated at his Seattle home that December, demanding a contract. The intimidation worked; soon after, Nirvana became one of the first bands in the label's growing stable of artists to land a formal agreement.

The terms of the contract called for a one-year deal running from January 1 to December 31, 1989, with two subsequent one-year options. The band was to turn in one album per year during the length of the agreement. In return, Sub Pop would pay $6,000 to the band for the first year. The second year would provide Nirvana with a $12,000 payout from the label, and the third would result in a $24,000 disbursement.

The Cling-Ons Had a Homecoming

Although Nirvana practiced in Aberdeen, they hadn't played a Grays Harbor gig in some time when a hometown show was booked at the Hoquiam Eagles hall, four days before Christmas. The December 21 show wasn't exactly a big draw, but a couple dozen former Cling-Ons and their associates, plus some family members—including Kurt's sister Kim—turned out for the gig.

In addition to a dozen originals, Nirvana treated the homecoming crowd to a rendition of "Immigrant Song," the classic Page/Plant composition that originated on 1970's *Led Zeppelin III*. The show was videotaped by Dana James Bong and, as evidenced by the footage, saw Novoselic performing in his underpants, while Cobain's neck was covered in fake blood.

Grunge Goals

Despite his initial pride in "Love Buzz," Cobain grew to loathe the single, confiding in friends that it was too commercial for his liking. As much as he had initially balked at the limited pressing, he would now convey his relief that there were only 1,000 copies in existence. He promised to anyone who listened that Nirvana's full-length album would be far less refined and way more volatile.

Christmas Eve at Reciprocal

Around midday on Christmas Eve, 1988, after spending the night of December 23 at the Seattle area home of Jason Everman (a friend of Channing's), Nirvana entered Reciprocal Recording Studios to begin tracking their debut studio album for Sub Pop.

Working again with Jack Endino to ready the disc for a March 1989 release, Kurt, Krist, and Chad completed one new original, called "Blew," during the five-hour session. Several other songs—including "Sifting," "Mr. Moustache," and "Swap Meet"—were attempted during the session but would be re-recorded at a later date. With the exception of "Blew," the tracks sounded dreadful.

According to Endino, the trio intentionally tuned their instruments to a lower setting than was usual. "I think Kurt was having trouble singing and wanted to make it a little easier for himself," the producer told *Goldmine*.

Later in the week, Nirvana returned to re-track the songs in their intended dropped-D tuning. Outtakes—save for those given to the band as rough cassettes—were few at the time. According to Endino, when the band was unhappy with a take they would erase it and try again until they were satisfied.

Christmas Single

Despite the fact Cobain was in Grays Harbor several times a week, he had not been to visit his paternal grandparents. He acknowledged this apologetically in a Christmas card he sent to Leland and Iris that month. Kurt informed them of how busy he was with the band, revealing their imminent plan to make an album, and boasted that Nirvana's debut single had already sold out.

The single was the gift Cobain gave to most immediate family members that Christmas, including his beloved aunt Mari, who couldn't have been prouder of Kurt's achievement. His mother Wendy was equally pleased with her son's maturity, which she gauged by the fact Kurt had been working and had a steady girlfriend plus a car and a respectable apartment. When she played "Love Buzz" on the family stereo on Christmas Day, though, it was clear she wasn't sure if her son had what it took to make it as a musician. She told him to be sure to have something to fall back on.

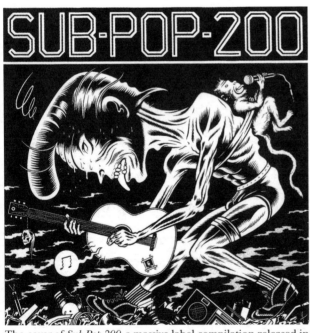

Sub Pop 200

On December 28, Nirvana's "Spank Thru" was released on *Sub Pop 200*, a new three-LP compilation designed to promote the label and the burgeoning grunge movement. It was the version the band had recorded at Reciprocal Studios with Channing that summer, as remixed on September 27 by Endino.

The sprawling project—which was issued with a limited pressing of 5,000 copies—included tracks by the likes of TAD, the Fluid, Mudhoney, Soundgarden, Fastbacks, Blood Circus, Cut Butt, Beat Happening, and Screaming Trees. The photo of Nirvana used in the booklet that accompanied

The cover of *Sub Pop 200*, a massive label compilation released in December 1988 and featuring Seattle grunge pioneers like TAD, Mudhoney, Green River, and Soundgarden. An early version Nirvana's "Spank Thru" was the third song on Side One of the original three-LP vinyl pressing.   *Author's collection* the project was shot by Charles Peterson in mid-1988 on Bainbridge Island, where Channing lived.

Sub Pop launched the set with a grand, two-night party at the Hollywood Underground in Seattle's U-district on the release date. Nirvana were among eight bands booked for the event and performed on the first night. According to attendees, performance artist and labelmate Steven Jesse Bernstein introduced the group as "the band with the freeze-dried vocals."

Melody Maker's Simon Reynolds reviewed the compilation and, upon hearing "Spank Thru," described that Nirvana as too complex for their own good. Six months later, speaking to the same publication's Everett True, Cobain defended the simplicity of his songwriting, adding, "Fuck that guy, what does he know?"

Too Many Humans

The day after the *Sub Pop 200* show, Nirvana went back into the studio with Endino to track "About a Girl," "School," "Negative Creep," "Scoff," "Swap Meet," "Mr. Moustache," and "Sifting" over three consecutive five-hour recording sessions that ran from December 29 to 31. The trio became sick during this second run of sessions, and according to Krist Novoselic, they were mixing codeine cough syrup from the Pierce County Health department with alcohol during this three-day period.

Despite the fact they were fighting nasty colds, the band experimented a bit, attempting the loud, sluggish "Big Long Now" before deciding it wasn't a good fit for the record. Cobain was of the belief that there were already enough slow, heavy tunes in the song sequence, so "Big Long Now" was removed from consideration for the album, which he was planning on naming *Too Many Humans*.

Meanwhile, after deciding they weren't happy with Channing's drumming on "Paper Cuts" and "Floyd the Barber," Cobain and Novoselic returned to the *Dale Demo* versions of the two songs, adding backing vocals to the former. They were then mixed along with the rest of the new tracks during two five-hour mixing sessions, held on January 14 and 24, 1989.

Ultimately, Cobain seemed pleased with the way the sessions had turned out and spoke proudly of the band's primitive approach to the studio the following year. "We wanted it to be as loud and as in-your-face as possible, as raw as we could," he told *Metal Forces* in 1990.

Getting the Knack

In late 1988, Cobain found himself obsessed with *Get the Knack*, the 1979 album by Los Angeles power-pop specialists the Knack. One Olympia friend, Damon Romero, thought Kurt was kidding when he pulled out the album one day with enthusiasm.

Cobain was obviously familiar with the record's flagship single, "My Sharona"—*Billboard*'s #1 song of 1979—but subsequently discovered the album's forgotten charms as he delved into the likes of "Good Girls Don't," "Oh Tara," and "Let Me Out" with great joy. He also extolled the virtues of the Doug Fieger–fronted foursome, who were obviously influenced by the Beatles, to the other members of his band. It's little coincidence, then, that Kurt's own power-pop nugget "About a Girl" surfaced at this time.

Especially the Smithereens and Celtic Frost

The Smithereens were another more recent band that Cobain liked who owed a debt of gratitude to the Fab Four. The New Jersey band's 1986 debut *Especially for You*—which featured hits like "Blood and Roses" and "Behind the Wall of Sleep"—was a regular presence in Novoselic's cassette deck during Nirvana's travels around this time.

Of course, the group also routinely offset those Pat DiNizio–driven pop sounds with the blistering thrash-metal tones of Celtic Frost. Speaking to *Rolling Stone* in 2001, Krist opined that both bands likely had an impact on the direction of Nirvana's debut album.

Dry and Crunchy

Despite the fact that Kurt had started moving toward pop/rock song structures, the sound of *Bleach* was steeped in '70s rock. The band used records by the likes of Thin Lizzy and AC/DC as a guide.

During tracking and mixing, Endino even kept the latter's *For Those About to Rock* on the turntable at Reciprocal for a reference. This—as Jack explained to Robert Hilburn in 2004—is why Nirvana's first album is such a "crunchy, in-your-face, dry record."

Banking on Everman

When all was said and done, Jack Endino billed the band for thirty hours of recording time, for a total of $606.17. Curiously, the bill was paid by Jason Everman, a respected local guitarist who had played in high-school bands with Channing, knew Dylan Carlson, and had some ties to Aberdeen, having lived there briefly as a child.

Everman, who had started working summers as a commercial fisherman in Alaska when he turned seventeen, had thousands of dollars in the bank, and volunteered to finance the project. At first it was a no-strings-attached proposition, but Cobain had another idea. Despite not actually playing on the record, Everman would be credited with doing so.

The chronology remains unclear regarding when Jason was approached by Cobain to see if he wanted to audition as Nirvana's second guitarist. Having seen the Skid Row show with Dale Crover at the Community World Theater a year earlier, Jason was seriously impressed with what Kurt and Krist were doing. With his old friend Channing already in the band, trying out seemed like a no-brainer.

Everman was a quick study. He learned to play all of the songs on the *Dale Demos*, and after playing at a few rehearsals he was asked to join Nirvana as second guitarist in February 1989.

Jason Who?

Jason Mark Everman was born in Kodiak, Alaska on August 16, 1967. He spent the first two years of his life in a village called Ouzinkie on nearby Spruce Island, while his father served as a commercial fisherman.

According to Everman, his young mother wasn't cut out for the primitive lifestyle Ouzinkie offered, and after a couple of years living in a remote two-room cabin with no running water, she left her husband and returned to the mainland. Growing up in logging towns on the Olympic Peninsula, Everman was exposed to the music his mom liked, including the Doors, Nancy Sinatra, and Leonard Cohen.

In 1975, Everman bought his very first album, *Kiss Alive*, which—as he told Music Life Radio's Dan Sauter in September 2010—"put the rock 'n' roll bug in me for sure." By 1978, Everman—then a fifth-grader—was hooked on Black Sabbath and Motörhead, and he continued to be drawn to heavy guitar records throughout junior high.

By ninth grade, he had expressed a desire to play an instrument. At first, he dreamed of playing the drums, but when his mother put an end to that idea, he set his sights on the guitar.

Around this time, Jason became consumed with a friend's ninety-minute homemade cassette compilation that included the likes of Black Flag and the Sex Pistols, plus the Zero Boys and Vicious Circle. He dubbed a copy for himself and, as he told Sauter, marveled at how the music was so exhilarating that it "made the hair on his arms stand up."

Unlike his favorite Sabbath tunes, which he felt too intimidated by to attempt to learn, the crude approach of punk music made Jason believe he could play the guitar. He taught himself the instrument and wound up playing with friends in high school. Eventually, he found himself playing alongside Chad Channing in the aforementioned Stone Crow, who drew heavily on another local band, Malfunkshun. The Bainbridge Island–based band, co-founded by Mother Love Bone's Andrew Wood and his brother Kevin in 1980, were—along with Green River, the U-Men, and the Melvins—among the area's grunge pioneers. But like many bands emerging in the Northwest around this time, Stone Crow's strongest original, "I'm Not Going," sounded more like a fusion of Black Flag and Black Sabbath than anything else.

Work for Love

In early 1989, Cobain had completely stopped working a day job. He had instead thrown himself entirely into his music career, making writing for and rehearsing with Nirvana his primary focus.

Kurt's longtime girlfriend Tracy Marander continued to support him while he pursued his rock star dreams. In an interview with the University of Washington newspaper the *Daily* that May, Cobain was certain to thank his "Nice, sweet, and wonderful" girlfriend for her support. Still, the economic imbalance in their relationship was starting to show signs of wear.

Sub Pop Saga

Nirvana's debut studio album may have been completed, but Sub Pop's continued money issues were still a stumbling block. Record label deals almost always had the company paying recording costs, but in Nirvana's case the band (or at least Everman) paid Endino directly for his production services.

Not long after their record was finished, the group—already miffed that they had to finance their own record—learned that the proposed March release date had been pushed to June. As Kurt told *Option* in 1992, "the excitement kind of left" as they waited for the record to hit store shelves.

A flyer promoting Nirvana's gig with the Melvins and Amorphous Head at the Covered Wagon Saloon in San Francisco on February 10, 1989.   *Author's collection*

Going to California

With little else to do, Nirvana decided to channel their frustrations with the label into something positive by broadening their scope as a touring act. They planned a run down into California in February 1989, and a week before that they made their public debut as a foursome, playing yet another Evergreen State dorm party.

The day before they set off, Novoselic outfitted his recently acquired, used white touring van with a bunk, which he built across the back, just below the windows, so that—if all else failed—the guys would have a place to crash. He also fixed the lock so that the back door couldn't be opened from the inside, thinking it might reduce the chances of their gear being stolen.

Traveling down into San Francisco, the band played a show supporting their old friends the Melvins at the Covered Wagon Saloon on February 10. Sadly, the gig had a low turnout. Hungry and out of money, the band and their entourage—which included roadie Dylan Carlson, Tracy Marander, Amy Moon, and a friend named Joe Preston—wound up going to a soup kitchen run by Hare Krishnas.

After spending the night spent on a friend's apartment floor, Nirvana teamed up with Mudhoney, with whom they had shared bills in Portland a month earlier, for a gig the next night at Marsuggi's in San Jose. During this show, Cobain left his audience of a few dozen awestruck as he played guitar standing on his head.

"[He] stayed there for a good long time," Mudhoney's Steve Turner told *Spin* in April 1995. "It was one of the coolest things I'd ever seen."

Canceled

Three of the shows Nirvana had booked during the tour were canceled when Cobain had to fly back home with Marander, who was suffering from the flu. A high-profile February 16 gig with Mike Watt's band Firehose and platinum-selling headliners Living Colour at UC Davis was scotched, as was a performance at the Chatterbox in San Francisco the next night. The band also pulled out of a Hollywood gig slated for two nights later at the world famous Coconut Teaszer with punk favorites NOFX and the Adolescents. Instead, Novoselic, Channing, and Everman drove home to Washington.

Friction

The California shows that the band actually played went reasonably well, but there was already some friction in the expanded Nirvana lineup. At times, Cobain and Everman seemed like polar opposites.

A disconnect was evident in their musical mind-sets. For instance, Jason was obsessed with speed metal like Testament and Celtic Frost. He was especially fond of "Aero Zeppelin" and loved playing Kurt's ode to classic rock. Yet to Cobain, it had become one of the songs of his own that he liked the absolute least. He was already shifting toward a more pop-influenced style of songwriting.

As much as Kurt welcomed the presence of an additional guitarist onstage, he didn't exactly relish the extra personality in the cramped quarters of Krist's van. The dynamic in the band had changed, and Cobain was already wondering if his decision to make Nirvana a quartet was a mistake.

Bleach Boys

During the band's first tour beyond Washington State, Nirvana's front man spotted an AIDS-prevention poster that caught his eye in San Francisco when the band had gone to the Haight-Ashbury free clinic to ask for more flu medicine. Aimed at needle users, the public-service advertisement warned heroin addicts to "Bleach Your Works" in order to avoid contracting the life threatening disease.

Cobain thought about the poster for a moment before turning to Novoselic, Channing, and Everman. He told them that their album had a new title: *Bleach*.

Four Bands for Four Bucks

On February 25, Nirvana were booked to play their largest concert yet when they appeared on a bill with the Fluid, Girl Trouble, the Legend, and Skin Yard. Branded as "4 Bands for Four Bucks," the gig—which actually featured five groups and was held at the East Ballroom of the Husky Union Building at the University of Washington in Seattle—was the first indication that the raw, hard-rock "grunge" sound was growing in the Northwest.

A crowd of 600 gathered, slam-dancing and stage-diving during Nirvana's volatile set. Cobain played calmly as he watched dozens of kids fly off the stage. Deep down he was elated by the idea that his music was the impetus for such bedlam.

The chaos—which culminated in damage to the venue as Nirvana destroyed their instruments—prompted university officials to suspend all additional live shows indefinitely. It also helped to build the buzz around the group, as word about Nirvana's destructive front man spread among the city's hipster elite.

Nirvana performed alongside the Fluid, Girl Trouble, Skin Yard, and the Legend at the University of Washington's Husky Union Building in Seattle on February 25, 1989. According to witnesses, damage that occurred to the venue while Cobain and Novoselic were destroying their instruments led to a ban on future concerts.
Author's collection

Melody Maker

Nirvana were given a brief write-up in *Melody Maker* along with labelmates like Mudhoney and TAD in the UK music weekly's March 18, 1989, issue. In a piece titled "Sub Pop. Seattle: Rock City," journalist Everett True wrote, "Basically this is the real thing. No rock star contrivance, no intellectual perspective, no master plan for world domination. You're talking about four guys in their early twenties from rural Washington who wanna rock, who if they weren't doing this, they would be working in a supermarket or lumber yard or fixing cars."

Later, True admitted in 2011's *Everybody Loves Our Town: An Oral History of Grunge* that he was an inexperienced writer on deadline at the time who had been flown into Seattle on the label's dime to assist Sub Pop in getting some international exposure. Although he was a little ashamed of his actions, he copped to copying Jonathan Poneman's description of Nirvana down word-for-word and using it as his own.

Confident Cobain

Nirvana's collective efforts as showmen grew as the band's crowd sizes improved into 1989. Cobain's enthusiasm was evident during a gig at the Annex Theatre in Seattle on April 7 as he fell back on top of the crowd and the audience passed him over their heads during "Blew." It was also during this show that Kurt smashed his brown wooden Fender Mustang—which he'd decorated with a Soundgarden sticker—to bits.

A week earlier, at a gig at Reko/Muse in Olympia, Tracy had taken the live action photo that the band would elect to use on the cover of *Bleach*.

Clowning Off

On April 14, Nirvana were booked to headline a bill of ten local bands at the Hal Holmes Community Center in Ellensburg. Despite the distinction, the band's show stopped after just two songs when Novoselic—who was once again back with girlfriend Shelli Dilly after a period of separation—got into an altercation with an employee after she was thrown out for slam-dancing and stage-diving.

To exacerbate matters, Cobain refused to leave the stage, and instead turned his amp to its loudest setting,

The photo used on the cover of *Bleach* was taken at Nirvana's show at Reko/Muse Gallery in Olympia on April 1, 1989. *Author's collection*

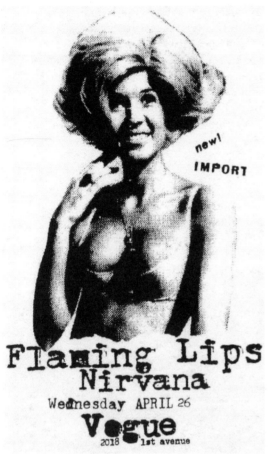

new!

IMPORT

Flaming Lips
Nirvana
Wednesday APRIL 26
Vogue
2018   1st avenue

Nirvana supported Oklahoma's rising psychedelic freaks the Flaming Lips, touring in support of their third studio LP *Telepathic Surgery*, at the Vogue on April 26, 1989. It was not the last time the bands would cross paths.

Author's collection

which didn't sit well with Steve Fisk (who would later produce the band). "I hated them," Fisk told Michael Azerrad in 1993, explaining how he walked out during the first song as Cobain tried to change one of his guitar strings. "They were just clowning off."

Screaming Trees front man Mark Lanegan was also in the audience and had the opposite opinion. "They completely blew me away," he told *Spin* in April 1995. "It was like seeing the Who in their prime."

Flaming Lips

Long before the Wayne Coyne–fronted Flaming Lips became one of the most revered experimental rock bands on the planet, the Oklahoma City–based group—founded in 1983—shared the stage with Nirvana on April 26, 1989, at the Vogue. The headliners were on tour in support of their third studio album, *Telepathic Surgery*, featuring the college-radio hit "Drug Machine in Heaven."

Montana noise-merchants Steel Pole Bath Tub were also on the bill that night and plugging their debut studio set *Butterfly Love* (released on Boner Records). Later that year, SPBT actually teamed up with Nirvana's chums the Melvins for a shared single, "Sweet Young Thing Ain't No More" / "I Dreamed, I Dream."

Looking back on his first impressions of Kurt from that night in a Twitter message exactly twenty-three years after the gig, Coyne said, "Cobain looked like he should be in Lynyrd Skynyrd."

Professional Artist

In between gigs, Cobain kept busy working on his art. He liked to paint over the board games he would buy for next-to-nothing in the area's thrift stores, happily mutilated album covers by forgotten classic-rock acts, and fruitlessly sought illustration work.

His apartment was cluttered with dolls, magazines, and old boxes, all which he might use for his creations. His birthday gift for Marander was an Iron Butterfly album cover, to which he painted a rendering of Batman and glued to it a naked Barbie Doll.

"He was a serious artist," Novoselic recalled in *Heavier Than Heaven.* "Some of it was morbid and twisted . . . His theme was pretty consistent. Everything was just a little fucked up and dark."

Yet Cobain was happy to become a professional artist in 1989, when his neighbor Amy Moon paid him for a painting. "I gave him his first, and probably only, commission," she told the *Seattle Times* in April 2004. "I had a dream and I wanted him to paint it."

At the time, Kurt was so broke that Moon had to front him the $10 canvas for the picture, of a deer that had been struck by a car at night. But the end result was well worth it. "The painting was amazing," she explained to the paper, without revealing what she paid him for the piece. "Exactly as I had described the dream."

In 1999, Moon also revealed to Charles Cross that prior to her commissioning Cobain to depict her dream, Kurt had shown her a different painting. He told her how he had given it a secret ingredient and showed her how shiny it was. When she asked him what caused that effect, he explained to her that the picture was shiny because it was coated with his dried semen.

Lame Fest '89 and More

As anticipation continued to build for the June release of *Bleach*, Nirvana booked a national tour and played a pair of shows in May. Following a show at the Central Tavern on May 9, the group performed a concert with Bible Stud and Skin Yard at Auburn's Green River Community College on May 26 that aired live over the school's radio station, KGRG-FM.

Then, on June 9, the band played a gig opening for labelmates TAD and Mudhoney at Seattle's Moore Theatre. Dubbed Lame Fest '89, the Sub Pop

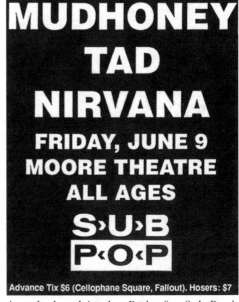

An ad placed in the *Rocket* for Sub Pop's Lame Fest '89 at the Moore Theatre. Nirvana were booked to open for labelmates TAD and Mudhoney. As would soon become customary, Cobain dove into Chad Channing's drum set.

Author's collection

arranged show was billed as "a one night orgy of sweat and insanity" in a label advertisement that appeared in the *Rocket*. The "Spring '89" ad was for an array of releases, including TAD's *God's Balls*, the Walkabouts' *Cataract*, the eponymous LP release by Swallow, the Mudhoney 45 "You Got It (Keep It Outta My Face)," plus the Fluid's *Road Mouth* LP, and, of course, *Bleach*.

The Moore Theatre gig found Kurt swinging his guitar around his neck by its strap like a hula-hoop. It also marked the first of many times he would dive into Channing's drum set in the next year. Although the band's set was intense—as many Nirvana shows had become by this point—the sound at the gig was downright unlistenable, as illustrated by video footage circulating on YouTube.

Ladies Man

With his piercing blue eyes and stringy blond hair, Cobain was always a good-looking young man, even though he wasn't always aware of his handsomeness. But as the front man and guitarist in Seattle's rising new band, Kurt couldn't help but earn the attention of the opposite sex, especially as he took his anger out on his equipment.

Kelly Canary, a member of the all-girl band Dickless, was rehearsing in a studio in the same building as Nirvana around this time. Speaking to Everett True, she spoke of how some of her bandmates had major crushes on Kurt. It got so serious that they made sure to do their hair and put on makeup before band practices in the hope that they might run into him.

"Do You Love Me?"

The night after Lame Fest, Nirvana accepted a gig at the Blue Gallery in Portland, pinch-hitting for labelmates Cat Butt. Aside from playing the songs from the forthcoming *Bleach* LP, the band didn't follow a set list that night. Their friend Rob Kader—who was arguably the group's first die-hard fan—shouted out requests for "Spank Thru" and "Big Cheese."

Although Novoselic declined Kader's request for the obscurity "Big Long Now," Nirvana did a live rendering of "Do You Love Me?," a Kiss song they had just recorded for a C/Z Records compilation, as the crowd (which included members of support act Thrillhammer) looked on.

Kiss This

"Do You Love Me?" was tracked at a studio on the campus of Evergreen State College at the request of C/Z owner Daniel House, also of local band Skin Yard. House recruited Nirvana to record their cover of the Kiss classic for a tribute album that he planned to release as a joint effort with Waterfront Records after

Sub Pop had passed on the idea. Waterfront was Nirvana's Australian label at the time, having licensed *Bleach*, plus records by L7 and TAD, from Sub Pop for release in that country.

The session was unique in that it was the only one ever to feature Jason Everman. The band also made an early attempt at "Dive," which they would re-record for release the following year.

Nirvana's Kiss cover wasn't released until August 1990. It appeared as part of *Hard to Believe* alongside recordings of other punk and indie bands like Bullet LaVolta, All, the Melvins, Chemical People, and the Hard-Ons, each paying homage to the iconic made-up hard-rock group.

Bleak *Bleach*

Asked to describe the overall mood of *Bleach*, Cobain spoke of the record's "gloomy, vengeful element based on hatred" in an interview with the University of Washington's *Daily* in advance of the album's release. Nirvana's debut was a reflection of Kurt's personality, with the bleak but aggressive nature of the music matched by the angry prose he wrote for the record.

Cobain would later divulge that he felt pressure from Sub Pop to conform sonically to the grunge style that the label and the Seattle music community as a whole had fully embraced by 1989. And while the general tone of the record was negative, it is interesting to note that by the time of *Bleach*'s June 15 release date, Kurt had already decided his next group of songs would take on a more accessible, pop-derived sound.

Negative Cover

Following the successful outcome of Nirvana's "Love Buzz" sleeve, a second photo session with Alice Wheeler was arranged for the *Bleach* cover, but the afternoon session down the street from her house didn't exactly go as planned. The group quickly dismissed the shots and—even though Pavitt was a fan of the pictures—the photographer herself shunned them, too.

"I don't want someone to have pictures they don't like of themselves for their record," Wheeler explained to *Goldmine* in 1997, adding that she understood why Nirvana passed on the "scary hick from Aberdeen" look that her photos gave them.

Instead, they used a reversed negative of a live shot of the band performing at Olympia's Reko/Muse gallery on April 1, as taken by Tracy Marander. While Cobain's live-in girlfriend took the enduring concert picture featured on the cover, a photo snapped by Charles Peterson at the HUB Ballroom at the University of Washington on February 25 was used for the limited-edition poster included with the second domestic vinyl pressing of the record.

Media Savvy

Interviewed for the aforementioned article in the University of Washington *Daily*, Cobain may have not had his album released yet, but he had already learned that giving a few good quotes to reporters would go a long way. He spoke of loving the Beatles, Led Zeppelin, and the Who, but insisted he loathed their respective singers, Paul McCartney, Robert Plant, and Roger Daltrey.

Aside from that rock 'n' roll blasphemy, he offered the following sentiment: "I'd like to live off the band, but if not, I'll just retire to Mexico or Yugoslavia with a few hundred dollars, grow potatoes, and learn the history of rock through back issues of *Creem* magazine."

Bleach Spills Out

On June 15, 1989, Nirvana's debut album was finally released. Although the record started slowly at college radio, it soon picked up steam with the help of Sub Pop's hype. The label's catalog promised "Hypnotic and righteous heaviness from these Olympia pop stars. They're young, they own their own van, and they're going to make us rich!"

Although only Cobain actually lived in Olympia, and the van was Novoselic's, the final point couldn't have been more tongue-in-cheek at the time it was written. Within three years, however, this hopeful prediction would become a bona fide fact.

Dismissing the Lyrics

Despite the vitriolic slant of Cobain's lyrics on *Bleach*, he would later dismiss them as insignificant in a 1993 *Spin* article. "[I] didn't give a flying fuck what the lyrics were about," Kurt explained in retrospect, adding, "I don't hold any of those lyrics dear to me."

Nirvana's front man conceded that he had finalized four fifths of the lyrics during the evening before the band entered Endino's studio, and even admitted he was still at work on the lyrics en route to Reciprocal. "It was like, 'I'm pissed off. Don't know what about. Let's just scream negative lyrics, and as long as they're not sexist and don't get too embarrassing, it'll be okay.'"

In the month Nirvana's debut was released, Cobain told punk fanzine *Flipside* that a strong melody, a memorable hook, and an overall energy were far more important. "Half the time I can't finish a subject, so I'll turn the rest of the song into something else," Kurt confessed. Sadly, the publication got his name wrong, addressing him throughout the article as "Kirk."

Funky Monks

If it wasn't immediately evident from his coarse, sing-scream style of vocalizing, Cobain drew from an unlikely influence when tracking his vocals on *Bleach*. In the aforementioned interview with *Flipside*, he expressed his admiration for the vocal power of the Gyuto Monks from Tibet.

Kurt credited their 1986 *Tibetan Tantric Choir* record for making him "feel spiritual" and "feel human," noting how it sounded as if "someone was really directing their energies." He marveled at how he was encouraged to use his own voice as if it was another instrument after hearing the chanting, in which the monks were able to reproduce three tonal chords simultaneously using a practice known as "throat singing."

"It has a very eerie effect on you," he explained.

Bleach Track by Track

Despite Cobain's dissatisfaction with the lyrics on *Bleach*, they were—to be fair—largely unintelligible. Kurt's vocal delivery, and the trio's presentation of the songs, resulted in an album that is consistently bleak, propelled by rage, and peppered with short, sharp shots of sarcasm. It certainly stood out from the other records that would infiltrate college radio in 1989.

A Sub Pop publicity photo of Nirvana (Cobain, Novoselic, and Channing) from 1989 that was distributed with media copies of *Bleach*.   *Author's collection*

"Blew"

Launching Nirvana's debut long player with "Blew" was a perplexing move, and ultimately a decision made by Sub Pop, which re-sequenced the record against Cobain's wishes (as explained below). Novoselic's throbbing, sluggish bass announces the song, colliding with Channing's stuttering drum work before giving way to Cobain's amalgam of feedback and twang.

Although "Blew" wasn't exactly the trio's most alluring or immediate number—as is typically the case with the opening tracks on the majority of rock debuts—its low tuning and heavy delivery help the intriguing tune stand up to repeated listening.

Some have suggested that "Blew" has sexual connotations—including the acts of masturbation, fellatio, or both—while others have interpreted Kurt's message, which is sung in a frigid, gasping drone, as being about something broader.

Cobain expresses a desire to "leave" and to "breathe" on the track. And, in his consequent actions in the first half of 1989, he did just that. Kurt broke free from society's expectations of a young man his age. Thumbing his nose at a traditional work plan, he was—at least in part—living out his rock 'n' roll dreams.

"Floyd the Barber"

A grinding, rhythmic number with the memorable refrain "Have a shave," Nirvana's hilarious ode to *The Andy Griffith Show*'s peculiar hairstylist makes quick mockery of the heavy metal the trio was weaned on. The song has a forceful delivery, while in his very own sonic episode of the show, Cobain imagines Floyd, Barney, Opie, and Aunt Bea as insane killers.

In the song's most pivotal verse/scene, the subject orders an unsuspecting customer to fellate him before Andy suffocates him. In a fitting end, the Mayberry locals in the shop hack him to pieces.

While "Floyd the Barber" may have been one of Nirvana's first finished songs—dating back to 1987—its fusion of the horrid and the humorous gave it staying power. Among underground-rock kids and college-radio hipsters—the core of the trio's early following—the campy "Floyd" was an instant favorite.

"About a Girl"

When Cobain's live-in girlfriend Tracy Marander griped that all of his songs were about murderers and masturbators, he felt challenged to write a song that could express his love for her. The net result was one of the finest numbers he would ever write.

With its Beatles-inspired foundation, the tune's simplistic but powerful rhythm and great, punky guitar riff make it impossible to ignore. If Kurt's vocals sound expectedly unrefined, this rough-but-ready number—which clocks in at just under three minutes—is bolstered by tremendously expressive guitar soloing.

According to drummer Chad Channing, when Cobain first introduced the song to the band it didn't have a formal title. He simply told them it was "about a girl." He had reportedly written it after spending the previous night listening to *Meet the Beatles*, the debut LP by the Fab Four.

According to Endino, Cobain was nervous about putting this heartfelt, contagious message to Marander out there for the world to hear. At the same time, he was fully aware that it was radically different from the ferocious tone of the other tracks on *Bleach*.

"I think the question was raised at some point, 'Gee, I wonder if Sub Pop's going to like this?'" Endino later told *Goldmine*. "And we decided, 'Who cared?' It's your album; put it on." For all of Cobain's worry, Sub Pop said nothing.

"School"

This fierce, riff-driven cut finds Cobain expressing his frustrations at the way that life—or, more specifically, the grunge-heavy Seattle music scene, and in particular the way his regional music peers had sat in judgment of his band on Sub Pop Sundays a year earlier—resembled high school.

With "School," Cobain didn't exactly rack his brains lyrically—the song only consists of two lines. But at just two minutes, it's far more glorious and rebellious than repetitious.

When Kurt barked the chorus—"No recess!"—it was an acknowledgment that life outside of the high-school walls isn't really much different from grades nine through twelve.

In 1990, Cobain sneered to Everett True, "If I could have thrown Soundgarden's name in, I would have."

"Love Buzz"

Nirvana's captivating debut single would also become the fourth song on the US pressings of *Bleach*. The Shocking Blue cover—remixed for the album without the sound collage heard on the original—landed the band early praise from their earliest international ally, *Melody Maker*'s Everett True, who branded it a "Single of the Week" and called it a love song for the "psychotically disturbed."

As much as Cobain enjoyed the acclaim the trio earned for reworking the tune, he would develop mixed feelings about it. "We made a mistake with 'Love Buzz,' because it's our best song as far as I'm concerned," he said in an April 1990 interview with Smith College's WOZQ. "There's nothing worse than when a band does a cover that's better than the original. Basically we took the rim—the bass line—and rewrote that song. We stripped it down."

"Paper Cuts"

Downright maniacal in its presentation, the musical accompaniment to "Paper Cuts" is nearly as sinister and brutal as the words Cobain barks throughout it. Spewing a horrific tale—based on a true story—of deranged parents who kept their kids imprisoned in the dim attic of their house, the song isn't totally unlistenable, but it sure is joyless.

Two years in advance of its release, Kurt read in the news about a mother so savage she pushed food to her children through a crack under the door. She also put down newspaper for them to defecate on like dogs.

That said, "Paper Cuts" may be the strongest early indication that something was really wrong with Cobain. It's certainly hard to imagine a sane person being compelled to pen an ode about such a sick individual. Hardcore aficionados Channing and Novoselic may have missed the meaning of their front man's indecipherable lyrics, though, as they simply got lost in the physical catharsis of playing the song.

Although it's the only track in the group's canon to mention the word "nirvana," it's evident that Kurt shouted it with a sense of irony. "Paper Cuts" was easily the rawest track on *Bleach*—and Cobain's tortured subjects knew no paradise.

"Negative Creep"

This heavy, hard-charging number is about as close to autobiography as Cobain would get during this preliminary stage in his songwriting career. For many, it's a defining moment in grunge rock, as sonic power collides with the front man's anger and depression.

In interviews, Kurt defined himself as a negative person. Based on the reprehensible acts he committed as a teen—be it his conduct with the mentally challenged girl several years earlier or his destructive and criminal behavior— "Negative Creep" was a way to own his past mistakes and try to cleanse his conscience.

If Cobain never actually took the innocence of "Daddy's little girl," the song embellishes things to make it so. Elsewhere, the tune's "stoned" chorus seems to acknowledge Kurt's rampant high-school drug abuse. Kurt would also acknowledge lyrical references to child abuse in a 1991 interview with music scribe Ann Scanlon.

Some have pointed out similarities between "Negative Creep" and "Sweet Young Thing Ain't Sweet No More," from Mudhoney's *Superfuzz Bigmuff*, in the years following the release of *Bleach*, and grunge elitists have even suggested that Cobain plagiarized elements of the latter for the line, "Daddy's little girl ain't a girl no more," although this has never been acknowledged by the Nirvana camp, nor pursued by their friends and labelmates.

"Scoff"

While the song itself is percussive and upbeat, the message behind "Scoff" is almost certainly directed at Kurt's parents and their respective spouses. As Krist and Chad pound out a sturdy rhythm, Cobain snarls about his own worth and reels against any notions that he is insignificant.

When Kurt utters the hook—"Give me back my alcohol"—like a teen who has just had his stash taken by a parental figure looking to exercise control, he isn't just effective; he's delivering one of the record's most memorable moments.

As the song continues, Cobain makes it evident that he—like any fragile young being—might go one way or the other, depending on the amount of love, support, and understanding available.

"Swap Meet"

Using a flea market as the backdrop for a portrait of an aging married couple, it's likely that Kurt found some inspiration for this song while growing up around his paternal grandparents. They bicker, smoke cigarettes, sell arts and crafts, and—once or twice a week—hit the early-bird special.

From a sonic standpoint, "Swap Meet" is long on heavy metal–style guitar lines. It's also somewhat atonal. Yet what it lacks in melody, it more than makes up for with its unique, well thought-out storyline.

"Mr. Moustache"

This punky, amphetamine-paced number is Cobain's first public knock at the macho mind-set that persisted with so many males in and around Aberdeen. With a nod to the Jam's feverish take on the *Batman* theme, Kurt takes aim at the homophobic, misogynistic, meat-loving meatheads who grew up around him in the late 1970s and early '80s.

These were the very same facial hair–wearing bullies who scorned him for being open-minded enough to accept homosexuals as friends and ridiculed him for exploring his artistic passions, including pursuing music over sports.

"Sifting"

Downbeat, heavy, and longer than necessary, "Sifting" features a peculiar bridge and a weighty affectation on Cobain's vocals. Perhaps on purpose, the track's presentation works to mask the past struggles Kurt sings about on the song, including his aforementioned woes in school, his homelessness, and his unsuccessful search for a religious identity at sixteen that came to an end soon after his baptism.

The Bio

In Nirvana's first official press bio, Sub Pop touted the quartet as "a heavy-pop/ punk/dirge combo spawned from the bowels of Seattle." Perhaps hopefully, the company used humor to exaggerate the then-unknown band's "success, fame, and a following of millions."

Purportedly penned by the label's then-publicist Jennie Boddy with input from Cobain, the document name-drops influences like the Bay City Rollers, Slayer, Lead Belly, and the Stooges. It also suggests that the band may soon need "groupie repellant," and that they want to "cash in and suck up to the big wigs in hopes that we too can GET HIGH AND FUCK" (repeating that last sentiment twice more).

Hype was one of Sub Pop's strong suits early on, as evidenced by its classic, strong-selling "Loser" T-shirts, which were all the rage around Seattle that year. And the bio for *Bleach*—with its air of wink-wink, nod-nod—was no exception.

For the college-radio music directors and fanzine writers who actually read the thing, though, it was amusing. Those who actually made it to the bottom of the page were warned that Nirvana were set on world domination—and that, while on tour, they would soon be looking to crash on their couches and use their stoves.

Out of Order

When Jack Endino went to sequence the record in preparation for mastering, he spoke to Nirvana on the phone and they read him the track list. According to the producer, "Floyd the Barber" was slated to open *Bleach*.

But, as Endino would eventually reveal, when Pavitt heard the running order that Cobain and Novoselic had selected, he didn't care for it, and asked them change it. Kurt and Krist then called their producer to break the news to him that "Blew" was now the album's lead track. As a result, Jack he had to re-sequence the entire record.

Critical Reaction

Upon the release of *Bleach*, the *Rocket*'s Gillian G. Gaar wrote, "Nirvana careens from one end of the thrash spectrum to the other, giving a nod towards garage grunge, alternative noise, and hell-raising metal without swearing allegiance to any of them." Several thousand miles away, Edwin Pouncey of the London-based *NME* called the record "the biggest, baddest sound that Sub Pop have so far managed to unearth," adding, "Nirvana turn up the volume and spit and claw their way to the top of the musical garbage heap."

On October 21, another UK music weekly, *Sounds*, explained, "the album thrives on gristly hooks onto which Kobain [sic] grapples his scarred, world-weary howl, a thousand years of life trapped in his young larynx."

Proud Mama

When *Bleach* was released, Cobain's mother was incredibly proud of her son's accomplishment. Mari Earl vividly remembered visiting her sister in the summer of 1989 and witnessing some surprising behavior.

"She was playing the album really loud on her stereo," Kurt's aunt told *Goldmine*. "Having it up that loud just about drove me crazy."

Off Drugs

Sub Pop arranged for an interview with the popular California punk fanzine *Flipside* to coincide with the album's release, and there were some interesting revelations on the band's behalf. Cobain and Novoselic revealed that they were both off drugs.

"I kinda reached my end of things to do as far as acid and pot and stuff," Kurt told the publication, adding, "Once you go past the learning experience, then you go into the downhill part. I never took drugs as an escape, I always took drugs for learning."

Territorial Pressings

In the US, Sub Pop's first run of 1,000 copies came pressed on white vinyl, while a subsequent run of 2,000 copies was produced on black vinyl. Poneman and Pavitt licensed the album for release in the UK on Tupelo Records, with the first 300 copies on white vinyl followed by 2,000 on green vinyl. In Australia, where the record was licensed to Waterfront Records, the first 500 copies were pressed on blue vinyl.

Aside from the issuing label, the UK pressing differed from its American version in another way. It omitted "Love Buzz"—which was exclusive to the Sub Pop Singles Club—in favor of "Big Cheese."

Commercial Performance

In its first two and a half years of release, *Bleach* managed to sell a modest 40,000 copies in North America on the strength of touring and college radio support. But the trio's independent record company would have sold a lot more copies with better distribution channels in place.

Later that year, kids would come up to Cobain and express frustrations over not being able to find the album. It was from this interaction with his new fans that Kurt thought long and hard about who he might do business with in the future.

After the success of Nirvana's 1991 commercial breakthrough and first major-label offering, *Nevermind*, Sub Pop reissued *Bleach*, appending "Big Cheese" and "Downer." This time, on the strength of Cobain's curious new converts, it sold 1.7 million copies, making it the Seattle label's best-selling album ever.

Jack Looks Back

Thinking back on *Bleach* in 1997, Endino explained that he would have liked the opportunity to work with Nirvana in less hurried circumstances. There was no time to discuss switching up amplifiers or using different drum sounds, he recalled; instead, they just set the microphones up and went to town.

The album was recorded on eight-track, but Jack acknowledged that they rarely used more than six or seven channels. "You basically just roll tape," he told Gillian G. Gaar. "And that's what's fun about indie rock, but that's also what limits it sometimes."

In 2009, Novoselic wrote a blog for *Seattle Weekly* about the album to coincide with the release of a twentieth-anniversary version of the record. He interviewed Endino about the project. "Considering it only took about thirty hours in the studio, and the equipment we used, I'm glad it sounds as good as it does," the producer told Krist.

10

Let Me Take a Ride

Nirvana's First National Tour

Road Rules

On June 21, 1989, the eve of Nirvana's first national tour, the quartet played a gig at the Vogue in Seattle. But instead of being excited, Cobain appeared irked by his hometown audience. Rampant stage-divers managed to step on his guitar cord, pulling it out of the instrument several times. At one point, Cobain apparently threw down his axe, climbed atop one of the venue's speaker stacks, and sang upside down.

The band had to be up extremely early the next day for a thirteen-hour drive to San Francisco, where they had a show scheduled the following night. Novoselic kissed Shelli goodbye, and Cobain said farewell to his girlfriend Tracy as they climbed into Krist's recently acquired, secondhand Dodge van for a planned two-month trek across the United States.

With the band lacking a tour manager, Novoselic stepped into the leadership role. He insisted that they alternate driving duties, but because of Cobain's tendency to drive, as Marander later put it, "like a little old lady," the others tended to keep him out of the rotation. Krist also required that they avoid a certain large gasoline brand whenever possible in the wake of the Exxon Valdez Oil Spill in Alaska that March. Additionally, at his insistence, and to conserve fuel, the air conditioner was kept off, and traveling above 70 mph was verboten.

Fudge Packin'

Space was tight in Novoselic's van between the band members, their equipment, a case of Mountain Dew given to them by a friend, and boxes of their new tour apparel. These black cotton items would eventually become one of Nirvana's most coveted and collectible pieces of merchandise—the now-legendary "Fudge Packin'" T-shirt.

The front of the T-shirt featured Nirvana's logo above an illustration of a bird's-eye view of the rings of a tree—a mocking tribute to their logging heritage. On the back it boldly and distinctly read, "Fudge Packin', Crack Smokin', Satan Worshippin', Mother Fucker."

A BENEFIT
for
Reko Muse
featuring:

LUSH

with
INDUSTRIAL
NIRVANA

Friday June 16
at REKO MUSE $3
112 State St. Olympia

Without Channing, Cobain and Novoselic performed this gig opening for Slim Moon's band
Lush at Reko Muse Gallery in Olympia. Backed
by Moon's drum machine, they were joined by
friends in the audience, including the Go Team's
Tobi Vail, who would later become Kurt's girlfriend.   *Author's collection*

Elvis Cooper

Nirvana's sense of humor went on display
when the band rolled into California that
month in the form of the stage banner
that served as their backdrop. They had
taken a tapestry of Elvis Presley and
glued a picture of Alice Cooper's head
to the top of it. The net result was "Elvis
Cooper."

"I fucking hate Elvis!" Novoselic told
Flipside. "Alice Cooper is cool." Cobain
echoed this sentiment, insisting, "Elvis
and the [Grateful] Dead just don't cut
it for us."

California

On June 22, at the Covered Wagon
Saloon in San Francisco, Nirvana shared
a bill with Bad Mutha Goose, led by Tim
Kerr, formerly of notorious Austin, Texas
punk band the Big Boys. In a promotional
poster for the gig, the band utilized the
cover of *Nirvana Girl,* a 1950s book about
teenage narcotic and sex addicts written
by H. R. DaMexico. The book's jacket,
which featured an attractive model surrounded by drug paraphernalia and
wearing a provocative dress, included the
line, "She traded her body for drugs—
and kicks!"

While the San Francisco show was
sparsely attended, the group's gig the
next day at Rhino Records in the Westwood section of Los Angeles had a decent
turnout. But in a bit of poor planning on Sub Pop's part, the label had only
managed to stock five copies of *Bleach,* meaning only a handful of the people
who were in the store for the performance could actually buy the album.

For their show at Al's Bar in L.A. the next night, Nirvana played with local
band Claw Hammer. "There were about fifty people there and it was a lot of
fun," Chris Bagarozzi, the band's guitarist and co-founder, told Junkmedia.org
in 2001. "I think [our bassist] bought a T-shirt off them."

Sun City Girls

Nirvana's tour next took them to clubs in Tempe, Arizona, and Santa Fe, New Mexico. At the first of these gigs, at the Sun Club on June 25, Novoselic was ecstatic about opening for the Sun City Girls, one of his favorite bands. (Krist had been introduced to the group in 1984 by Buzz Osborne, who owned their first album, which was released on Placebo Records.)

"Their performance drew me into their own world—just like good art is supposed to," Novoselic remembered in a piece for the *Seattle Weekly* in 2010. "Bass player Alan invited the crowd to 'swing on the pendulum.' There was no such physical device—rather, the listener was asked to follow the group to the far edges."

According to Krist, the headlining act drew an eccentric, "postmodern" crowd. In his estimation, their brand of Northwest grunge "didn't fit" with the deep, esoteric sound of the experimental desert trio, which consisted of guitarist Richard Bishop, his aforementioned bassist brother, and drummer Charles Gocher.

Despite Novoselic's positive memories of the gig, the club's management managed—according to the tour's booking agent, Danny Bland—to screw Nirvana out of their $50 guarantee.

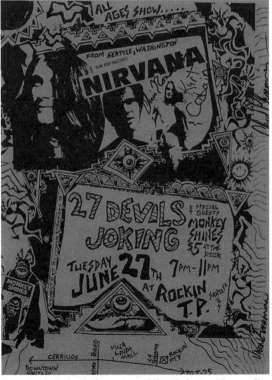

Texas

Nirvana arrived in San Antonio, Texas, on June 29, and were booked to play a private birthday-party show with local acts the Swaziland White Band and Happy Dogs two days later. They stayed for two nights at the home of Happy Dogs guitarist Milton Robichaux before playing the gig in front of approximately forty attendees.

The group's gig at the Axiom in Houston on July 1, to a crowd of around one hundred people, was followed by club dates in Fort Worth and Dallas over the next two nights at the Axis Club and the Electric Jungle. Drummer

An autographed flyer signed by Cobain, Novoselic, Channing, and Jason Everman promoting Nirvana's concert in Santa Fe, New Mexico, June 27, 1989.

Author's collection

Lyman Hardy, who played in the Bayou Pigs at the time, also played at the Fort Worth show. When he was asked by the *Houston Press* in 2004 for a memory of the show, however, Hardy had little recollection of the band.

A late night show at Dallas' Electric Jungle took place the next night. According to a flyer posted around the venue, the admission fee was $3, and included free beer. Insiders who knew a special password were given free access.

Gator Aid

With no other accommodation available in between their Texas gigs, the young men of Nirvana crashed in their van one night in the woods near a national park adjacent to swampland. Perhaps they were all too tired to acknowledge the signs throughout the area that warned them to "Beware of the Alligators."

According to a story relayed by Channing to Everett True in 2005, the band kept a couple of baseball bats in the van for protection. That night he, Cobain, Novoselic, and Everman clutched them as they slept.

Midwest

As the last note rang out in Dallas, Nirvana quickly loaded out and hit the road in order to make the 542-mile trek to Carbondale, Illinois, where the band was booked to play on the evening of July 4, 1989. For all their efforts, the Pizza 611 show only attracted ten fans. The next night, the band was billed with Sub Pop labelmates Blood Circus for a show at Gabe's Oasis, where a maximum of twenty attendees heard Cobain sing "About a Girl" and "Polly," among other numbers.

Less-than-spectacular turnouts in Minneapolis and Madison, Wisconsin— where the group opened for Canadian favorites the Tragically Hip—on July 6 and 7, led up to a respectable show at Chicago's Club Dreamerz on July 8. However, holes in the group's tour routing required the band to drive 415 miles across Indiana and Ohio to make a gig in Wilkinsburg, Pennsylvania, on July 9. Only twenty people made the gig at the Sonic Temple, which also featured a local act known as Worm Art, but it didn't stop Kurt from smashing another Fender Mustang.

Road Diet

The group lived on a diet of horrendous fast food during the tour. According to Channing, Cobain's appreciation of corn dogs at this time was notable. Everman was happy to dine regularly on McDonald's, and Novoselic—who had become a vegetarian at this point—preferred to frequent grocery-store salad bars.

As for the cassette deck, it was occupied on this trek by albums by Lead Belly, Talulah Gosh, the Vaselines, Led Zeppelin, Soft Machine, and Shonen Knife. These recordings, plus releases by Seattle outfits Mudhoney and Soundgarden, were all in regular rotation as the miles elapsed.

Krist's Beer

In addition to their $50 guarantee, Nirvana were entitled to a case of beer from each host venue. This meant that alcohol was usually in ample supply, even if cash was scarce.

For Novoselic—the only member of the band who enjoyed playing music intoxicated—this provided an opportunity for him to get wasted on many nights of the trek. Remembering the tour in *Come as You Are*, Cobain told Michael Azerrad, "Krist drinks to the point of oblivion and literally turns into a retard, unable to speak, gesturing and knocking things over. I've known so many people who drink, it seems quite ordinary."

East

After a few days off, Nirvana checked into J.C. Dobbs in Philadelphia on July 12 for a gig with regional hardcore outfit Napalm Sunday. A look at historic YouTube footage of the quartet playing the likes of "Polly" and "Love Buzz" at the celebrated South Street venue offers some interesting tells.

Cobain, Novoselic, and Channing appear to playing together in total sync, while Everman seems out of step. With his giant hair and showy moves encroaching on the front man on such a small stage, it couldn't help but suggest that a lineup shift was forthcoming. This was Kurt's band, after all.

Tearing It Up in Hoboken

The next night, at the legendary venue Maxwell's in Hoboken, Nirvana teamed with Sub Pop's own TAD. According to *Sounds* reporter John Robb, who had flown in from the UK to cover the show, there were just twelve people in the room. "They tore the place apart in one of the best ever gigs I've seen," Robb wrote in a blog post in 2009. "Their raw power was intense and the songs were already amazing."

Nirvana ended the gig with an exercise in destruction, as Novoselic threw himself to the ground and Cobain shoved his guitar into the ceiling before falling back on top of Channing's drums. Kurt's guitar was completely trashed after the gig.

The show reminded Robb of the Who circa 1965. When he asked Krist about it for *Sounds*, the bassist explained, "It seems to becoming more common at our gigs. The more people screaming at you the more you are into smashing everything up. It's definitely not a contrived thing."

Hangin' with Moore and Mascis

Among that dozen or so people in the New Jersey club to witness the chaos were East Coast indie-rock luminaries like Dinosaur Jr.'s J. Mascis and Sonic Youth's

A rare eight-by-ten glossy publicity picture of Nirvana during the short-lived Jason Everman era. The picture was shot in Hoboken, New Jersey, by the banks of the Hudson River in July 1989, around the time of the group's historic Maxwell's performance.
Author's collection

Thurston Moore. They not only made the show but also hung out backstage and befriended Nirvana's principals.

It was there, on July 13, 1989, that Cobain asked Mascis—then riding high on the strength of the indie anthem "Freak Scene" and a boss cover of the Cure's "Just Like Heaven"—to team with Nirvana. "Kurt said, 'you should join my band,'" Mascis told *Spin* in October 2012. "I think he was sick of the guy Jason [Everman] who was in the band at the time, and thought I should play guitar. I didn't think much about it."

Still, these interactions marked the start of some important friendships. The next night, Krist and Kurt were Moore's guests backstage at the Ritz in New York when Sonic Youth teamed with Mudhoney as part of the New Music Seminar.

Green Street Trade

Nirvana's gig in Jamaica Plain, Massachusetts, was notable for the fact it was the only time that Cobain played with his band without a guitar. He had managed to damage his only guitar, a Fender Mustang, at the end of the Hoboken show, and was left to do nothing but sing the likes of "Big Cheese" and "Negative Creep," leaving Everman to cover all of the guitar parts.

After the gig, Nirvana crashed with a guy named Sluggo, who happened to have a broken guitar hanging on his wall. Kurt thought he could fix Sluggo's axe and asked if he wanted to trade it for his trashed Mustang. His host agreed and they switched, but only if Kurt would sign the guitar he was trading. Instead of signing his name, he wrote, "If it's illegal to rock 'n' roll, throw my ass in jail," signing it "Nirvana."

MIT

Cobain made do with his just-acquired, patched-together six-string, and the band used it to play a private "Eating Club" fraternity party at the nearby Massachusetts Institute of Technology that night. Although Kurt had at first resisted playing among a bunch of elitist intellectuals and instead sat pouting on a pool table, he knew the group needed the money to fill their gas tank, so he took the payday.

Still, things got dicey at one point when an intoxicated Novoselic dismantled the frat's letters from the basement wall on which they hung. Krist, who hadn't been to college, didn't realize that what he had done was the ultimate sign of disrespect. A fight nearly ensued, but the band took their money and split before anyone had summoned up enough courage to come after the towering bassist.

The Pyramid

Crashing on the floor of friend and publicist (and future manager) Janet Billig's Manhattan apartment on 7th Street between Avenue B and C, Nirvana had returned to New York for a New Music Seminar concert on July 18 at the Pyramid. For the show, Nirvana made an effort to stand out against Cows, God Bullies, Lonely Moans, and Surgery, the other acts on the bill. In a chaotic performance, the band played a frenzied thirteen-song set that left an impact on many NYC scenesters, including punk icon Iggy Pop, who was in the audience.

"[Kurt] hopped around like a muppet or an elf or something, hunched over his guitar, hop hop hop, hippety hippety hop, I loved that," Iggy told *Spin* in 1995. "At the end of the set he attacked the drum kit and finally threw himself into the audience. He was little, with stringy blond hair and a Stooges T-shirt. I felt proud."

According to eyewitnesses, a stage-crasher grabbed the mic during the group's second song, "Floyd The Barber," and screamed "fucking shit" before being forcibly removed. Everman purportedly went after the fan, which didn't sit well with Cobain. Although Jason may not have known it at the time, this show wound up being his last with Nirvana.

Homeward Bound

After the New Music Seminar show, Cobain told Novoselic he wanted to cancel the rest of Nirvana's tour to return home to Washington. He had a list of reasons, including being without a suitable guitar, or the money to acquire one, since he totaled his a week earlier. Furthermore, he was homesick, coping with a recurring stomach ailment that was causing him to vomit frequently, frustrated by the lack of attendance during the first half of the band's national tour, and increasingly at odds with Everman.

Novoselic agreed, and the band's planned shows in Montreal, Toronto, Newport, Detroit, Champaign, Denver, Salt Lake City, and Boise were scrapped. As the band rolled across 3,000 miles in three days, stopping only for gas and food, Cobain thought of how he might fire Everman. Letting people go was never easy for him, and days after their arrival home, on July 22, he still hadn't broken the news to Jason.

Everman, Out!

Whether Jason Everman quit Nirvana or whether he was fired depends on who you ask. According to Cobain and Novoselic, he was fired, but in interviews soon after the exit of their second guitarist, they addressed the question gingerly. In October of that year, Kurt told the *Rocket* that the split was due to artistic differences and was a "very mutual decision."

According to Janet Billig—in *Nirvana: The True Story*—Cobain and Novoselic very nearly left Jason in New York so that they wouldn't have to travel home with him. They asked her if they could leave him behind, but she told them, "No. You can't leave him here."

Kurt explained to writer and future Sub Pop publicist Nils Bernstein that Jason "just wasn't into exactly the right type of music, especially for the direction that we're going now." In reality, Everman was a hair-throwing metal-head— albeit a talented one—who may have been jealous of Kurt and Krist's camaraderie, and also took exception to their destructive treatment of band equipment.

Everman also wanted to bring his ideas to the material, but Cobain wasn't having any of it. Jason told *MusicLifeRadio* in 2010 that he "left Nirvana when I realized I wasn't going to be able to participate in songwriting, which is fine—it wasn't my band." He says he was planning on taking a break from music after his experience with Nirvana when he got a call that September from Soundgarden's Kim Thayil. After an audition, he joined the band, replacing founding bassist Hiro Yamamoto. Jason played with the band for a year, on the world tour in support of *Louder Than Love*, until friction with the group's front man, Chris Cornell, led to his firing in late 1990.

Everman then joined the band Mind Funk in time to play on their second album, *Dropped*, which was recorded for Megaforce Records in 1993 after the band had been released from their major label deal with Epic. He ultimately left music and joined the US Army, where he became a Special Ops Army Ranger. Everman has also spent time as a Nepalese monk and a bike messenger, and as recently as 2010 he was studying philosophy at Columbia University.

It's Something Else, It's Something New

Fall 1989

Back Home

U pon returning to Seattle, Kurt—at the insistence of Krist and others—sought medical help for his ongoing stomach ailment from a specialist at Tacoma's St. Joseph Medical Center. Meanwhile, the band regrouped as a trio and planned to make up many of the Midwest dates it had canceled that fall. In August, the reconstituted trio played a handful of shows in smaller halls, including the Hoquiam Eagles Lodge, the Bellevue VFW, and Olympia's Washington Center on Contemporary Art (CoCA).

A month earlier, while the band were on the road, Cobain made his first non-Nirvana appearance on record, on a 45 by the Go Team called "Scratch It Out" / "Bikini Twilight," released through K Records. The project was spearheaded by K Records owner Calvin Johnson (also of area favorites Beat Happening) and Tobi Vail of Bikini Kill, and was one of a dozen planned monthly singles released in 1989.

Meanwhile, Cobain and his friend Mark Lanegan—front man of Sub Pop's Screaming Trees—wrote a series of songs together that summer and even got Jonathon Poneman's approval to make an album. They recruited Novoselic and Trees drummer Mark Pickerel to play with them as the Jury (a name that won out over Kurt's choice, Lithium). Unfortunately, when they went into the studio with Jack Endino on August 20, things fell apart. The Jury wound up tracking a Lead Belly cover called "Grey Goose" but little else. (These extramural releases are detailed elsewhere in this book.)

CMJ Love

Bleach began to receive instant national attention at US college radio and specialty radio after the *CMJ New Music Report* praised Nirvana in its August 12 edition. Featuring the band's album on its cover, the bi-weekly music bible for radio stations to the left of the dial described the band as "action comic metal for the post-stoned generation."

"Nirvana is a retro-fueled blast of Sabbath-like mega-sludge riffs supplied with feedback and other nifty '70s tricks," the publication insisted, calling Kurdt—as he was then known—"the best rock throat since Chris Cornell . . . and he doesn't have to sing bare-chested to prove he's a man."

Timed with Sub Pop's servicing of the record to most reporting stations across the US, and coupled with the return of many college-radio staffers to the airwaves at the outset of the fall '89 semester, these accolades pushed the record up the *CMJ* survey. Its competitor, *Rockpool*, saw a similar response from its reporting stations.

Ice Cold

At the aforementioned CoCA gig, held on August 26, Nirvana experienced their biggest Seattle reception yet on a bill with Mudhoney and another Sub Pop band, Cat Butt. At the time, the packed venue lacked air conditioning, causing the performing musicians to seek other ways to keep cool.

It was here that Cobain asked Cat Butt's James Burdyshaw to dunk his head into a beer tub full of ice water. Kurt stayed under so long that Burdyshaw began to worry, until he finally came up for air with a resounding "Yeah!"

Fisk Sessions

In September 1989, Nirvana teamed with producer Steve Fisk at the twenty-four-track Music Source Studios in Seattle to record tracks for a planned EP, which would be released in Europe in conjunction with the trio's European trek. The EP was recorded over two late night sessions, a week apart. The first found the band recording the basic tracks to "Polly," "Been a Son," "Stain," "Even in His Youth," and "Token Eastern Tune." The second session was reserved for vocals, guitar parts, and mixes.

According to Fisk, Nirvana's equipment was pretty much trashed from the tour. Channing's fiberglass drums were cracked and duct-taped together, and Cobain and Novoselic's amps were worn out from road abuse, causing a rumbling effect. On the day of the session, Krist—who had been throwing his bass into Channing's drums like a hatchet on the road—attempted to have his bass repaired, but it didn't do much good.

Fisk felt that "Stain" might have had hit potential, although Cobain littered it with repeated use of the word "fuck." Meanwhile, "Been a Son"—which was supposedly about Don Cobain's disappointment that his daughter Kim hadn't been born a boy—was unique as it featured a Novoselic bass solo rather than a traditional guitar break. Both songs, which would see release at the end of '89 on the *Blew* EP, highlighted a more infectious, pop direction than had been suggested by the bulk of *Bleach*, particularly in terms of the drum sound.

"Polly," originally known as "Cracker" and "Hitchhiker," was about a 1987 incident in which a young girl was kidnapped, raped, and tortured. Cobain had written the song from the perspective of her savage captor, but as strong as the song seemed, it was left unfinished. Alongside "Even in His Youth" and "Token Eastern Song," it sat unreleased. The plan was to finish these unfinished numbers at a later date, but Fisk and Nirvana never got around to it.

Dancing with Themselves

Upon completion of "Been a Son," Cobain and Novoselic were so excited by the mix that they asked Fisk if they could dance on tables at his Capitol Hill studio. The producer was hesitant at first but OK'd the mischievous idea and even embraced it.

"So they jumped up on one table and they rocked," Fisk told *Goldmine* in 1997. "And I jumped up on another and rocked. Me and Chris were almost up to the ceiling and Chad was in the other room watching TV or something. And as we listened to the song, we rocked. Ah! That's cool! That's fucking cool. Not a lot of people ever got to do that. I got to nail the mix and jump up on the furniture and rock with Nirvana."

Bleach-ing Europe

In late August 1989, *Bleach* was finally released in Europe through Tupelo Records. The UK version of the record supplanted "Love Buzz" with "Big Cheese." To help promote the band to foreigners, Sub Pop publicist Jennie Boddy readied a revised artist bio that informed overseas media that the band was a trio.

The one-page document listed Cobain as "Kurdt" and described him as "perfecting the garage attendant style." A few lines down, Novoselic—still billed as "Chris" and jokingly referred to as a competitive tree-climber—says "99% of the music out there is bullshit." As for Channing, he is described as looking "perpetually stoned."

While it was not exactly a brilliant document, the bio did its job in sparking curiosity among tastemakers abroad. As Nirvana's first tour of Western Europe supporting their friends in TAD was being planned for the final two months of 1989, the group began to land a decent amount of European press coverage.

Two-Week Tour

When Nirvana embarked on its rescheduled Midwest trek in September '89, the increased presence of *Bleach* on the college airwaves helped them draw 200-plus fans to shows in locales like Chicago and Ann Arbor, although gigs with Steel Pole Bath Tub in Champaign and Kalamazoo were still modest draws. This time out, the band had a gig guarantee of $100 to $200 per night, which meant they could afford to rent a U-Haul truck to carry their equipment for the two-week tour and bring along a soundman, Craig Montgomery, and a roadie, Ben Shepherd, a friend and former bandmate of Channing's.

The first time Ben Shepherd had met Cobain, it was when Channing brought him to a party in Olympia. Kurt was sitting on one end of the couch alone, and Ben—who was a little guarded in a crowd—took the seat on the other side.

Throughout the night they passed an acoustic guitar back and forth, entertaining each other and admitting that they often sat alone with guitars at parties. "[We] didn't really know anybody and didn't really want to," Shepherd told True. "Not in the mood for it."

NIRVANA
DICKLESS
KNIFE DANCE
September 26   Tuesday
VOGUE

A souvenir flyer from Nirvana's gig at the Vogue in Seattle on Tuesday, September 26, 1989.   *Author's collection*

After a warm-up show at the Vogue on September 26, the tour got underway two days later at the Uptown Bar in Minneapolis. However, Cobain's stomach woes were still unresolved and unpredictable, leaving Shepherd to fill in on guitar during soundcheck while Kurt endured a vomiting attack behind the venue. A show the next night at Marquette University was canceled due to Cobain's nausea.

A gig at Chicago's Cabaret Metro found Kurt in better health as Nirvana opened for local hopefuls Eleventh Dream Day (who had just signed to Atlantic Records on the strength of their '88 disc *Prairie School Freakout*) and their new friends in Sonic Youth (who were still supporting their acclaimed double LP *Daydream Nation*). As Nirvana's set ended, Kurt dived into Channing's drum kit, leaving both acts with a tough act to follow.

Nirvana teamed with the Flaming Lips and Steel Pole

Bath Tub in Ann Arbor at the Blind Pig on October 3, and the show drew a decent crowd of students from the University of Michigan, who were treated to two renditions of Nirvana's opening number. After the first performance of "School," the trio realized Cobain's vocals had been inaudible, so they played it a second time. Later, after the band broke down their gear, they watched with laughter as the Flaming Lips' smoke machines packed the place, much to the club owner's frustration.

Following sparsely attended gigs in Toledo and Cincinnati, the band played a show with Black Rock Coalition outfit 24-7 Spyz at the Outhouse in Lawrence, Kansas, which drew 150 people. During this concert, Channing became frustrated that his floor tom kept falling over—so much so that he eventually threw it into the crowd during Nirvana's set.

Such irritations aside, even when the crowds numbered only two dozen or so people, the shows could be uplifting. Nirvana left the audience at the Liftticket Lounge in Omaha chanting for more tunes and then got an unexpected encore, breaking out "Paper Cuts," "Even in His Youth," a Novoselic-steered jam on Lead Belly's folk staple "Where Did You Sleep Last Night," and "Breed" to satisfy the small but demanding crowd.

Before the trek wrapped in mid-October, Nirvana teamed up with Colorado-based labelmates the Fluid for a well-attended gig at the Garage in Denver on the 11th. Two days later, the group played to just twenty people at Boulder's Penny Lane Coffeehouse.

Throughout the tour, Nirvana's "Fudge Packin'" T-shirts sold well, fans in larger meccas actually knew their tunes, and the band earned enough money to not only break even but come away with $300 each in profits. It wasn't much, but it was something.

Roadie Ben

Ben Shepherd very nearly joined Nirvana as Jason Everman's replacement on second guitar. During his brief time served as the band's roadie, Ben proved himself to be a great fit with the others in the group and auditioned at Kurt's request, passing up an offer he received a day later to play bass in Soundgarden.

While on tour in Ann Arbor, Cobain asked Shepherd—a songwriter in his own right—if he would mind exclusively playing someone

```
TICKETMASTER.

BP1003
EVENT CODE        PRISM PROD PRESENTS
2.00              FLAMING LIPS
SERVICE CHARGE    W/SPECIAL GUEST
109 0               NIRVANA
1743              THE BLIND PIG
20CT9       TUE OCT 3, 1989 DO 9PM
ADULT
ADMISSION     GEN. ADMISSION        ADULT
                                    ADMISSION
10.00 GEN.   GEN   ADM CA      10.00
PRICE    SEC/BOX    ROW    SEAT  CN 23987
1X        CALL FOR TIX 313-645-6666
          SERVICE CHARGE NOT REFUNDABLE
```

Nirvana reconnected with headliners the Flaming Lips for this October 1989 show at the Blind Pig in Ann Arbor, Michigan. Note the cost of admission: just $10 to witness these two historic bands in their formative years.
Author's collection

else's songs. Ben understood that Nirvana was Cobain's group and said he would be happy with such terms.

However, after very nearly asking Shepherd to join his band, Kurt changed his mind on the advice of his friends in Screaming Trees, TAD, and Mudhoney, who felt that an additional guitarist took away from the group's sound. Surprisingly, there was no bad blood between Cobain and Shepherd, who would later admit that he, too, thought Nirvana were better—and more direct—as a trio.

Later, in *Come as You Are*, Cobain told Azerrad, "I still kind of regret that because I like that guy a lot—he would have added to the band, definitely. He was kind of crazy sometimes, but that's okay. I'd rather have that than some moody metal-head."

A flyer announcing Nirvana's Omaha gig at the Liftticket Lounge, where a sparse audience of just two dozen insisted on an encore after the band began packing up their gear. Cobain obliged, and a frantic version of "Paper Cuts" followed.   *Author's collection*

Ironically, instead of taking Everman's spot in Nirvana, Shepherd did finally join Soundgarden, and in fact wound up taking Jason's place in that band in late 1990.

Earth

With a week off before Nirvana were set to embark on their first European dates, Cobain agreed to help his close friend Dylan Carlson's project Earth with the song "A Bureaucratic Desire for Revenge," which Carlson was preparing for release on an EP of the same name.

Earth initially came together after the breakup of Lush, Carlson's band with Slim Moon. The pair went on to form a new band with Cobain on bass, but because they only had a right-handed bass, which Kurt was unable to play, he was sacked. Moon was then booted out over a dispute about the way Dylan wanted him to sing.

Putting these issues aside, during the third week of October 1989, Kurt went to track guitar and vocals in a Portland recording studio with Carlson. The end product finally saw release via Sub Pop in 1991 on the *Extra-Capsular Extraction* EP.

Russell Warby

On October 22, Nirvana took off from SeaTac en route to the United Kingdom, where they would launch an extensive six-week club tour. The initial shows had Nirvana opening for TAD, with support from the Cateran—a Scottish quintet heavily influenced by Hüsker Dü who were then on tour in support of their latest album, *Ache*.

In fact, it was Cameron Fraser from the Cateran who had first got Russell Warby, an agent at Nomad Artists, to consider booking Nirvana after turning him on to the "Love Buzz" seven-inch some months earlier. Then, when *Bleach* became available in the UK on import in the summer of '89, Warby began pestering Sub Pop about the band, expressing his fondness for them.

When the time came to arrange a European trek to support the proper European release of the record, Russell's eagerness earned him the trust of Sub Pop to book the tour, which Warby did out of his bedroom. He also went to retrieve both bands and the tour's soundman, Craig Montgomery, at the airport.

Speaking to *Mojo* in 1998, Warby remembered Cobain as "this funny little fella with bleached hair." He also recalled just how pleased Kurt, Krist, and Chad were to learn that they would be able to stay at inexpensive bed-and-breakfasts after crashing on floors during their first two US tours.

The band spent their first night at a B&B called the Dalmacia in the Shepherd's Bush, London. Cobain stayed in, fighting bronchitis, as his bandmates ate Chinese takeout with Tad Doyle and his band and hit the pubs.

Sounds Good

To coincide with their October tour, both Nirvana and TAD graced the cover of UK music weekly *Sounds*. It was a major coup for publicist Anton Brookes, who had started representing Sub Pop acts in the UK in 1989 and was now getting exposure for groups like Soundgarden, Mudhoney, and Screaming Trees. As Brookes would explain to *Mojo* in 1998, he loved Nirvana for their "energy, power, presence and songs," adding, "They were like Zeppelin meets the Beatles."

Journalist Keith Cameron, who covered both bands for the piece, wrote of the natural evolution of American underground bands—how outfits like Big Black and Sonic Youth gave way to the Pixies and Dinsoaur Jr.—and, then, Nirvana. The tension in the trio's live shows stayed with the *Sounds* freelancer, who was especially excited by the way they trashed their equipment. When Cobain threw his guitar at Novoselic, and Krist smacked it with his bass like a baseball bat, Cameron found the destruction "magical."

Bass for Your Face

Nirvana had taken a significant step up, and now, with the help of the *Sounds* cover, the shows attracted new fans as word spread among friends. Launched at Riverside in Newcastle on October 23, the thirty-six-date, forty-two-day trek got off to a contentious start when one of several hundred fans threw a beer bottle, hitting Novoselic in the head.

In a fit of rage, Krist took his brand new bass—acquired just before the trek—and smashed it into a pair of rental amplifiers. He then threw his bass on the floor, breaking the neck of the instrument. After taking half of their £500 guarantee, the band fell instantly into the red as a result of the damaged equipment. Of course, they would make it back eventually, and the mayhem and rebellion of their live show captivated their awestruck audience.

Smashing Good Time

The buzz on Nirvana continued to build as shows in Manchester and Leeds, on October 24 and 25, respectively, drew impressive crowds. At the former, Cobain dived into the audience, losing his microphone temporarily until a fan handed it back to him when he threatened to stop the show. As the set ended, the band refused to play an encore, claiming they had no additional songs to perform.

The Leeds performance, held at the Duchess of York Public House, was as energetic as ever, although it was very nearly absent of wrecked equipment—that is, until the band's publicist reminded Novoselic as he walked offstage.

An advertisement promoting Nirvana's show with TAD in the Student's Union at Manchester Polytechnic, October 24, 1989. UK band the Cateran opened the show. *Author's collection*

"I said to him, 'Krist, you didn't throw your bass across the stage,'" Anton Brookes told *Mojo*. "And he goes, 'Oh yeah.'"

Novoselic then catapulted his bass backward over his head. The audience watched in amazement as the instrument flew overheard and then, with exact precision, knocked over both of the group's microphone stands.

Peel Again

On October 26, Nirvana settled in at London's Dalmacia Hotel before entering Maida Vale Studios for their first "Peel Session," a radio performance recorded for the iconic BBC personality and producer John Peel, who by now had worked with everyone from AC/DC to the Wedding Present.

Ironically, the set—which featured "About a Girl," "Love Buzz," "Polly," and "Spank Thru"—was not produced by Peel but by Dale "Buffin" Griffin, a founding member of Mott the Hoople, who handled Peel's overflow. It was engineered by Ted de Bono and first broadcast on November 22, 1989.

Advance Praise

A week ahead of the band's proper London debut, *Sounds* called Nirvana "natural descendants of Mudhoney and Dinosaur Jr" and "a high energy explosion resulting in a trail of smashed gear and beat anthems." This was weighty praise indeed, and it undoubtedly caught the attention of savvy indie-rock kids in and around the English mecca.

In the same piece, when asked where the group fit in among their Sub Pop stablemates, Novoselic told John Robb, "If there's anything we're really close to, it's the Stooges—the momentum and the energy."

In *Melody Maker* that same week, Kurt set the record straight on Nirvana's place in the burgeoning flannel-clad grunge scene at home. "I feel like we've been tagged as illiterate, redneck cousin-fucking kids that have no idea what's going on at all. That's completely untrue."

Doubling Up

When Nirvana and TAD took the stage at London's School of Oriental and African Studies (SOAS) Student Union for a gig on October 27, they learned the show had been oversold by twice its capacity, prompting fire officials to consider canceling it. The media coverage had worked well—maybe a little too well.

Things got so frenzied that at one point, as fans pushed toward the stage, Brookes, Warby, and tour manager Alex McLeod were forced to hold the monitors and other equipment in place. Cobain came offstage at one point, unsure of what to do next. Brookes suggested that he let off a fire extinguisher. Kurt did so, and the show became legendary.

Hell in a Bucket

Cobain wasn't the only person on the tour with a stomach ailment. Tad Doyle suffered from gastrointestinal woes that resulted in a daily vomiting ritual every morning around the time of the band's 10:00 a.m. departure.

This intrigued and excited Kurt, who was prone to vomit bile or blood. In Cobain's eyes, Tad's colorful puke was a work of art, and he held a plastic bucket waiting in the rented Fiat van for Doyle to heave. As TAD guitarist Kurt Danielson told Charles Cross, "No one else got to hold the tub; it was his delight."

During the tour, Cobain would write the song "Immodium" about Doyle's over-the-counter diarrhea medication. Kurt had a strange fascination with bodily functions, and he was purportedly interested in deviant pornography, including scatophilia.

Holland Insults

On Halloween 1989, after an eight-day run through the UK, Nirvana and TAD left England by ferry, arriving in Hoek Van Holland to begin a brief tour of the Netherlands. Upon arrival at Amsterdam's Quentin Hotel, the band were about to settle in when Novoselic—who had drunk a whole bottle of whiskey by himself on the ferry—insulted one of the proprietors, whom he felt resembled Queen's Freddie Mercury. According to a 1994 interview with tour manager Edwin Heath in Dutch magazine *Oor*, Krist yelled, "Fuck you, Freddie Mercury fag!" forcing the group to scurry to find different lodging. (He later apologized).

The band eventually settled in at the Acro Hotel for a five-day stay that found them playing shows in places like Hilversum—where they tracked "About a Girl" and the as-yet-unreleased "Dive" for radio station VPRO—Groningen, Utrecht, and Appeldoorn. Most of these shows were plagued with sound problems, and the latter devolved into an exercise in destruction after just twenty minutes of music.

Despite such iffy shows, Nirvana's final Netherlands gig of the tour, held at Melweg in Amsterdam, was a shining moment for the group. The eighteen-song show—bolstered by an interlude of Lipps, Inc.'s "Funkytown" in the midst of "Stain"—was downright triumphant. At the end, to the awe of the crowd, Cobain smashed his guitar during a jam that would eventually become known as "Endless, Nameless."

The Sound of Music

The members of Nirvana listened to everything from the Pixies and Shonen Knife to the Beatles and the Vaselines as they crisscrossed Europe that fall, and these records would help shape the feel of the trio's next studio album.

Seventies rock acts like Queen and Badfinger also helped pass the time away as tour manager Edwin Heath did virtually all of the driving. Rather than Novoselic's bunk-fitted ride at home, the bands were now traveling in an enormous white rental van with nine seats that did not recline, and—with TAD's four members in tow, plus equipment for both acts—each spot was occupied.

Whenever they needed to take the edge off, they were drawn to ABBA's *Greatest Hits*. Something about the mood and tempo of "Waterloo" and "Dancing Queen" felt like a good match as they traveled the European countryside.

The Walls Came Down

On November 7, Nirvana began an eight-date run through West Germany at B-52 in Mönchengladbach, with stops the following nights in Cologne, Hanover, and Enger, West Germany. On November 11—two days after the Berlin Wall came down—Nirvana and TAD played at Ecstasy in Berlin.

Although the show wasn't going Cobain's way—sound problems prompted him to throw down his guitar in frustration, prematurely ending his trio's set—outside of the club, history was being made. Because of all of the activity outside, just a third of the expected 600 attendees caught the show.

"We didn't even know what was going on until a little before we got to the border and there were all these little cars crammed full of people offering us fruit," Novoselic told the *Rocket* the following month—to which, Cobain added, "I heard one man cried at the sight of bananas."

Two decades later, in November 2009, Novoselic wrote in *Seattle Weekly* of how East Germans came to the West in their Trabant cars. "Emotional Germans were at the borders with arms wide open and eyes welling with tears of joy," he explained. "Instead of the shame and humiliation associated with WWII, this was a time of hope."

The Reeperbahn

Two nights later, Nirvana and TAD played a club called Fabrik in Hamburg, and while the show wasn't memorable, Novoselic accompanied Doyle and his musical co-conspirators to the Reeperbahn, the district known for its strip clubs, brothels, and pornography retailers.

Inside a porn shop, Krist saw something disturbing that stayed with him for twenty years: photos of people smeared with feces having sex. He ran out of the shop screaming in horror.

School
Scoff
Love Buzz
Floyd the Barber
DIVE
Polly
Big cHEESE
About A girl
mR moustache
Token Eastern Song
Stain
Negative creep
BLEW
Sifting - paper cuts - Trophy - swap meat - BAD moon - 112

A handwritten set list from Nirvana's concert in Hanover, West Germany, on November 9, 1989, marks the return of an early number, "Mr. Moustache," which Cobain had penned about his former drummer, Dave Foster.

Author's collection

"Molly's Lips" and More

At the Circus in Gammelsdorf on November 17, Nirvana gave their version of "Molly's Lips," originally by the Vaselines, its live debut after rehearsing it at the soundcheck earlier that evening. The song would become a recurring part of the band's set lists for the duration of the tour, and would become one of their favorite covers.

"I'm a Boy"

On November 22, at the U4 in Vienna, Novoselic had an onstage exchange with some intoxicated male members of the audience. These hooligans had been harassing some of the women in the crowd and it didn't sit well with Krist, who had been drinking himself.

In an extended diatribe, the bassist lectured the audience about the appropriate way to treat women, before telling them that he was a woman himself. From there, Novoselic started singing the classic Who song "I'm a Boy" until Kurt resumed control of the situation.

According to NirvanaLiveGuide.com, a video of this Austrian show was once offered on eBay with a minimum bid of $250,000. It went unsold.

Teriyaki Asthma

In November 1989, while Nirvana were overseas, the first track from the group to appear through a label other than Sub Pop surfaced when "Mexican Seafood" was included on the C/Z Records EP release *Teriyaki Asthma, Vol. 1.* It was taken from the Endino demo tracked with Crover earlier that year after C/Z owner Daniel House—who had played shows off and on with Nirvana in their first year and loved what he heard—asked to release the song. Cobain and Novoselic happily obliged, and Nirvana were teamed with the likes of Coffin Break, Helios Creed, and Yeast for the seven-inch EP, which was pressed in a run of 1,500 copies.

Jumper

After playing to very sparse crowds in Austrian cities like Graz and Hohenems, the band's shows in Fribourg, Switzerland, and Mezzago, Italy, were modest successes, with audiences of around 500 and 900, respectively. When the 300-pound Tad Doyle passed out from the heat at Bloom in Mezzago, Cobain stepped in and sang TAD's songs "High on the Hog" and "Loser."

By the time they got to the Piper Club in Rome on November 27, however, Cobain was fried from touring. Backstage food fights and onstage destruction couldn't help Cobain fight his homesickness. Although Cobain had forged a new friendship with Kurt Danielson, his touring roommate, he missed Tracy and he missed his mom. He even considered asking his mother to wire him the money to fly home.

The front and back covers of C/Z Records' 1989 *Teriyaki Asthma* compilation EP, which marked the recorded debut of "Mexican Seafood" and also featured songs by Helios Creed, Coffin Break, and Yeast. Nirvana's track would of course later be reissued as part of 1992's *Incesticide*. *Author's collection*

NIRVANA ("Mexican Seafood") KURDT KOBAIN — Guitar, Vocals / CHRIS N OVOSELIC — Bass / DALE CROVER — D rums HELIOS CREED ("America is I n Good Hands") HELIOS — Guitars / D. HOUSE — Bass / JASON FINN — Dr ums COFFIN BREAK ("Hole in the G round") PETER LITWIN — Guitar, Vo cals / ROB SKINNER — Bass / DAVE BROOKS — Drums YEAST ("Solid All igators") BORGVARD ALBERTI — Pork / BON PLANT — Chicken / HERSHEY F LETCHER — Beef Engineered by JA CK ENDINO / Design by ART CHANTRY

C/2009

C/Z records

Cobain's stomach troubles were irritated by stress and remained an issue throughout the tour. If they were worsened by Kurt's reliance on corndogs, the appearances of Pavitt and Poneman—who had flown in for the show—only aggravated the Nirvana front man. This was a no-frills tour for Sub Pop's bands, as the label was struggling to make ends meet—yet somehow Bruce and Jon were able to finance their own excursion to Rome.

Kurt was irked; he did his best to channel his aggression, taking the stage after Doyle's rousing chants of "Fuck the pope," but things weren't working. He cut Nirvana's set short midway through after smashing his guitar during "Spank Thru" and climbing atop a stack of speakers.

"I'm going to kill myself!" he announced, threatening to jump to his death as the audience, the bouncers, his bandmates, and his touring companions all begged for him to come down. Instead, Cobain navigated his way through the rafters to the venue's balcony, where he threatened to throw chairs at the audience.

Backstage, Nirvana were interrogated by the Piper Club's soundman about some broken microphones. As tour manager Edwin Heath looked on, Kurt argued that the equipment looked fine before tossing the microphones to the ground to ensure they were broken. This irritated Heath, who threatened to quit his position. Cobain also announced he was quitting the tour and going home to his girlfriend. According to author/reporter Everett True, Novoselic and Channing also quit the band that night.

Stolen Passport

After the Piper Club gig, Poneman managed to talk some sense into Cobain, who agreed to hang in there and finish the final two weeks of the tour. That day, as they toured Rome's historic Coliseum, the band patched things up.

As this flyer asserts, Nirvana got top billing over TAD for this show in Geneva, Switzerland, on November 29, 1989.

Author's collection

Meanwhile, Jon had promised Kurt he would buy him a new guitar when they arrived in Geneva for their next gig. He also bought him a train ticket from Rome so that he could have some time out of the cramped quarters of their touring van.

Unfortunately, Kurt fell asleep on the train and woke to discover that his wallet, shoes, and US passport had been stolen. He spent six hours on November 28 at the US consulate in Berne, Switzerland, waiting to get new paperwork so that the band could travel on to their shows in Geneva and Zurich on November 29 and 30.

Legendary in London

Following shows at venues like Fahrenheit in Issy-les-Moulineaux, France, and Democrazy in Ghent, Belgium, on December 1 and 2, Nirvana returned to London for Sub Pop's Lame Fest UK '89 at the oversold 1,000-capacity Astoria Theatre on December 3. Booked to play a show that also featured TAD and Mudhoney, Nirvana didn't just give the headliners a run for the money—they crushed them with a chaotic set.

Having driven from Dover to London on a cold, foggy night, the trio made it to the theater just twenty minutes ahead of their set time. Nirvana and TAD had missed their planned ferry ride over from Belgium, and were forced to wait for another boat.

Upon arrival, Kurt lost the coin toss with Doyle, so Nirvana took the stage first, without a soundcheck. They performed for a mere half-hour, but Kurt played like his life depended on it. According to reports, he destroyed four guitars in the course of just ten songs; the fourth and final axe was demolished by Novoselic after Cobain threw it at his bassist. In an act of retribution, Krist stomped on the guitar and smashed it to bits, using his own instrument like a baseball bat.

When Kurt came offstage, his knees were bleeding through his holey jeans from where he had jumped four or five feet in the air from his amps and landed on the stage. The following week, the UK music weeklies *Melody Maker*, *NME*, and *Sounds* all heralded the trio.

In *Come as You Are*, Poneman called the gig "one of the proudest moments in my life." Of course, the members of Mudhoney—somewhat jealously—thought Nirvana flat out sucked that night. And they weren't the only ones. Novoselic thought Nirvana were equally awful, later telling Everett True, "It stunk. On a scale of one to ten, it was a zero."

Ironically, Nirvana had been on the brink of collapse a week earlier. Now, members of the influential British music press were treating them like the second coming.

Blew Goes #1

Nirvana canceled their final week of European live dates, nixing scheduled shows in Italy that were scheduled between December 4 and 10, 1989. While Kurt and Chad flew home to Washington, Krist was met by Dilly and together they traveled on to visit with his dad in Yugoslavia.

Despite the cancelation of these dates, the group's impact on the music world was becoming more and more significant each week, as evidenced by their overseas record sales. Nirvana's debut album was selling well, reaching the UK Indie chart's Top Ten thanks to regular airplay on John Peel's radio show.

The legendary DJ also got behind their brand new UK-only EP, *Blew*, which was released via Tupelo Records just after the tour ended. It had originally been slated to drop ahead of the group's European trek before being delayed. Still, all 3,000 copies of the EP, which was issued on vinyl and compact disc, were in high demand. To everyone's surprise and delight, *Blew* peaked at #1 on the Indie charts the following month.

Aside from the title track—which was excerpted from *Bleach*—the extended-play release also included "Love Buzz," which had been left off UK pressings of the album as it was initially exclusive to Sub Pop, plus the previously unreleased new tracks "Been a Son" and "Stain," recorded with Steve Fisk earlier in the year. By this point there was already a small but loyal swell of Nirvana fans in both the US and Europe—kids who couldn't wait to get their ears around any new material by the group. They were sold on the fresh, more contagious songs Cobain, Novoselic, and Channing were now playing.

Explaining the group's new, more accessible direction of their material, Krist told *Pulse* writer Richard T. White in December '89 that the plan was to establish "a good grab-bag of songs."

In the same piece, Kurt spoke of his desire to diversify Nirvana's songbook. "I think it is easy to write one hit song and then write an album's worth of retreads that just sort of feed off of that . . . We want the songs on our records to be different and away from where the previous song was."

12

Bruises on the Fruit

From "Sappy" to "Sliver"

Krist Gets Hitched

On December 31, 1989, just weeks after becoming engaged during their trip to Yugoslavia, Krist Novoselic and Shelli Dilley were married in a small ceremony in their Tacoma apartment. Mudhoney's Matt Lukin served as Novoselic's best man as family and friends—including Cobain and Tracy Marander, Dan Peters, and the members of TAD—looked on.

Later, after copious amounts of alcohol had been consumed, Novie looked on with glee as Tad Doyle and his guitarist Kurt Danielson participated in a wrestling match. Cobain—who had no interest at the time of making a marital commitment to Tracy—spent a large part of the night by himself, getting drunk on the roof of the building that Krist and Shelli called home.

Lizards and Flipper Babies

A week earlier, Cobain had given Marander a $100 coffee-table book called *The Art of Rock* as a Christmas present. Although it was a thoughtful choice, and probably more than he could afford, it was hardly the romantic gift that Tracy was hoping for after nearly three years together.

Cobain was pulling away from his girlfriend, and she couldn't help notice that he was becoming more and more peculiar. After reading a journal entry that February, in which he wrote that he was "lactating" and revealed that his breasts were sore, she couldn't help think that Kurt was having mental problems.

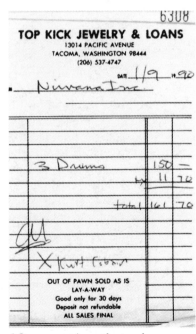

After pawning three drums on December 20, 1989—presumably as a loan for Christmas gifts—Cobain took them out of hock on January 9, 1990, as evidenced by this autographed slip from Tacoma's Top Kick Jewelry & Loans.

Author's collection

When he also confessed in his diary that he hadn't masturbated in months due to lack of imagination, she was sure something was wrong with her twenty-three-year-old boyfriend.

"I close my eyes and I see my father, little girls, German Shepherds, TV news commentators, but no voluptuous pouty-lipped naked female sex kittens wincing in ecstasy," he wrote in his notebook. "I see lizards and flipper babies."

Vampire Dreams

As long as Kurt and Tracy had been together, he had had difficulty sleeping and suffered from recurring nightmares about people trying to kill him with knives. He also had similar dreams where he was attacked by vampires. It wasn't unusual for him to wake up crying, covered in sweat. While Tracy was happy to comfort him like a mother would console a little boy, she couldn't imagine how he was coping with his nightmares on the road.

"Sappy"

As Nirvana entered 1990, they had plans to track a new studio album and hopes of a summer release. To gain momentum, the trio went into Reciprocal Studios on January 2 and 3 with Jack Endino to record a new tune called "Sappy."

The results of the ten-hour, $500 session were mixed, largely because Cobain was obsessed with trying to get a particular drum sound akin to those heard on records engineered by Chicago producer Steve Albini, a veteran of the bands Big Black, Shellac, and Rapeman who had overseen records by the Pixies, Urge Overkill, the Jesus Lizard, and Pussy Galore.

After Kurt had the band attemp the song several times without success, Endino came away with the verdict that "Sappy" was inferior to the tunes he had previously tracked with Nirvana. As they parted company, Endino told Cobain to spend some time writing and come back. At first this rubbed Kurt the wrong way, but he accepted the challenge.

Junkie Zombie

Following a gig with TAD on January 6, 1990, at the University of Washington—which resulted in Nirvana being given a lifetime ban from the institution's venues because of the damage they caused to their equipment and the stage—Cobain spent much of the next month writing in his apartment. He crafted a number of tracks, including "Lithium" and "Opinion," during this time, while Nirvana rehearsed for a memorable Olympia gig at Rignal Hall on the outskirts of the city on January 19.

The show found Nirvana sandwiched between two of Kurt's favorite bands: the Melvins and Beat Happening. For this special event—the second of three

Northwest gigs with the Melvins—Kurt dressed up as a "Junkie Zombie," using stage blood to draw needle marks on his arms. In fact, he looked so believably deathly that his joke was lost on folks in the crowd, who began to speculate about whether the Nirvana front man was using heroin. Meanwhile, Novoselic was outfitted in a ladies' dress and slurped a jug of wine during his set.

Later, Kurt was seen in the front row, rocking out during the Melvins' headlining set. But the night belonged to Nirvana, as evidenced by the way the crowd thinned out after their powerful set.

Arm and Dangerous

Nirvana supported the Melvins the next night at Legends in Tacoma—a sellout show that earned the trio a whopping $500. If it was one of their biggest paydays yet, it was more memorable to Kurt because it was the night that he finally earned the acceptance of Mudhoney's Mark Arm.

The Mudhoney front man and Seattle tastemaker had resisted Nirvana for two years, but on the strength of *Bleach*—and under the sway of Poneman, Pavitt, and his bandmates Dan Peters and Matt Lukin— Arm finally came around. It was all the more exciting for Cobain to look into the audience and see Mark—someone he had long admired—rocking out to his band throughout their explosive set. From the opening strains of "School" to a Novoselic-sung Beatles medley of "All You Need Is Love" and "If I Fell" and the final notes of "Blew," Arm was transfixed, and was now firmly a fan.

Meanwhile, Lukin led a pack of several dozen stage-divers who caused chaos throughout, leading to multiple fights between bouncers and the principal offender. Matt would use his backstage pass to casually walk to the edge of the stage—and then jump. When security stopped the show three times, Cobain apologetically cautioned them, saying, "He's our friend."

This January 1990 gig at the Reko Muse Gallery in Olympia offered a dream bill for Cobain, who found his trio sandwiched between two of his all-time favorite bands, the Melvins and Beat Happening. During the show, Novoselic donned a dress and drank jug wine, while Kurt took the stage with fake blood and hand-drawn needle marks on his arms.   *Author's collection*

Pine Tree Janitorial

In the winter of 1990, Cobain was broke again and needed a job to tide him over until Nirvana's next tour. With Novoselic also out of work, Kurt hatched an idea for them to start their own janitorial business, based on his experiences of a few years earlier. He named the proposed operation "Pine Tree Janitorial" and even drew up flyers, which they hung up around Olympia as a means to solicit business.

"We purposely limit our number of commercial offices in order to personally clean while taking our time," the hand drawn flyer—which featured caricatures of Kurt and Krist—promised. Nobody hired them.

Best Coast

On February 9, Nirvana and TAD began a West Coast tour with a gig at the Pine Street Theatre in Portland that received international coverage when Everett True's review ran in the March 3 edition of *Melody Maker*. Offering comparisons to Dinosaur Jr's then-popular brand of pop noise, True chronicled the band's destructive nature, declaring, "Nirvana shows an instinctive understanding of the joys of rock 'n' roll normally taken to far greater, more horrendous extremes."

Elsewhere, the band's shows in San Jose and Sacramento were notable for Novoselic's impromptu covers, which typically occurred when Kurt needed to change a guitar string. At the first of these gigs, he broke into a humorous rendition of "I Want to Hold Your Hand" before Kurt started into "Polly." At the latter concert, Krist and Chad played an unexpected treat for the punks—a rendition of the Dead Kennedy's "California Über Alles."

Nirvana played two shows in one day in San Francisco, rocking the Rough Trade Records retail store on Valentine's Day afternoon before taking the stage that evening at the Kennel Club. TAD and Nirvana were billed as "hot hunks" at the nighttime show, which drew a sizable audience.

Trucker Hats

Cobain and Novoselic took the opportunity to poke fun at their own backgrounds by buying redneck-style box caps branded with slogans about hunting and fishing at a truck stop early into the tour; Channing's bore the CBS Sports logo.

Jeans and flannel shirts were already part of their touring uniform, and hats like Cobain's Day-Glo orange "I'd Rather Be Hunting" cap presented a perfect way to subvert the redneck look. Their new disguises came in handy, too, in preventing them from getting harassed on the road by—you guessed it—intolerant rednecks.

Satanic Road Music

Passing the hours on the highways of California that February, the men of
Nirvana listened to a diverse assemblage of cassettes by acts including Gong, the
Fugs, the Rolling Stones, Marine Girls, and, of course, the Vaselines. Speaking
to *Melody Maker* for its March 17 edition, Novoselic joked that their favorite on
the road song was the Brady Bunch's tepid rendition of the 1970s hit "Me and
You and a Dog Named Boo."

It wasn't the only oldie on their road mixes. Cobain extolled the virtues of
Witchcraft Coven, who had a hit single with the song "Ode to Billy Jack."

"On one side are sappy songs and on the other there's a Satanic sermon,"
Cobain snickered to the music weekly. "[It] sounds like Bob Barker or some TV
announcer saying stuff like 'Kiss the goat,' 'Satan, the Leviathan.' So we turn
that up really loud at intersections."

Guitar Surgery

Most nights on the West Coast tour, Cobain was smashing at least one guitar if
not two. Sometimes the destruction came from a happy place, but usually Kurt's
rage was driven by frustration or boredom. After all, smashing a guitar was a
great feeling, and an even greater release. Why else would he trash a vintage
Fender Mustang in front of two dozen people in Pittsburgh?

If it seemed like a costly way for Kurt to get his jollies, Novoselic defended his
bandmate, explaining to reporters that used guitars could be had on the cheap
in Tacoma, where he lived, and where Cobain often tracked down his supply.

According to Channing, Kurt had also become a hell of a guitar surgeon by
this point. It got to the point where Kurt had an assortment of guitar pieces at
the ready, including multiple necks, bodies, and an assortment of inner parts;
when one axe was smashed to pieces, he would salvage the electronic guts and
make another.

Crumbling Drums

Novoselic joined Cobain in the art of instrument destruction on February 14,
when he completely destroyed his bass at the end of Nirvana's legendary gig at
the Kennel Club in San Francisco. But an even greater spectacle occurred the
following night in Hollywood, following the trio's 400-mile drive to Los Angeles.

At the end of the group's gig at Raji's—played before a packed crowd of
400 people—Kurt purposely fell backward, crashing into Channing's drums.
His actions gave Charles Peterson an ideal photo opportunity, and resulted
in a picture that would be published weeks later in *Melody Maker* and go on to
become one of the indelible images of grunge.

Peterson's iconic photograph captured Kurt sprawled out on top of Chad's
crumbling kit in an apparent daze, decked out in his Converse sneakers, torn

jeans, and flannel lumberjack shirt. As triumphant as the show was, it's hard to imagine how Cobain walked away uninjured.

Hanging with Jesse Reed

Following a night spent on the floor of L7 bassist Jennifer Finch's L.A. apartment, Nirvana left for a show down at Bogart's in Long Beach the next evening. Afterward, the trio arranged to meet up with Kurt's old friend Jesse Reed, who was now living outside San Diego, on their way to a gig in Mexico.

The plan was for Reed to join the group on their border-crossing excursion to Tijuana. After scooping him up in the parking lot of the San Ysidro McDonald's—site of the mass murder/suicide of twenty-two people in July 1984—they played Iguana's, a notorious rock club in the city.

That night, Cobain and Reed celebrated their reunion and Kurt's forthcoming twenty-third birthday by snorting the crystal meth Jesse had acquired. The pair also downed a half-gallon of hard alcohol. It was around this time that, despite his stomach troubles, Cobain resumed binge drinking.

Kurt on "Grunge"

As Nirvana's profile increased, Cobain began increasingly concerned about being exclusively labeled a grunge band. Although he copped to Everett True about being a part of the genre in March, he insisted on distancing himself from his touring companions in TAD and Sub Pop labelmates Mudhoney.

"We consider ourselves a bit more diverse than just full-out raunchy heavy music," Kurt explained in *Melody Maker* that month. "We're aiming towards a poppier sound."

Two months later, Cobain had had just about enough of the genre, telling a Smith College radio announcer, "There's only so much distortion you can take . . . We don't want to milk the sound as far as we possibly can."

Big Plans

Nirvana's West Coast trek with TAD concluded with two uneventful gigs at the Mason Jar in Phoenix, Arizona, and Blue Max in Chico, California, on February 17 and 19, respectively. Kurt spent his twenty-third birthday with his bandmates, traveling the 500-plus miles home to Olympia.

Back home, the group had received word that Sub Pop wanted to move forward with a new release, and although it wasn't quite clear if Nirvana would be tracking an album or an EP, plans called for the group to head out to Wisconsin's Smart Studios to record with producer Butch Vig. These April 1990 sessions would give way to a seven-week tour through the midwestern, eastern, and southern United States.

For the next month, Cobain would hone the material he had in mind for the session, and the band would rehearse regularly at the Dutchman, their new rehearsal space in south Seattle. In advance of their trek, Nirvana played a show in Canada at the Town Pump in Vancouver, with TAD and the Bombshells, on March 12.

Evergreen Video

On March 20, Nirvana entered the television studio at Olympia's Evergreen State College to record some performance footage for a planned long-form video they hoped to release at some point in 1990. Cobain, Novoselic, Channing, and director Jon Snyder had intended to include external footage shot in and around Aberdeen for the project, plus snippets of footage Kurt had taped off of television. The project was never fully realized, however.

During the taping, a series of jams and a failed attempt at "School" gave way to a full rendition of the latter song, plus live takes of "Big Cheese," "Floyd The Barber," and a new tune, "Lithium." For their trouble, Snyder and cameraman Alex Kostelnik were fed pizza and paid $40.

A clip of "School" featuring the band playing as Donny and Marie tap-danced in the background was released that year as part of the Sup Pop Video Network. SPVN was an inexpensive promotional tool for the label, which serviced VHS tapes of its acts to key journalists, television contacts, and radio people in the hope of getting added exposure.

The label also released a clip of "Big Cheese" that year, with Kurt's childhood Super-8 movie footage of mutilated dolls plus parts of a silent mail order film about witches interspersed with Nirvana's performance.

Falling Apart

In late March, Nirvana left Washington State behind for the Midwest, where they would launch a seven-week tour and record songs for what would presumably be their next Sub Pop release. Marander was sleeping when Cobain left, but he would later discover a goodbye note from her in his journal. Tracy wished him good luck on the road and in the studio and she pledged her love to him.

Leaving a note meant that neither of them would need to face the uncomfortable silences that had plagued their relationship since Kurt's return home in late February. Kurt continued to have little interest in sex—which was somewhat unusual for a twenty-three-year-old male—while Tracy craved intimacy. It was the beginning of the end.

Trashing Chicago

During their first tour stop—a high profile gig at Chicago's Cabaret Metro on April 1, opening for local favorites Eleventh Dream Day—Nirvana knocked 'em dead, premiering a memorable new song, "In Bloom." At the end of the set, during "Blew," Cobain fell into Chad's kit while Channing continued to play; he and Novoselic then trashed their instruments. When all was said and done, the audience was left stunned by the excitement.

Instead of hanging around to see how the night's headliners might top their mind-blowing finale, the trio left immediately, traveling through the night to arrive at Butch Vig's Madison studio on the morning of April 2, as planned.

Get Smart

Nirvana arrived in Madison, Wisconsin, with plans to record a second full-length album during their five-day stay at Smart Studios with Vig. Unlike during the sessions for *Bleach*, however, the songs Cobain brought with him were far less developed, which hindered progress.

Ironically, Vig wasn't an instant Nirvana convert. As he explained to writer Gillian G. Gaar, "I wasn't crazy about *Bleach* the first time I heard it, except 'About a Girl.'" Still, he saw something in them, and following Poneman's persuasion he took on the production assignment. The band's main instruction was for him to make them sound "very heavy."

Thankfully, in addition to his growing resume as a producer of groups like Die Kreuzen, Killdozer, and Urge Overkill, Vig was a veteran drummer, having played in the band Fire Town, who had a minor hit on Atlantic called "Carry the Torch" in 1987. Because of his kit experience, he was able to satisfy Kurt's wishes in relation to Channing's drum sound. However, Chad's drumming abilities were hit-and-miss in Kurt's eyes, and Cobain let his frustrations be known in the studio and in the weeks that followed on the road.

During the five-day session, Kurt's moodiness became increasingly evident to Vig as the front man would occasionally go off into a corner and sulk. Perhaps it was his realization that there just wasn't enough time to complete an album's worth of material.

When the week was over, Nirvana had tracked seven originals, plus a cover of "Here She Comes Now" for a Velvet Underground tribute record. They had recorded their powerful new number "In Bloom" (a song inspired by Cobain's friend Dylan Carlson) and reworked "Polly" into an acoustic presentation, with Kurt using a beat-up five-string guitar. They had also tracked "Dive," "Pay to Play"—which took aim at shifty club owners that required bands to pay money up front in order to perform—the melodic "Lithium" and "Immodium," a song that paid homage to Tad's diarrhea medicine.

Thinking back on the session in the liner notes for the 2004 boxed set *With the Lights Out*, Vig wrote, "I noticed right off the bat that Kurt wrote amazing songs and Krist wrote super hooky bass lines. The bass lines are really melodic, and the hook under the song was in the bass, at least musically. And that works so well with Kurt's vocal melody. They have a cool, interweaving quality."

Sheep

Kurt planned to call Nirvana's next studio record *Sheep* and half-jokingly imagined how the masses would flock to it. "Because you want to not," he wrote in an imaginary ad in *Journals,* "because everyone else is." Later on in his proposed ad copy, Cobain added, "Steal *Sheep.* At a store near you. Nirvana. Flowers. Perfume. Candy. Puppies. Love. Generational Solidarity. And Killing Your Parents."

As we all know, Kurt's plans for *Sheep* were stalled. Still, the tracks wound up comprising one of the finest and most notorious demo tapes of the rock era.

Kurt's Kharisma

Following Nirvana's final afternoon in the studio with Butch Vig, they went over to Madison's Club Underground to play what the producer would describe in *Come as You Are* as a "very loose" gig, noting that the trio were "pretty messed up" during their set. At one point, after Novoselic kept repeatedly knocking the head of his bass into the venue's low ceiling, he took a sock and stuffed it into the hole he had created.

The band moved on with TAD to play shows in Milwaukee and Minneapolis. That second show, held at the notorious 7th Street Entry on April 9, is where Cobain had an opportunity to meet the Amphetamine Reptile label's owner, Tom Hazelmyer. Hazelmyer—who has released records by Killdozer, Helmet, and the Cows—was stunned by Cobain's magnetism. "Even after years of being 'round shitloads of bands I've never sensed that level of charismatic presence again," Hazelmyer recalled, in 2009's *Nirvana: The Biography.*

Chad Abuse

Nirvana's gig at the Blind Pig in Ann Arbor was as chaotic as ever, with Cobain jumping into the audience before Novoselic damaged Channing's drums by standing on them and trapping the kit man under the wreckage. By the time the group got to Lee's Place in Toronto on April 16 for one of two Canadian dates, Kurt began to throw bottles at the wall behind Chad midway through the show. The audience followed suit.

Later in the week, Cobain's frustrations with Channing's playing became more public than ever after he threw a full pitcher of water at the drummer during a concert at ManRay Nightclub in Cambridge, Massachusetts, on April 16. Perhaps drawing on his past baseball skills, Kurt very nearly hit Chad in the head.

Senior Haus

After a show at the Olde Club on the campus of Pennsylvania's Swarthmore College on April 20, Nirvana returned to Cambridge for the second time in a week to play a show at Massachusetts Institute of Technology. The April 21 gig was slated to be an outdoor event, with a stage constructed in a campus court-yard in the band's honor, but due to rain the show was moved to the basement of Senior Haus, a nearby co-ed dormitory.

As the show progressed, Novoselic's destructive instincts kicked in, and he defaced the dorm's historic skull and bones crest, replete with the motto "Sport Death." He used one of two bones he tore from the display to slap at his bass, which did not sit well with residence-hall officials at the gig. When the show was over, Novoselic issued a half-hearted apology to those he had offended.

Pyramid

Five days later, Nirvana played the Pyramid in New York for a pack of luminaries, including members of Sonic Youth, their Geffen A&R head Gary Gersh, and punk legend Iggy Pop, who reportedly loved the band. After the show, photographer Michael Lavine introduced Kurt to Iggy, which was a personal thrill for Cobain.

When the meeting was over, however, Kurt thought about how the band had played that night, and he was bothered. So was Krist. Despite the applause, there were sound problems, not to mention the fact that Channing's timing was off. An attempt at "Been a Son" had to be abandoned and started over, and the night's finale was an epic failure, with Cobain quitting on Chad midway through "Negative Creep." Kurt was so upset that he again took his frustration out on the drummer's duct-tape-covered kit—much to the elation of the audience.

New Tracks

During the tour, Cobain began dubbing off copies of the band's sessions with Vig and circulating them. Lacking a budget for blank tapes, he would simply put Scotch Tape over the holes of his stash of promotional *Bleach* cassettes and hand them out to journalists, photographers, industry contacts, and friends from other bands.

Songs like "In Bloom" and "Lithium" were urgent and alluring, and caught the attention of everyone who heard them. Now, following the lead of Sonic Youth—who had signed to Geffen and planned to release a new album, *Goo*, in July—Kurt and Krist wanted to take their band beyond the distribution problems and financial limitations of Sub Pop.

Anton Brookes opened a package from Cobain one day that spring with a cassette inside titled *New Tracks*. He would eventually tell *Mojo*, "I thought these were some of the best songs I'd hear in my life."

Shaved Head

Nirvana were back in Massachusetts on April 27 to headline an Amnesty International Benefit at Hampshire College in Amherst on a bill featuring seven other bands. The next night, the trio teamed with the Jesus Lizard for a show at Maxwell's in Hoboken.

Sub Pop shot footage from this show—including Cobain smashing his guitar—for an early "In Bloom" video that would be sent out that summer as part its Video Network promotional effort. After the show, Krist Novoselic shaved his head, eyebrows, and body hair in atonement for the band's performance at the Pyramid.

The next morning, the group filmed additional scenes for "In Bloom" in downtown Manhattan. As a result, Novoselic can be seen with and without hair in the original clip for that song.

Kurt Cobain, Comedian

When Cobain felt like toying with an interviewer, the results could be hilarious. In the aforementioned Smith College radio interview for WOZQ, Kurt's sarcasm was on full blast. When asked if Nirvana made a concerted effort to jump around onstage, he offered this snarky reply: "Yeah. We choreograph it. There's tape marked all over the stage."

The interview took place just after Novoselic had shaved his head, and the DJ first mistook him for one of the security people at the group's show. Kurt jokingly referred to Krist as a Nazi, and explained that his bassist had just discovered Minor Threat.

If that wasn't enough, when asked about what Nirvana did for the recent Earth Day celebration, Cobain snapped, "We collected as many plastic and poly-styrene goods as we could find and built a big bonfire." As for the trio's recycling practices on tour, Kurt said, "We throw everything right out the window."

Trashed Florida Condo

After a rundown the Eastern Seaboard in the last week of April that included stops in Philadelphia, Washington D.C., and North Carolina, Nirvana pulled into the Masquerade in Tampa on May 4. A fan at the show offered the band lodging for the night at his dad's lavish condominium. It was a big mistake.

Novoselic and Cobain were fried on acid much of the night and woke to find no one home. According to soundman Craig Montgomery, the band took all of the food out of the cabinets and the refrigerator and completely ransacked the kitchen. To top things off, a hairless Krist strolled the high-class neighborhood without any clothes on, shouting at the top of his lungs.

As penance, Novoselic left a $100 bill on the kitchen counter to cover the cost of whatever they had destroyed, and Nirvana left to play a show that night at Einstein a Go-Go in Jacksonville Beach.

Firing Chad?

The final two weeks of the band's tour took in venues in Atlanta, Columbus, Cincinnati, Tulsa, Lincoln, Denver, and Boise. The last of these, on May 17, 1990, at the Zoo with black rock band 24-7 Spyz, would mark Nirvana's final performance with Chad Channing on drums.

After nearly two years in Nirvana, Chad—who was a multi-instrumentalist, capable of playing guitar, bass, and violin, and writing songs—had grown increasingly frustrated with his role as Cobain's drum machine. According to Everett True, when Chad shared some of his original songs with Kurt, the singer dismissed them as "dorky." At the same time, Channing—who knew he would never be allowed to make much of a contribution under Kurt's direction—had grown sick of piecing his drums back together, night after night.

Two weeks after Nirvana's return to Washington, Cobain and Novoselic drove out to Channing's house in Bainbridge Island without warning. Although they liked Chad as a person, having him as their drummer just wasn't working. He just wasn't playing hard enough for Kurt. And so that afternoon they fired him. Or did they?

According to Chad, he quit. In the book, *Nevermind/Nirvana*, he cited "Creative differences," and said, "I was losing interest, and it was totally showing. Kurt and Krist realized it. It should have come up a lot earlier, and I should have brought it up. I made the situation to be one where they had to come up to me and say, 'This isn't working out.'"

Splitting with Tracy

Cobain's relationship with Tracy Marander wasn't working out either, and on April 27—her birthday—he phoned her from Massachusetts to explain that things weren't what they had once been for him and suggest they no longer live together. Never comfortable with direct conflict, Kurt had taken the easy way out.

During the final weeks of the tour, Cobain slept with a woman he had met on the road, later revealing what he had done to Marander upon his return to Olympia. By July, Tracy had moved home to Tacoma.

13

Spring Is Here Again

Getting with Grohl

Major Decision

By the conclusion of Nirvana's spring tour, Cobain and Novoselic had committed themselves to landing a major-label deal. Independent companies like Touch and Go or SST, with which Kurt once aspired to sign, were no longer desirable because they faced many of the same financial troubles and distribution struggles that plagued Nirvana's existing label.

In the meantime, Sub Pop was in talks with CBS over a lucrative major-label deal of its own that would allow the latter to distribute the former's artists' records—including those by Nirvana—on a much broader scale. During this process, Sub Pop prepared a new, thirty-page contract for the band to consider. But with the label's ongoing financial struggles, a lack of promotion for *Bleach*, questionable accounting for royalties, and the idea that Soundgarden, the Pixies, and Sonic Youth were already on majors (and thriving), Kurt was reluctant to sign.

Cobain and Novoselic consulted Susan Silver, manager of Soundgarden, who told him they should get an entertainment lawyer, who could in turn help them get their own deal.

Mintz

Nirvana heeded Silver's advice, and in May, on her recommendation, Kurt and Krist flew to L.A. to talk to music business lawyer Alan Mintz. Mintz—who represented the Rolling Stones, Kiss, Poison, and the Bangles at the time—had already heard and liked *Bleach* and the Vig demo, but he was less impressed with Cobain and Novoselic's unkempt appearance.

Regardless, he agreed to take on Nirvana as clients and started shopping the Vig tape to major labels. The reaction was remarkable, with a half-dozen record labels—including Columbia, MCA, Atlantic, Charisma (a division of Virgin), and Geffen—all expressing serious interest in the band.

Being Courted

By the summer of 1990, Nirvana were being taken to dinner by a host of A&R representatives. Kurt and Krist took advantage of the hospitality, even bringing friends like Dale Crover along for free food, booze, and schmooze as the executives came calling by limousine to Olympia.

"It's not really hard to keep your dignity and sign to a major label . . . Most people don't even have any dignity in the first place," Cobain told *Sounds* that October, revealing he was mulling over eight label offers. "I feel we're experienced enough to deal with it now. I hope that we are."

Sub Pop Shocker

Perhaps naively, Poneman and Pavitt were caught off guard when they learned from Olympia insiders that Nirvana were being lured by companies with tremendous resources. Still, it hurt deep, seeing as the pair behind Sub Pop had nurtured Nirvana and helped the band build a following.

"It was a shock," Pavitt told Charles Cross. "Even though we were constantly broke and in some ways dysfunctional, the least we deserved was to have some honest communication with the group."

Tobi Vail

By the summer of 1990, Cobain had started pursuing Tobi Vail, a friend of Tracy's for whom he had developed feelings. Vail first became friendly with Cobain in mid-'88, when she was just nineteen and Kurt was old enough to buy her beer.

They began dating in mid-July, although it was a far different relationship than the one he had with Marander. Vail was busy between her college classes, job, and juggling playing drums in three bands, which left her little time to wait on Cobain the way he was used to. She was also allergic to Kurt's cats, and a little put off by his graffiti-covered apartment.

Just the same, they were in love. He was struck by her natural beauty and long brown hair, and impressed by her musical knowledge and creativity, coupled with her feminist beliefs. According to reports, the first time he slept with her he was so nervous he threw up.

Clearly Vail, who is widely credited for conjuring up the phrase "Riot Grrl," was in a different league from his nurturing ex. Tobi got things done for herself, whether it was launching her fanzine *Jigsaw* or starting her own flagship band, which she did in October when she co-founded the iconic punk quartet Bikini Kill with singer Kathleen Hanna, guitarist Billy Karren, and bassist Kathi Wilcox.

The Bathtub Is Real

During their courtship, Cobain and Vail recorded together using her father's four-track machine, taping a number of subdued, minimalist pop songs (for which they shared song ideas) during 1990.

The couple alternated vocal and drum duties, laying down material like "Israeli Donkey" and "The Bathtub Is Real." The latter was misunderstood as their band's name, since it was handwritten on the demo, and the moniker stuck.

Working with Kurt, Vail was struck by his approach to songwriting. He told her to decide on a singing style and use her voice as an instrument—an idea she would later call a "revelation."

Peters In

That June, it looked as if Mudhoney might be on the verge of splitting up. Guitarist Steve Turner wanted to return to college and, with the acclaimed Seattle band's future in doubt, Dan Peters suddenly became available.

Nirvana began playing with Peters after Krist's wife ran into him one night at the Vogue and suggested he could fill their vacancy. Dan—along with Mudhoney's Matt Lukin—had since become a huge Nirvana fan, and playing with them seemed like a great idea. Without hesitation, he made contact with Kurt and Krist, who were both encouraged by Peters' suggestion.

However, when Cobain and Novoselic asked Peters to join them on an August tour with Sonic Youth, he revealed that he was already committed to playing conflicting European festival dates with Mudhoney. As a result, old friend Dale Crover was tapped to join Nirvana on the road that summer, but it was understood that Dan would rehearse with the band and assume live duties from September.

Peters' new bandmates even bought him a massive, beat-up drum kit, thinking that his minimalist setup in Mudhoney might not be adequate. Dan took the bass drum but left the rest, and they got to work.

Sonic Youth tapped Nirvana to open their August 1990 West Coast tour, which included this show at the Crest in Sacramento. With Nirvana between drummers, Dale Crover filled in for the nine-day run.   *Author's collection*

Tracking "Sliver"

Nirvana may have been looking for a better label deal, but they still had an obligation to Sub Pop, and agreed to record a quick single for the label for autumn release. A new song called "Sliver" came together quickly during rehearsals with Peters at the Dutchman early that July.

Days later, on July 11, Nirvana cut the single with Jack Endino in just ninety minutes at Reciprocal during TAD's lunch break. Using borrowed instruments, Kurt, Krist, and Dan cut the tune while Doyle and his band sat around eating.

The finished product was a hook-injected keeper—arguably Nirvana's most accessible number yet. Kurt's semi-autobiographical lyric about a little boy being dropped off at his grandparents' house against his will was, as *NME* writer Push would declare, "a hell of a pop song."

Talking to Dawn Anderson about the single soon after its release, Krist said, "It was so spontaneous. The song kind of jelled together in three or four days, then we jumped right in there and recorded it."

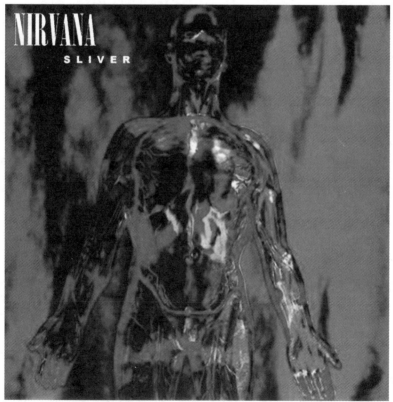

Released on vinyl by Sub Pop in September 1990, Nirvana's single "Sliver"—which featured Mudhoney's Dan Peters on drums and was recorded during a TAD studio session that July—was backed with "Dive."   *Author's collection*

Supporting Sonic Youth

Sonic Youth's West Coast tour in support of *Goo* began on August 13 in Long Beach, California, with Nirvana's opening slot serving as an endorsement to fans of the headliners. Attendees were left awestruck by the trio's performances, even if Cobain and Novoselic's destructive urges were kept in check.

Dale had made it clear to them that his treasured drum kit was off limits for the tour, and Kurt and Krist honored his request. During the two-week run, the music was Nirvana's only spectacle, and concertgoers were plenty receptive.

During the band's set at the Hollywood Palladium on August 17, Cobain jumped into the crowd during "Love Buzz" and let members of the audience play his guitar before he returned to the stage. The audience was enthralled.

Two nights later, at the Casbah in San Diego, the group incorporated pieces of Iggy Pop's "TV Eye" and the Melvins' "Eye Flys" into the set, which opened with "In Bloom" and closed with a new song, "Verse Chorus Verse." Meanwhile, large club and theater shows in markets like Las Vegas, Sacramento, San Francisco, Portland, and Vancouver were well received.

After the band completed the tour with a hometown stop at Seattle's Moore Theatre, Crover was astonished to note that his longtime friends hadn't smashed one single guitar during their trek.

Nice Scream

En route to Long Beach to begin the tour, Nirvana pulled into San Francisco a few days earlier to pick up their temporary drummer from Buzz Osborne's place, where he'd been staying. Dale wanted to take Krist and Kurt to see his friends in Scream, a Washington D.C. punk band with memorable tunes, at the I-Beam.

It took some convincing at first. Cobain had seen Scream in October 1987, at Tacoma's Community World Theatre, and—having been so fond of early Scream—he wasn't impressed. This time it was different. The band's drummer, Dave Grohl, left a lasting impression.

Later, speaking to Buzz, Kurt expressed his wish to find a drummer who could hit as hard as Grohl. He didn't know it at the time, but the following month his wish would come true.

Pignapping

Following the show at the Casbah, Cobain reportedly wound up—quite uncharacteristically—sleeping with a female fan, according to publicist Anton Brookes. The rest of the group went to get gas while waiting on their front man for the return trip to Los Angeles, and it was then that Novoselic saw a pig walking around at a nearby farm.

Novoselic, still intoxicated from the after party, became concerned that the pig might be slaughtered, so he decided to try and kidnap it and bring it home with him. Thankfully, his attempts were thwarted, and soon enough he gave up.

First Impressions

During the tour, Cobain took the opportunity to continue to educate himself about Sonic Youth's approach to the music business. He remained impressed with how Lee Ranaldo, Steve Shelley, Kim Gordon, and Thurston Moore were able to collectively survive and thrive at a time when most bands of their ilk still such had limited resources.

Sonic Youth received minimal publicity, and radio play was scarce outside of the college market. Still, Kurt couldn't help but be impressed how the band, with the help of managers John Silva and Danny Goldberg, had achieved success on their own terms.

By the time things got underway in Vegas, Cobain struck Ranaldo as reserved, albeit elated, to be opening for one of his favorite bands. Speaking in *Nirvana: The True Story*, the guitarist fondly remembered his first impressions of the trio, saying, "I thought they were incredibly exciting and, like everyone else, relished their great combination of raw power, energy and pop Beatlesque sensibility."

John Silva and Danny Goldberg

While in L.A. for their Palladium gig, Cobain and Novoselic were introduced to Sonic Youth's manager, John Silva, and his boss at Gold Mountain Management, Danny Goldberg. Silva was already representing revered Hollywood band Redd Kross and modern folk/blues band House of Freaks when he landed Sonic Youth as clients, just prior to the release of *Goo*.

The men at Gold Mountain were immediately impressed with Thurston Moore's musical knowledge, plus his reputation among, influence over, and connections with new artists, including his touring companions in Nirvana. After Moore talked up the band to Silva, they arranged a meeting. And because Kurt and Krist had faith in Thurston's judgment, experience, and business acumen, Nirvana promptly signed with Gold Mountain.

Getting Grohl

After seeing Grohl's performance in San Francisco six weeks earlier, Cobain and Novoselic agreed that if they ever had the chance to ask him to join their band, they would do so. At the same time, Scream was falling apart. The band's drug-addled bassist, Skeeter Thompson, had quit the band, and Dave was living in the Los Angeles area, tiling floors to make ends meet.

When Dave phoned Buzz Osborne, whom he had befriended on tour with Scream, to see if he had any knowledge of any drummer vacancies, the Melvins front man told Grohl that his friends in Nirvana were looking for a drummer and gave him Novoselic's phone number. Dave—who had been chatting with Crover and Osborne backstage that night—knew exactly whom Buzz was speaking about.

"Krist was all over the room, drinking and laughing," Grohl told *Mojo* in 2005. "And Kurt was so quiet. I remember asking someone, 'Who are those guys? That's Nirvana? You're kidding me, no shit!'"

Dave ran into Kurt again while on tour in Olympia that August. After their show, Grohl and his bandmates were invited back to a party at Slim Moon's that Cobain also attended. During the festivities, Dave left a bad impression with Kurt by making fun of Tobi's performance on the same bill earlier that evening.

Dave would remember Vail to Azerrad three years later as a "sad little girl with the bad fucking songs." Kurt's negative impression of Dave was exacerbated when the drummer tried to play his Primus cassette, *Fizzle Fry*, at Moon's party. But despite Grohl's behavior, Kurt couldn't shake his respect for his drumming.

A few days after making contact with Osborne, Grohl got up the courage to give Novoselic a call. Unfortunately, he was instructed that Nirvana had already asked Dan Peters to join the band. That night, however, both Krist and Kurt called Dave. They spoke about music and discovered they had a lot in common—everything from Neil Young to D.C. hardcore to Public Enemy.

Grohl agreed to fly to Seattle. But first he went to the record store to get a copy of *Bleach*. He listened to it repeatedly as he dismantled his drums. He packed them in a large U-Haul box, threw the rest of his belongings in an old army duffle bag, and hopped on a plane. He arrived at SeaTac on Friday, September 21, with Kurt and Krist picking him up in their van.

Peters Out

On September 22, Nirvana played alongside the Dwarves in support of the Melvins at Motor Sports International Garage in Seattle. It was the only time the band played a gig with Dan Peters on drums. In the audience was future drummer Dave Grohl, who had flown up from Los Angeles the day before to try out.

The next day, Peters sat in on a Nirvana photo shoot and interview for UK music weekly *Sounds*. Little did he know that Kurt and Krist were replacing him.

Somewhat awkwardly, Grohl was also hanging around during the interview—which occurred during a barbecue at the Novoselics' home—trying to be discrete. Understandably, Peters was pissed off when he found out later that all this was going on behind his back. "None of those fucking guys had the balls to tell me," he told Charles Cross.

Eventually, Kurt called Dan to explain that they had found someone else. Peters—who hadn't always gotten the warmest vibes from Kurt—was relieved.

Cobain later told journalist Push that while they weren't unhappy with Peters' drumming, they had found someone who could match their needs even more—and someone who could take care of the backing vocals. "It was a stressful situation," Kurt explained, "but it now looks like Dan will rejoin Mudhoney, and they'll carry on as before." (After much deliberation, Steve Turner had decided to stay on in Mudhoney, so the band could continue.)

KAOS Announcement

On September 25, the night after Grohl's audition, Cobain was invited to perform on Calvin Johnson's *Boy Meets Girl* radio program on KAOS. He took the opportunity to announce that Nirvana's new drummer was Dave Grohl, describing him as a "baby Dale Crover." It was the best compliment he could pay his new kit man.

For the show, Kurt played acoustic renditions of "Lithium," a new song called "Dumb," "Been a Son," and "Opinion." The latter took aim at the holier-than-thou music snobs creeping around Seattle and Olympia in the autumn of 1990.

Nirvana were on the rise, making changes and planning to shift to a major label. The song was Cobain's way of getting in front of the backlash he was anticipating from the underground during the group's transition.

14

Son of a Gun

Dave Grohl's Childhood

Grohl Is Born

David Eric Grohl was born at Trumbull Memorial Hospital in Warren, Ohio, on January 14, 1969. He was the second child of James and Virginia Grohl, who were also parents of a daughter, Lisa, born in February 1966.

Virginia and James

Virginia Jean Hanlon was a student teacher working in a Trumbull County community theater when she first met up-and-coming newspaper reporter James Harper Grohl. Both had musical backgrounds: she had sung in an a capella group called the Three Belles as a teen, and he was a jazz enthusiast who had been classically trained phenomenon on the flute.

Virginia was of Irish descent and had a deep appreciation for poetry and literature, and in particular beat generation writers like Jack Kerouac and Allen Ginsberg. James' ancestors came from Germany and were, as Dave would explain to the *Cleveland Plain-Dealer* in 2003, "an old Pennsylvania Dutch family where everyone is pretty frugal and hard-working."

By the time of Dave's arrival, James was a writer and reporter for the Scripps Howard newswire service in Columbus. The young family settled in the nearby town of Niles, where James had been raised and where Grohl's paternal grandparents and uncles also lived.

Kent State

In May 1970, Dave's father was called upon to cover the student protests at Ohio's Kent State University. The university body had come together to protest President Richard Nixon's announcement on April 30 that US troops had invaded Cambodia, and his ongoing failure to end the war in Vietnam (as he had promised to do when elected in November 1968). The military action in Cambodia, adjacent to Vietnam, was evidence that the war had escalated.

On May 1, a demonstration was held on the campus of Kent State, followed by intermittent rioting in the town of Kent. As matters intensified, James Grohl was on hand to document the happenings as Governor James Allen Rhodes called on the National Guard to restore order to the municipality and the University.

Two thousand people attended a subsequent protest at the Kent State campus on May 4. When they failed to disperse as ordered, the National Guard fired tear gas and—when that failed to clear the area—live ammunition. Four students were killed.

As sad and unnecessary as the Kent State massacre had been, James Grohl's reporting of it would earn him national attention. In 1972, he was asked by Scripps Howard if he wanted to move to Washington D.C. to cover national politics. He accepted the offer and, along with his young family, relocated to the Washington suburb of Springfield, Virginia.

Jackson Five

A year earlier, two-year-old Dave had caught his first concert when the family went to see the Jackson Five at the Ohio State Fair. Thanks to James' press pass, Dave, Lisa, and their parents got to catch thirteen-year-old Michael singing classics like "I Want You Back," "ABC," and "The Love You Save," with backing from his musical siblings.

Understandably, Grohl has no recollection of the show. "I was only two but they were my first musical encounter," he told *Visions* in 2000. "So maybe subconsciously, I want to be Michael Jackson."

Life in Springfield

Springfield was only a few miles outside of Washington, D.C., and in close proximity to the Pentagon, which made it—along with other Northern Virginia towns like Arlington and Alexandria—a popular choice for young families. Just fifteen minutes outside of D.C., Springfield was a mix of well-connected politically affiliated businessmen and working class Virginians.

The Grohls' small, single-family home was located on a cul-de-sac at 5516 Kathleen Place. Dave was an energetic and lovable child who as a toddler carried a stuffed Winnie the Pooh toy with him at all times.

Before long, Grohl began to roam the white, middle-class neighborhood on his Big Wheel trike. In the fall of 1974, Dave started kindergarten at North Springfield Elementary; his sister Lisa was in the third grade at the time.

Taft and Teaching

Not long after the Grohls' arrival in Washington, James quit journalism to take a position as a campaign manager and speechwriter for republican senator Robert

Taft Jr, who was also an Ohio native and the grandson of retired US president William Howard Taft. Virginia went to work as a teacher of English and drama at Thomas Jefferson High School in Alexandria. With her warm personality and unique approach to teaching, Mrs. Grohl soon became one of the most liked and respected teachers at the school.

Divorce

James and Virginia separated in 1975 and divorced soon after. Although the split was hard on the family—especially for Dave's older sister Lisa—for a six-year-old boy, the scenario was hard to process.

"By the time I got a hold of the situation, it was too late for me to have a freak-out," he told *Kerrang!* in 1997. "It just seemed abnormal for all my friends to have a father. I thought growing up with my mother and sister was just the way it was supposed to be."

Getting By

After the divorce, James Grohl returned to Ohio, where he continued to work as a speechwriter for the Republican Party. Virginia, meanwhile, had established roots in the area, as had her children, so she elected to stay in Springfield.

As a teacher, Virginia earned around $18,000, which wasn't much in the mid-'70s. As a single mother with two young children to support, she knew that she would need to supplement her salary with additional work to make ends meet, so she took on part-time work and summer employment to help pay the bills. She clerked in the evenings at a local department store, and on Saturdays she would give estimates to customers of a nearby carpet-cleaning outfit.

Despite Virginia's strong work ethic, times were often lean, and the family wasn't above dining on peanut butter and pickle sandwiches.

UFO Fascination

Dave once admitted to having an obsession with unidentified flying objects. In the era of movies like *Star Wars* and *Close Encounters of the Third Kind*, it wasn't uncommon for kids to have a fixation with UFOs.

On summer nights, Dave could be found lying in his backyard staring up at the stars, hoping to spot a spaceship of some sort. "I had amazing UFO dreams," he told music writer Mike Peake. "I wanted them to abduct me."

"I believe that there could be something else other than little planet Earth with all the little planet Earth people," Dave explained to *Time Out*'s Mike Higginbotham in 1995. "Wouldn't you be bummed if you found out it was just us? It's nice to imagine something else."

All of this helps explain why Grohl would eventually name his own vanity label Roswell Records after the site of an alleged UFO incident. The UFO crash that purportedly occurred there in either June or July 1947 has long been a pop-culture phenomenon

"Frankenstein"

Although the Grohls didn't have a working record player, Virginia would borrow one from the high school where she worked and allowed her children full access to her record collection. When Dave was seven, he eyed up a K-Tel hits compilation album called *Block Buster* during a shopping excursion with his mother, and she bought it for him.

Boasting "20 original hits," the 1976 collection featured smashes like K. C. & the Sunshine Band's "That's the Way (I Like It)," Silver Convention's "Fly Robin Fly," War's "Why Can't We Be Friends," Jigsaw's "Sky High," and the Edgar Winter Group's "Frankenstein." The latter would quickly become one of young Dave's favorite songs.

Recorded in 1972, "Frankenstein" peaked at #1 on the *Billboard* singles charts in May 1973 on its way to becoming a million-selling 45. In January 2001, Grohl told BBC Radio 1's *Evening Session* host Steve Lamacq that the song "was the most bad-assed thing I'd ever heard in my life—it's got all these crazy keyboards and a drum solo in it."

Kiss

On October 31, 1976, seven-year-old Grohl watched Kiss—the most popular hard-rock band in the land—lip-synch hits like "Detroit Rock City" and "Beth" on ABC-TV's *Paul Lynde Halloween Special*. He couldn't help but be taken by the makeup-clad rockers as they ripped through "King of the Night Time World," and very soon after that he was bugging his mom for a Kiss album.

Virginia Grohl acquiesced, and Dave was soon studying the moves of Paul Stanley, Gene Simmons, Ace Frehley, and Peter Criss as he listened to his very own copy of 1976's *Rock and Roll Over*, which was released on November 11 that year and produced the singles "Calling Dr. Love" and "Hard Luck Woman." A year later, he would also pick up Kiss' second concert album, *Alive II*.

Stairway to ABBA

At one point during 1976, Dave got his first earful of "Stairway to Heaven," the lengthy, iconic classic-rock opus by Led Zeppelin, which was played regularly on his mom's favorite radio station. It wasn't until later, however, that he fully discovered the merits of guitarist Jimmy Page and drummer John Bonham on songs like "Trampled Underfoot" and "No Quarter."

It was also around this time that he came to appreciate Swedish pop sensations ABBA, who were riding high with the success of *Arrival* and hits like "Fernando" and "Dancing Queen."

Dad's Guitar

In 1973, when Dave's parents were still together, Virginia bought her husband an acoustic guitar, but he never found time to play it. By the time Dave turned nine he had broken four of the six strings on the nylon-strung, flamenco-styled instrument while attempting to make a racket on it. Somehow, with the two remaining strings, he was able to figure out Deep Purple's legendary hard-rock number "Smoke on the Water." It was the start of his fascination with the guitar.

Hyperactive

Dave had developed a number of interests by his tenth birthday. He played trombone and was an avid soccer player, competing in Springfield's youth league, and had seemingly boundless energy.

In the eyes of his teachers, Dave was hyperactive. Or, as Grohl remembered it to *Kerrang!* in August 1997, "David could be a great student if he could just stay in his fucking seat!"

Another outlet for Dave during this time was acting. Between the ages of nine and twelve, he worked with several professional D.C.-area theater groups.

Chip Moves In

By 1979, Virginia's boyfriend, Chip Donaldson, had moved into the home. Donaldson—a Vietnam veteran turned English teacher—became an important male figure in Dave's life, and his record collection was an essential part of Dave's musical development as he delved deep into the sounds of Jethro Tull, the Grateful Dead, Bob Dylan, Led Zeppelin, the Rolling Stones, and Lynyrd Skynyrd.

When Dave was blown away by the guitar solo on the latter group's classic hit "Freebird," Donaldson encouraged him to think that if he practiced long and hard enough, he too might be able to play like that someday. During the few years that Chip and Virginia were together, Donaldson opened Dave's eyes to the outdoors, taking him on nature walks and teaching him to hunt.

"Chip was a fucking brilliant man," Grohl told *This Is a Call* author Paul Brannigan in 2009, marveling at how Donaldson's presence changed his life at a critical time. Chip's deer antlers, gun rack, and milk crates full of classic albums also helped turn the Grohls' Springfield living room into "a hunting lodge with really good music."

The B-52s on *SNL*

On January 26, 1980, Dave snuck out of the house to hang out with his sister Lisa at a nearby babysitting job. When 11:30 rolled around, the siblings caught America's leading late-night sketch-comedy show, *Saturday Night Live*, which was hosted that evening by the actress Teri Garr. As musical guests the B-52s took the stage just before midnight, for the first of two songs, Grohl couldn't help but be taken aback and mesmerized at the same time.

Singers Kate Pierson and Cindy Wilson had giant bouffant hairdos and colorful dresses, front man Fred Schneider was dressed in an oversized suit jacket, and the band—which included guitarist Ricky Wilson and drummer Keith Strickland—moved about in a chaotic, quick-jerking manner. As the Athens, Georgia group played their new single "Rock Lobster," Grohl couldn't believe what he was seeing and hearing.

"I remember that moment like some people remember the Kennedy assassination," he later told Brannigan. "It made me want to be weird. It just immediately made me want to give everyone the middle finger and be like, 'Fuck you, I wanna be like *that!*'"

Jim Craig

In early 1980, Grohl was heavily impacted by the United States ice hockey team's win over Russia during the Winter Olympics. Dave was more than just a fan of the sport—he had begun playing hockey and lacrosse by this point—and was stunned by the efforts of the team's goalie, Jim Craig.

"I was really into the Olympics that year," Grohl told MTV's Kurt Loder in 2002. "I wanted to be a hockey goalie more than anything, I think, just because they had the most gear or the cool big things on the legs. But he was just a kick-ass goalie, too. I mean, the guy was really something else."

Craig had become such a hero to Grohl that the eleven-year-old even started stalking the Olympic star. When Dave found out that Craig lived in Worcester, Massachusetts, he called directory assistance to see if he could track the goalkeeper down. The operator came back with several people by the name of Jim Craig who lived in the vicinity of Worcester. Grohl took down all the numbers and called to say congratulations to each of them. Sadly, none of the people on the receiving end of the calls wound up being the hockey player, but Grohl eventually got to meet Craig and thank him for inspiring him as a child in person, just minutes before a Foo Fighters performance at the 2002 Winter Olympics.

Let There Be Rock

By the fall of 1980, Dave had lost most of his interest in academia. As his obsession with music grew, his interest in school deteriorated. And with his mother always at work while school was in session, he began ditching classes.

Dave would retreat to his room, where the walls were adorned with posters of the Sex Pistols, Kiss, and AC/DC. He imagined he was Malcolm Young, the rhythm guitarist in his new favorite band.

By early 1981, twelve-year-old Dave was taken with AC/DC's explosive new album *Back in Black*, and he and his friend Larry Hinkle went to catch a midnight showing of the band's concert film *Let There Be Rock* at a theater in downtown Washington. The night gave Grohl his first exposure to marijuana, as the odor of pot smoke filled the theater, while the volume inside the theater gave him a rebellious urge.

"I just wanted to tear that movie theatre to shreds, watching this rock 'n' roll band," he told *Q* in October 2010. "It was fucking awesome."

Larry and Jimmy

Dave and his friends Hinkle and Jimmy Swanson all had similar interests in rock 'n' roll. Hanging out, they would listen to Washington's rock station, DC101, and mimic guitar solos and lip-synch along when the station played the likes of AC/DC, Led Zeppelin, Cheap Trick, the Who, or Van Halen.

Dave and his friends got into typical fifth- and sixth-grade trouble. On one occasion they teased a female classmate on the school bus, taking her purse and tossing it out the window, for which they were called down to the principal's office. During Saturday-night sleepovers at Grohl's, they would sneak out to a nearby road and throw crab apples at cars.

Pillow Drumming to Devo

Devo's "Whip It"—culled from *Freedom of Choice*—topped the US singles chart in the fall of 1980. Around this time, Grohl became fascinated with the band and even managed to get his hands on the group's 1978 LP *Q: Are We Not Men? A: We Are Devo!*, which featured the band's jerky rendition of the Rolling Stones' "(I Can't Get No) Satisfaction" and originals like "Mongoloid" and "Jocko Homo." Grohl was taken with the unique new-wave outfit from Akron, Ohio, and imagined they had "been beamed from some parallel universe."

The idea that the band had conquered New York and signed to Warner Bros Records from Dave's home state of Ohio only added to the appeal. Besides, their music was simple enough that he was able to start drumming along to it in his bedroom, using drumsticks he had bought on the cheap to tap out rhythms on pillows he set up on his bed.

Grohl began studying percussion at school, but because of space restrictions and lack of money at home, a drum kit of his very own was still several years away.

A Secondhand Silvertone and *The Complete Beatles*

In December 1981, Dave was given his first electric guitar as a combination Christmas and twelfth-birthday gift. The gently used axe—a gift from his mom— was a 1963 Sears Silvertone with an amplifier built into the instrument case. Dave was ecstatic and spent most of Christmas day—if not his entire holiday vacation—plucking out "Smoke on the Water," the only song he knew.

In addition, Dave received two essential Fab Four albums that Christmas: *The Beatles 1962–1966* and *The Beatles 1967–1970*, unofficially known as "The Red Album" and "The Blue Album," respectively. These legendary compilations boasted every great Lennon/McCartney single, from 1962's "Love Me Do" to 1970's "The Long and Winding Road."

Then, on his official birthday, Virginia bought her son *The Complete Beatles*, a songbook containing transcriptions and chord charts for all of their songs. Dave occupied much of his time by putting the albums on and playing along to songs like "Ticket to Ride" and "Day Tripper."

"If it weren't for the Beatles, I would not be a musician," Grohl wrote in the 2012 notes for the iTunes-exclusive compilation *Tomorrow Never Knows*. "From a very young age I became fascinated with their songs—their groove and their swagger, their grace and their beauty, their dark and their light. The Beatles seemed to be capable of anything."

The H. G. Hancock Band

Before long, classmates Grohl and Hinkle began plotting their own band. The group was named in a manner similar to Southern rock stars Lynyrd Skynyrd, who had taken theirs from a gym teacher and morphed the spelling. Similarly, Grohl and Hinkle took the last name of their own physical education instructor and affixed the initials of their own last names to the beginning.

The H. G. Hancock Band—as it was known—was just a duo. Together, they'd work at covers of Stones and Who numbers that Dave was learning in guitar lessons. Dave's mother was so tired of hearing "Smoke on the Water" that she gladly paid to help widen her son's repertoire, and he was a quick learner who quickly discovered he could play by ear.

One of Dave's first compositions was called "Bitch," written about his dog, BeeGee. Another of the songs he played for Larry was called "Three Steps." Later that day, he admitted it wasn't his—it was a copy of Skynyrd's "Gimme Three Steps" that he passed off as his own.

2112

Canadian power trio Rush ruled the airwaves in 1981 with rock anthems like "Tom Sawyer," "Limelight," and "Red Barchetta." Dave was hooked on Alex Lifeson's driving guitar lines, Geddy Lee's high-register vocals and, perhaps most importantly, Neil Peart's innovative, impressive drumming. When a cousin gave him a copy of the band's 1976 album *2112*, Grohl's interest went much deeper than the trio's airwave standards.

Dave taught himself to play along with Peart on a makeshift kit comprised of furniture, with a pillow as his snare, a chair as the hi-hat, and his bed as toms and cymbals. As he told *Modern Drummer* in 2004, "I would play to these records until there was condensation dripping from the windows."

X Marks the Spot

In 1981, twelve-year-olds Grohl and Hinkle decided to mark their musical allegiance in a permanent way—by giving themselves tattoos. For Dave, this was the start of an appreciation for tattoos that would continue into his later years.

Ironically, Dave forgot about the tattoo for a number of years until one day, around his twenty-first birthday, when he was sitting in traffic and saw the small marking—which had been made with a Biro—reflecting back at him in his side-view mirror.

Despite the tattoos, the H. G. Hancock Band didn't last much longer. When Larry's parents' split the following year, the boy moved to Maryland with his dad. Although he and Grohl still hung out whenever they could, their days in a band together were over.

Nick Christy

With Larry out of the picture, Grohl sought out a new musical companion, quickly teaming up with a neighborhood kid named Nick Christy, a Massachusetts native just a few months older than Dave who was a strong singer and capable guitarist.

Nick had hoped to start his own band to play Beatles, Who, and Rolling Stones covers. One afternoon he invited Dave over to jam in his basement. At first they did duets, playing to classmates at Christy's house. They graduated to an open-mic night at a local restaurant called Treebeards, where they would play in front of the Wednesday-night crowd thanks to the encouragement of their chaperone, Mrs. Grohl.

Tracy Bradford

In the summer of 1982, Virginia, Lisa, Dave, and his friend Larry Hinkle traveled to Evanston, Illinois, to visit Mrs. Grohl's friend Sherry Pelz Bradford and her family. Bradford had been Virginia's best friend since they attended Ohio's Boardman High School and sang together in the Three Belles.

Sherry's daughter Tracy was considered a "cousin" to Dave and Lisa because of the sister-like relationship of their moms. But this shaven-headed fourteen-year-old girl was unlike anyone the Grohl kids had ever known.

Tracy was a bona fide punk rocker who sang in a band called Verboten and was a regular in the small Chicago punk scene in 1982. She had had her head turned a year earlier by a Dead Kennedys show with support from locals Naked Raygun and Articles of Faith.

When Tracy answered the door of her parents' mansion in combat boots, bondage pants, and an Anti-Pasti shirt, Dave was instantly captivated. She proved to be a great teacher of all things punk, with an amazing record collection. Grohl listened to every one of her punk singles and made a note of the ones that he found most exhilarating.

Naked Raygun

During the Grohls' two-week stay in Evanston, Tracy offered to take Dave and Larry with her to see Naked Raygun and Articles of Faith team up for a gig at Cubby Bear, a rock club across from Wrigley Field.

Throughout the show, thirteen-year-old Grohl (one of the younger kids in the room) was captivated by the collective excitement. Be it the amphetamine-paced music, his first time slam-dancing, or the thrill of being introduced to the headline group's singer, Jeff Pezzati, after the gig—Dave was hooked.

The small, fully engaged audience made Grohl's first concert experience a memorable one, and the experience only added fuel to his desire to pursue music. In 2002, Dave told the *Times* of London, "I stood there and thought, 'I could do this, I can play drums, and you don't even have to sing—you can just scream your balls off.' And so I just dived into the whole punk rock thing."

Washington Punks

As Grohl was making a list of singles to buy—his first would be "Nazi Punks Fuck Off" by San Francisco's Dead Kennedys—he noticed a few had addresses in close proximity to his hometown of Springfield. On the back of singles by S.O.A. and Minor Threat he would see the name of the Dischord label, which was based out of Washington, D.C.

A photo of Nirvana's future kit man Dave Grohl with his mother Virginia in 1982.   *Courtesy of WWYY FM*

Tracy continued to play releases by Dischord acts like Faith and Void for Dave, and she also introduced him to another D.C. outfit, Bad Brains. Grohl was enthralled by the idea that he could act locally on his newfound passion for hardcore. While it took some time before he had the courage (and his mother's permission) to venture into the city on his own, by mid-1983 he had become fully immersed in the punk movement.

Therapy

Dave's new musical direction, coupled with the punk outlook that went with it, didn't exactly sit well with his conservative father. James felt it would be beneficial for his son to get some professional help, but the therapy sessions he arranged only served to increase the distance between the Grohl men.

"My mother and father had been divorced, and I wasn't really getting on with my father," he told *Flipside* in 1999. "He thought we needed to go to family counseling. It kind of backfired. I didn't feel like I needed help. It just didn't really work."

Sandy Moran

By the time Grohl had entered the eighth grade at Oliver Wendell Holmes Middle School in the fall of '82, he was smitten with a girl named Sandy Moran. Dave dated the feathered-hair beauty for a mere two weeks, but he would describe her to *Melody Maker* in 2000 as "the hottest chick in the whole school."

When Sandy dumped him, thirteen-year-old Dave rebounded quickly. That night, he dreamed that he was a rock star, playing guitar onstage in an arena as the audience worshipped him. Then, as he looked down into the front row, he saw Sandy crying.

As a way to fall asleep—and as a means to sidestep therapy—Dave began talking about his problems into a tape recorder he kept by his bed. When he was through, he would rewind the tape and listen to himself as he fell asleep.

Not So Quiet

When Grohl and Hinkle returned from Illinois, they attended a weeklong lacrosse camp at the University of Maryland with punk rock on their minds. Dave went down to the local record store in College Park, where he picked up *Back from Samoa*, the 1982 second album by L.A. group the Angry Samoans.

Dave was energized by the sounds of "Gas Chamber," "My Old Man's a Fatso," "Tuna Taco," "They Saved Hitler's Cock," and the band's take on the Chambers Brothers' classic "Time Has Come Today." That summer, he also threw himself into the double-LP punk compilation *Not So Quiet on the Western Front*, issued in conjunction with the punk publication *maximumrocknroll*. The set boasted tracks by forty Bay Area bands, including Flipper and Millions of Dead Cops.

From there, Dave bought Bad Brains' *Rock for Light*—produced by none other than the Cars' Ric Ocasek—and the Dead Kennedys' 1981 EP *In God We Trust*, which included such memorable songs as "Religious Vomit," "Moral Majority," and a cover of "Rawhide," as well as the aforementioned "Nazi Punks Fuck Off."

Dave was no longer interested in Rush or AC/DC. The excitement he felt for the music he had just discovered consumed him. He had never heard many of the records he bought until he got them home. When he put the needle down, he regularly had his mind blown.

Rock Against Reagan

On July 3, 1983, Grohl and Hinkle traveled to the Lincoln Memorial in Washington, D.C., for the Rock Against Reagan concert, a hardcore festival that boasted a headline set by the Dead Kennedys plus performances by M.D.C., Dirty Rotten Imbeciles, Toxic Reasons, Reagan Youth, Crucifucks, and Washington's own Scream. The show was sponsored by a leftist organization known as the Youth International Party, which sponsored the legalization of marijuana, among other issues.

Nearly 1,000 punks from the D.C. area and beyond gathered to slam-dance, mingle, and buy merch. On the fringes, frat boys and hippie chicks looked on in amazement as cops on horseback gave punks their lumps with police department–issued nightsticks.

Just before sundown, Jello Biafra and the rest of the Dead Kennedys took the stage, launching into "Holiday in Cambodia" as police helicopters flew overhead. "It was so unbelievably moving," Grohl told *Mojo* in November 2009. "It was like our own personal Altamont, our Woodstock. And that's when I said, 'Fuck the world, I'm doing *this*.'"

Three Bars

At some point in 1983, Grohl became so caught up in punk that he gave himself another tattoo. This time, he planned to brand himself with Black Flag's indelible four bars logo using a needle and pen ink, prison style.

Dave had picked up the technique by watching *Christiane F.—Wir Kinder vorn Bhanhof Zoo*, a 1981 movie about the drug epidemic in Berlin. Unfortunately, the fourteen-year-old only made it to the third of the four bars, leaving his skin tribute to Black Flag incomplete.

Soccer Rocker

In his freshman year at Thomas Jefferson High School for Science and Technology in Alexandria—where his mom taught, and his sister was a senior—Dave had a haircut to fit the times. The Police were the biggest band of the year, and U2 were closing in. In keeping with their respective front men, Sting and Bono, the fourteen-year-old Grohl sported what he called a "soccer rocker"—not quite a mullet, but close to it. In 2003, he admitted to *Blender*, "Everybody on the soccer team had a haircut like Sting's in 1983."

Scream

Hailing from Bailey's Crossroads in Northern Virginia, Dischord act Scream were fresh off the release of their '83 debut *Still Screaming* when Grohl discovered his favorite new local band. Bad Brains had moved to New York, Minor Threat had called it a day, and now Scream—initially comprised of singer Peter Stahl, his guitarist/brother Franz, bassist Skeeter Thompson and drummer Kent Stax—filled a void in the punk scene.

In addition to their debut album, Dave was drawn to Scream's willingness to go beyond the hardcore status quo of numbers like "Bedlam" and "Laissez-Faire." The group took chances, playing covers like Steppenwolf's "Magic Carpet Ride" and breaking into trippy jams before firing back into their own ferocious originals.

Bad Brains

Bad Brains had become one of Grohl's favorites bands, especially after he caught them live at the 9:30 Club in 1983. At a time when most hardcore bands were thin white straight-edged kids with shaved heads, this dreadlocked, Rastafarian African-American D.C. punk collective was like nothing else out there. Their gigs were as intense as they were explosive.

"It was like if James Brown was to play hardcore," Grohl told the *Melody Maker* in 1999. "It was so smooth and so fuckin' powerful—they were Gods, man, they were way more than human . . . It was just fuckin' unreal.

The Key Club

One afternoon, Grohl and Christy were playing Beatles and Rolling Stones numbers for the residents of an Alexandria nursing home, having volunteered to do so as part of their membership in the Thomas Jefferson High School's Key Club. The show offered a way for them to play out in public and provide service to the community, but the real reason they joined initially was to meet people and get invited to keg parties.

A local drummer and upperclassman named Tony Morosini spotted the duo and approached Christy about joining his band as the singer, but Nick explained that he would only join if his friend Dave was included.

Nameless

By late 1983, Grohl and Christy had become part of Morosini's band, expanding the trio to a five-piece. Together, they worked up versions of the Who's "My Generation," some classic Stones numbers, and even "Louie Louie."

Having played a few backyard parties that spring, the quintet signed up for their school's annual variety show in June. When pressed for a name upon registration, they said they were nameless. As show time approached, they were billed as "Nameless."

During the show they played the Who's "Squeezebox," Chuck Berry's "Johnny B. Goode," and Kenny Loggins' recent #1 hit "Footloose." Unfortunately, they lost the competition to another band, Three for the Road, whose members included Chet Lott, son of one-time Mississippi senator Trent Lott.

Perhaps Nameless might have won if Grohl had been playing Morosini's drums. In between songs during rehearsals at Tony's that spring, Dave would hop behind the drums whenever he could, disrupting practice and irritating his bandmates.

"He'd just start wailing on those frigging drums," Christy told Paul Brannigan. "I'd be saying, 'Cut the shit, dude, we've gotta practice and you're not a fucking drummer.'" Of course, time would tell that the opposite was true.

Virginity Lost

In the spring of 1984, toward the end of his freshman year, fifteen-year-old Dave had an intimate encounter with a junior on the girl's basketball team. Sadly, it wasn't the great experience Grohl had hoped.

"She ruled me like a caged animal," Dave admitted to *Blender* in 2003. "It was like *2001: A Space Odyssey*, just silent until the monolith came crashing down."

D.C. Bound

In the summer of 1984, Grohl was mowing lawns all week to make enough cash to get into Washington on the weekends. As he pushed his mower to the sounds of Minor Threat and Black Flag coming through his Sony Walkman, he would dream of his future as he plotted out how he might get to the next Scream or Rites of Spring gig.

He lived for punk shows at miniscule venues like d.c. space and Food for Thought (a restaurant that held after hours gigs). Sometimes his sister would drop him off in the city; other times he would take the Metro.

At the time, D.C. was downright volatile, plagued with weekly if not daily murders, with the highly addictive drug crack cocaine on the rise. Another substance called love boat—essentially marijuana mixed with PCP—was also being blamed for the uptick in street violence. Regardless, the fifteen-year-old Grohl was determined to be a part of the city's punk movement.

Making the Scene

Walking into a show at a venue like Space II Arcade, Dave would strike up conversations with people selling fanzines and giving away stickers, and musicians waiting to go onstage. If the equipment was iffy at times, the energy was always high. Grohl was quick to learn that crowd participation was key.

Through new friends, he would trade tapes as a means to discover new bands. Through the fanzines—most notably Tim Yohannon's *maximumrocknroll*—mail order helped a suburban kid like Dave get his hands on singles that were impossible to find at his local store.

Of course, there were parts of the scene that Grohl couldn't buy into. Straight-edge kids—initially inspired by the Minor Threat song "Straight Edge"—embraced a lifestyle that was free of inebriation, but Dave was already smoking pot and attending beer parties. He liked both, and he had no intention of slowing his roll.

John Denver's Nightmare

In 1984, Grohl sent Xeroxed letters to punk bands that he had read about in the fanzine *Warning*, soliciting song contributions to a punk mixtape he was planning to release called *John Denver's Nightmare*.

In the letter, obtained by the website *Death and Taxes* in 2011, he wrote, "Me and my friend are putting out a compilation tape of about 15 different bands from all over," adding, "It's gonna be sold at almost all of the D.C. shows, so it won't be a waste of time."

Dave's letter advised that bands with names like Presidential A.I.D.S., the Dead Ends, and Chips Patrol were already onboard. It's unclear if the compilation ever surfaced.

Lisa's Modern Rock

For every Dirty Rotten Imbeciles album or Egg Hunt 45 Dave brought home, his sister Lisa had an R.E.M. or Siouxsie & the Banshees cassette to match. Lisa had become exposed to new bands that were still considered left-of-center through word of mouth and the local alternative-rock radio station, WHFS.

Lisa exposed him to records he might have otherwise missed, like the Buzzcocks' now-classic compilation *Singles Going Steady*, R.E.M.'s *Murmur*, and albums by David Bowie and Talking Heads. At times they would discover they were already listening to the same thing, as was the case with Hüsker Dü's *Zen Arcade.*

Vice President

In the fall of his sophomore year at Thomas Jefferson High, Grohl—who had become quite popular—was elected vice president of his class. With his position, he was occasionally given the opportunity to take over the school's intercom system after making his announcements. He treated his classmates to the sounds of the Circle Jerks and Bad Brains, leaving many to ask him later about said bands. It was his way of spreading the word about the music he loved.

Dope

By early 1985, Dave had become an avid pot smoker, and was using marijuana multiple times a day. "I was such a burn out, I was smoking all day long," Dave told *Metal Hammer* in 1996.

His grades—which had been pretty good until this point—began to falter. With weed being his main pursuit outside of music, he admitted to *Kerrang!* writer Dave Everley in '97, "I couldn't give a shit about anything."

15

Six Color Pictures, All in a Row

From Freak Baby to Scream

Freak Baby

In the fall of 1984, Dave Grohl met a likeminded punk kid named Brian Samuels at a Void show at the Wilson Center in D.C. Samuels, a 270-pound skinhead who played bass in a band called Freak Baby, soon discovered that Grohl played guitar and suggested he audition as the band's second guitarist.

Grohl dropped in for a tryout on rhythm guitar in drummer Dave Smith's basement. If Grohl was proficient, he didn't leave any of Freak Baby's members awestruck. However, his liveliness, passion, and wit were all quickly evident. Dave was hired into the group, which also featured lead guitarist Bryant Mason and singer Chris Page. To avoid confusion with two Daves in the band, Mason and Page gave their younger counterparts distinguishing handles: Smith became Smave and Grohl became Grave.

It wasn't long before Freak Baby made their first demo with a young local producer named Barrett Jones, who recorded bands at his Laundry Room Studio when he wasn't playing in his own R.E.M.-influenced band 11th Hour. At the time, the studio was in his parents' Arlington home; the main control room was in the actual laundry room, while the acts performed in his adjacent bedroom.

With the tape complete, the band managed to get local punk record store Smash to stock it. For Grohl's live debut, they booked one key gig, opening for area favorites Trouble Funk that winter at Arlington's alternative high school, H-B Woodlawn.

Mission Impossible

Despite having brought Grohl into the picture, bassist Brian Samuels was kicked out of the band in late 1984 after attacking Dave during practice. Grohl had been messing around on Smith's drum kit when Samuels lost patience with him and pulled him to the ground. Grohl wasn't hurt by this unexpected act of violence; singer Page broke up the scuffle, and practice dispersed.

When the band reconvened as a four-piece, it was decided that Smith should move to bass, and Grohl—who had impressed the other members in practices— left the guitar for a place behind Smith's drums. They also assumed a new name: Mission Impossible.

With Samuels out of the band, there were few dissenting opinions as Mission Impossible crafted their own new and unique material. Grohl was thrilled to play real drums, and once his bandmates could see what he was capable of, they were amazed. Soon enough, the quartet had become the fastest punk band in the D.C. area. Aside from his speed, Dave played with power and ingenuity.

Mission Impossible recorded a new twenty-song demo in early 1985, again with Jones, for which they reworked some Freak Baby holdovers and cut new hardcore winners like "Butch Thrasher," "Life Already Drawn," and "Neglect." Elsewhere, the foursome showed a comic side with their take on the "I'm Stuck on Band-Aid Brand" jingle and their own rendition of the *Mission Impossible* TV theme, which became their signature opening number.

The 1986 split seven-inch EP *Getting Shit for Growing Up Different*, released by Sammich Records, included three songs by Mission Impossible, featuring Dave Grohl on drums.   *Author's collection*

Grohl's Originals

Grohl brought two of his own original songs to the demo session. The first was a seventy-four-second sonic bomb called "New Ideas" that was easily the quickest song in their repertoire, while "To Err Is Human" showed a much different side of Mission Impossible. Sonically, it resembled Hüsker Dü, who—with the release of the aforementioned *Zen Arcade*—had become one of Dave's favorite bands. According to Paul Brannigan, one mainstream reviewer would list it as one of Mission Impossible's better songs and compare it to something one might have heard on the Clash's classic *London Calling*.

The lyrics, inspired by the issues Dave had been experiencing with his father James, started as prose in his notebook, not long after his sixteenth birthday; sung forcefully by Page, they served as a challenge to Grohl's dad: *"To err is human / So what the fuck are you? Working so hard to make me perfect too."*

Closet Metal Head

Unlike many of his peers on the independent D.C. punk scene, Grohl wasn't an elitist. He began exploring underground metal bands like Slayer, Metallica, Mercyful Fate, and Venom, and he renewed his appreciation for Motörhead— even if he kept it from his Mission Impossible bandmates at first.

As with hardcore, Dave identified with and was drawn to the aggression, rebellion, and energy he heard in underground metal. Of course, there were distinct differences between the two genres. Metal was slightly more polished, its subject matter more diverse, and its presentation definitely nastier. At the same time, it was far more accepting than the typically elitist hardcore movement.

Dave's Drum Influences

At a time when rock 'n' roll was increasingly segregated by subgenre, Grohl's influences were broader than those of most young drummers. He continued to learn fills by his favorite drummers—including Rush's Neil Peart, punk players Earl Hudson (of Bad Brains), Jeff Nelson (of Minor Threat), John Wright (of No Means No), and metal kit men like Slayer's Dave Lombardo and Metallica's Lars Ulrich—at home on his makeshift bedroom set.

With nowhere for Dave to keep a drum kit in his mom's cramped house, coupled with the fact that he had Dave Smith's drums at his disposal, he held off on buying his own for the immediate future. Because he was used to playing on pillows, with no rebound to them, and used marching sticks, Grohl played extremely hard. When he got on Smith's kit, he would often break his sticks, because he hit the snare, toms, and cymbals with such power.

Disagreements with Dad

If the distance between Grohl and his father wasn't hard enough on their relationship, philosophical differences were inevitable. Dave followed his mother's more liberal-minded approach to life, and his commitment to punk rock flew in the face of nearly everything that staunch Republican James stood for.

Grohl found his speechwriter father intimidating throughout his teen years, and he joked to the *Times* of London in 2002 that he'd get "the State of the Union address" if he stepped out of line. Without a strong father figure in his life day-to-day, Dave believed he became more accepting of the differences in people around him, including the homosexuals he encountered during his years in theater, and the many eccentric people he met in the punk scene. He couldn't help but have some conflicts with his rigid dad.

When it came to music, for instance, James took issue with his son calling himself a musician, because his background was steeped in classical and jazz. Rock—and especially punk rock—was just noise. It wasn't until Dave became a rich and famous musician that James Grohl changed his mind-set.

77KK and the Second Demo

Mission Impossible's demo earned them a place on Washington, D.C.'s regional *Metrozine* compilation *Can It Be?* in the late spring of 1985. The featured song was Grohl's "New Ideas," and its release led to the band landing a mention in Tim Yohannon's *Maximumrocknroll*.

Soon after, French punk label 77KK tapped the band to appear on its debut compilation, with Mission Impossible's "Life Already Drawn" featured next to D.O.A., Youth Brigade, and a slew of other North American and French punk outfits.

The band had already tracked their second official demo with Barrett Jones, recording six new songs that marked a sonic evolution. MI was still a punk band, per se, but they had become stronger and more confident on songs like "I Can Only Try," "Into Your Shell," "Paradoxic Sense," "Wonderful World," "Helpless," and "Now I'm Alone."

First Love

When Grohl was sixteen, his first really serious girlfriend, Wendy, moved from Arlington to Arizona. He was devastated.

He spent weeks pining for her while listening to Led Zeppelin's "All of My Love." As Dave told the London *Times* in 2005, "All I wanted to do was drop out of high school and drive to be with her."

Just Maniacal

During the summer of 1985, Dave Grohl befriended D.C. punk icon Ian MacKaye after the Minor Threat singer and Dischord Records co-founder dropped in to see Mission Impossible play with Lunchmeat at the Lake Braddock Community Center in Burke, Virginia, on July 25, 1985.

"Everyone said, 'You gotta see this drummer, this kid, he's sixteen, he's been playing for two months and he's out of control,'" McKaye told *Mojo* in November 2009, describing Grohl's performance as "just maniacal." Although Dave had actually been playing on a real drum kit for six months, Ian was stunned—as was Grohl when one of his heroes walked up to him to explain that he played just like D.O.A., Black Flag, and Circle Jerks veteran Chuck Biscuits.

Dave was floored by the compliment, and that summer he and his friend Bobby Sullivan hung around from time to time at Dischord House in Arlington. Bobby was the younger brother of Mark Sullivan, a one-time bandmate of McKaye's in the Slinkees. McKaye remembered Grohl as fun to be around, with his warm, upbeat personality and wide smile.

Pizza Boy

That summer, Dave worked at a Shakey's Pizza. "That job fucking sucked," he told *FHM*, remembering how he reeked of pepperoni. When asked if he was hygienic, he told the magazine, "I'm sure my hands had been in places the pizza lovers wouldn't want to know about."

Dave's memory of the experience may have been tainted by the fact that he was required to work to pay for his own schoolbooks, which would no longer be provided now that his parents had decided he needed a stern learning environment.

Bishop Ireton

In the fall of 1985, Dave was sent to Bishop Ireton High School in Alexandria. Run by priests and nuns, the school had a rigorous disciplinary philosophy, which was just what James and his ex-wife Virginia felt their sixteen-year-old soon needed.

Following his poor grades and general devotion to music over school, the last straw came when Virginia found a bong (a water pipe used to smoke marijuana) under the front seat of her Ford Fiesta. Dave's perpetual weed use with Jimmy Swanson had finally caught up with him. Sort of.

Dave would still get high before morning prayers at his new school. But for a teenage boy who had rarely been to church, there was something ironic about having to study the Bible. As Dave griped to *Q* in 2007, "It's like, 'Dude, all I did was take acid and spray-paint shit! Why am I here?'"

Mission Impossible Splits

Mission Impossible disbanded when their founding members, front man Chris Page and guitarist Bryant Mason, left for college in September of 1985. Two swan-song gigs were set for the end of August—one at Lake Braddock Community Center, followed by a final show at Fort Reno Park with the local band Age of Consent.

Alongside another band on the Lake Braddock bill, Lunchmeat, Mission Impossible were asked to participate in a split-seven-inch EP for Sammich Records, the label run by Ian MacKaye's sister Amanda. Featuring the three best numbers from MI's April '85 demo—"Helpless," "Into Your Shell," and "Now I'm Alone"—the EP, titled *Thanks*, was readied in the weeks that followed the foursome's demise. When all 500 copies sold out, the record was re-released under a new title: *Getting Shit for Growing Up Different.*

Reuben Radding

Soon after Mission Impossible split up, Grohl received an offer to join Minor Threat guitarist Brian Baker—who was just off a short tenure with the Meatmen—in his new band Dag Nasty, but he passed. He was no longer interested exclusively in punk. He also wanted to keep playing with Smith, who had become one of his best friends and his rhythmic counterpart.

Grave and Smave were evolving stylistically, and now sought to find a front man who was looking to do the same. They approached Smith's childhood friend Reuben Radding, who just happened to be Barrett Jones' roommate. Radding's band Age of Consent had also just broken up, and, like Grohl, he had a newfound appreciation for Led Zeppelin.

If Grohl was steeped in hardcore, Radding had been schooled in the experimental post-punk sounds of Gang of Four, Television, Mission of Burma, and Public Image Ltd. Zeppelin was their common ground. When Smith and Grohl asked him to join forces with them, it was with the expectation that he would be their singer and switch back to guitar. Reuben agreed.

Bonham

For Grohl, it wasn't just that weed went together perfectly with Led Zeppelin. *Houses of the Holy* featured "The Rain Song," one of Dave's favorite Page/Plant compositions, and, as a drummer, he couldn't help but be taken by the work of the late John Bonham, who died tragically in 1980 of asphyxiation.

Dave studied each and every one of "Bonzo's" drum rolls, and he loved how his new hero played with equal parts power and soul, never forgoing the groove. As Grohl would tell *Mojo* in 2005, he was taken with Bonham's "recklessness" and "his precision," explaining, "When he hit a groove it was so deep it was like a heartbeat."

Dain Bramage

If the name of Grohl's new trio sounded cool at the time, he had second thoughts with twenty years of hindsight. "I don't know where the hell we got that name," he chuckled to the *Independent Magazine* in 2005.

The group's fall 1985 rehearsals, leading up to their first live gig, were usually productive. During their very first rehearsal they got high, plugged in, and wrote four songs.

The songs may have come easy, but that's not to say they were popular when they played their debut show at the Lake Braddock Community Center on December 20. Any fans of Grohl's earlier bands who came expecting punk would in fact hear something very different when Dain Bramage played the moody new number "In the Dark."

As Dave told *Mojo* in 2009, "Nobody fucking liked us."

The Energizer

Not only were Dave and his bandmates outsiders, they took pride in being different. Dain Bramage might not have won everyone over, but they did catch the interest those who could appreciate the group's unique fusion of influences—everything from Tom Verlaine and Neil Young to Metallica and Black Sabbath. Although Radding was out in front, it wasn't unusual for most eyes to be on Grohl, an explosive, animated drummer with a killer smile and boundless energy.

Grave's stage presence was a reflection of his wind-up-toy personality. He would go for hours and then conk out. After a twenty-minute nap he was back at it. Because he kept going and going, Smith and Radding nicknamed him "The Energizer."

Drugs

Despite his longstanding appreciation of marijuana, Grohl was initially hesitant to try harder drugs as a teenager. He even resisted taking acid during a 1985 trip with friends to Ocean City, Maryland, but relented when his buddies—who had already taken the drug—told them they would put it in his drink. He liked it so much that he dropped another tab six hours later.

Alongside pot, hallucinogens continued to play a part in Dave's recreational drug use throughout his junior year in high school. During a Christmas party hosted by his mother for all of the family's friends that December, one of Dave's pals gave him mushrooms as a present. He wound up tripping while Christmas carols played in the background.

Fartblossom

In early 1986, Dain Bramage recorded a pair of demos with Barrett Jones. During the first session, they tracked the aforementioned "In the Dark," plus titles like "Cheyenne," "Watching It Bake," "Space Car," and "Bend."

A second turn at Laundry Room resulted in the trio's own innovative rendering of Grand Funk Railroad's 1973 smash "We're an American Band," plus eight original numbers including, "Flannery," "Give It Up," "The Log," "Baltimore Sucks (But Booje Needs the Bucks)," and "Home Sweet Nowhere."

That spring, the group shared demos with people in and around the D.C. scene, but purposely avoided Grohl's friend Ian MacKaye, thinking that their sound was an ill fit for the now-revered punk label. Eventually, Corrosion of Conformity's Reed Mullin handed the demo to Bob Durkee, the head of Pomona, California's Fartblossom Records, who called and offered to sign the band. They took the deal.

I SCREAM NOT COMING DOWN

Dain Bramage's 1986 album *I Scream Not Coming Down* was released on Fartblossom Records and included the liner note: "David Grohl destroys Tama drums exclusively."
Author's collection

I Scream Not Coming Down

In June 1986, following an inexplicable falling out with Barrett Jones, Dain Bramage planned a Friday-to-Monday session at RK-1 Studios in Crofton, Maryland, where they would record their Fartblossom debut. Engineered by the facility's owner, E. L. Copeland, and Radding's friend Dan Kozak, who had played guitar in Age of Consent, the project was plagued with power problems due to a violent thunderstorm.

Just the same, Copeland's soundproofed garage facility produced a ten-song album that included the title track, "I Scream Not Coming Down," plus "Swear," "Stubble," "Drag Queen," and more.

WHFS

As Grohl anxiously awaited the autumn release of his band's debut album, the trio arranged to get themselves played on the Sunday night *Local Licks* program on WHFS-FM, the area's alternative rock station, in November 1986. "I remember thinking that it was so fucking cool that there was a DJ introducing one of our band's songs, going out to maybe a couple of thousand people," Dave told *Kerrang!* in 2002.

Despite that high point, the months dragged on, and the album never materialized, even though Fartblossom ensured the members of Dain Bramage it would. Dave was uneasy about his future and wondered where he'd be in a year, when all of his classmates shipped off to college. Then, as fate would have it, he stopped in at a local music store for some new drumsticks, and his life changed.

Joining Scream

Grohl was on his way out the door of Rolls Music in Fall's Church, Virginia, when a flyer caught his eye: "Scream looking for drummer. Call Franz." To some, this ad might not have meant much, but to Dave—who had been following the Dischord band since their 1983 debut *Still Screaming*, and cherished the 1985 LP *This Side Up*—it was an epiphany.

Dave tore the flyer off the wall, folded it into his pocket, and hurried home to Kathleen Place. He picked up the phone and called the number. When guitarist Franz Stahl answered, he asked how old Grohl was. Dave told him he was twenty. At first, Stahl resisted, because of Grohl's age, but eventually, after a second call, the drummer convinced him.

Grohl knew the work of former Scream drummer Kent Stax—who was departing to raise a family—better than Stahl could have ever expected when he finally showed up for an audition at the band's practice space below a Northern Virginia head shop. When Franz asked if he wanted to start with some covers, Dave said he'd rather play tracks from Scream's first album. "So I said, 'Oh, how about *Still Screaming*,'" he told *Metal Hammer* in 2003. "And they went, 'Which song?' So I said, 'The whole thing.'"

After deliberating for some time with his vocalist/brother Pete and bassist Skeeter Thompson, Franz asked Grohl to join the band. Dave was elated and totally freaked out in equal measure. Scream had toured the US and Europe, and had another trek planned to support their third album. Their newly hired drummer had never been beyond Illinois before, and—although they were unaware—was still a high-school senior.

Passing on Fugazi

In between the time of his Scream audition and his subsequent hiring, Grohl was invited to try out for rising gore-rockers Gwar. He graciously declined the offer.

More serious was an invitation to come to Dischord House in Alexandria to jam with Ian MacKaye. Along with Joe Lally, it was Grohl who drummed during the formative stages of the band that would become Fugazi. When MacKaye asked Dave to join the band, however, he had to pass, as he had already accepted his slot in Scream.

Dropping Out

After several days of hemming and hawing, Grohl told his parents that he was dropping out of school to join his dream band. It wasn't an easy discussion for Dave to have with his mother, especially since she was an educator herself. "When I told her I was leaving school, she said, 'All right. Well, you better get a job and you better be good at this,'" Grohl told radio host Howard Stern in 2011.

When word reached his conservative absentee father James—who envisioned his son going into the military—there was tremendous resistance. But by that point, Dave had his mind made up. As he told *X-Ray* in 2003, "I knew that in ten years, I wouldn't be using much trigonometry."

Quitting Dain Bramage

As luck would have it, the week after Grohl told his Dain Bramage bandmates that he had secured a spot behind the drums in Scream, copies of the trio's record, *I Scream Not Coming Down*, arrived on Reuben Radding's doorstep. The LP was officially released on February 28, 1987.

Radding and Smith didn't take the news well. They had been brothers in arms for a year, and in Smave's case they had been playing together for several years. It put a strain on their friendships, but Dave knew he was making the best choice for himself.

Scream

The origins of Scream date back to 1979, when guitarist Franz Stahl and his freshman classmates Skeeter Thompson (bass) and Kent Stax (drums) came together in his parents' Bailey's Crossroads home to play covers of their favorite rock songs. By 1981, and with Stahl's older brother Pete brought into the fold on vocals, the group shifted to hardcore and began playing out in the Washington, D.C. area.

With a style that merged Minor Threat's blistering hardcore with Bad Brains' reggae-laden bombast, Scream became notorious on the local scene. They recorded their debut LP, *Still Screaming*, for Dischord in 1983. Before the release of their acclaimed second album, Scream added a second guitarist, Robert "Harley" Davidson. The result was what many—including Grohl—considered to be the band's best effort, 1985's *This End Up*.

Scream's final album with Stax, and their last for Dischord, *Banging the Drum* was released late the following year. It marked a shift toward modern rock—which was becoming more popular with the recent commercial successes of bands like R.E.M. and U2—while still holding on to Scream's punk foundation.

Road Dog

In the spring of 1987, Grohl—just eighteen years old—embarked on his first US tour. Traveling in Scream's Dodge Ram van with his new bandmates and his best friend Swanson, who was hired as the group's roadie, Dave crisscrossed North America, living on cheap cigarettes and Taco Bell.

The quintet played gigs in venues like the Botanical Center in Des Moines and Fender's Ballroom in Los Angeles during the two-month summer caravan. Dave struck the Stahls as a star in the making. In addition to being a monster drummer, he was a kid who loved the touring lifestyle and was excited to be out rocking in the free world.

Found Out

Midway through the trek, Pete Stahl uncovered the truth about Dave's age. At first he was pissed, but because Dave was a legal adult in most respects—and one hell of a drummer—he relented, and Scream trudged onward.

Before long, Stahl—who was a decade older than Grohl—took the drummer under his wing and showed him how not only to survive on the road but to have fun, thrive, and even score with the ladies.

Dope Behind the Wheel

One night, the band was traveling down a dark stretch of American highway with Grohl behind the wheel and Swanson in the passenger seat. With the rest of the group fast asleep in the back, Jimmy pulled out a new bong they had just acquired, and together he and Dave tested its merits.

Passing the Easy Rider Aqua Pipe back and forth, Grohl and Swanson proceeded to get stoned very quickly. As the van filled up with marijuana smoke, they went into a fit of hysterics, and Dave lost control of the vehicle.

The van rode over the warning bumps on the shoulder of the road at seventy miles per hour, prompting the drummer to regain control just short of going into a ditch. He woke the rest of the band in the process—and, as a result, Grohl was stripped of his driving privileges for the rest of the tour.

Europe

Following a run of autumn tour dates, Grohl returned home to Springfield for Thanksgiving 1987, with instructions to obtain a valid passport. The Stahls informed Dave that a European tour was slated for the following February.

The group—now a quartet, following the departure of Davidson—flew standby via Martinair from Washington to Amsterdam, where they based their operations. Staying in squats occupied by fans, the group traveled to the UK for a

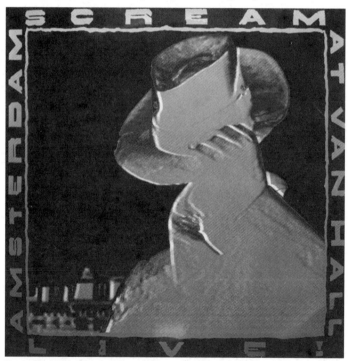

Scream's 1988 concert album, *Live at Van Hall, Amsterdam*. Recorded live on March 28 of that year, Grohl, singer Peter Stahl, guitarist Franz Stahl, and bassist Skeeter Thompson, played to an enthusiastic Dutch audience.

Author's collection

series of gigs with Subhumans and journeyed to various other European cities, including Turin, Italy.

"They're burning the mattresses 'cause they have scabies all over them," Grohl told the *Independent* in 2005. "You walk in with your gear and they're still trying to figure out how to steal electricity from the building next door."

These illegal dwellings would often double as makeshift venues, and although the pay was negligible—usually only gas money—the hospitality and sense of community stayed with the drummer. "[They would] make you the biggest bowl of pasta you've ever seen in your life—and smoke you out! It was great."

Perhaps the most important gig of the trek took place on March 28 in Amsterdam, where the band's Van Hall gig was broadcast live on Dutch radio. The explosive concert—which found Scream sounding as powerful as ever—would be released late in the year as the concert album *Live! At Van Hall Amsterdam* throughout Europe on Konkurrel Records.

Discovering Dale

During some downtime staying with a friend of the Stahls' in Amsterdam between gigs, Dave went through his host's record collection, playing everything he was unfamiliar with that intrigued him. Midway through the stack, he uncovered the Melvins' *Gluey Porch Treatments*. While Dave anticipated it would be just another hardcore album, it was much more.

"When I put it on, it really fucking blew my mind," Grohl told *Mojo* in 2004, marveling at how the band's drummer, Dale Crover, could play so slow and still keep time. "This was the moment I fell in love with the dirge aesthetic."

Zeppelin Tattoo

Before flying home to Washington in late March, Grohl decided to add to his growing number of tattoos. Following his first attempt at tattooing himself with Led Zeppelin's three-circle logo at the age of sixteen, he had an Italian friend named Andrea have a second go at John Bonham's 1971 symbol—first seen as part of the album art for *Led Zeppelin IV*—using a "tattoo gun" made from a doorbell machine.

"When my mother saw it, she was like, 'David!'" he told *Rolling Stone* in 2009. "I was like, 'Mom, I've done a lot worse shit than this, believe me. Look at my other arm.'"

Monsters of Rock

Aside from the punk shows he had seen and played in during his teen years, it wasn't until Dave turned nineteen that he saw his first real rock show. The lineup for the "Monsters of Rock" tour, which touched down at RFK Stadium on June 10, 1988, boasted the Scorpions, Van Halen, Dokken, and Metallica.

"Metallica were fucking great," Dave told *Visions* in 2000. "It was just before they released . . . *And Justice for All.*" Still, he didn't really enjoy being in the cheap seats of the stadium, where he was forced to squint at drummer Lars Ulrich, who looked like he was the size of an ant in the distance.

"I was watching the drummer and the sound was taking three seconds to get to me," he explained to *NPR*'s Jacob Ganz in 2011. "I thought, 'This is insane.'"

No More Censorship

In 1988, Scream signed with RAS Records, a reggae label whose initials stood for Real Authentic Sounds. Founded in 1979 by Gary Himmelfarb, the company was looking to break into new markets and hoped Scream would be a part of the launch of its new rock division.

If Scream's earlier albums were punk records flirting with rock, *No More Censorship* felt like the opposite. High points included the album's title track and "Fucked Without a Kiss," which explores the subject of prison rape. Less effective was "Run to the Sun," an obvious stab at the mainstream (and possibly the result of label pressure to sound commercial), and inferior numbers like "Building Dreams."

The album—a fusion of rock styles that left the band without any clear musical identity—was deemed a commercial failure within months of its August 1988 release. It sold just 10,000 copies, and by mid-'89 the band was dropped.

Tower

In between tours, Dave found work in a nursery, as a stonemason, and in a furniture warehouse. For a spell in 1989, he even wound up manning the registers at the D.C. branch of the legendary (but now defunct) Tower Records.

Often, as Grohl told *Spin* in 2000, he would retreat to the storeroom on his breaks, where he "used to smoke weed on the sly."

Skeeter's Drug Problems

Like Dave, the Stahls had jobs between tours, while Thompson's main source of income was selling drugs. As a weed dealer, Scream's bassist kept everyone well supplied with marijuana, but his access to harder drugs like cocaine eventually led to problems with addiction.

Skeeter's behavior became erratic. During one 1989 tour of Europe, he vanished, returning home without telling the band. Luckily, roadie Guy Pinhas was able to play bass, and he filled in for Thompson, who later explained his quick departure had come as a result of girlfriend woes.

With North American tour dates planned, Thompson took a hiatus from the band to sort through his personal issues, and Scream tapped veteran punk musician Ben Pape for the tour. But when Pape was hired by producer and Def Jam co-founder Rick Rubin to join L.A. hard-rock group the Four Horsemen, Scream had to act fast. The Stahls asked their old friend J. Robbins—who had played in Government Issue and would form Jawbox and become a revered producer of punk acts like Jawbreaker, Against Me!, and Paint it Black—to step in in his place.

Quitting Drugs

In 1989, after witnessing the effects drugs were having on Scream's bassist, Grohl—aged just twenty at the time—quit taking drugs altogether. His appreciation of pot had waned—it began giving him panic attacks—and he had long outgrown his interest in acid.

Dave claims to have never tried coke, out of fear. His reliance on cigarettes and coffee made him realize he had an addictive personality, and he had seen a friend have a heart attack in a 7/11 parking lot after taking the drug.

"Gods Look Down"

In late 1989, and without a label, Scream tracked a new round of demos that sounded like a return to form. The band played viciously, and with equal parts frustration and fervor. When word spread as the tapes made the rounds, it looked as if the foursome—who had again welcomed Skeeter back into the fold—might have a lifeline in their sights after being contacted by Glenn E. Friedman, a respected photographer in the punk and skateboard scenes who had recently befriended Rick Rubin and his Def Jam partner Russell Simmons. Friedman was planning on launching a label called World Records, with Rubin and Simmons' backing, and as a longtime fan of the band, he was interested in making Scream his first signing.

Among the songs on the demo was a Grohl original named "Gods Look Down," which Dave had originally demoed as a solo performer at Laundry Room with Barrett Jones a year earlier. It was one of the obvious standouts from the Scream basement sessions.

In exchange for some weed, Jones helped Dave record his first studio number in around twenty minutes. Dave tracked all of the parts himself, and when the song was completed, Barrett was amazed at how great it sounded.

"I realized you could go into a studio and write and record everything yourself," Dave told *NME* scribe Liz Evans in December 1995. "I wanted to see if I could do it, so I did." Dave would share the tapes with his mother and his buddy Swanson. "I never considered them to be demos for anything. It was just for fun."

Fumble

In December 1989, Grohl, Thompson, and the Stahl brothers descended on Inner Ear Studios in Arlington, where they recorded what they believed would be their fifth studio album with producer Eli Janney. In addition to "Gods Look Down," Scream tracked titles like "Crackman," "Caffeine Dream," "Dying Days," and "Poppa Says."

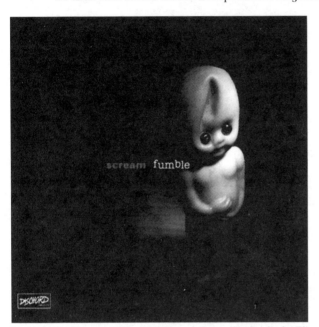

Back together and in top form, Scream were playing what many considered to their best-ever shows in the spring of 1990. Together, they recorded another live album on May 4 at the Oberhaus in Alzey, Germany, for the German label Your Choice.

When Scream returned from their triumphant, tightly booked, three-and-a-half-week, twenty-three-date tour, they were in high spirits. That was until they learned that the proposed deal with Friedman was on hold.

Recorded in January 1989 at Arlington's Inner Ear Studio by Eli Janney, *Fumble*—Scream's final studio album with Grohl—was eventually released in 1993 on Washington, D.C.'s revered punk label Dischord Records. *Author's collection*

When World Records never materialized, Scream continued to make tour plans with the hopes that another deal might surface. Unfortunately, what became the band's final record remained unreleased until July 1993, when Dischord put it out as *Fumble.*

Dying Days

After more than three years in Scream, Grohl had become increasingly frustrated with the band's slow progress. Dave turned twenty-one in 1990, and one day, while waiting for hours on a New Orleans street for his bandmates to retrieve him, he began to worry about being homeless. He had grown tired of worrying about his next meal. As he told *Mojo* in 2009, "I just wanted to go home and work at the Furniture Warehouse, and have somewhere to take a shower, and go to bed every night and be with my friends and my family."

The future of Scream was iffier than ever by the time the group pulled into Los Angeles for their gig at the Gaslight. Once again, Thompson was a no-show, prompting Franz to cancel the show. When Skeeter failed to surface the following day, a show in San Diego was called off.

Broke and dejected, Dave, Pete, and Franz crashed in the L.A.-area house that the Stahls' sister Sabrina was renting with two of her mud-wrestling co-workers from the Hollywood Tropicana. While the girls treated them well, Grohl was becoming restless.

Stuck in Hollywood, and with no money to get home to Springfield, Dave began tiling floors on the cheap just to pay for food and cigarettes. He knew he had to make something happen, and soon.

When Grohl saw an ad in the *L.A. Weekly* announcing an upcoming Melvins show, he knew that seeing the band would help him out of his depression. He called front man Buzz Osborne—whom he had befriended when Scream and the Melvins had previously crossed paths in Amsterdam—and asked to be put on the guest list. Backstage, over a few beers after the show, Buzz told him Nirvana needed a drummer.

Quitting Scream

Leaving Scream for good to join Nirvana was not something Dave did lightly. He thought of Franz and Pete as brothers, and even though the band was coming undone, stepping away weighed heavily on his mind. He called his mom for advice. Although Virginia was fond of the Stahls, she told her son to look out for himself.

"I had the hardest decision of my entire life," Grohl told *Mojo* in 2009. "I remember saying to Franz that I was going up to try out for the band, and he just shook his head and said, 'You ain't coming back.' And deep down I knew it too."

16

I'm Lucky to Have Met You

Gettin' with Geffen

An Important Cornerstone

The day after Cobain's announcement on KAOS, Sub Pop prepared a press release to confirm Grohl's joining Nirvana. It read, "This new kid on the block can't dance as good as your MTV favorites, but he beats the drums like he's beating the shit out of their heads."

Written by Cobain, the document proclaimed that Grohl "passed through the grueling Nirvana initiation ritual with flying colors and is now an important cornerstone in the Nirvana institution."

North Shore Surf Club

At first, Grohl lived with the Novoselics in Tacoma as the band prepared for their upcoming European tour with L7, with the new lineup's debut set for October 11, 1990. Until then, the trio rehearsed in a nearby barn that boasted a brown shag carpet.

"There was no sun. There was no moon. There was just . . . the barn," the drummer explained in his 2013 SXSW Keynote speech. "Every practice would begin with an improvisational, free-form jam, which kind of served as an exercise in dynamic and musical collaboration/communication . . . We spoke to each other with our instruments."

The chemistry within the band was instantly better than ever. In rehearsals, Dave was amiable, fun-loving, hard-working, and creative—a perfect fit. That notion was confirmed when they took the stage.

Sold out with just one day's warning, the new lineup made their debut at the 300-capacity North Shore Surf Club in Olympia. The power tripped twice during the trio's opening rendition of the Vaselines' "Son of a Gun" and also interrupted "Molly's Lips" and "D-7." When the shirtless Grohl hit his snare drum so hard he broke it, Cobain picked it up excitedly to show the crowd, which responded noisily.

For Dave, the sight of 200 people lined up down the block when he and Cobain went to get some dinner before the show was stunning. Usually, Scream shows were a lot smaller. Later, he called his mom, stunned at the reception. Sure, he was nervous—he didn't know anyone in the crowd, and he barely knew his new bandmates—but his fear faded when he realized just how great they sounded.

When all was said and done, Kurt and Krist knew they had their guy. Thinking back on that night, with Grohl and his big kick drum now in the fold, Novoselic marveled, in *Of Grunge and Government*, "Nirvana was now a beast that walked the earth."

Selling Out

After a few years of opposition to the idea of corporate rock, being on a major label started making more and more sense to Cobain. "I just don't see independent labels running their businesses any better," he told journalist Keith Cameron that October, taking an obvious shot at Sub Pop.

With Sonic Youth's Geffen arrangement as a guide, Kurt felt confident that he, too, had enough experience on the road and in the studio, and adequate business acumen, to deal with a big company. Above all else, Cobain knew he had some great songs. Stateside record executives knew it too. That fall, Nirvana had eight major labels hoping to sign them. The ultimate goal was to find an A&R man whose outlook was compatible with theirs.

Talking about the situation with *Option* magazine a little over a year later, Kurt balked at cries of sellout: "What were we gonna do? Stay on Sub Pop? You couldn't even find our last record."

Poneman Responds

With a seven-inch single for "Sliver"—Nirvana's catchiest song yet—on the way, Jonathan Poneman was guarded when asked about the notion of losing Sub Pop's biggest act. Citing his contract with the band, he told *Sounds* of a lack of communication between parties and revealed fears of getting "fucked over." He made no mention of the company's distribution woes.

But with a contract in place, Cobain still felt some loyalty to Poneman and Bruce Pavitt. It wasn't a secret that Nirvana were being wined and dined regularly, and Kurt was optimistic in interviews from this era that a deal would be worked out that would be mutually beneficial to both sides.

Billboards

Despite worshipping indie rock, Kurt thought long and hard about ways to make Nirvana huge. It went far beyond his journals. In a 2009 interview, Novoselic revealed that Cobain imagined buying roadside billboards as a means of promotion.

After years on the fringes, the idea of becoming a successful band became more and more of a possibility. "It was starting to change," Novoselic told John Hughes, citing 1990's gold- and platinum-selling US modern-rock bands. "You had bands like Faith No More and Jane's Addiction—they were more like alternative or edgy. They paved the way for Nirvana."

New Roommates

That October, Grohl moved in with Cobain at 114 North Pear Street. In a scenario similar to *The Odd Couple*, Dave found himself cleaning up after Kurt—a total slob—doing his front man's laundry, and adjusting to the foul odors coming from the aquarium and the kitchen.

"The apartment we lived in was an experiment," Grohl told *Mojo* in 2005. "You walked in and there [were] sculptures and paintings, there were turtles and medical books and Leonard Cohen records. It was chaos, but it was, like, 'This is Kurt.'"

Although it was quirky, Grohl liked the arrangement, which required him to crash on the couch and cut through Kurt's bedroom to use the bathroom. They lived together for eight months, with Dave, who was usually broke, surviving on a diet of convenience store corn dogs—three of which could be had for a buck at the AM/PM down the street.

At night, after Dave retired to bed, Kurt would retreat to his room and write in his notebooks before turning out the light. They became close during this time, although Dave never really felt accepted by Cobain's elitist indie-rock friends. When Slim Moon nicknamed Grohl "The Rocker," it was not out of flattery but sarcasm.

Teen Spirit

Just the same, some folks in Olympia found themselves drawn to Grohl. It was during this time that Dave briefly dated Tobi Vail's Bikini Kill bandmate, Kathleen Hanna. The couples hung out, partied, rode skateboards, and committed vandalism around town.

One night, after catching a whiff of Cobain, Hanna noticed that Kurt smelled like Tobi's brand of deodorant. She took a can of spray paint and wrote "Kurt smells like Teen Spirit" on his bedroom wall.

Around this time, Cobain was hard at work on a new, infectious song called "Anthem," but because Vail's band already had a song of the same name, he agreed to change it. He took the new title, in part, from Hanna's graffiti.

In an early working version of "Smells Like Teen Spirit," Kurt asked, *"Who will be the king and queen of the outcast teens?"* He imagined that he and Tobi might fill those roles.

Peel This

On October 21, Cobain, Grohl, and Novoselic landed at London's Heathrow Airport before being shuttled to John Peel's BBC Radio 1 studios in Maida Vale, to record material for an upcoming broadcast. Nirvana recorded four cover songs during their second Peel Session: the Wipers' "D-7," Devo's "Turnaround," and renditions of the Vaselines numbers "Molly's Lips" and "Son of a Gun."

The latter three of these four songs would initially appear on Nirvana's 1992 Australia-only EP *Hormoaning*, but would eventually see global release when the trio dropped the rarities compilation *Incesticide* in December '92.

As for the Vaselines tracks, Grohl had been playing them without ever hearing the originals, which left him to drum and sing in his own way. Plans to track numbers by Fear, Leonard Cohen, and Beat Happening were discussed for a subsequent Peel Session that never happened.

Astoria and Beyond

Nirvana's week-long UK trek kicked off on October 23 at Goldwyn's Suite in Birmingham, England, and found the band playing to packed audiences of 600 or more during shows in Leeds, Norwich, and Nottingham. A much larger, celebratory gig on the 24th at London's Astoria Theatre drew more than 1,200 people, who gave the trio rapturous applause amid a sea of stage-divers.

On the strength of a substantial write up in *Sounds* and the band's reputation for ferocious, volatile gigs, the shows were sellouts. "If any of the US underground bands are likely to break through into the mainstream, then its got to be Nirvana," the music weekly wrote. It sounded like fate.

When the tour wrapped, the good news was that Nirvana were finally a profitable touring act. They each returned home with a modest amount of cash in their pockets.

On the Road with L7

L7—who had just signed to Sub Pop—turned out to be great touring companions. The all-female band liked to kill time by getting drunk, just like the guys in Nirvana. That week, they repeatedly watched *This Is Spinal Tap* and had food fights backstage. Cobain took the opportunity to dye his hair a shocking shade of blue, while the two groups continually pulled pranks on each other.

Meanwhile, Grohl began cuddling up with bassist Jennifer Finch. Dave and Jennifer had first become acquainted when she booked a gig with Scream and Bad Religion in Los Angeles a year earlier. The two quickly reconnected backstage, and before the Birmingham gig was over they were hooking up.

According to Finch, she and Grohl had an instant chemistry. They liked a lot of the same bands, and she was an attractive, well-connected punk chick who grew up on the California music scene. In addition to having played with Hole's

Courtney Love and Babes in Toyland's Kat Bjelland in the short-lived, mid-'80s San Francisco band Sugar Babydoll she also played with L.A. all-girl band the Pandoras, who were briefly signed to Elektra. She joined L7 around 1987.

Meeting the Vaselines

For Cobain, the highlight of the UK tour was easily the October 26 show the band played with two of his favorite bands, Shonen Knife and the Vaselines, at Calton Studios in Edinburgh. Despite having split up in 1989, the Vaselines had been asked to reunite for the show, and front man Eugene Kelly was surprised to find out that Cobain was nervous to meet him.

Calling their music "some of the most beautiful songs I've ever heard," in a *Melody Maker* interview from 1992, Cobain praised Kelly and his partner Frances McKee as "the Captain & Tennille of the underground."

"I was intrigued to find out why they were so keen on us, because we'd split up and we were incredibly obscure," Kelly would tell *Q*. "I thought only about a thousand people in the whole world knew about us."

It's True

In response to the positive exposure that journalist-turned-friend Everett True had given Nirvana in *Melody Maker* over the previous two years, the group arranged a unique second encore for their gig at Trent Polytechnic in Nottingham. After the band wrapped their set with "Stay Away," the crowd had started thinning out when Cobain returned to the stage to announce a special guest.

As True took the stage, Kurt strapped his left-handed guitar over his shoulder. Then he and Krist retreated to Grohl's drum kit to add percussion to "Do Nuts," True's own Sub Pop single. After two short minutes, Kurt trashed Grohl's kit.

House Shopping

For a fleeting moment, Kurt started thinking about buying a home in Olympia. Even though he was usually broke, he imagined his prospects would soon change, with all of the label interest that autumn.

Cobain even acquired a list of available properties, and with his friend Mikey Nelson, from Fitz of Depression, he went and visited a series of rundown commercial properties. His idea was to build his own recording studio in the front half of a building and set up house in the back. Of course, at this stage in his career, he was still unable to buy anywhere.

Heroin

Although Cobain had scorned his friend Jesse Reed for wanting to try heroin in 1987—even lecturing Reed about how it could kill him—he developed a much different mind-set about the drug after he started shooting up in the fourth quarter of 1990 and discovered it was one of the few things that helped with his stomach ailment.

When he told Novoselic about it just before Nirvana's trip abroad, Krist was somewhat curious to find out what it was like, but mostly worried after the death that April of Andrew Wood, singer for the Seattle band Mother Love Bone. Krist warned Kurt that he was playing with fire, and Kurt agreed. He promised his friend he wouldn't take heroin again.

A few weeks after the UK tour, Grohl flew down to L.A. to spend time with Finch and to fill in on the drums with L7 at a November Rock for Choice benefit show. When he called back home to Novoselic to check in, Krist broke the news that Cobain—who had since become Grohl's roommate—was using heroin. When Dave flew home he confronted Kurt about his drug use. Kurt told him that he wasn't enjoying it and wouldn't do it again. Dave had little choice but to believe him.

But these were promises Kurt couldn't keep—he was already taken with the drug's effects. He bonded with Dylan Carlson—who had also started using around the same time—and the pair relied on a local dealer named Jose to supply them with their junk.

At first, their lack of income and the will to avoid becoming addicts kept them from using daily. Instead, shooting heroin was something they would save for certain weekends and special occasions, disappearing together to cheap hotel rooms away from concerned friends.

Kurt's heroin use wasn't a secret, however. When Novoselic told his wife, Shelli, word circled among her friends—including Tracy Marander. Since their split a year before, Tracy and Kurt had become friendly again. But when he called her one night, she suspected he was high and confronted him about it. He said he had only done it a few times.

Marander tried not to judge, but she couldn't help but worry about Kurt. A week later, after they had been out party-hopping with friends, Kurt asked to stop home to use the toilet. When he didn't come out for a long time, Tracy went in and found him passed out with a needle in his arm. Despite this scary event, however, Cobain had yet to become a daily-dosing junkie. At this point, he was still a recreational heroin user.

Kurt Dumps Tobi

Over the years, Nirvana lore had it that Cobain started using heroin because Vail dumped him. The truth is less romantic—Kurt actually broke it off with her that October, but not before she threated to stop seeing him because of his drug use.

Still, based on the songs that he wrote and continued to revise around the time of their unraveling, he certainly made it seem as if she was the heartbreaker. The material from this era is pained, be it the lovesick lines of "Aneurysm" or the angst of "Teen Spirit." Another number, "Drain You"—initially titled "Formula"—was a somberly sung expression of gratitude, while "Lounge Act" was a song about denial—Cobain's way of coping with the heartache he brought about.

In the days and weeks after, Cobain would shut down around his bandmates, especially his housemate Grohl. The drummer became alarmed about this behavior until Kurt explained during one late-night ride home from rehearsal that he was basically in mourning, but that he was working his way past the sadness he had been feeling.

Open Book

Kurt left his diary around the house for all to see, including Grohl's new girlfriend Jennifer Finch. After flipping through one of the books Kurt had left out on the kitchen table, she became deeply concerned about his drawings and journal entries, many which chronicled his own self-loathing. Something wasn't right with him.

One of Cobain's pictures depicted an alien with his skin being torn off; another showed a woman flashing her vagina while sporting a Ku Klux Klan hood. There were multiple allusions to rape and other disturbing themes. One entry began, "When I grow up I want to be a faggot, nigger, cunt, whore, jew, spic, kraut, wop, sissie, whitey hippie." In another, he imagined kicking an elderly woman's legs. Suicide, heroin fantasies, and notions of self-mutilation were also present, including one in which Cobain envisioned himself as Hellen Keller, using a knife to puncture his ears and remove his voice box.

"Friend of a Friend"

That winter, Nirvana were rehearsing most nights between 10:00 p.m. and 1:00 a.m. Aside from sleeping, Grohl looked for ways to pass the time. He picked up the guitar and began writing again. One song, which he wrote in early 1991 while residing with Cobain, would eventually surface on the Foo Fighters' 2005 album *In Your Honor*.

The pensive "Friend of a Friend" made reference to Kurt's need to sleep in a locked bedroom, remain painfully silent much of the time, and write on an old guitar. "It was fucking depressing," Dave told writer Craig McLean in 2005, adding, "Of any song that I've written, [that] is most blatantly about my time in Nirvana."

A&R Dinners

By November 1990, Nirvana's members found themselves being invited to expensive meals by a number of record label executives, some who had flown up to Seattle from Los Angeles to court the band at the time of their November 25 show at the Off Ramp.

For a trio of young men who lived on convenience store food, Kraft Macaroni and Cheese, and cheap pizza, it was an opportunity to eat big thanks to the droves of A&R men with big expense accounts looking to sign Nirvana. Only Krist struggled with the sophisticated menus, as he had recently become a vegetarian.

That month, Cobain and Novoselic flew down to L.A. to meet with Bret Hartman at MCA Records. But after speaking to the label's then-president Richard Palmese for just seconds, Nirvana's co-founders were turned off when he unintentionally snubbed them. (He had to leave for a lunch meeting.) Regardless of the money on offer, Palmese's conduct meant that MCA was a no.

There were plenty of other offers. "They all came sniffing," Novoselic chuckled to *Kerrang!* writer Mike Gitter that year. "MCA, Capitol, Charisma, Columbia, Slash, Polydor, PolyGram . . . all the Polys."

"Suddenly we were thrown into a bidding war of A&R guys with fancy shoes from Fred Segal, and radio-promo dudes with little one hitters in their glove compartments, closets full of complimentary box sets, and fucking Benihana every fucking night," Grohl remembered in his 2013 SXSW Keynote speech.

At one point, the band met with Columbia head Donny Ienner in his New York high-rise office. The label boss, sitting behind his large oak desk, asked Cobain what he wanted. According to Dave, Kurt's reply was, "We want to be the biggest band in the world."

Dave Grohl, Record Executive

During these meetings, Grohl enjoyed grilling the executives and finding out about their backgrounds. He was surprised to learn that many of them had worked at Tower Records, just as he had. For fun, he took to collecting their business cards and reusing them.

Still relatively unknown around the Northwest, the drummer would walk up to bands he disliked and tell them he was a record executive interested in signing them. In one instance, Dave approached a lounge band in Tacoma and told them to give him a call next week, when he would be back in L.A. Of course, when they called, they would learn they had been suckered.

Gold Mountain

While in L.A. on MCA's dime, Krist and Kurt went back to see John Silva, and were reassured they had hired the right management firm when they found out he had once cohabitated with Dead Kennedys' front man Jello Biafra. It also helped that Gold Mountain head Danny Goldberg had worked with Zeppelin in the 1970s.

Goldberg was equally impressed by Nirvana's drive. Kurt had decided he wanted hits, fame, and wealth, and he was committed to making it happen. In his 2008 autobiography, *Bumping Into Geniuses*, Goldberg affirmed Cobain's commitment. "You know who wanted to reach more people—the most of the three of them? Kurt, he wanted to make it big."

Several months earlier, Gold Mountain had put Cobain and the others on a $1,000 monthly retainer. Then, during their L.A. meeting, Silva advised Krist and Kurt that signing with Geffen really made the most sense. After all, the company—under the direction of A&R man Gary Gersh—had already proved its worth with Sonic Youth's recent critical and commercial success. In fact, *Goo* was ideally timed, having recently sold several hundred thousand copies without losing an ounce of underground credibility.

"Sliver"

Although "Sliver" was released as a Sup Pop single in September 1990, most reviews didn't emerge until the end of the year. *Melody Maker* scribe Push called it "one hell of a pop song" in the December 15 issue. Cobain agreed, calling it "the most straightforward song we've ever recorded."

Meanwhile, *Sounds* dubbed it "a great, powerful pop single that'll boost the band's reputation still higher."

Kurt's Publishing Advance

In late 1990, Cobain had received a $3,000 advance after signing a deal with Virgin Publishing. The president of Virgin, Kaz Utsunomiya, had flown to Seattle for the meeting. When Kaz showed up at Cobain's apartment, he was stunned at Cobain's living conditions.

Upon receipt of the check, Kurt paid his rent and took the rest to the South Sound Mall with his friends Mikey Nelson (from Fitz of Depression) and Joe Preston. He spent nearly half the money on a number of unique items, including a pair of BB guns that resembled M15 rifles, a Nintendo gaming system, two PixelVision video cameras, and a number of plastic Evel Knievel action figures.

Kurt also bought fake dog mess, fake vomit, and a pair of severed hands made from rubber at a novelty store. Later, he plunked down $20 on a used child's Swinger bicycle, which he rode for hours until darkness despite the fact he was way too big for the thing.

According to Preston, Kurt used the BB gun to shoot out the windows of the Washington State Lottery's administrative building, which was on 4th Street, right around the corner from his apartment in Olympia.

A *Sliver* CD EP was pressed soon after by the band's U.K. label, Tupelo. Featuring alternate artwork, it added live versions of "About a Girl" and "Spank Thru," which were caught live on February 9, 1990, at the Pine Street Theater in Portland.   *Author's collection*

Cheryl Arnold

On the rebound from Tobi, Kurt had made a new acquaintance in Cheryl Arnold. They hung out, either alone or with Cobain's friends Dylan Carlson and Ian Dickson, watched horror movies like *Texas Chainsaw Massacre*, and even returned to Kurt's mom's house in Aberdeen to would visit with Wendy and Kurt's baby sister Breanne.

Arnold—who implies in *Nirvana: The True Story* that she and Kurt were romantically involved—watched him interact with his turtles, and together they would get drunk, shoot his BB guns, play his video games, and throw eggs at passing cars. She says she even watched him dance around in high-heeled platform shoes and dress up in women's clothes.

By her observation, Cobain lived on a steady diet of Fruity Pebbles and pizza during their time together, and Cheryl marveled at how the boxes piled up in his apartment. "He had a really fucked-up stomach," she told author Everett True. "He was in pain all the time."

Kurt and Cheryl went to a demolition derby with Carlson in the first week of July of 1991, and also took a trip to the ocean but wound up retreating to an Aberdeen hotel called the Flamingo because the beach was too crowded. Within weeks, however, things between them would dissolve. Cobain had become infatuated with a woman named Courtney Love.

Home for the Holidays

Grohl flew home to Virginia for nearly a month around Christmas 1990, where—in addition to seeing family—he dropped by a party at Dischord House to catch up with D.C. friends Ian MacKaye and J. Robbins, among others. Dave was extremely proud of a new Nirvana song, "Smells Like Teen Spirit," and played them an early version that they had recorded in practice.

Everyone who heard the tune was impressed. When Grohl told them that a label deal seemed imminent, nobody—especially MacKaye—seemed surprised. Ian told him it sounded like a hit—not in the formal sense, but one that would be embraced by the growing punk masses who would also buy 250,000 copies of Fugazi's *Repeater*.

Back in Olympia by New Year's Eve, Grohl rejoined his bandmates that night for a gig at Portland's Satyricon, headlining over four other local bands, including Caustic Soda and Thrillhammer. Despite the fact that Cobain was smashed on Jack Daniel's and Coke, witnesses called the show fantastic.

Load Up on Guns

With Grohl out of the picture for a while, there were no proper Nirvana rehearsals, and Kurt was without his roommate and daily companion. His drug buddy Dylan Carlson filled the void, and together the two drank, smoked marijuana, and kept occupied with other pursuits when heroin was unavailable.

Carlson was a firearms fanatic who brought Cobain into the woods and began to show his friend how to aim and fire his shotgun and pistol. They shot at empty beer and soda cans, and Kurt even offered up some of his inferior art pieces for target practice.

Kurt also spent time around the holidays shopping with friends like Mikey Nelson in local thrift stores, in one of which he found Charles Manson's lone album, *Lie*.

IBS

In the second week of December, Cobain's stomach issues finally led him to seek help from a Tacoma doctor who diagnosed him with irritable bowel syndrome. But his prescription for the drug Lidox didn't seem to improve matters. After contracting bronchitis during Christmas week, he stopped taking what the doctor ordered.

New Year's Day Session

Nirvana hit the studio with soundman/producer Craig Montgomery on the first day of 1991, tracking "Aneurysm" and a new version of "Even in His Youth." Based on Montgomery's recollection to biographer Charles Cross, they were evidently hungover from the previous night's revelry, and were not playing on top form.

They had also mistreated some of their equipment at the Portland gig the night before, which was having an impact on the sound quality. Still, this session is noteworthy because the band took their first stab at the song "All Apologies," along with a few other new ideas.

Farmer Kurt

On January 2, Cobain joined Jesse Reed on a trip back to Aberdeen to visit his family. During the drive, Reed remembered Kurt talking about hoping to return one day to Grays Harbor County.

Nirvana's front man spoke of his love for the landscape and the people of the area, and how he might like to plunk down his label advance on a farm near Satsop. Kurt thought of doing what Neil Young had done in California, two decades earlier. He talked about throwing big parties someday at his farmhouse, where his band could play as loud as they wanted, whenever they wanted.

Uncle Patrick

January 2, 1991, turned out to be a sad day for Cobain, his mother, and the entire Fradenburg clan. It was the day that Wendy's brother Patrick succumbed to AIDS in California, aged just forty-six. This somber occurrence pulled Kurt and Wendy closer together than they had been in recent years.

Patrick's family had always been in denial about his sexual preferences, and they struggled to accept the idea that he was homosexual even after he proclaimed it himself. Out of shame, the more controlling members of the family opted to leave Uncle Patrick's cause of death out of the obituary, declining to list the name of his "special friend" and life partner.

For Kurt, who had been supportive of homosexuality since high school, this cover-up was upsetting. He declined to attend the memorial service, explaining he had to prepare for his upcoming album.

Kurt's Tattoo

In early 1991, after a quick lesson from Grohl, Cobain gave himself a homemade tattoo of the letter "K" using a needle and India ink. It was the impetus for Kurt to then visit an Olympia tattoo parlor, where he had the K Records logo—a letter K inside a shield—properly inked on his left forearm.

Of course, in addition to being the name of Calvin Johnson's record label, the letter was also the initial of Cobain's first name. But Kurt insisted the tattoo was a tribute to the label. In the January 1992 issue of *Option*, Cobain spoke of his admiration for K Records. "They've exposed me to so much good music, like the Vaselines, who are my very favorite band ever," he insisted. "They reminded me of how much I really value innocence and children and my youth . . . of how precious that whole world is."

The Off Ramp

On January 25, Nirvana headlined a show at Seattle's Off Ramp that also featured appearances by Holy Rollers, Heavy Into Jeff, and Dylan Carlson's band Earth. They played one of their most diverse sets yet, introducing a series of newer numbers like "Aneurysm," "Oh, the Guilt," "Verse Chorus Verse," "Something in the Way," and "Radio Friendly Unit Shifter," which would appear on Nirvana's third album in 1993.

Midway through the set, during "Dive," the show was stopped as the club had gone past its curfew for alcohol sales. The band started back up with "Dumb," another song that wouldn't be released until 1993. The show also marked the reappearance of Nirvana's versions of the Velvet Underground's "Here She Comes Now" and Lead Belly's "Where Did You Sleep Last Night."

The gig was only Grohl's fourth stateside appearance with Nirvana in the four months since he joined. While the band continued to write and rehearse each day, perfecting the songs they envisioned recording once a new record deal was finalized, it felt strange for Dave. It was a major shift in approach from the gonzo touring he had grown used to during his years in Scream.

So Long, Sub Pop

In January 1991, Nirvana released "Molly's Lips," their final single for Sub Pop. A split 45 with the Fluid—who served up the song "Candy"—the single was limited to just 4,000 limited green vinyl copies and 3,000 more black vinyl pieces.

Nirvana's cover of the Vaselines tune was tracked during the band's February 9, 1990, gig at Portland's Pine Street Theater. Although Cobain wasn't pleased with the band's version of the song, it was a condition of the trio's exit deal with Sub Pop.

The word "Later" is etched into the run-out groove on Nirvana's side of the 45. It is not known if this was the band's idea or the label's doing.

Signing to Geffen

Throughout the early spring of 1991, Nirvana's management worked through the nuts and bolts of their agreement with Geffen's new music imprint, DGC. The trio would receive an advance of $287,000, with another $75,000 payable to Sub Pop in order to buy out the group's existing contract. Furthermore, Sub Pop's logo would be featured on Nirvana's first two records, and the label would be entitled to a percentage of royalties on said discs. In accordance with the contract, the group would be given full creative control.

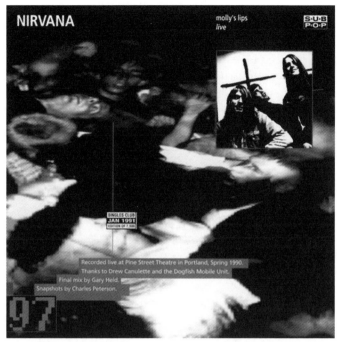

Released in January 1991 as part of a split Sub Pop seven-inch single with the Fluid, Nirvana's live cover of the Vaselines' "Molly's Lips" was recorded on February 9, 1990, at Portland's Pine Street Theater. Although Cobain was hesitant to release the single, because he didn't think it was up to par, he ultimately relented. It was issued as part of the band's buyout agreement with Sub Pop, cementing the band's major-label deal with DGC Records.   *Author's collection*

Nirvana had received large advance offers from other labels—and had even made a verbal commitment on a deal with a $200,000 advance from Charisma Records—but because they were keen to minimize their debt and take a higher royalty rate, they wisely agreed to go with DGC. Alongside Sonic Youth and Seattle power-pop act the Posies, Nirvana gave Geffen a blast of indie credibility. Not long after aligning with DGC, the group's Scottish friends Teenage Fanclub—whom they had met in Edinburgh through Eugene Kelly—also signed to the label.

Although Nirvana didn't actually sign their formal Geffen contracts until April 30, 1991, when the band arrived in L.A. to begin work on their major label debut, they may as well have by the time they sat down again with *Backlash* writer/publisher Dawn Anderson that March.

"DGC just seemed hip, you know?" Novoselic told the fanzine.

"They have an alternative young staff," Cobain added. "They have some credentials in the underground."

Just the same, Kurt acknowledged that inking a major-label deal was kind of like playing Russian roulette. Only time would tell if Geffen would promote them properly—and that was something that quickly soured them on Sub Pop.

For Kurt, the very idea that he would have his albums available in stores everywhere was something he couldn't wait for. That year, he told *M.E.A.T.* scribe Karen Bliss, "It will probably be available in K-Mart! Filed right between Nelson and N.W.A."

Calling Don

While it had been many years since Cobain had had a proper conversation with his father, upon signing to Geffen Records he called Don to check in and share the news.

If the conversation was a little uncomfortable, and quite short, Don was pleased when Kurt asked about his stepsiblings and Don's current position as an investigator with the Washington State Patrol. Kurt spoke about performing, and his father said that he would love to see him play some time.

Hiring Vig

When it came time to make a shortlist of producers for what was still known as *Sheep*, Cobain came up with some major names, including Bill Price (the Clash, Sex Pistols, Guns N' Roses), Scott Litt (R.E.M.), George Drakoulias (Black Crowes), David Briggs (Neil Young & Crazy Horse), Dave Jerden (Jane's Addiction, Social Distortion, Alice in Chains), plus the team of Steve Thompson and Michael Barbiero (Metallica, Guns N' Roses).

It was clear that Kurt wanted to choose a producer who would make a major impact. For a while, it looked like Dixon would produce and Vig would engineer, as Butch was still relatively unknown, despite having just finished work on *Gish*, the soon-to-be-released debut album by Chicago band Smashing Pumpkins. But after talking it over with Krist and Dave, Cobain pushed for Butch, and Nirvana's label and management agreed.

At the eleventh hour, Vig got a call asking if he could come to Los Angeles the following week. He agreed to fly to L.A. to produce the band. With a recording budget of $65,000, the sessions were slated to last three weeks and would begin in May 1991 at Sound City Studios in Van Nuys, California.

OK Hotel

In April, and in anticipation of their trip to L.A., Nirvana booked an afternoon gig on the 17th at Seattle's OK Hotel. Part of the reason was that they were broke, and were playing the one-off show in order to get enough gas money to make the long trip southward.

Following sets by Bikini Kill and Fitz of Depression, Nirvana walked out onto the stage. Cobain greeted the audience by saying, "Hello. We're major-label corporate rock sellouts." Midway through the set, he introduced the song that was just six months away from changing his life. "This song," he declared, "is called 'Smells Like Teen Spirit.'"

Despite being short on funds, Cobain threw $250 of the band's take from the gig to help out Fitz of Depression's Mikey Dees (a.k.a. Nelson), who had some unpaid traffic violations and whose band was about to embark on their own tour with the Melvins.

City of Angels

In the last week of April, the members of Nirvana departed for Los Angeles. Novoselic and his wife Shelli planned to leave a few days after Cobain and Grohl, traveling with the band's equipment in his VW bus.

Kurt and Dave set out in the front man's aging Datsun B210, with plans to stop in San Francisco to hang out with Osborne and Crover. Twenty minutes outside of Olympia, however, the Datsun's engine began to overheat. They pulled over to put water into the radiator. It cooled down, and they took off. Ten minutes later, it happened again.

This went on for five hours. By the time they reached Oregon, the pair had decided to turn around and head back home—but not before taking out their aggression on Kurt's car. "We were so pissed off, we pulled into a quarry and stoned the fucking car for half an hour," Grohl remembered, on the television series *Classic Albums*.

Five hours later, after smashing out the B210's windows in frustration, they left the junked car in front of Novoselic's house, where they found their touring van waiting. They fueled up and hit the road, visiting with their chums in the Melvins to break up the eighteen-hour trip to L.A.

According to some reports, Cobain and Grohl also stopped on the way at Universal Studios, so that Kurt could go on some of the same amusement rides he had been on with his grandparents, Leland and Iris, fifteen years earlier.

The Retards

While in the Bay Area, Cobain and Grohl went with Crover to catch a Flipper reunion gig. They also formed a short-lived group called the Retards with bassist Debbi Shane. According to Shane, it was during this session that Cobain developed what became "Drain You." After cutting the song on Dale's four-track with Dave, they brought it with them to Los Angeles, where they would continue working through it with Krist.

17

All Our Pretty Songs

Nevermind

The Cokewoods

I n the final days of April 1991, the members of Nirvana settled into the Oakwood Corporate apartments. With their close proximity to Sound City, these short-term residences, which the band and Vig called the Cokewoods, were often used by struggling actors and aspiring musicians.

During the sessions for what would soon be known as *Nevermind*, Swedish pop-metal band Europe—best known for their 1988 hit "The Final Countdown"—lived down the hall. Child actors were a common sight around the complex, and Grohl even bumped shoulders with hip-hop/comedy duo Kid 'n Play.

Dave Meets Butch

Upon his arrival in Los Angeles, Dave Grohl met Butch Vig for the first time. In advance of their introduction, Cobain had called Vig to tout Grohl's amazing drumming skills. If Butch—who had received boom-box tapes of material from the band's practices at home—was skeptical, Kurt's claims about Dave's strengths were validated during their first afternoon in rehearsals.

Before proper recording began, Vig took notes and instructions—most notably on Cobain's desire to sound heavy—and marveled at just how loud Dave could play without his drums being miked. Like anyone else who encountered the drummer at this time, Vig was also impressed with Dave's energy, humor, and remarkably upbeat attitude.

In an effort to prevent Nirvana from burning out on the material before the sessions, Vig kept the rehearsals brief. For Butch, the one song that stuck out above all the others was "Smells Like Teen Spirit."

Working at Sound City

Recording got underway on May 2 in Van Nuys at the Sound City facility, which was notorious for being the birthplace of Fleetwood Mac's classic 1977 album *Rumours*. The band was billed $500 per day to work in the studio that had also given rise to Neil Young's *After the Gold Rush*, Cheap Trick's *Heaven Tonight*, Tom Petty's *Damn the Torpedoes*, and records by the Jackson 5, Foreigner, the Grateful Dead, and many others.

When the band pulled into the parking lot of the facility for the first time, however, Sound City seemed unimpressive. Located in a San Fernando Valley warehouse area, it was different from the kind of big-budget Hollywood recording complex the band had imagined. There was brown shag carpet on the walls and crummy old furniture. As Grohl joked to a 2013 SXSW audience, "It looked like a Chi Chi's that had a fire."

The trio would roll in around 3:00 p.m. after Butch had been prepping for a few hours, and would start warming up by playing covers of Aerosmith and Led Zeppelin songs. From there, they would put down Dave and Krist's rhythm tracks and then finalize the basic tracks, including Kurt's live guitar and scratch vocals for a pair of songs. By 11:00 p.m. after completing the basic tracks for a pair of tunes, they would call it a day and head out into the L.A. night.

For the sessions, Grohl elected to rent a Tama Artstar II kit, which he pounded with such force that he needed to change the heads every other day. He also picked out a brass Black Beauty snare drum, which he nicknamed "The Terminator." It was exactly like the one Lars Ulrich played on Metallica's *Master of Puppets*. A ten-day rental on the drums cost $1,542.

Despite Kurt's desire to keep the sound of the record "pure" and true to the punk aesthetic, Vig encouraged him to try new things with his songs. Cobain was reluctant, but he eventually gave into the idea of double-tracking his guitar and vocal parts when Butch reminded him that even John Lennon used such studio techniques.

"I got the band to do some things I think they didn't necessarily want to do," Vig told *Goldmine* in 1997, referring to his use of vocal and guitar overdubs and multitracking Butch was "trying to make it sound larger than life. 'Cause that's how they played live."

Nirvana's hard work back home in Seattle had prepared them well for their time in Sound City, meaning that major changes to the framework of the songs were unnecessary. Despite this focus, Vig suggested Cobain make subtle changes to the arrangement on "Teen Spirit," which Kurt agreed to. In a few instances, Novoselic's bass parts were redone to ensure they were locked in with Grohl's drum parts.

Kurt's live guitar lines were usually flawless, with overdubs layered on top. As for his vocal takes, Butch would typically get just three or four performances per song before the front man lost his voice from singing so hard. Vig would then go through and pick the best parts from each to craft the best possible track.

At times, Vig could tell he was pushing Kurt too far. At one point during "Lithium," for instance, Cobain threw his guitar down. Another time he just walked away from the microphone.

Kurt's mood could go the other way, too. A case in point was the moment when pop-metal band Warrant returned to Sound City to retrieve the gear they had used in the session before Nirvana's. With a heavy dose of sarcasm, Cobain took over the facility's paging system and began yelling, "Bring me some 'Cherry Pie,'" in reference to that group's 1990 single. Butch, Dave, and Krist were in hysterics.

"There would be times when we would really connect—smile and laugh and feel like a band. And there were times when you felt lost and questioned what you were doing there," Grohl told *Rolling Stone* in 2001. "There were times when I had to back off completely and think, 'I'm just the drummer in this band.' When we'd all share something really beautiful, like a show or recording or just a vocal harmony, that's when you really felt like you were part of something great."

The facility's recording room—located in a large, converted warehouse where Vox amplifiers were once manufactured—helped too. The studio's big live sound, coupled with its aging Neve mixing desk and excellent microphones, lent itself to the production of amazing sounding records.

"When we went there for sixteen days, we weren't making that album with the intention that we were going to change the fuckin' world," Grohl told *Rolling Stone* in 2013. "We just wanted it to sound good."

The drummer came away with such an emotional connection to the facility that when he heard it was closing years later, he made the 2013 documentary film *Sound City* about the importance of the studio.

Cover Concept

During the band's stay at the Oakwoods, Cobain hatched the idea for the album's cover, which would depict a baby underwater with an erection. "Kurt was watching this special on underwater birth," Novoselic said in a 2011 *Sirius XM* special. "It was this really beautiful, innocent, slo-mo image of babies swimming underwater."

The band approached Geffen's art director Robert Fisher with the idea of using images of water births, but because the stock photos he located were either too graphic or too expensive, Fisher hired photographers Kirk Weddle and Rick Elden to shoot the cover. Five pictures were in consideration, including one of Elden's three-month-old infant son Spencer. A dollar bill with a fishhook was added to the shot, giving the appearance of the baby reaching for money.

When the cover was finalized in the summer of 1991, both the band and the label were expecting the image of the baby's penis to be censored by some retail stores. In preparation, Geffen readied an alternate cover without the penis, although little if any pushback materialized.

Cobain suggested to *Flipside*, in its May/June 1992 issue, that they had also planned to put a sticker over the penis that said, "If you are offended by this you're probably a closet pedophile."

The back cover of the record consisted of a photograph of a rubber monkey standing in front of a collage created by Kurt. Cobain's artwork—which had been taped to his Olympia refrigerator for some time—collected photos of raw beef from a supermarket circular, pictures of diseased vaginas from medical photos he had acquired, and images from Dante's *Inferno*. The front man also suggested that if fans looked close enough, they could see a miniscule rendering of the band Kiss standing on a piece of meat.

Sheep No More

As the sessions at Sound City progressed, Cobain became tired of the record's provisional title, *Sheep*. After discussing it with Novoselic toward the end of May, he recommended that they go with *Nevermind*. Kurt liked the idea that the title fitted in with his often-indifferent outlook on life. The notion that it was grammatically incorrect appealed to him, too.

Hollywood High

While in Los Angeles, Grohl—who still had friends and former bandmates in the city—bought an $800 motorcycle to get around. At night, after his work was complete, he would jump on his bike and ride through the Hollywood Hills and out to Venice Beach, pondering his future.

He also reconnected with the Stahls, which usually meant fun, such as the time Pete stopped in to hear the rough mixes of Nirvana's album. But it could also mean trouble. In one instance, Franz and Kurt—both drunk and high and in the company of Dave—went to score drugs at the Tropicana in Hollywood, and nearly got themselves caught in the middle of a police sting. Cobain—who had developed a fondness for cough syrup—and Grohl's former guitarist could also be found buying drugs at the crack-plagued French Cottage hotel.

Feeling Evel

During the sessions at Sound City, Cobain claimed to have stolen the master tapes to Evel Knievel's eponymous 1974 studio album. He called his buddy Dale Crover up to brag that he snuck them out of the facility and had them shipped home to Olympia.

Drunk Driving Bust

On the evening of May 17, 1991, Novoselic was arrested after an evening celebrating his twenty-sixth birthday by attending a concert by the Butthole Surfers, Redd Kross, and L7 with Vig, Grohl, and Cobain. En route to the gig at the Hollywood Palladium in his VW bus, Novoselic was guzzling Jack Daniel's as he drove.

Following the show, the men in Nirvana were headed back to the Oakwoods when Novoselic was pulled over in Laurel Canyon. After failing a sobriety test,

Krist—who had continued to drink throughout the evening, and was also high on mushrooms—was taken into custody.

As the police took the bassist away, Dave and Kurt were reportedly left stranded and without cash, nearly seven miles from their apartment, and forced to walk home.

The next afternoon, Vig—who had taken a taxi home when he lost the others—called Gold Mountain to find out why the band hadn't shown up at the studio. They were running late, John Silva told him, because Novoselic had just been released.

Courtney Love

Cobain had met Courtney Love before, if her subsequent claims are to be believed, during a 1990 Nirvana gig at the Satyricon in Portland, and at a Dharma Bums gig in 1988. But the May 17, 1991, concert at the Hollywood Palladium was the first time the two had formally aligned.

Love—twenty-six to Kurt's twenty-four—tackled Cobain while he was rough-housing backstage with the writer Everett True, and the two quickly hit it off. Nirvana's front man was high on mushrooms and cough syrup when they found each other. He liked that she looked like Sid Vicious' late girlfriend Nancy Spungen. When she pinned him, he gave her a sticker of Chim Chim, the *Speed Racer* monkey he loved, as a reward. She put it on her guitar case.

Born Courtney Michelle Harrison, Love—front woman for the L.A. band Hole—was a close friend of Grohl's then-paramour, Jennifer Finch. The troubled daughter of one-time Grateful Dead tour manager Hank Harrison and therapist Linda Carroll, Courtney had spent her childhood living in L.A., Portland, and New Zealand before going to live with a family friend in Eugene, Oregon.

As a teen, Love ran away, becoming a stripper in Japan before briefly study-ing at Trinity College in Dublin, Ireland. As a quick-talking networker living in Liverpool, England, Courtney befriended members of Echo & the Bunnymen and the Teardrop Explodes. She also sang in an early incarnation of Faith No More before teaming with Finch in Sugar Baby Doll.

If that wasn't enough, Courtney had acted in Alex Cox's 1986 movie *Sid and Nancy* and starred in alongside the Clash's Joe Strummer in his spaghetti western *Straight to Hell*. At some point, she had married Falling James, the cross-dressing front man for Leaving Trains—a Los Angeles–based band signed to SST Records.

By 1989, Love had settled in L.A., where she launched Hole after answering guitarist Eric Erlandson's ad in the *Recycler*. He was seeking "people into Big Black, the Stooges, ABBA, and Fleetwood Mac." They released the Sub Pop single "Dicknail" the following year before recording their Caroline Records debut LP, *Pretty on the Inside*, which was produced by Don Fleming and Sonic Youth's Kim Gordon.

It didn't take long before Grohl—who had known Courtney through Finch— became the go-between. When Love told him that she had a crush on Kurt, he let her know that the feeling was mutual. That summer, Courtney even gave Grohl a heart-shaped box—which would inspire the 1993 Nirvana track—to hand-deliver to his bandmate. Inside the silk-and-lace box, which she bought in a New Orleans antique shop, she placed three dried roses, painted seashells, a miniature teacup, and a small porcelain doll, which Cobain adored.

"During that time I knew that I liked her a lot, but I wouldn't admit it," Kurt told the *Advocate* in 1993. Later, in August 1991, when Nirvana and Hole crossed paths at England's Reading Festival, they reconnected. It was during this time that their romance started.

"I really pursued him," Love told *Sassy* scribe Christan Kelly in January 1992. "Not too aggressive, but aggressive enough that some girls would have been embarrassed by it."

Andy Wallace

When Vig played back the rough mixes for the band, "Smells Like Teen Spirit" left them all stunned. It rocked harder than they ever could have imagined. With each successive track, the band's skill and intensity came through.

But when they all sat down to mix the record, Butch and the members of Nirvana were displeased with the final result. The band went back to DGC for input and the label provided a list of producer-engineers, including the aforementioned Scott Litt and Ed Stasium, who had worked with the Ramones and the Smithereens.

At the bottom of the list was the name Andy Wallace—the man who had co-produced Slayer's recent album *Seasons in the Abyss*. Cobain and his bandmates knew how heavy that record was, and when he pointed his finger at Wallace's name, Novoselic and Grohl instantly agreed.

Using special-effects boxes, Wallace stepped in and worked through a track a day, finishing up his work in June. When the album was finished, Kurt, Krist, and Dave all loved the final mixes. It wasn't until the record made Cobain a star that he began to express his disdain for Wallace's efforts, blaming him for making Nirvana's music sound "candyass."

That August, a month before the record hit the stores, Novoselic heralded Wallace's work. "Andy used the magic dust, man!" he told Mike Gitter. "He stole Slayer's soul and now they're soulless! We have their souls now."

Mastered

On August 2, 1991, Wallace's final mix of Nirvana's DGC debut *Nevermind* was forwarded to Howie Weinberg, who prepared the recording for pressing. Working at the Mastering Lab in Hollywood, Weinberg—who had previously mastered albums for acts like the Beastie Boys, Camper Van Beethoven, the Clash, and Hüsker Dü front man Bob Mould—got started on the process alone when the members of Nirvana, Wallace, and Gary Gersh failed to arrive on time.

In fact, Nirvana and their associates were so late that by the time they showed up, Howie had mastered the bulk of the album. As a result, initial pressings of Nevermind had what Cobain considered to an egregious error: the final, hidden track, "Endless, Nameless," was inadvertently left off of the album.

When Cobain discovered this, after listening to a finished copy of the record, he flipped his lid and called Gersh to insist that any and all subsequent pressings be corrected.

"In the beginning, it was kind of a verbal thing to put that track at the end," Weinberg explained in the book *Classic Rock Albums: Nevermind*, admitting that he had failed to write down the request from the band and the record company. "Maybe I misconstrued their instructions, so you can call it my mistake if you want."

Although the first 46,351 copies of the record were missing the extra song, all ensuing versions were fixed to accommodate Cobain's wishes, putting ten minutes of silence between the final listed track, "Something in the Way," and "Endless, Nameless."

Nevermind Track by Track

Nirvana's second album signified their desire to break free from the Seattle grunge movement with which they had been associated. Embracing the soft/loud dynamic Cobain had first heard on Pixies records, and the production values evident on Sonic Youth's 1990 DGC debut *Goo*, the band recorded what would become 1991's most important rock album, following its release on September 24. The unexpected success of *Nevermind* marked a cultural shift away from innocuous pop-metal. Within six months, the album had sold three million copies, as mainstream rock kids left their Nelson, Warrant, Winger, and Slaughter CDs behind for good.

"Smells Like Teen Spirit"

Before it became the greatest rock song of the 1990s, "Smells Like Teen Spirit" was merely the lead single and opening number on *Nevermind*. Penned in Nirvana rehearsals by Cobain, Novoselic, and Grohl just weeks before they entered Sound City studios, the song was the first of several numbers on the band's DGC debut to use the soft verse–loud chorus formula. With its four-chord riff in the introduction and chorus, "Teen Spirit" resonated immediately with indie rock kids, metal-heads, and general rock fans.

"I was trying to write the ultimate pop song. I was basically trying to rip off the Pixies. I have to admit it," Cobain told *Rolling Stone* in January 1994, expressing his love of the Boston band who had produced such classics as 1988's *Surfer Rosa* and the following year's *Doolittle*. "We used their sense of dynamics, being soft and quiet and then loud and hard."

Kurt had the main riff and the hook when he brought the song into the practice room. Together, he and his bandmates played the main riff for an hour and a half before it dawned on Novoselic to slow the song down in the verses. Incorporating Krist's memorable bass line and Grohl's drumbeat, which gave it the added stamp it needed, the song that became the group's biggest hit was given a shared writing credit.

Despite having different chord progressions, the song's double-tracked guitar line has been compared by some to Dinosaur Jr.'s "Freak Scene" and by others to Boston's 1976 classic "More Than a Feeling." Cobain agreed with the second comparison. He called it "such a clichéd riff," in 1994, explaining to writer David Fricke, "It was so close to a Boston riff or [the Kingsmen's] 'Louie Louie.'"

According to producer Butch Vig—who advised the band to trim the chorus—the trio made three attempts at the basic track, selecting the second version. Kurt cut just three vocal takes, and Vig cherry-picked the best parts of each for the final version. In 2001, Grohl remembered the band being shocked the first time it came through the speakers. "We were used to hearing it sound like a shitty bootleg," Dave told *Rolling Stone* in September 2001. "All of a sudden, you have Butch Vig making it sound like *Led Zeppelin IV*."

Cobain once suggested that, after spending time spray-painting buildings around Olympia and discussing punk rock and anarchism with Kathleen Hanna, he felt that the aforementioned graffiti ("Kurt Smells Like Teen Spirit") left by her on his bedroom wall had rebellious implications.

"'Teen Spirit,' it's basically just about friends," Kurt said in a transcript of a 1991 interview with the *Seattle Times*. "We still feel as if we're teenagers, because we don't follow the guidelines of what's expected of us to be adults. We still screw around and have a good time. It also has kind of a, like a, teen revolutionary theme to it too." Cobain was supposedly unaware that Hanna had been referring to the scent of Tobi Vail's deodorant brand, Teen Spirit.

In fact, he contended, he did not know that such a product even existed until long after the single had been released. In a September 2007 *Seattle Weekly* column, Novoselic wrote that upon seeing the spray-painted phrase on Kurt's wall, he thought, "Too much cheap red wine!"

Released to radio on August 27, 1991, followed by a commercial release on CD on September 10, the single grew legs in markets where the band had existing fans, exposure on modern-rock radio, or both. Neither Geffen's marketing department nor the band's management at Gold Mountain expected the song to be a proper "pop" hit but merely one that would help earn attention on the FM dial and on MTV and, ultimately, lure in album buyers. But when the people started to hear the song, as manager Danny Goldberg would tell Michael Azerrad, "It was instantaneous . . . They heard it on alternative radio, and then they rushed out like lemmings to buy it."

MTV picked up the video for the song in October, giving the clip its world premiere on the weekly alternative program *120 Minutes* before putting it in heavy "Buzz Bin" rotation, where it stayed until the end of the year. Meanwhile, the song had become a favorite on the network's metal show, *Headbangers Ball*, giving Nirvana—like Faith No More and Jane's Addiction before them—the rare distinction of reaching all of rock's radio formats, from hard rock and album rock to modern rock and college radio.

If Top 40 radio was slow to catch on because of the group's harder sound, by the time 1991 ended, "Smells Like Teen Spirit" had made it all the way to #6 on *Billboard*'s pop singles survey. It was named the best single of 1991 in the *Village Voice*'s "Pazz & Jop" critic's poll and, of course, would also catapult *Nevermind* to the top of the album charts around the globe. Eventually, the single would earn an RIAA platinum certification for one million copies sold, and the track was the main impetus for its parent album to sell more than ten million copies in the US alone.

"Smells Like Teen Spirit" would earn Grammy nominations in the categories of Best Hard Rock Performance with Vocal and Best Rock Song. It lost the latter to Eric Clapton's *Unplugged* reworking of Derek & the Dominoes "Layla." Still, such recognition—critics suggested the song was "the anthem of a generation"— left the men in Nirvana uncomfortable. The song received such overexposure that by the end of 1993 Cobain felt embarrassed and was reluctant to play it. Yet its legacy has not diminished in subsequent years. In 2000, MTV and *Rolling Stone* ranked the song third on their joint list of the one hundred best songs of all time, behind the Beatles' enduring "Yesterday" and the Rolling Stones' rock classic "(I Can't Get No) Satisfaction."

When asked by Fricke in 2001 if he had any sense of what was to come on the eve of the song's release, Grohl said, "It didn't seem possible," citing the pop fare of Mariah Carey and Michael Bolton that had been ruling the charts. " It seemed like we were about to make another pass through the underground. One of the first people to say they thought the album was going to be huge was Donita Sparks of L7. And I didn't believe her. I was going, 'There's absolutely no way.'"

"In Bloom"

In 2011, Butch Vig told a story of Dave Grohl trying to hit the high harmony vocals on "In Bloom"—the second song on *Nevermind*, and the fourth and final single from the album—in the recording studio. According to the producer, Grohl's voice sounded "amazingly like Kurt's and it blended really well."

"[Dave] said, 'I have to pull a Keith Richards,'" Vig told *Billboard*. "So he'd take a sip of Jack Daniel's and a puff from a cigarette. He'd get halfway through a line and his voice would start to break up. I remember all of us laughing and laughing. By the time he got the vocal done, I think he had drank half a bottle of Jack Daniel's."

Prior to this, Cobain's lead vocals continued to get increasingly loud during the making of the song, which forced Vig to alter the input levels to keep the volume balanced between the verses and the choruses. As with Kurt's vocals, which were double-tracked, Dave's parts were recorded twice.

"In Bloom" was one of the first tunes attempted at Sound City, and because Nirvana had previously recorded it a year earlier during its Smart Studios session with Vig, they all agreed it made a good starting point. Like the other carryovers from that April 1990 session, the song remains largely unchanged, with the exception of the differences in Grohl and Chad Channing's playing styles.

In one interview, Novoselic explained that "In Bloom" had originally reminded him of a Bad Brains number, until Cobain went home and morphed it into a pop song. Kurt employed the quiet verses–loud choruses approach when he performed a revised version of the tune for the bassist over the telephone.

Cobain biographer Charles R. Cross has called the song a "thinly disguised portrait" of Kurt's friend Dylan Carlson, who "liked to shoot his guns" and was particularly fond of the group's "pretty songs." Others have suggested that it had a broader meaning, and was directed at newer fans of Nirvana who were from outside of the underground and misunderstood the band's intentions. But the reality is that, while tracking the song at Van Nuys in May, or during the original sessions in Madison a year before, no one in Nirvana could have predicted that so many jocks and metal-heads would flock to the band that fall.

By the time the single was commercially released in the UK—where it reached #28—on November 30, 1992, Nirvana had ballooned into one of rock's biggest bands. In the US, there was only a promotional release, as a DGC had already turned its attention to a new rarities compilation, *Incesticide*, due for release on December 14 that year.

"Come as You Are"

When Cobain and Novoselic were growing up in Aberdeen in the 1970s and '80s, there was a Christian church on Market Street that invited passersby to "Come as You Are." It is from this sign, encouraging people to walk into the house of worship, that many—including Doug Barker, managing editor at local newspaper the *Daily World*—believe Kurt got the idea for one of Nirvana's most successful songs.

Cobain told Australia's Triple J radio station that the song—which uses paradoxes like "Take your time/hurry up"—was "really contradictory," adding that it was about "people and what they're expected to act like." About the line "And I don't have a gun," Kurt added, "Just because I say 'I' in a song doesn't necessarily mean it's me. It's just the way I write; [I'll] take on someone else's personality or character. My life is kinda boring, so I just take stories from things I've read, and off the television, and in stories I've heard, maybe even some friends."

Cobain recorded three vocal takes of the song at Sound City, of which Vig used and then double-tracked the first. Butch also employed Kurt's second attempt at the guitar solo. According to music writer Jim Berkenstadt, Nirvana's front man mistakenly sang "And I don't have a gun" too soon while overdubbing the harmony vocals. Vig also took a sample of Cobain singing "memoria" midway through the track and used it twice near the end of the song.

The mid-tempo recording launches with Kurt's distinctive, twangy, eight-second riff, which he played through an effects pedal designed to give his guitar a "watery" sound. By the time Nirvana and their management were considering the song for *Nevermind*'s second single, they were well aware that the song's signature guitar part resembled a slowed down version of the riff heard on Killing Joke's explosive 1984 hit "Eighties." In fact, Danny Goldberg told *Rolling Stone*'s Carrie Borzillo-Vrenna in 2003 that "Kurt was nervous because it was too similar."

They went for it anyway, releasing "Come as You Are" as a single on March 3, 1992. The song went on to peak at #9 in the UK before reaching #32 on the US *Billboard* Hot 100, and its popularity helped drive further sales of *Nevermind*.

That same year, Killing Joke claimed that Nirvana's song plagiarized "Eighties," although a copyright infringement lawsuit was never filed. Borzillo-Vrenna's report cited "personal and financial reasons," which has led many to believe that the Nirvana camp eventually paid for the UK band's silence.

"Breed"

Originally known as "Immodium," the fourth song on *Nevermind* was a hold-over from the Smart Studios era and offered a stylistic link to the approaches on *Bleach*, notably the repetitive lyrics. A powerhouse of a song, propelled by Grohl's rhythmic attack, it conjures up images of what life might be like if things had worked out for Kurt and Tobi Vail. He appears to be singing her thoughts and/or capturing her dialogue, as evidenced by the reappearance of the phrase "She said."

As on most of *Nevermind*, Kurt appears to be reeling from life without Vail, and their past conversations seem to inform the lyrics. Forgoing the pressure of raising a family ("we don't have to breed") and just cohabitating ("We can plant a house / We can build a tree"), it ends up being one of the record's most candidly personal tracks, and one of its most musically forceful.

"Lithium"

The fifth track on *Nevermind*, and the album's third single—released commercially on July 21, 1992—"Lithium" tells the tale of a man who turns to God after thoughts of killing himself. When asked about the song that year, Cobain described the partly autobiographical, partly fictional song to a fanzine writer named Cake. "The story is about a guy who lost his girlfriend, I can't decide what caused her to die, let's say she died of AIDS or a car accident or something, and he's going around brooding and he turned to religion as a last resort to keep himself alive. To keep him from suicide. Sometimes I think religion is OK for certain people. It's good to use religion as a last resort before you go insane."

In the same interview, Kurt went on to cite his aunt Mari as an example of someone he knew and loved deeply who became disillusioned with her life and wound up feeling suicidal before becoming a born-again Christian. By turning to religion, he explained, she had kept herself alive, for which he was clearly grateful. He also conceded the following year in *Come as You Are* that the song was infused with some of his own experiences, including his time spent with Jesse Reed's family.

Unlike a lot of Cobain's songs, which were pieced together from various poems and musical ideas, "Lithium" was one he had managed to write from start to finish. During recording, the band struggled to keep a steady tempo. Kurt kept speeding up his playing, with the band following suit. "Kurt wanted to be able to play the guitar very . . . not methodical—it needed to have this space," Butch Vig told Azerrad. "It had to be relaxed." Whenever Kurt sped up, Butch made him redo it, eventually suggesting they use a click track. He also recommended that Grohl and Novoselic simplify the song's rhythm.

Upon its release, the CD single—which included full lyrics for the *Nevermind* album, cover art by Cobain, and a sonogram of the front man's then-unborn unborn daughter, Frances Bean—stalled at #64 on the *Billboard* Hot 100, even as its parent album continued to ride high in the album survey. A UK pressing—which boasted the cassette-only "Curmudgeon," a live version of "Been a Son," and a cover of the Wipers' "D-7" tracked during the band's 1990 Peel session—peaked at #11.

"Polly"

Arranged for acoustic guitar, the song "Polly" is based on a June 1987 incident in which a fourteen-year-old Washington girl was kidnapped and raped by a man named Gerald Arthur Friend after he picked her up hitchhiking home from a rock concert at the Tacoma Dome. After Friend tortured her with a whip, a razor, and a blowtorch, the teen likely saved her own life by somehow managing to persuade her abductor to untie her. Later, she escaped from his van when he stopped at a gas station and caused a commotion, which led to his capture and conviction.

The song was known as "Hitchhiker" when Kurt wrote it in 1988, and later as "Cracker." Speaking to *NME* in November 1991, he acknowledged rape as one of the "most terrible crimes on earth," and opining that while women should be taught to defend themselves, men should be taught not to rape. "I was talking to a friend of mine who went to a rape crisis center where women are taught judo and karate," he continued. "She looked out of the window and saw a football field full of boys, and thought, those are the people that should really be in this class."

"Polly" was initially a contender for *Bleach*, but Cobain and Novoselic left it off that record because it seemed out of place alongside the record's heavy material. The version on *Nevermind* comes from Nirvana's sessions at Vig's Wisconsin studio in 1990, and features cymbal playing by then-drummer Chad Channing.

"Territorial Pissings"

Nirvana recorded this explosive, punk-inspired track directly into the sound-board at Sound City in May 1991. It begins with Novoselic's off-key bastardization of the chorus from the Youngbloods' 1967 hippie anthem "Get Together," and was purposely sardonic.

"I really don't have an explanation for that song," Cobain told *NME* in August '91, when asked about its meaning. "A lot of the time I write a song and when someone asks me about it, I'll make up an explanation on the spot, because a lot of times I write the lyrics in the studio and I have no idea what I'm talking about."

Despite such claims, the lyrics to this cathartic shot of rock 'n' roll suggest Nirvana's creative chief was pretty clear on what he wanted to say. "Territorial Pissings" found Kurt projecting his support of feminist viewpoints and singing out about paranoia and alienation.

According to Everett True, "Territorial Pissings" stemmed partly from *The SCUM Manifesto*, a scathing criticism of men written by Valerie Solanas. The militant feminist led the Society for Cutting Up Men, and Kurt supported her idea that women should rule the earth.

The song would live in infamy after the band performed it on NBC's *Saturday Night Live* in January 1992, destroying their instruments at the end of the appearance. Later in the year, during a slot on UK TV's *Tonight with Jonathon Ross*, the band again trashed their instruments to the song, stunning the show's producers, who had booked the group to play "Lithium."

"Drain You"

Some suggest that this mighty *Nevermind* number was a chronicle of Cobain's split from Vail, while others believe it was about his struggle with heroin, specifically in the line, "I travel through a tube and end up in your infection." The reality is that it may be about both, but when pressed for a meaning, Kurt was quick to suggest it had no real meaning, telling reporters much of it had been made up on the spot.

One thing is for sure: this song features more studio trickery than the others on *Nevermind*. Despite Cobain's aversion to overdubs, "Drain You" is loaded with six layers of guitar work, with Vig having supposedly bamboozled Kurt to record them by telling him that some of the takes were flawed. In the bridge, engineer Andy Wallace took a rubber duck Kurt had brought into the studio and manipulated the quacking sound through a digital delay. The sound of an aerosol can and rattling chains can also be heard during this experimental interlude.

"Lounge Act"

With an opening bassline taken from Shocking Blue's "Send Me a Postcard," the mid-tempo "Lounge Act" was perhaps most memorable for its confessional lyrics. According to Krist—by way of Charles Cross—the song was specifically written about Tobi.

When Kurt sings "I'll arrest myself, I'll wear a shield," he is referring to the K Records tattoo on his forearm, acquired to impress Vail. Elsewhere, he sings about fighting jealousy, feeling smothered, and feeling no regrets.

In a January 1992 *Musician* interview, Kurt stated that several of the songs on *Nevermind*, including this one, stem from "some very personal experiences, like breaking up with girlfriends and having bad relationships, feeling that death void that the person in the song is feeling—very lonely, sick."

"Stay Away"

On the cathartic punk communiqué "Stay Away," Cobain takes aim at fickle "fashion shits" who blindly follow trends and movements and reveals that he'd "rather be dead than cool." The lyrics seem to point aim at the Seattle grunge scene he was looking to distance himself from. The song's original title, "Pay to Play," also suggests his dissatisfaction with the Emerald City music environment.

Late in the song, Kurt sings, "God is gay," a phrase he once spray-painted on a homophobic Weatherwax classmate's car. It was also his way of coming out in support of gay rights and warning any small-minded curiosity-seekers to steer clear of his band. Following the meteoric rise of Nirvana, however, and much to Cobain's disappointment, his message was seemingly lost on some of the millions who bought the record.

"On a Plain"

One of *Nevermind*'s many gems, "On a Plain" was penned by Kurt Cobain in 1990 and originally recorded with Nirvana's sound engineer Craig Montgomery in a Seattle studio session on January 1, 1991. The song—which was released as a radio single in the summer of '92—was then cut in Van Nuys with Vig. According to the producer, Cobain brought a little toy train into the vocal booth during the session at Sound City.

"He had all these little toys on there and he was playing with them during the song," Vig told *Billboard* in 2011. "I remember saying, 'OK, are you ready for the vocals?' And he said yeah, so I started rolling the tape and recorded. But he didn't sing; he just recorded all these odd little things through the song. And I thought it was interesting. Then I'd say, 'Are you ready to do a vocal?' And he said, 'OK, Butch, I guess so.'"

When it was suggested by *Flipside* in its May/June 1992 issue that the song's vibe resembled Cheap Trick on *Dream Police* or *Live at Budokan*, Kurt was taken aback. "That's weird!" he said, revealing he had just been listening to both of those records that same day, before opining, "That song came out way too clean. I'm not happy with the way that came out at all. It should have been a lot rawer; we play it a lot better live I think. I'll admit I like Cheap Trick—that first record is great. I keep forgetting how punk rock it really is. It's pretty raw for a commercial rock record."

"On a Plain" begins with an audible handclap and the sound of guitar noise before giving way to the hook-injected elements of the song. Cobain's lyrics sound as if they spilled out of him quickly, but the words aren't without meaning, despite the line, "What the hell am I trying to say?" There's a lucidity to the song, which touches on Kurt's struggles with addiction, his issues with writer's block, his feelings of selfishness, and his careening emotional state.

"Something in the Way"

After early attempts at a full-band version of "Something in the Way" failed, Cobain sat down with his old Stella twelve-string guitar (strung with just five nylon strings) and performed a solo rendition of the tune for Vig. The producer loved what he heard and—after silencing the studio's telephones and air conditioning—he set the control room up to capture Kurt's fragile, unaccompanied version.

With Cobain seeping into the couch, Vig was floored. "His performance stunned me," the producer told *Rolling Stone* in 1996. "He had gone deep inside himself and brought out a haunting portrait of desolation, weariness and paranoia."

From there, Novoselic and Grohl dubbed their restrained parts. On the final day at Sound City, a guest musician named Kirk Canning was brought in to write and play the cello lines that would augment the recording.

The decision to add strings to the song was totally spontaneous and last-minute. Canning, who was friendly with Novoselic, happened to be at the band's L.A. apartment when Kurt came up with the idea. When Kirk revealed he played the cello, it felt like fate. They brought him with them to Van Nuys the following day.

Cobain played "Something in the Way" live for the first time on November 25, 1990, at Seattle's Off Ramp Café, having written the song earlier that same year. The myth that it was written during a time when Cobain was homeless and slept under a bridge near his mother's home in Aberdeen, Washington, was squashed by Novoselic in Charles R. Cross' 2001 book *Heavier Than Heaven*, who said it never happened.

"Endless, Nameless"

This impromptu instrumental jam was recorded by Vig and appended to the second and all subsequent pressings of *Nevermind* as a "hidden track," appearing long after the album's finale proper winds down.

When asked about the song by Cake in early 1992, Kurt revealed that the band had been working with noise and guitar effects pedals. "It's a little taste of what our next album might sound like," he explained. "I don't want to get too experimental to where we turn into a punk rock version of Rush or Yes! I hope we have enough sense to know when to quit."

Outtakes

There were very few outtakes from *Nevermind*. The band came in with fifteen song ideas, leaving just three or four incomplete, including a Cobain original called "Song in D" that had a contagious, R.E.M.-inspired feel.

According to Vig, Kurt left two other songs unfinished—a punk-inflected number and bluesy acoustic tune. Cobain eventually lent elements of the latter to Courtney Love for the Hole song "Old Age."

Photo Shoots

For band photos, art director Robert Fisher had wanted to try to get the members of Nirvana in a pool, but the one photographer Kirk Weddle had hired out had a broken pump, and as a result the water was cloudy. This coupled with the fact that it was a windy overcast day meant the shoot didn't go as planned. "Kurt was really, uh, sick," Fisher recalled in *Nirvana: The True Story*. "He'd sit at the top of the water and kick to try and go underwater and he couldn't do it."

On May 23, New York photographer Michael Lavine was sent to Sound City to take the press pictures that would accompany promotional copies of the record. During the photo shoot, it was evident to Lavine that Kurt was an addict—his teeth were rotting away from his gums. In an effort to make it through the day, Cobain drank an entire bottle of Jim Beam.

Jabberjaw

On May 29, 1991, Nirvana took the stage at L.A.'s Jabberjaw, playing a last-minute gig at the venue as a means to prevent their friends in Seattle's Fitz of Depression from having to cancel their show. Kurt, Krist, and Dave plowed through a seventeen-song set that included newly recorded numbers like "Lithium," "On a Plain," and "Come as You Are."

At one point, Kurt was so wasted on drugs (he had started taking Quaaludes) and alcohol, it took him several minutes to change a guitar string, the audience cajoling him all the while. But the show was made memorable by a rare, unexpected performance of Wild Cherry's 1976 smash "Play That Funky Music" and the presence in the audience, once again, of Iggy Pop.

Longing for Tobi

Despite their breakup, Cobain and Vail reconnected at times in the months that followed. In an unsent letter to Tobi written in late May, Kurt admitted he taking a lot of drugs during his stay in Los Angeles, expressed his displeasure with his lack of nourishment and sleep, and complained about the heat in Southern California.

"It might be time for the Betty Ford Clinic or the Richard Nixon Library to save me from abusing my anemic rodent-like body any longer," he wrote to Vail, before professing his love to her.

Double That

Nirvana's six-week stay at the Oakwoods ended in early June. By the time they left the complex, the apartment Kurt and Dave had inhabited was covered in graffiti.

If Gold Mountain's security deposit on the place was a goner, it wasn't the only unexpected expense. By the time *Nevermind* was finished, the band had nearly doubled their $65,000 budget, running up a tab of $120,000.

18

Here We Are Now, Entertain Us!

Building a Buzz

On the Road with Dinosaur Jr.

It's no secret that the members of Nirvana were fans of Dinosaur Jr.—Everett True even went so far as to suggest "Smells Like Spirit" was inspired by "Freak Scene." So it made sense for Cobain's trio to open for J. Mascis' band when they hit the road that June in support of their own major label debut, *Green Mind*.

After a brief trip home to Olympia—which found Nirvana playing one last warm-up dorm party at Evergreen State—Kurt, Krist, and Dave stepped up to theaters, launching two weeks of roadwork on June 10 at the Gothic Theater in Englewood, Colorado.

Tour stops at Salt Lake City's Pompadour Rock & Roll Club and the Warfield Theatre in San Francisco gave way to shows in Tijuana, Sacramento, and Santa Cruz. The latter show, at the Catalyst on June 18, marked the public debut of a new song, "Rape Me." At the time Cobain unveiled it, Novoselic and Grohl had never even heard it before. It went over so well, though, that he played it again on the last night of the trek at Portland's Melody Ballroom.

Considering the Mainstream

If the band's Hollywood Palladium gig that month offered Cobain another opportunity to mingle with Courtney Love, whose band Hole opened for Nirvana and Dinosaur Jr., business came before pleasure. Backstage, Kurt spoke to a reporter about the notion of getting as big as Metallica or Guns N' Roses, and explained he just didn't see it happening.

At the time, Cobain felt really connected to Nirvana's audience. He was also happy with the idea that many of those who followed the band shared the same points of view. He simply couldn't imagine hard-rock fans liking Nirvana, and besides, as he said that night in an unpublished interview later acquired by NirvanaClub.com, "I just can't accept that mainstream macho-dickhead attitude.

Nirvana supported Dinosaur Jr.—and Kurt befriended Hole's Courtney Love—during this memorable gig at the Hollywood Palladium on June 14, 1991.   *Author's collection*

I wouldn't be comfortable having that many people in my audience every night like that."

Moving Away

Nirvana returned to Washington in late June. Early the next month, Grohl informed Kurt he was moving out.

Dave had grown tired of sleeping on the couch and decided he would rent a house with his old friend Barrett Jones, who had recently moved to the Northwest. The producer/engineer had been crashing with his girlfriend in a van in front of the Novoselics' place, waiting to take occupancy of their new digs in west Seattle.

With Cobain now living on his own, he felt free to do heroin whenever he wanted. Whenever he had the cash, and the drug was available, he was happy to escape by shooting up.

Quisp and Stew

Cobain's behavior had become more and more erratic that summer. In a patriotic mood, and with July 4 approaching, he decided to dye his white male kitten Quisp red, white, and blue using Kool-Aid.

If that wasn't odd enough, friend and neighbor Ian Dickson claims that Kurt even let the cat have intercourse with Stew, his female rabbit. Despite the fact that Quisp had damaged Stew's reproductive tract, Kurt enjoyed watching them go at it. When they were through, he would push the rabbit's insides back using the eraser end of a pencil.

Valiant Effort

Although Cobain—who was behind on his rent—came home from touring with a pocket full of cash from Nirvana's merchandise sales, he spent the money elsewhere. Instead of making good on the hundreds he owed on Pear Street, he plunked down $550 on a 1963 Plymouth Valiant on June 24 to replace the Datsun that had long since been towed to a salvage yard.

In mid-July—just days before Kurt was due in Los Angeles to finalize the album art for *Nevermind*—he sold his beloved turtles for a mere $50. When Tracy Marander asked why he had let them go, he explained he was broke and needed the cash.

Weeks later, while Cobain was out of town in Los Angeles, plotting the album's artwork and upcoming promotional campaign with Silva, Goldberg, and the staff at DGC, he was locked out by his landlord for failure to pay rent. He came home in late July to find his belongings on the curb. His neighbors had contacted Marander to come for his animals.

Homeless again, Kurt resumed the couch-surfing lifestyle of his teenage years. When all else failed, he slept in the light brown Valiant alongside all of his worldly possessions. He wasn't terribly worried. He knew he merely had to get by for the next couple of weeks, until Nirvana's tour got underway.

Showcase

On August 15, Nirvana returned to Los Angeles to play an industry showcase at the Roxy on Sunset Boulevard. Before the entire Geffen Records staff, radio and media people, and other key music-business contacts, the band took the stage using rented gear (theirs had already been shipped overseas for their imminent European tour) and played what some have called the best Nirvana show of all time.

The audience was treated to an opening set by Franz Stahl's new band Wool, and had been whipped into a frenzy by the time Cobain, Novoselic, and Grohl took the stage. Opening with "School," they mixed *Bleach* highlights with all-new winners like "Drain You," "Smells Like Teen Spirit," and "Lithium."

At one point, things got so crazy with stage-divers that Cobain had to warn his intruders to be careful not to step on his effects pedals. During the show, the band announced plans for their next music video, which was to be shot that coming weekend, and urged fans to show up to be cast as extras.

While no one in attendance could have predicted how successful Nirvana would become at the time of this gig, Geffen's staff knew on the basis of crowd reaction, media response to the advance cassette, and the strength of the album itself that *Nevermind* would at least match the sales of Sonic Youth's *Goo*. Soon, the idea of the record breaking the 500,000-copy sales barrier was not inconceivable. Such an achievement would put Nirvana in the company of giant alternative-rock bands like Jane's Addiction and the Red Hot Chili Peppers.

Years later, *Kerrang!* magazine went so far as to rank this gig at the top of its list of "The 100 Greatest Gigs of All Time." It's certainly the concert most Nirvana fans wish they had witnessed.

World Debut of "Smells Like Teen Spirit"

On the afternoon of the Roxy show, Nirvana appeared on the influential college-radio station KXLU in Los Angeles to plug the gig and their upcoming album. They were also on hand for the debut airing of their DGC debut single, "Smells Like Teen Spirit."

Geffen's radio-promotions man John Rosenfelder had brought along a test pressing of the tune, and everyone present marveled at just how great the song sounded on wax.

This flyer was circulated around Los Angeles in mid-August 1991, soliciting young adult fans to appear in Nirvana's upcoming music video for "Smells Like Teen Spirit." The handbill included a map to the Culver City Soundstage and instructed participants to "adapt a high school persona, ie. Preppy, punk, nerd, jock . . ." for the clip.   *Author's collection*

Making the "Teen Spirit" Video

Word spread about the "Smells Like Teen Spirit" video shoot following the Roxy gig, thanks in part to an announcement on KXLU. The flyers handed out during and after the gig called for extras, aged eighteen-to-twenty-five, to arrive at the GMT Studio in Culver City on August 17 for a day of shooting. So many kids turned up at Stage 6 that hundreds had to be turned away.

Inside, the soundstage resembled a high-school gym, complete with basketball hoops and cheerleaders clutching pompoms. The idea for the video was Cobain's, and stemmed from the Ramones' cheesy 1979 film *Rock 'N' Roll High School*, but Kurt wanted to take it to another level: the pep rally from hell.

In Cobain's vision, cheerleaders would wear anarchy symbols on their uniforms; the mosh-pit punks would be the cool kids. From the outset, there was a disconnect between Kurt and director Samuel Bayer, with the two engaging in a screaming match during the shoot. It didn't help that Nirvana's front man was drinking whiskey during the filming. Nor did the director's Napoleonic approach to filmmaking delight the band or their extras.

Still, when all was said and done, the resulting clip looked pretty damned cool—and the powers at MTV thought so, too. Heavy rotation was just around the corner.

Readying for Reading

After a twenty-four-hour stopover back home in Seattle, Nirvana—with Cobain's friend Ian Dickson in tow—flew out of SeaTac to Dublin, Ireland, on August 19, 1991. The two-week European tour that followed was exciting and celebratory, culminating in the trio's biggest-ever festival gigs, including a high-profile spot at the Reading Festival.

Alcohol was in abundance, with Novoselic and Cobain practically guzzling Glenfiddich and Absolut, respectively. Kurt shared his ample supply of vodka with his touring roommate Dickson, although his beloved Covonia cough syrup with codeine was off limits. Grohl meanwhile found a new appreciation for red wine.

The tour began with a pair of Irish gigs with Sonic Youth at Sir Henry's in Cork and the Top Hat in Dun Laoghaire. Both bands were filmed during these shows for Dave Markey's alternative music documentary *1991: The Year Punk Broke.*

At 3:00 p.m. on Friday, August 23, Nirvana took to the stage of the Reading Festival. They had been sandwiched between two British shoegazing bands,

A rare ticket from Nirvana's gig opening for Sonic Youth in Cork, Ireland, on August 20, 1991.   *Author's collection*

Silverfish and Chapterhouse, and wiped the stage with both acts. Their explosive set began with "School" and "Floyd the Barber," before the band invited Eugene Kelly of the Vaselines onstage to collaborate on a version of his song "Molly's Lips." Later, an unexpected jam on the Doors' "The End" gave way to "Blew." At the end of the show, during "Endless, Nameless," Cobain dived into Grohl's drum kit, dislocating his shoulder in the process, but he was brought back onstage later on during Sonic Youth's set, which preceded a headlining performance by Iggy Pop.

Monsters of Spex

That Saturday, Nirvana traveled to the Monsters of Spex festival in Cologne to appear alongside Bob Mould, Dinosaur Jr., and Sonic Youth, among others. The band had a 4:00 p.m. set time, but when that hour approached, they called the promoter to inform him that they had been caught in traffic and were stuck at customs.

Organizers scurried to shift the lineup around to make sure that Nirvana could still play, and the band wound up with a far more desirable 6:00 p.m. spot. Later, their agent Christof Ellinghaus would reveal that the delay was a complete scam—the trio hadn't been detained, but just preferred to play later in the day.

Pukkelpop

On Sunday, August 25, Nirvana traveled to Hasselt, Belgium, where they opened for An Emotional Fish, the Pogues, Ride, House of Love, Dinosaur Jr., the Pixies' Black Francis, Sonic Youth, and the Ramones. They had been booked at the last minute after the cancelation of the Limbomaniacs.

During Black Francis' performance, Kurt—always happy to cause a little chaos—sprayed a fire extinguisher on the stage. He had already spent the afternoon with his bandmates jumping atop the two acts' trailers, which were parked close together, as well as switching Nirvana's nametag with the one on Francis' bus, and had also gotten into a "fruit war" with the members of Sonic Youth before starting a full-scale food fight with the group and their entourage inside the catering tent.

If that wasn't enough, while Ride were onstage, Kurt orchestrated the theft of champagne from the group's trailer. He took their flowers and candy, too.

Burning Up in Bremen

Midweek gigs with Sonic Youth in Bremen, Halle, Stuttgart, and Nuremberg were relatively uneventful, save for the fire Cobain started inside the band's rented tour van. That occurred in Bremen, on August 27, midway through an interview to promote *Nevermind*, while a representative from MCA Germany (Geffen's local distributors) waited outside. The same label employee had already been insulted when a note reading "Fuck you" was taped to a basket of candy and magazines she had brought to welcome the band.

After Novoselic shot off a fire extinguisher backstage, ripped up the magazines, and tossed the candy across Sonic Youth's dressing room, the woman from MCA lost it. She regained her composure temporarily—until the fire began. When she went back to the label to explain what had happened to her, Nirvana's camp began damage control. When MCA's German arm threatened to pull distribution for Nirvana's forthcoming album, the band formally apologized for what Cobain would characterize in a *Melody Maker* interview that November as "classic rock 'n' roll angst."

Rotterdam and Peel

At the Ein Abend in Wein festival in the Netherlands, Nirvana had a lot of downtime, which left plenty of opportunity to get into mischief before their set and after the final notes of "Negative Creep" had been played.

Alcohol again played a part in Kurt's actions with Dickson. In fact, they were so drunk on vodka that they elected to dress up in medical facemasks and gowns they had mysteriously obtained. At one point, Ian was rolling Kurt around backstage in a wheelchair.

Most visitors to their dressing room were met with splashes of wine and orange juice. And when Courtney Love showed up to introduce her boyfriend, Smashing Pumpkins front man Billy Corgan, to the members of Sonic Youth and Nirvana, he was awkwardly received. According to witness Everett True, as Love walked away, Kurt—who still had a crush on her—took a magic marker to the wall, smiling as he wrote "Courtney + *Gish.*" *Gish*, of course, was the name of the Pumpkins' recent debut album.

Nirvana's performance was delayed because Australian rocker-turned-poet Nick Cave was busy reciting prose on a nearby stage. As Cave continued, an intoxicated Cobain grew impatient and started playing "Polly."

The drunkenness didn't help Nirvana's performance. They had to restart "Sliver" and "In Bloom," and Kurt basically gave up on "Negative Creep," tossing his guitar and taking his rage out on the equipment with help from Dave and Krist. As they walked offstage, some of the venue staff voiced their displeasure to Cobain. A fight ensued, but was broken up before things got too heated.

Two days later, Nirvana returned to England, where they visited the recording studios of BBC radio DJ John Peel for a third time. The group recorded a new song called "Dumb" plus versions of "Endless, Nameless" and "Drain You." They went out in London that night, and Cobain took ecstasy for the first time.

Homeward Bound

During the last two weeks of August 1991, Nirvana had gone from being up-and-comers to bona-fide stars, playing to an ecstatic crowd of 70,000 at the Reading

Festival. Unfortunately, when Kurt came home to Olympia on September 4, he was faced with the sobering reminder that he was homeless, and would once again be living out of his car.

Why *Nevermind*?

When pressed for an explanation of his new album's title, Kurt explained that it had to do with ideas that come and go. It bothered him how people would give up on their ideas—whether it was grabbing a can of spray paint or starting a band—almost as quickly as they would come up with them.

He spoke of spray-painting "Kill George Bush" repeatedly on a wall, telling the *NME* in August 1991, "Whether that would have an impact on anything or not it doesn't matter, it's still fun to do it . . . Many times I've been arrested."

Accessible Crap

09/22/91 Atlanta, GA
09/23/91 Boston, MA
09/25/91 Providence, RI
09/26/91 New Haven, CT
09/27/91 Trenton, NJ
09/28/91 NYC, NY
09/30/91 Pittsburgh, PA
10/01/91 Philadelphia, PA
10/02/91 Washington, DC
10/04/91 Chapel Hill, NC
10/05/91 Athens, GA
10/06/91 Atlanta, GA
10/08/91 Memphis, TN
10/09/91 Columbus, OH
10/10/91 Cleveland, OH
10/11/91 Detroit, MI

10/12/91 Chicago, IL
10/14/91 Minneapolis, MN
10/16/91 St. Louis, MO
10/17/91 Lawrence, KS
10/19/91 Dallas, TX
10/20/91 Houston, TX
10/21/91 Austin, TX
10/23/91 San Diego, CA
10/25/91 Los Ageles, CA
10/26/91 San Francisco, CA
10/27/91 Hollywood, CA
10/28/91 Portland, OR
10/29/91 Portland, OR
10/30/91 Vancouver, BC
10/31/91 Seattle, WA

An advertisement from a September 1991 issue of college-radio tip-sheet *CMJ New Music Report*, plugging Nirvana's then-upcoming tour.
Author's collection

Asked to describe Nirvana's second record in advance of its release to the press, Cobain relayed to readers that they should expect a substantial progression from the band's first album. The album was a fusion of heavy music and Kurt's own unique definition of pop, which he rationalized by noting that even the Butthole Surfers, the Clash, and the Sex Pistols had simplistic pop songs in their repertoires.

"I think it's a fine mixture of radio friendly accessible crap and still reminding you of what our *Bleach* album sounds like and what we sound like live," he told *NME* journalist Keith Cameron that August. "Like if Cheap Trick were to have a lot of distortion in their guitars."

Sarcasm and Controversy in *Melody Maker*

Asked by *Melody Maker* for its September 14 issue about how Nirvana completed their new album, Cobain offered scandalous replies that seemed like jokes but were partially true. "We downed a lot of hypodermic cough syrup and Jack Daniel's," he said, explaining how his increased drug use had helped him combat stress while making the record. He also copped to lounging on the studio couch for days in a row.

Kurt even joked that, during the sessions, the band had considered acquiring songs from music stars of various genres—including Dinosaur Jr.'s J. Mascis, Gloria Estefan, and Warrant—if they failed to meet their time commitments at Sound City.

"J.'s got a shit-load of songs floating around," Cobain quipped. "He's always trying to palm them off on people too—'Here, you wanna buy a song for a quarter?' That's a quarter of a million dollars . . . We can afford that 'cause we're on a major label now."

Meanwhile, Novoselic admitted to having smoked hash the night before the interview and referred to himself as "a pothead philosopher." With a sardonic grin, he also admitted that he had been practicing a mantra of "pyramid power lotus love meditations" to deal with Nirvana's potential ascent.

Junkie Decision

Upon Nirvana's return from Europe, Cobain made the choice—according to a document written by him later on, in a drug-treatment program—to use heroin on a daily basis. He was doing so, he explained, to cope with the stomach ailment he had been dealing with for several years. His disorder made it painful for him to swallow food, and had gotten so bad that it made him consider killing himself.

According to Kurt's confessional letter from rehab, he would "experience an excruciating, burning, nauseous pain" in the upper part of his stomach lining, which was exacerbated on tour because of trouble maintaining a proper eating regimen. After claiming to have seen fifteen different doctors and tried around fifty different types of ulcer medication, he determined that heavy opiates, such as heroin, were the only things that worked.

"I decided if I feel like a junkie as it is," he wrote, "I may as well be one."

Radio Silence

On Friday, September 13, in advance of that night's party to celebrate the release of *Nevermind*, Nirvana went on a tour of Seattle's rock radio stations. Instead of being excited to talk about the record, however, Cobain seemed to shut down.

After weeks of phone interviews with newspapers and arts weeklies to plug the album, Cobain was growing tired of music writers' redundant questions. When he realized that radio personalities were no different, he clammed up.

During a lunchtime visit to KXRX, Kurt said little, letting Dave and Krist field most of the questions instead and throwing pizza slices at his rhythm section while they took questions in the studio. It was his way of embracing what he called the "J. Mascis Fifth Amendment," a reference to the Dinosaur Jr. guitarist's silence around the media.

Something about the notion of explaining himself over and over seemed asinine to Cobain. Before long, he had given up on most radio interviews altogether.

Love Doll Liar

Nirvana's front man began coming up with extravagant lies just to see how gullible journalists were and what he could get away with. In a key interview with the *Seattle Times* during the week of *Nevermind*'s release, he told writer Patrick MacDonald a hilarious lie about how he had bought an inflatable love doll and cut off the hands and feet. He explained that he intended to climb inside the doll and wear it onstage.

David Grohl   Kurt Cobain   Chris Novoselic

NIRVANA

DAVID GEFFEN COMPANY

© 1991 The David Geffen Company. Permission to reproduce limited to editorial newspapers and other regularly published periodicals and television news program

A DGC-sanctioned publicity shot serviced to music journalists in mid-September 1991 with advance cassettes and finished promotional copies of Nirvana's major label debut.
Author's collection

Nevermind Triskaidekaphobia

Cobain, Novoselic, and Grohl arrived at Re-Bar at 1114 Howell in Seattle on the night of the radio interview to a mobbed crowd of journalists, local musicians, and other scenesters. Invitations for the event read "*Nevermind* Triskaidekaphobia, here's Nirvana."

Inside, Cobain seemed uncomfortable with the attention, hiding inside a photo booth for part of the night. That is until the Jim Beam he and his bandmates had been guzzling took effect. An intoxicated Kurt then started a food fight by dousing Krist in ranch dressing. All hell broke loose, and control was only regained after the men in Nirvana were thrown out of an event held in their honor.

As the evening progressed, the members of Nirvana went to a celebration in a friend's loft where Novoselic—who had had too much whiskey—decided to shoot off a fire extinguisher. Party over.

The boozing and antics continued at an after-party held in the Seattle apartment of Susie Tenant, who handled local promotion of DGC releases. At one point that evening, Cobain—who was wearing one of Tenant's dresses—took a gold sales plaque for pop-rock labelmates Nelson down from the wall and melted it in the microwave out of disdain.

Kurt arose around mid-afternoon the following day to announce his plans to those still hanging around at Susie's place. He was off to the grocery store to buy a rump roast, which he and Carlson then planned to shoot.

Beehive

On Sunday, September 15, Nirvana descended upon Beehive Records in Seattle for an in-store performance and album signing. When 200-plus kids showed up for the event—instead of the anticipated fifty—it became apparent that Nirvana had already struck a nerve with "Teen Spirit," which had been picking up speed on local radio.

As they hid out in the nearby Blue Moon Tavern, the trio drank to calm their nerves. "Holy shit," Kurt said to Krist, completely stunned at the length of the line outside the store.

An advertisement in *The Rocket* promoting a *Nevermind* listening party to be held at University Beehive on September 16, 1991.

Author's collection

Inside, the first commercially available copies of the album soon sold out. The store was so crowded that people were standing on top of the CD racks to see the band play a set of twelve songs plus an impromptu jam of Fleetwood Mac's "The Green Manalishi (with the Two Prong Crown)."

As Novoselic and Grohl jammed away, Cobain changed a guitar string and looked around the room. He felt stunned and uneasy, and he couldn't help thinking, throughout the forty-five-minute set, that Nirvana were on the verge of something big.

Taste of Fame

After signing dozens of autographs, Kurt went out to the parking lot for a cigarette. Two old friends from Montesano, Scott Cokely and Rick Miller, came up to him and asked if he would sign their "Sliver" singles. Doing so felt strange to Cobain as he made small talk with these guys he knew from home. In fact, it felt uncomfortable. He started to wonder if he was a good fit for the stardom everyone kept telling him was coming. *Nevermind* wasn't even out yet, and he was already becoming dissatisfied with fame.

"Things started to happen after that," Krist told Charles Cross. "We weren't the same old band. Kurt, he just kind of withdrew . . . It got complicated. It was more than we bargained for."

Mary Lou Lord

The following weekend, after packed shows at the Opera House in Toronto and Foufounes Électriques in Montreal on September 20 and 21, respectively, Nirvana flew to Boston. Excited by the prospect of a night off—Nirvana's next show was the following day—and the prospect of hanging with his pals in the Melvins, Kurt made his way to the Rat after a restaurant dinner spent throwing ribs around with his bandmates.

The doorman hadn't yet heard of Nirvana, but a pretty blonde singer/songwriter with a cherubic face—known around the city for playing her songs in the subway—had. Not only did she vouch for Cobain, she informed the venue employee that Nirvana would be playing the WFNX Birthday Bash the following night.

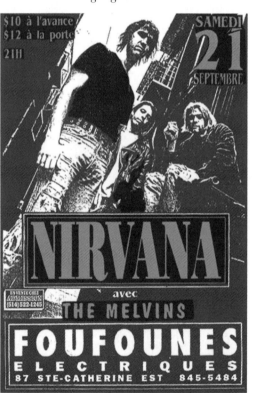

A handbill advertising Nirvana's concert at Foufounes Électriques in Montreal on September 21, 1991.

Author's collection

Although the club's staff still made Kurt pay, he struck up a conversation with the singer, Mary Lou Lord, forgetting for a while about his old friends, Crover and Osborne. He was taken with her, and the attraction only grew when he learned that Mary Lou loved the Pastels, the Vaselines, and Teenage Fanclub, and was knowledgeable about many of the other bands Kurt worshipped.

They hung out all night, and Cobain went to her apartment the next day to find a picture of Lester Bangs hanging on the wall. Lord sang him a pair of songs—not her own songs, but covers of two tracks from the still-unreleased Nirvana record.

That afternoon, Kurt opened up to Mary Lou as they walked around Boston, telling her about his recent fascination with an Eastern religion known as Jainism, his troubled childhood—including how he once witnessed his dad kick a dog—and his feelings about his ex-girlfriend Tobi. He also spoke of how he used drugs to treat his stomach problems, and asked Lord if she had ever tried heroin, which alarmed her.

Kurt also expressed an interest in busking in the Boston subway like his new friend, but after spending part of the afternoon trying to track down a left-handed acoustic guitar, they gave up and went into Cambridge instead, hitting up a few record stores during their travels.

As they walked into the Axis—the location of Nirvana's show that night on a shared bill with the Smashing Pumpkins, Cliffs of Doneen, and local act Bullet LaVolta—Kurt held Lord's hand and carried her guitar. When soundman Craig Armstrong asked who Lord was, Kurt told him she was his girlfriend. The next night, Lord joined Cobain in Rhode Island for Nirvana's show at Club Babyhead.

Lord would later tell Everett True that it was "a brief but nevertheless real relationship where you learn the person's entire history in a very short time." Although their relationship only lasted around two months—until Courtney Love entered the picture and pushed Mary Lou out of Kurt's life—for Lord the chemistry between them was unforgettable. "It was like I had known him for years and we were just getting reacquainted. It was as special as it gets."

A–

In advance of its street release on September 24, 1991, promotional copies of *Nevermind* made their way into the hands of music journalists, who were overwhelmingly receptive to Nirvana's DGC debut. *Entertainment Weekly*'s David Browne gave the record an A– grade; *Select* gave it four stars out of five, ranking Nirvana among the likes of the Pixies, Sonic Youth, and Jane's Addiction. In the *New York Times*, Karen Schoemer wrote, "*Nevermind* is more sophisticated and carefully produced than anything peer bands like Dinosaur Jr. and Mudhoney have yet offered." And in *Melody Maker*, Cobain loyalist Everett True called it "an album that would blow every other contender away."

Boston Globe critic Steve Morse was less enthusiastic, describing *Nevermind* as "generic punk-pop" and insisting "the band has little or nothing to say, settling for moronic ramblings by singer-lyricist Cobain." Ira Robbins' three-star assessment of the album in *Rolling Stone* was mixed. "If Nirvana isn't onto anything altogether new," he wrote, "*Nevermind* does possess the songs, character, and confident spirit to be much more than a reformulation of college radio's high-octane hits."

By year's end, the trio had the last laugh when *Nevermind* was voted as the best album of the year in The *Village Voice*'s renowned "Pazz & Jop" critic's poll.

Crisco Kid

On September 24, as *Nevermind* was released across America, Kurt was holed up with Lord, waiting to play a second, all-ages gig at the Axis. The album was major news, with a perfectly timed MTV piece about the band—which showed

Novoselic playing Twister backstage in his underpants the night before while covered in Crisco Oil—running that day.

When Krist and Dave went down to Newbury Records with DGC's Mark Kates, they saw what seemed like a thousand kids clamoring to get their hand on the disc. With mainstream rock radio slow to pick up "Teen Spirit" (which debuted at #27 on *Billboard*'s Modern Rock chart on September 21) and alternative radio still a miniscule piece of the market, much of the buzz about the band came courtesy of a twenty-two-year-old named Amy Finnerty, a young MTV programmer who believed in the record so much that she threatened to quit her job if it wasn't added to the channel's playlist. Her bosses acquiesced.

Meanwhile, at the Axis show, Nirvana opened with a cover of the Vaselines' "Jesus Doesn't Want Me for a Sunbeam," worked out a new song called "Pennyroyal Tea," and played a version of the Rolling Stones' "Satisfaction" in the style of Devo's cover of the song.

East Coast Run

With the Melvins in support, Nirvana's tour resumed on September 25 at Club Babyhead in Providence, Rhode Island, where the group unexpectedly revisited "Vendetagainst" before jamming on the Stooges' "Dirt."

The next night, at the Moon in New Haven, Connecticut, the trio played part of Led Zeppelin's "Dazed and Confused" at the outset of a gig plagued by Cobain's guitar woes, which resulted in two attempts at "Blew."

The artwork on this in-store hanging display was lifted from Nirvana's *Nevermind* LP, depicting a baby underwater and being lured by the almighty dollar. The image became a controversial talking point during the fall of 1991.   *Author's collection*

In Trenton, New Jersey, at the legendary punk venue City Gardens, New York's Das Damen—veterans of Twin/Tone Records, SST, and Thurston Moore's Ecstatic Peace label—took over as the opening band, promoting the *High Anxiety* EP, their first release for Sub Pop (and ultimately their swan song). Nirvana then played an efficient fifteen-song set before taking Route 1 up to New York, where they checked in to the Roger Smith Hotel for the weekend.

Big in the Apple

Saturday, September 28, was a big day for New York–area Nirvana fans, some of whom got to witness the group perform a rare, eight-song semi-acoustic set at the Manhattan branch of Tower Records. Aside from tracks from the new record, Cobain strummed his way through the Vaselines' "Sunbeam" and the unreleased numbers "Dumb" and "Pennyroyal Tea."

According to witnesses, Kurt recorded the packed performance on his own personal boom box and treated himself to Oreo cookies and milk during the set. When the show was over, the trio threw the remaining cookies out into the crowd.

That night, at a sold-out Marquee show, Nirvana reteamed with opening act the Melvins for an incendiary sixteen-song set that was notable for its inclusion of the recently written "Rape Me."

Disco Kurt

Cobain had called Mary Lou Lord and asked her to come to New York for the Marquee gig, so she hopped on a Greyhound to New York with a friend and arrived when the show was nearly over.

Lord wrote about this night in a 2010 blog post for Oedipus1.com called "About Me and Kurt (What You Don't Know)," explaining, "I made it backstage and Kurt came up to me with a huge smile [saying] 'There you are!'"

After introducing Mary Lou to Kim and Thurston from Sonic Youth, among many others, Kurt took her to a late-night party and then on to a club with a jukebox full of disco, where they hung out until 5:00 a.m. "Kurt Cobain himself—I know, hard to picture—danced his ass off!"

Kurt's Deal

After friend and journalist Everett True told Cobain backstage at the Marquee that he was in New York that weekend to cover the Breeders, Cobain insisted True introduce him to front woman Kim Deal, who, of course also doubled as the Pixies' bassist. Deal was recording the follow up to her band's 1990 album *Pod* in a nearby studio when they showed up the next day at the sessions for what would become 1993's *Last Splash*. According to True, Kurt was very shy and nervous about meeting one of his heroes.

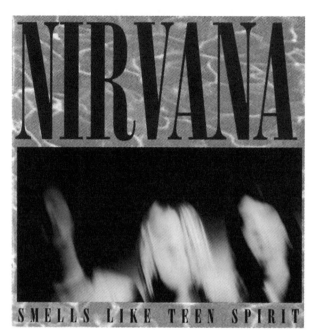

SMELLS LIKE TEEN SPIRIT

The 1991 45 sleeve for the French pressing of "Smells Like Teen Spirit." *Author's collection*

"That's Me!"

The first time Cobain saw himself on MTV was in his Manhattan hotel room on September 29. He called his mother excitedly, repeatedly telling her, "That's me! That's me!" Mary Lou Lord personally witnessed his reaction. For a brief moment, Kurt felt his accomplishment was worth celebrating, even if his early brushes with fame hadn't been what he had imagined.

Like Hotcakes

Nirvana's handlers underestimated what they had with *Nevermind*, and as a result the initial pressing of the album was quickly deemed too short for demand. When it debuted at #144—moving half of its available copies in the first week, largely on the strength of the first airing of "Teen Spirit" on MTV's *120 Minutes*—the company quickly ordered more.

Within days, the network moved the clip into daytime rotation, and as a result, in many US markets, the record was sold out. Within weeks, thanks to increased video airplay and the unexpected radio success of the single, the album achieved a gold certification from the Recording Industry Association of America for sales of 500,000.

Playing with Fire

The *Nevermind* tour progressed into Pennsylvania, where the band played at Graffiti in Pittsburgh on September 30. Backstage following the gig—which saw Kurt shove his guitar neck into Dave's snare drum—and after an altercation with club personnel, Cobain reportedly took his frustration out on the couch, setting it alight with a pack of matches. When the local Fire Marshall arrived to arrest Nirvana's road manager, the club's operator declined to press charges. (Kurt had already left the building.)

The next night, in Philadelphia, Kurt's stomach ailment was making him miserable, prompting Nirvana to cut the show short and skip the encore. Fans inside J.C. Dobbs screamed "Sellout!" It was ironic, considering the miniscule venue held a few hundred people at best, as did most of the venues on the first leg of the tour in support of the album.

Buck's Party

By the time the tour rolled into Athens, Georgia, on October 5, Nirvana had been playing nightly for a solid week in spaces like the 9:30 Club in Washington, D.C., and the Cat's Cradle in Chapel Hill.

During a drunken but reportedly amazing performance at the 40-Watt Club, Cobain jumped up and pulled a projector screen out of the ceiling. The destruction continued as Grohl kicked his drums over before beating them with live microphones. The audience was encouraged to join in the fun, and

A set list in Cobain's handwriting from Nirvana's gig at J.C. Dobbs in Philadelphia on October 2, 1991.   *Author's collection*

when all was said and done, Kurt, Dave, and Krist piled up their equipment in the middle of the stage and said goodnight.

Despite all the chaos, local hero Peter Buck—guitarist in R.E.M.—invited the band back to his Athens home for a party. This, of course, was a secret thrill for the members of Nirvana—especially Cobain, who had long admired the band.

Lord Lost

Five days later, Nirvana arrived in Cleveland, Ohio, for a gig at the Empire Concert Club. Despite a playful opening to the show that included a brief jam on Queen's "Another One Bites The Dust," Cobain was in a bad way backstage, according to Mary Lou Lord, who had come to Ohio to see her boyfriend.

Although Lord was unaware at the time (as were Kurt's bandmates), he had been withdrawing from drugs. He was miserable, cursing and complaining much of the time about how small the venues were, and how bad the sound had been the night before at Stache's in Columbus.

The next day, October 11, Lord traveled with the band to Detroit's Saint Andrew's Hall, but she flew home to Boston the following morning, despite Cobain's pleas for her to come with him to Nirvana's next gig in Chicago. She was worried she might lose her job, but mostly she had concerns about becoming a burden on the band. Plus she didn't want to frighten Kurt away.

Leaving him alone and headed toward Chicago would soon become one of Lord's biggest regrets. "If I had only known how much he had wanted to be loved," she told Everett True, "I would have shown him exactly how I felt."

Here Comes Courtney

With Windy City natives Urge Overkill opening, Nirvana astounded the audience at the Metro on October 12, wrapping up their show with a fit of destruction. After switching instruments with Grohl, Cobain destroyed Dave's drums, forcing the band's tour manager to buy him a new kit.

Backstage was Courtney Love, who had arrived in Chicago earlier that day to surprise her boyfriend, Smashing Pumpkins front man Billy Corgan. Love had borrowed money from her attorney Rosemary Carroll (who happened to also be Danny Goldberg's wife) to make the trip, but their relationship came to an abrupt end after she showed up at Corgan's place to find him with another girl.

Hours later, upon discovering Nirvana were playing that night, Love took a strategic cab ride to the Metro. That night she reconnected with Kurt, and before long Love—who had once worked as a stripper at Jumbo's Clown Room in Hollywood—was sitting on his lap for everyone in the room—including Danny Goldberg, Butch Vig, Corgan's Pumpkins bandmates, and the guys in Urge Overkill—to see.

To Kurt, Courtney was blunt but charismatic and full of excitement. He couldn't help but be attracted to her. Things got hot and heavy quickly as the couple retreated to the Days Inn hotel room Cobain was sharing with Grohl. Confronted by a "Do Not Disturb" sign, Dave opted to crash in soundman Craig Montgomery's room instead.

"I Feel Fine"

The next day, Love flew home to Los Angeles, and Nirvana went north for two performances in Minneapolis. Cobain seemed happy strumming songs on an acoustic guitar inside the record store Northern Lights. A quick version of the Beatles' "I Feel Fine," affirmed his outlook.

Grohl had yet to replace his drum kit, and that night at First Avenue—as with the next few nights' shows—he made do with Urge Overkill drummer Blackie Onassis' kit as Nirvana played a lengthy, twenty-two song set that concluded with "Rape Me."

"Fuck It!"

By the time Nirvana took the stage at Mississippi Nights in St. Louis on October 16, it had become more apparent than ever that the trio's ever-growing popularity could no longer be contained in such small venues.

As slam-dancers and stage-divers collided with the security down the front, things got violent, and when Cobain was repeatedly struck by fans and bouncers alike he became visibly annoyed. Finally, Novoselic warned the audience to "mellow out," but when a bouncer stepped on his effects pedal and broke it, Kurt stopped the band and gave the offender a piece of his mind.

When the band had to stop the show for a fifth time, Kurt—frustrated with the way the venue's security had treated its audience—yelled, "Fuck it! You all want to get up on the stage? Well come on up!"

Most of the club stampeded forward. Grohl left the stage while Cobain and Novoselic bravely stood among the crowd. Fifteen minutes passed before order was restored, and another fifteen before the band could play the rest of their forty-five-minute set.

Punched Out in Dallas

Parts of Nirvana's gig at the Dallas nightclub Trees were captured on video and can be found easily enough on YouTube. The footage shows Cobain getting pushed in the face by a bouncer after smashing the venue's monitor board with his guitar. Kurt had been made angry by the fact that the club had been oversold tickets in a flawed attempt to meet demand. And while it was the inferior sound system that first set him off, the fact that he was suffering from the flu and was mixing alcohol, cough syrup, and antibiotics didn't help matters either.

Staggering to the stage, Kurt led the band through four songs before taking aim at the board as if his guitar was a hatchet. When security came after Kurt, ready to fight, Novoselic and Grohl stepped in and broke it up. The trio walked offstage to chants of "Bullshit, bullshit" and went back up into their dressing room.

The venue's management was livid, but after both sides realized there might be a riot if the show didn't continue, soundman Craig Armstrong managed to get some of the undamaged channels on the monitor console working enough that the band could resume playing.

When the band returned to the stage, the aforementioned bouncer taunted Cobain for the next five songs. Then, when Kurt jumped into the crowd with his guitar during "Love Buzz," the security guard came after him, pretending to save him from the savage audience while grabbing his hair and punching him in the ribs. Later, the same bouncer punched Cobain in the back of the head and kicked him when he was down on the ground.

"I swung the butt-end of my guitar into his face," Cobain told *Melody Maker* in 1993. "He bled and proceeded to beat the shit out of me."

The band nearly got away after the show when their tour manager quickly stuffed them into a taxi, but somehow the bouncer and a pack of what Kurt described as his "heavy metal vomit friends" caught up with them. The bouncer stuck his bloody hand into the taxi and attempted to choke Cobain before the driver pulled away.

Smashing In-Store

Additional shows in Texas with openers Sister Double Happiness at the Vatican in Houston and Liberty Lunch in Austin on October 20 and 21 were sandwiched either side of a fully acoustic, afternoon record-store performance at Austin's Waterloo Records, where the band played a short take on Lynyrd Skynyrd's "Sweet Home Alabama" in response to audience heckling for "Freebird." Following a partial performance of "Dumb" and full renderings of "Polly" and "About a Girl," Cobain smashed his acoustic guitar.

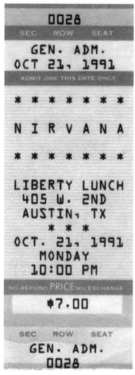

A ticket stub from Nirvana's show at Liberty Lunch in Austin, Texas. By this point in the *Nevermind* tour, the band had begun to open all of their shows with the Vaselines' "Jesus Doesn't Want Me for a Sunbeam," instead of "Drain You" or "Aneurysm."

Author's collection

Tijuana

On the afternoon of October 24, Nirvana played another in-store gig at Off the Record in San Diego. Although it was announced as an acoustic event, the record store failed to secure a left-handed guitar for Cobain, and as a result the band ripped through a six-song electric set comprising "Dumb," "Here She Comes Now," "About a Girl," "Polly," "On a Plain," and "Been a Son."

Afterward, the band signed copies of *Nevermind* before departing for that night's show at Iguana's in Tijuana, Mexico. From the start of their set, the Tijuana show was troublesome, as fans on the balcony began jumping down eighteen feet and landing on the backs of audience members below.

Meanwhile, the mosh pit turned violent as some of the kids in the crowd got trampled into the concrete floor after repeatedly swarming the stage and diving off. According to attendees, the venue's insufficient security watched dumbfounded as kids staggered around injured. Understandably, the Nirvana camp couldn't wait to leave and never come back.

Headbanger's Dress

One of the most hilarious moments in Nirvana's career occurred on the after-noon of October 25, 1991, when Cobain and Novoselic filmed their segment for MTV's heavy-metal show *Headbangers Ball*. At the time, Nirvana were crossing over to the hard-rock audience, but instead of embracing it the band's founders resisted while going along with their promotional obligations.

Kurt showed up for the interview wearing a hideous yellow ball gown. When asked about it by host Riki Rachtman, Cobain said that he was bothered by the fact that his bassist had refused to wear a tuxedo. "You didn't get me a corsage," he balked.

When asked about the quick rise of the band, Cobain snapped, "Everyone wants to be hip." After a few more insipid questions, Kurt looked incredibly bored as he sat smoking a cigarette and wearing sunglasses.

An ad from music industry trade magazine *HITS* touting the power of "Smells Like Teen Spirit." At the time, Geffen executives were hoping to make Nirvana a pop crossover success. They succeeded.

Author's collection

Meanwhile, Krist did his best to humor the host before Rachtman introduced "Smells Like Teen Spirit" as that week's #5 "Skullcrusher."

"We have a big bandwagon and we have a bunch of Clydesdale horses, multi-colored horses pulling it," Novoselic said sarcastically. "People are just jumping on. It's kind of like a Ken Kesey acid trip–type thing, passing Kool Aid around, and we're like the Merry Pranksters."

"We hope that we can turn people on to more music than just these mainstream Harley-riding rock bands," Krist continued. "All the bands that I support are really real and have good values."

If Nirvana's co-founders felt awkward as Rachtman introduced a video by Infectious Grooves (a band that had recently opened for Ozzy Osbourne), Kurt let his freak flag fly to the metal world, listing his influences as Lead Belly, Bikini Kill, the Breeders, the Pixies, R.E.M., the Melvins, Patsy Cline, the Vaselines, and Public Enemy.

In one final amusing remark, Novoselic explained how Kurt would bring his song ideas for the band to collaborate on. "It's kind of like the Play-Doh fun factory," he smirked. "We just stuff it in and it comes out."

Slick

For all Kurt and Krist's sarcasm and disinterest, the MTV appearance was remarkably effective. Within a week, *Nevermind* had sold 500,000 copies.

Not that Cobain was happy about crossing over into the hard-rock and heavy-metal world. Loathing the idea that his trio had found a following with Guns N' Roses' fans, he began to speak out against *Nevermind*'s production, pointing the finger at the album's engineer, Andy Wallace, when expressing his dissatisfaction.

"This album is so slick-sounding," he told *New Route*'s Michael Deeds that month for the magazine's December issue. "I've probably offended my own beliefs as a self-proclaimed punk rocker. A few years ago, I would have hated our band."

Rock for Choice

Nirvana headlined the Palace in Los Angeles that night as part of the Rock for Choice benefit show after the leader of the Feminist Majority Foundation called and personally requested the band. Because Grohl was tight with L7, and Cobain an advocate for the feminist movement, the band signed on alongside tour openers Sister Double Happiness and Hole, who had also played with the trio a night earlier in Tijuana.

Ironically, L.A.'s often-misogynistic heavy metal hoi polloi came out to watch their favorite new band. In front of such high-profile performers as Mötley Crüe's Tommy Lee and Guns N' Roses front man Axl Rose, Novoselic spoke about his political views, including the right to equality, keeping abortion legal, and getting then-president George H. W. Bush out of the White House. Message aside, Nirvana's performance left everyone inside the Palace amazed by the band's sheer power.

Shooting Up for Love

After a week spent keeping in touch by telephone prior to their shared gigs in Tijuana and Los Angeles, Kurt and Courtney became closer and closer. When they finally got together again for the first time since Chicago, they got drunk and had sex in the back of Nirvana's tour bus. The party continued in Kurt's hotel room at the Beverly Garland after the gig as the couple watched the evening broadcast of *Headbangers Ball*.

According to Charles Cross, that same night Cobain and Love—a recovering addict—arranged to score heroin on Kurt's suggestion. At first Love was reluctant, but she wanted to be with him, so she agreed to do it that one time. Courtney was afraid of needles, so Kurt injected her dose.

On October 26, Nirvana went up to San Francisco to play a concert at the Warfield Theatre with L7, Sister Double Happiness, and Urge Overkill, but the next day they were back in Los Angeles for another gig at the Palace with support from the Wipers' Greg Sage and Hole. That night, Cobain and Love took heroin together once again.

Although Courtney was hesitant at first, Kurt pouted when she said she didn't want to shoot up again, and she relented. As she told Everett True, "I thought, 'I'll go back to this, I guess.'"

Robes

Onstage at the Warfield, Nirvana wore red-and-black terrycloth robes that featured their logo embroidered on the back in honor of Bill Graham. The robes were a gift from the revered San Francisco concert promoter, who had died in a helicopter crash in inclement weather the night before when his helicopter flew into a high-voltage tower on the way back from a show by Huey Lewis & the News at the Concord Pavilion. As one of the most important figures in the concert business from the late 1960s until his death, Graham had produced the Philadelphia portion of the 1985 Live Aid concerts, plus the Amnesty International tours A Conspiracy of Hope (1986) and Human Rights Now! (1988).

Halloween Homecoming

Nirvana wrapped up the first leg of their tour in support of *Nevermind* with three Northwest shows that also featured support from their friends in Mudhoney.

The original plan, when these gigs were booked two months earlier, was for Mudhoney to headline. But in recent weeks, based on the massive response to Nirvana's new album, it was decided that Mark Arm's band would open for Cobain, Novoselic, and Grohl at the Fox Theater in Portland and the Commodore Ballroom in Vancouver. The group's Seattle gig was also moved from the Moore Theater to the larger capacity Paramount Theater to accommodate the large demand for tickets.

For this gig, Cobain had his friends Ian Dickson and Nikki McClure serve as onstage go-go dancers. Meanwhile, John Silva and the powers that be at DGC had hired a video crew—to the tune of $250,000—to document the event. The backstage area was full of industry types, friends from around the I-5 Corridor, and family members.

Somewhat awkwardly, Kurt's ex-girlfriend Tobi Vail—the inspiration for much of *Nevermind*—was also there, as he had asked Bikini Kill to open the show. They hung out that night, and Vail wound up sleeping in Kurt's hotel room. This time, however, she was on the floor, as were a handful of other friends.

Uneasy with Fame

That night at the Paramount, Cobain went outside to get some air and saw Mudhoney's Matt Lukin and his old Cling-On buddy Steve Shillinger smoking a joint. Shillinger needled Kurt about his quick ascent to fame, marveling at how "Teen Spirit" was on MTV every three hours.

Nirvana's front man felt defensive and uneasy about his newfound stardom. He snapped back about how he was unaware of such things, pointing out that he didn't have a TV in his car—not that he was really homeless anymore, between his tour-bus bunk and his nightly hotel rooms with regular access to cable television.

Although his life had changed drastically in just two months, Kurt was tired of the constant ass-kissing from writers, DJs, and hangers-on. "I'm really tired of people telling me they like our music," Cobain said in the November 2 issue of *Melody Maker*. "I wish someone would come up to me and say we suck."

As Grohl would explain to David Fricke a decade later, Kurt began to feel remorseful about their success—as did Dave and Krist, to a lesser extent. "Kurt felt, in some way, guilty that he had done something that so many people had latched onto," Dave explained, citing the band's shift into larger and larger venues. "We were all in such a weird state. It was such a whirlwind that no one really had any time to feel comfortable with it."

19

For This Gift I Feel Blessed

Blowing Up

Duck!

In early November 1991, *Nevermind* reached #35 on the *Billboard* 200. When pressed for an explanation of the record's meteoric ascent—the quickest yet for a band of Nirvana's ilk—Geffen head Ed Rosenblatt was left scratching his head. "We didn't do anything," he told the *New York Times*. "It was just one of those 'Get out of the way and duck' records."

After peaking at #4 in the weeks before Christmas, the album reached #1 in the US on January 11, 1992, bumping Michael Jackson from the top spot. In early 1992, the disc was selling a staggering 300,000 copies a week.

Writing of the record's surprising sales figures in the *New York Times* in 1992, Jon Pareles marveled, "Suddenly, all bets are off. No one has the inside track on which of dozens, perhaps hundreds, of ornery, obstreperous, unkempt bands might next appeal to the mall-walking millions."

As a result, major labels were throwing piles of money at alternative-rock bands. A perfect example was one-time Amphetamine Reptile band Helmet, who signed to Interscope in early 1992 for $1 million.

"Nirvana came along and delivered the goods—they made the Cars album, the Knack album for punk rock," Thurston Moore would note in a June 1991 interview posted on Nirvanaclub.com, describing the band's allure. "It was what people were waiting for—the best of metal meets the best of R.E.M."

Teenage Wasteland

Nirvana flew to the United Kingdom on November 4 and began a monthlong European trek at the Bierkeller in Bristol the following night. For parts of the tour, the trio were supported by Eugene Kelly's new band Captain America (eventually renamed Eugenius after a lawsuit by Marvel Comics) as well as Urge Overkill and Hole.

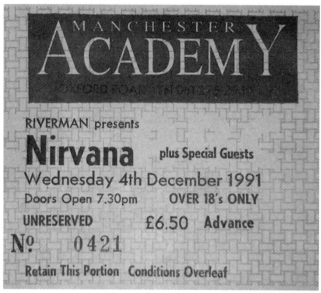

A ticket stub retained from Nirvana's Manchester Academy show
from December 4, 1991.   *Author's collection*

These shows—which included stops at London's Astoria Theatre, the Loft in Berlin, Austria's Vienna Arena, Teatro Castello in Rome (for a show that was broadcast on the Italian television channel Videomusic), and the Queen Margaret Union at the University of Glasgow—featured regular appearances by "Rape Me," "Dumb," and "Pennyroyal Tea," all of which were in consideration for Nirvana's next record.

On the final night of the tour, at Salle Omnisports in Rennes, France, on December 7, the band opened with a surprise rendition of the Who's 1971 anthem "Baba O'Riley." Nirvana were clearly in a playful mood, with Novoselic and Grohl providing lead vocals on the song.

Oh, Lord

Nearly three weeks had passed since Cobain last saw Mary Lou Lord when she surprised him by flying to the UK in early November. Although they had been talking on the phone four or five times a week in their time apart, Kurt was stunned when she surfaced backstage in Bristol.

His fame aside, Lord knew something had changed with Kurt. His stomach ailment appeared to have gotten worse, and she suspected he had been using heroin. He was well aware of her disapproval of his drug use. The next day, in London for the Astoria gig, Lord asked Kurt if he had met someone else. Although he had fallen for Courtney Love, he lied and told Mary Lou he was just tired.

They went back to his hotel room, where Lord sat several feet away as Love called Kurt to confront him about Mary Lou at 3:00 a.m. London time. A Boston DJ had told the Hole front woman that day during an interview that his friend Lord was Cobain's girlfriend. This obviously didn't sit well with Courtney, who barked back, "I'm Kurt's girlfriend!"

Love laid down the law via the long-distance line, with Kurt being very careful to speak cryptically, so as not to upset his guest. He used words like "yes" and "OK" when Courtney warned that if she even heard the name Mary Lou Lord again, their relationship was over.

The next morning, Cobain—who just weeks earlier would have done anything for Lord—asked her how she was going to get to Wolverhampton, the location of Nirvana's next gig. Lord lied and said she still had things to tend to in London.

Although she wasn't entirely sure, she took this to mean their relationship might be over, until Kurt gave her a copy of his tour itinerary and a goodbye kiss. Despite the mixed messages, she would know they were truly done when she heard what Kurt had to say when Nirvana appeared on television the following night.

Cranky Cobain

During their time in London, Nirvana were summoned to an *NME* photo shoot cold Brixton studio for a cover feature that was to run later in the month. But despite the attention (not to mention the record sales) Cobain wasn't just irritable—he was in drug withdrawal, and feeling serious discomfort in his stomach.

With Kurt hunched over on his side in a fetal position, smelling of vomit, having just thrown up, the band's publicist offered him a piece of gum. In front of writer Mary Ann Hobbes, Cobain snapped at his handler, "I'll do the fucking pictures, OK?" adding, "I just want to be left alone."

The Word

On the afternoon of November 8, Nirvana went to Limehouse Studios in London to film an appearance on *The Word*. The band played a spunky rendition of "Smells Like Teen Spirit," and an unprovoked Cobain announced to the audience, "I just want everyone in this room to know that Courtney Love, the lead singer for the pop group Hole, is the best fuck in the world."

Cobain's language caused a stir, which only earned the band more notices in the UK papers. When word reached Love, who was still in the US with Hole, she was secretly thrilled. Kurt had publicly proclaimed her as his lover.

Lord was stunned and understandably crushed. She flew home to Boston a few days later, intent on putting Cobain in her rearview mirror. But instead of that being the end of it, she claims Love started harassing her via her answering machine. For a period of time lasting into early 1992, Courtney was relentless, leaving numerous disturbing messages at all hours, despite the fact Mary Lou says she never tried to reconnect with Cobain.

Stickers

By the time Nirvana rolled into Frankfurt on November 12, Cobain had begun to miss some of the group's soundchecks. Working with soundman Craig Armstrong and Urge Overkill drummer Blackie Onassis, Novoselic and Grohl tried to keep things light by working through a version of Led Zeppelin's "Heartbreaker."

In advance of the show, Novoselic covered his shirt with stickers he took from a recent issue of *Metal Hammer* magazine. As he began to perspire, the stickers—featuring logos of bands like Metallica, Alice Cooper, Ozzy Osbourne, and Extreme—fell to the floor, at which point he picked them up and pressed them against the foreheads of the kids in the front row.

At the end of the show, Kurt dived into the crowd. As the crowd passed him around, he was stunned to find some of the audience members sticking their hands into his pants pockets in search of souvenirs and cash.

Throwing Fruit

On November 17, before Nirvana's gig in Mezzago, Italy, began, Cobain took a basket of fruit and sandwiches from the catering table and started throwing them into the crowd. But this rock star move backfired, and as Nirvana launched into "Drain You," the fruit and other items were tossed back at the band.

If that wasn't enough, Novoselic had been having problems with his bass during that opening number

An Italian magazine advertisement promoting Nirvana's November 1991 shows in the country in support of *Nevermind*.
Author's collection

and tossed the instrument skyward in frustration. When it came back down, it smashed to the ground and was left beyond repair.

The show finally got started after Krist borrowed Urge Overkill bassist Eddie "King" Roeser's bass, and after a second crack at "Drain You" a few minutes later, the concert carried forth in front of Nirvana's rabid Italian following.

Destruction in Belgium

Hole joined the trek for Nirvana's gig in Ghent, Belgium, on November 23. Back together again with Love, Kurt seemed genuinely happy. It showed midway through the concert when he dived into the crowd and solicited fans to go-go dance atop the band's speaker cabinets for the rest of the gig.

For a rendition of Lead Belly's "Where Did You Sleep Last Night," Novoselic and Grohl switched instruments. Dave played Krist's bass on his back until Hole guitarist Eric Erlandson ran out onto the stage to tackle Cobain for fun. Just as Kurt threw his guitar, Dave got up and out of the way.

The show culminated with Krist—who was playing bass naked—and Kurt smashing their instruments into the stage in tandem. When large pieces of Novoselic's bass flew into the crowd, one fan was struck in the mouth, knocking out a tooth, causing serious bleeding, and sending the fan into shock with uncontrollable convulsions. Krist felt horrible about what had happened and tried to comfort the injured fan as medics tended to him backstage.

Two nights later, on the afternoon before the band's gig at the Paradiso in Amsterdam, the Belgian fan who had been hit by a piece of guitar showed up in the company of a law-enforcement official, looking for Nirvana to right some wrongs.

For several hours, Nirvana's equipment was impounded. The band's tour manager worked to right the wrongs and a financial settlement was reached just prior to the band's stage time. An undetermined amount of cash was handed over to the victim, and the equipment was released. The show went off without a hitch.

Lenny Kravitz Calling

When Cobain and Love had to spend time apart that month, they assumed secret hotel-check-in aliases. In joking tribute to the headline grabbing Hollywood couple of the moment, Kurt became *Mama Said* rocker Lenny Kravitz, while Courtney played the role of Lisa Bonet, star of the smash 1980s sitcom *The Cosby Show*.

The names made it slightly easier for them to reach one another by telephone in their respective rooms. As they would talk to each other multiple times a day, one has to wonder how many European hotel desk assistants heard Cobain say, "This is Lenny Kravitz calling for Lisa Bonet."

Hilversum

Nirvana tracked radio sessions for Dutch radio stations VPRO and VARA on November 25. Although the group had been asked to play "Polly" and "Teen Spirit," respectively, for the Nozems-a-Gogo and Twee Meter de Lucht In programs, they did not honor the request. Instead, they performed an unknown song for which Kurt and Krist switched instruments, plus their well-known Lead Belly and Velvet Underground covers, and a jam with Grohl alone on guitar and vocals.

Tracked in under an hour in Jingle Production Room 2 at NOB Radiostudio, this Netherlands performance wasn't exactly Nirvana's finest moment. When all was said and done, Cobain and Grohl apparently ran from the facility, while according to Nirvanaguide.com, Novoselic told those on hand, "We know when we fuck up," as he walked out the door with a shrug.

Top of the Pops

Days after reteaming with openers Captain America and bringing in additional touring companions Shonen Knife—the all-female Japanese pop-punk group who were among Kurt's favorites—Nirvana went into Studio C at BBC's Elstree Centre in London to perform "Smells Like Teen Spirit" for the weekly chart show *Top of the Pops*. However, while most bands to appear on the show would lip-synch to their pre-recorded song, Kurt refused to mime. After much deliberation, Kurt was allowed to sing live over Nirvana's backing track. It wound up being one of the most memorable and hilarious examples of the ridiculousness of miming to records ever filmed.

Feeling especially defiant, Nirvana's front man performed his vocals in a much different style than usual, sounding more like Sisters of Mercy's Andrew Eldritch or the Misfits Glenn Danzig than Kurt Cobain. Strumming his guitar with a grin at first—and then not at all—he was clearly making a mockery of the pop-music program, at one even point shoving the microphone into his mouth as he sang.

Meanwhile, Novoselic barely mimed his part, swirling his bass around his head as Grohl poked his drumsticks high in the air while flashing a wide, unforgettable smile. As the audio faded out at Kurt's solo, some kids in the crowd jumped on the stage and Cobain dropped his live microphone to the ground.

Later, in the car ride back to his hotel, he cracked a wry smile. He knew he had enough fame and power to pull off such a stunt. It was November 28, the same day *Nevermind* passed sales of one million copies in the US.

Teen Spirit in Edinburgh

With a night off in Scotland on December 1, the members of Nirvana made a covert appearance at the Southern Bar in Edinburgh. Planned as a charity concert for a local children's hospital, the show had been organized by their friends from the Cateran, several of whom were now playing as the Joyriders.

As a means to ensure a capacity crowd, the Joyriders had circulated handbills for the gig indicating that they would be playing with some "very, very special (American) guests)" during Nirvana's show at the nearby Calton Studios two nights earlier. Only two dozen audience members remained at the Southern Bar, however, when it was eventually announced that Nirvana would not be playing. Instead, Cobain and Grohl took the stage sans Krist to play a five-song set that included "Polly" and a cover of "Twist Barbie" by Shonen Knife, members of which band happened to be at the Southern Bar that night, with this homage by Kurt providing a secret thrill.

Three Bottles of Bordeaux

If Novoselic's alcohol use continued to be overshadowed by Cobain's own excesses during the European tour, Krist was still in a bad way and his wife Shelli, who was trying to keep up with him, was not much better off. Nirvana's bassist had developed an appreciation for Bordeaux and was downing three bottles of wine on his own each night. He was also smoking hash whenever he could.

A ticket stub from Nirvana's show at Rock City in Nottingham, England, December 3, 1991. Captain America—fronted by Eugene Kelly of the Vaselines—opened this and several other shows on the band's UK tour.   *Author's collection*

Marital Musings

By the tail end of the tour, Kurt and Courtney were using heroin whenever they got together. On the morning after Nirvana's concert at Kilburn National Ballroom, they decided to get married.

Courtney couldn't wait to share the news with anyone and everyone, but her friends responded with concern. As she explained to *Rolling Stone*'s David Fricke three years later, "Kim Gordon and Julie Cafritz told me when me and Kurt got serious, they spelled it out. 'You know what's going to happen? You'll become junkies. You'll get married. You'll OD. You'll be thirty-five. You'll try to make a comeback.'"

"I don't give a fuck," she continued. "I love this guy."

Jonathan Ross

Nirvana were booked to play their forthcoming single "Lithium" on the UK TV show *Tonight with Jonathan Ross* on December 6. And after two soundchecks of the song—one with and one without Cobain—at the Greenwood in advance of the band's taping, it appeared as if, for once, Kurt might not thumb his nose at the medium of television.

Guess again. The band deviated from the plan and played a fiery rendition of "Territorial Pissings," much to the frustration of the show's host and producers. At the end of the performance, they smashed their instruments to bits. Ross was caught off guard but made good fun of the unexpected change, telling the audience after the performance that Nirvana were available for children's birthday parties and bar mitzvahs.

Wendy's Letter

While Cobain was in Europe, his mother Wendy couldn't keep her pride over her son's success to herself. She fired off a letter to the Aberdeen *Daily World*, which the paper printed under the headline, "LOCAL 'TWANGER' MAKES GOOD, MOM REPORTS."

Mrs. O'Connor boasted about the fact that Nirvana—also featuring Aberdeen's Novoselic—had just sold one million records via Geffen, and were currently near the top of the *Billboard* album survey. "I know the chances of making it are slim-to-none for many, but two boys who never lost sight of their goals, Kurt and [Krist], have something to really smile about these days."

Hilariously, Cobain's mom closed the letter by reminding him—if he happened to be reading—to brush his teeth and eat his vegetables. "You are truly one of the nicest sons a mother could have."

Canceled

Following Nirvana's performance at France's Transmusicales Festival on December 7, the group elected to scotch their six remaining gigs. Shows in Ireland and Scandinavia were shelved. Cobain cited his stomach woes and stress.

A House and a Baby

Back home in Seattle that month, the Novoselics decided to buy a home in Greenlake. With the proceeds he had earned from sales of *Nevermind*, Krist put a sizable down payment on the $265,000 home.

Cobain also returned to Washington and spent time with his good friend Carrie Armstrong. A week before Christmas, he returned to his mother's home for some pot roast. He spent time with his six-year-old half-sister Breanne, giving her an early Christmas gift of art supplies, and found his stepfather Pat treated him differently now that he had become a star. It made him uncomfortable.

That night, December 17, Armstrong and some other friends joined Kurt on a journey to Seattle in a rented Pontiac Grand Am. They were off to see his beloved Pixies play at the Moore Theater in support of their fourth and final album, *Trompe Le Monde*.

Days later, Courtney Love flew to Seattle, where she and Kurt planned to spend the holidays together. In the company of Armstrong, Kurt introduced Courtney to his mother. The meeting went surprisingly well.

It was around this same period that Cobain likely learned that his fiancée was pregnant with his child. She had conceived at some point during Nirvana's European tour.

Touring with Pearl Jam and the Chili Peppers

Just after Christmas, Nirvana embarked on a West Coast tour with the Red Hot Chili Peppers, who were experiencing the best sales of their career with new album *Bloodsugarsexmagik* and its lead single "Give It Away." The funk-punk collective's fifth album (and first for Warner Bros) had been released on September 24, 1991—the same day as *Nevermind*.

Pearl Jam, a Seattle band formed from the ashes of Mother Love Bone, were tapped to open the shows. Fronted by enigmatic vocalist Eddie Vedder, the quintet were on the rise with their debut Epic album *Ten*, released that August and propelled by the single "Alive."

The five gigs—in noticeably larger, 20,000-capacity venues—started on December 27 at the Los Angeles Memorial Sports Arena and wrapped on January 2 at the Salem Armory Auditorium. For Nirvana, and especially Kurt, touring had become a circus. Backstage, publicists, managers, label people,

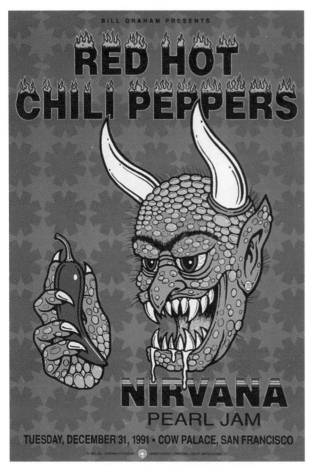

A poster from Nirvana's historic 1991 New Year's Eve concert supporting the Red Hot Chili Peppers. The opening act that night was Pearl Jam, another Seattle band who had just released their debut album, *Ten*.   *Author's collection*

and concert promoters were pulling him in a million different directions, while Hollywood types like River Phoenix and Keanu Reeves sought his attention.

Kurt had no interest in any of it. His only real source of solace and security was Courtney. When he was reserved, she became his protector. A perfect example was the sign she put on the door of their San Francisco Hotel after Nirvana's New Year's gig at Cow Palace: "No Famous People Please. We're Fucking."

Although additional two shows were booked at the Seattle Center Arena and the Pacific National Exhibition Forum in Vancouver on January 3 and 4, they were canceled after both Cobain and RHCP singer Anthony Kiedis became ill.

BAM!

In advance of the Los Angeles show, Cobain was still in a bad way with heroin. According to interviewer Jerry McCully's article for *BAM*, which ran the first week in January, Kurt had "pinned pupils, sunken cheeks and scabbed, sallow skin," and was "nodding off occasionally and in mid-sentence."

Although Kurt didn't ever reveal publicly that he was using heroin, his situation was clearly visible to the people around him. He did confess to McCully what insiders had known for weeks: that he and Courtney were planning to marry. Although he looked like a wreck, he explained, "I've never felt so secure in my life and so happy. It's like I have no inhibitions anymore." He also spoke about having a family, suggesting he was already aware of Courtney's pregnancy.

Hotel Hell

Although Novoselic and Grohl had been aware of their front man's drug problems, it hit home just how messed up Cobain and Love had become when they went to see Kurt in his hotel room one day. "They were nodding out in bed, just wasted," Grohl told Michael Azerrad in 1993. "It was disgusting and gross."

They're All Wasted

That night, in Los Angeles, Cobain felt out of his element in such a big hall. As a result, the band broke into the Who's "Baba O'Riley" for just the second time ever to start their set.

"We just got on the stage and I'm like, 'Krist, I feel like we're the Who!'" Cobain told *Flipside* the following spring. "He said, 'Hey, let's play "Teenage Wasteland!"' We didn't know how to play it, but the 'Louie, Louie' chords worked out."

Kurt the Ghoul

According to Eric Erlandson, Kurt and Courtney spent part of this same week sleeping on the floor of his apartment—until he threw them out for using heroin.

As the tour progressed, Novoselic realized he needed to get himself together, partly in response to seeing what was happening to Kurt. He decided it was time for him to dry out.

"He looked like shit," Krist would tell *Musician* magazine in October 1993. "He looked like a ghoul. But what am I going to do? It's his fucking trip, his life, he can do whatever he wants."

Novoselic Quits

On January 1, 1992, Krist Novoselic quit drinking, for three months, at least. He later claimed that he decided to give up booze after he smacked his head on an overhead heater in a hotel room. When he woke up the next day covered in blood, he realized he had had enough.

"I had to learn how to deal with [success]," he told *Melody Maker* that summer. "Either ignore it or deal with it like a mature adult instead of running away into booze."

When he did return to alcohol consumption later in the year, following the group's tours of Japan, Australia, and Hawaii, it was on the condition that he would not drink when the band played. He also embraced moderation.

Like a Hurricane

Fame affected each of the three members of Nirvana very differently. When things got crazy for the band in late 1991, Cobain took it hardest, as he was the face of the band.

"Nirvana was caught up in this hurricane," Dave Grohl told the Cleveland *Plain Dealer* in 2003, "but unlike Kurt, I was able to stand outside of it all." Grohl—and to a lesser extent Novoselic—would reap the perks of being in one of the biggest bands in the world without having to deal with being the focus of everyone's attention.

For example, Grohl could hang backstage at rock shows and never get hassled. In the press, Novoselic spoke proudly of going to the local Safeway and buying his own fruits and vegetables without a spectacle. Of course, he didn't care if people stared or pointed at him. He went on his merry way.

Cobain had the opposite reaction to Nirvana's newfound notoriety. It got to the point that when he tried to go see bands, he would get heckled by drunken concertgoers who would congratulate him on his band and his fame and then criticize him for his drug problems. Now, almost any time he went out in public, he was getting hassled. In another instance, he found himself harassed by a group of jocks who threatened to beat him up, hoping to make him cry.

As Grohl told *Kerrang!* writer Joshua Sindell in 2001, "I think that for someone like Kurt, whom millions of tortured kids related to, it was difficult for him to live his own life . . . I felt for him."

When asked about it directly in the May 1992 issue of *Flipside*, Kurt responded with a question. "You mean, what is it like being in the Beatles?" he asked. "I hope to eventually someday turn into Pete Best—just brush it under the carpet and forget about it." At the time, Kurt was still reeling from the *BAM* article, and felt bitter about how the magazine made him out to be "this self-destructive-heroin-taking little dork."

When asked how it felt to be at the top of the *Billboard* album charts during Nirvana's weekend in New York, Cobain revealed his mixed feelings. "It's like being #16, only even more people kiss your ass," he told *Melody Maker*.

SNL Rehearsals

On January 8, Nirvana flew to New York for their first appearance on NBC's legendary sketch-comedy series *Saturday Night Live*. Cobain brought Carrie Armstrong, his mother, and his fiancée along for the trip. While the rehearsals on the Thursday were upbeat, Kurt was taken aback when members of Nirvana's road crew told him how "hot" his forty-seven-year-old mother was.

On Friday evening, the band's *SNL* rehearsals focused on the two songs slated for the next evening's broadcast. In addition to the obligatory version of "Smells Like Teen Spirit," the band had agreed on "Territorial Pissings." The show's producers weren't pleased with the choice, but Nirvana had enough clout—with their record having just gone to #1—that they wouldn't be swayed.

Sassy

Despite requests from the likes of *Rolling Stone* and the *New York Times*, Kurt agreed to just one interview during Nirvana's stay in New York, and it was on the condition that Courtney was included. That Friday, January 10, they were interviewed by and photographed for a cover story in the teen magazine *Sassy* about rock 'n' roll love.

When Christina Kelly's article ran two months later, fans learned that Kurt had bought Courtney a vintage engagement ring from 1906 with a ruby in the middle and that he too wore an ornate band on his finger. Elsewhere in the piece, Cobain revealed a penchant for cross-dressing, and how Love preferred him in floral-print baby-doll dresses.

Following the *Sassy* interview, Cobain went to meet up with Nirvana at MTV's New York studios to record a live nine-song mini-concert (eight originals plus "Molly's Lips") for the network's alternative-rock show *120 Minutes*. The performance, which depicted Nirvana sounding far rawer than on their recent album, was edited down into individual clips of tracks like "Drain You" and "On a Plain."

Alphabet City

Despite his fame, Cobain bought his own heroin in the Alphabet City neighborhood without fanfare during the band's Manhattan visit. Meanwhile, following the publication of the *BAM* article, Novoselic and Grohl made Nirvana's handlers at Gold Mountain aware of the extent of Kurt's drug problem. Silva and Goldberg prayed for things to go off without a hitch and worried about what to do with their junkie rock star.

At a New York photo shoot that afternoon with Michael Lavine, Kurt—by now a full-blown addict—was so strung out that he was falling asleep standing up. His plan was to shoot up early in the day, sober up in time for the *SNL* broadcast, and then inject again after the show.

When he wasn't nodding off at Lavine's, Kurt was alert enough to hand-draw the fish logo from Flipper's 1982 debut *Album—Generic Flipper*, rendering the crudely stenciled logo right onto the T-shirt he would later wear on television.

Are You a Hooker?

Days into their New York trip, Kurt and Courtney shifted hotels to the Omni Park Central, which had just undergone a $60 million renovation. Despite Cobain's fame, the couple—whom some had started calling Kurtney—stuck out like a sore thumb in the company of the hotel's millionaire guests.

At one point, Love got locked out of Cobain's hotel room after she went to buy a pack of cigarettes in the lobby. Hotel reception and security thought she was either a prostitute or a thief, or both, and tried to have her arrested, until Carrie Armstrong came to retreive her. It didn't help that she was incoherent and wearing only her underwear.

Sobered Up for *SNL*

En route to NBC Studios at 30 Rockefeller Plaza that afternoon, Cobain—who refused to take a limo like a typical "rock star"—was throwing up. Backstage in the band's dressing room, he lay on a sofa in agony. A request for a brief visit by the show's host, actor Rob Morrow, went ignored. When the daughter of the network's president sought out an autograph, Kurt wouldn't comply.

Deep down, Nirvana's front man was filled with anxiety and fear. "It was really scary," he would confess to *Flipside*. "There's a lot of stress to play

Recorded with WFNX Boston radio host Kurt St. Thomas on January 12, 1992, *Nevermind, It's an Interview* was a promotional-only release issued by Geffen that year. The interviews were recorded in New York on the night of Nirvana's *Saturday Night Live* debut.   *Author's collection*

on a television show live, you can hear every little note that's missed. I don't know, it kinda bugs me."

Somehow, when it came time to perform "Teen Spirit," Kurt felt well enough to play. He looked like hell—all sickly, with a strawberry Kool-Aid dye job, torn jeans, and a worn cardigan sweater—yet he didn't just pull off a great performance: he triumphed.

Of course, Kurt didn't do it alone. A shirtless Grohl attacked his drums while Novoselic—now sporting a big beard—jumped up and down like a crazy person.

Forty-five minutes later, Nirvana returned to the stage to take on "Territorial Pissings," destroying their instruments at the song's conclusion. Grohl's drum kit flew off its riser, Novoselic threw drums in the air, and Cobain jammed the neck of his guitar into a speaker. It was as destructive and exultant as rock 'n' roll television would ever get.

Kiss This

Minutes later, as the *SNL* credits rolled, Novoselic—sporting a Melvins T-shirt—gave Cobain a French kiss directly in front of the cameras. While Kurt would claim it as his idea—a way of riling any homophobes who might be watching—Novoselic remembered it differently.

He knew how hard Cobain had been struggling with his newfound fame and was deeply worried about him. "I just wanted to make him feel better," Krist explained to Cobain biographer Cross. "At the end of it all, I told him, 'It's going to be OK. It's not so bad, OK?'"

Saturday Night Dead?

In the early morning hours of January 12, 1992, after Nirvana had successfully rocked *Saturday Night Live*, Cobain skipped the cast party in favor of a two-hour late-night interview with a journalist. Afterward, according to Charles Cross, he retreated to his suite at New York's Omni hotel and shot a lethal dose of pure "China white" heroin into his arm.

Sometime around 7:00 a.m., Love reported woke up and found Cobain stiff and unresponsive. His skin was an aqua-green color. Fearing Kurt was dead, Courtney panicked as she worked to resuscitate him. Splashing cold water on his face, she moved his arms and legs, eventually punching him in the solar plexus twice until he started gasping for air and finally became conscious.

Despite Cross' account, Nirvana author/insider Everett True and photographer Michael Lavine both contend that Cobain didn't actually overdose in Manhattan on this night. According to True, Kurt's OD came a year later, after Nirvana's 1993 Roseland Ballroom show.

The Legacy of *Nevermind*

By the time Nirvana made it to the Salem Armory Auditorium, they had learned that *Nevermind* had sold a staggering two million copies. In the early months of 1992, it continued to sell at a pace of about 300,000 copies per week in the US. In a stunning achievement, Nirvana—with their sophomore record and defiant outlook—had become the voice of Generation X.

In the years that followed, *Nevermind* continued to be a steady catalog seller as new, younger fans discovered the band. In March 1999, it was certified by the RIAA for sales of ten million.

As Michael Azerrad would explain in his 1993 book, the band's timing was perfect. "This was music by, for, and about a whole new group of young people who had been overlooked, ignored, or condescended to."

Unaware of what was about to happen, Cobain spoke of his aspirations, and of filling that void, to Mike Gitter in August 1991. "It'd be nice for a fifteen-year-old kid in Aberdeen to have the choice of buying a record from a band like us," Kurt said, revealing how he'd read about punk bands in *Creem*, but because of where he lived he couldn't act on it until the Melvins saved him from his Iron Maiden albums. "That wasn't an opportunity I had when I was growing up."

When asked by Gibson.com in September 2011 about what made *Nevermind* such a classic record, Novoselic pointed to the album's diverse mix of sonic approaches. "The individual songs have personality, and that's because we approached ever song for its own sake," Krist said. "And, of course, those hooks! Kurt Cobain was a gifted artist and he knew how to write a song."

20

Don't Expect Me to Lie

Controversies

Nirvana's honest outlook on the music business and celebrity was as refreshing as it was hilarious. Not since the Sex Pistols provoked the UK by using foul language on national television in December 1976 had the music industry seen such rebellion. Cobain, Novoselic, and Grohl used the media to ridicule the things they thought were lame. From products to celebrities to the government, little was safe from their chastisement.

Anti-Budweiser

While on tour in Europe in August 1991, Nirvana came out against America's behemoth brewer Anheuser Busch. When asked what kind of beer they get brought backstage, Cobain bemoaned Budweiser. "The stuff tastes like piss," he told *Rockview*. "It's not even real piss with really good vitamins, it's just watered down piss."

Grohl and Novoselic agreed with Kurt's assessment of the brand, as the front man added, "It just proves [that] you could feed the general public anything, whether it's Vanilla Ice or pissy beer."

Trashing Guns N' Roses

A year before Nirvana had their public showdown with Guns N' Roses at the 1992 MTV Awards, Krist and Kurt had begun criticizing the band in interviews. Speaking backstage at the Reading Festival in 1991, a month before the release of *Nevermind*, Novoselic called GNR "assholes" in an interview with writer Crazy Chris, criticizing them for "throwing whiskey bottles around."

Cobain took it one step further, rejecting the idea that Guns N' Roses' tattoos, alcoholism, and supposed rebellious image did anything to make them special, and referring to them instead as "obnoxious idiots." To Kurt, GNR's version of rebellion was fake, while Nirvana's was authentic. "If anyone has a brain, they'll realize that [Nirvana] is more sincere than Guns N' Roses."

Dice—"A Stupid Fuck"

Speaking to *Kerrang!* writer Mike Gitter the same month, Cobain revealed that he took exception to comedian Andrew "Dice" Clay's hateful comedy about women. Kurt spoke openly about how Clay truly offended him, calling him an "asshole" and "a stupid fuck."

"I hate people like that," he raged. "[He] should be shot."

Economic Collapse

By November 1991, Nirvana were the hottest rock band in the United States, but that didn't stop Novoselic from putting down the land of the free in an interview with *NME*. Calling America a "fucking police state" and an "awful place" where education was bad and citizens were spoiled by their cable television and cheap gasoline, an irate Krist opined how nobody cared that "the USA is completely fucking over the Third World."

If that wasn't enough, Novoselic expressed hope for a total economic collapse and blamed President Bush for his inferior efforts to preserve the economy. He was adamant that that a new depression was forthcoming that would make the '30s feel like a vacation.

Dissing Pearl Jam and Alice in Chains

Speaking to *Flipside* in early 1992, Cobain took aim at fellow Seattle acts Pearl Jam and Alice in Chains, revealing that he objected to having Nirvana lumped in with them. Calling them "corporate puppets" who jumped on the alternative-rock bandwagon, Kurt griped that these groups were once a part of the "hairspray/cock-rock scene" but had suddenly stopped washing their hair and started wearing flannel.

Two months later, speaking to *Rolling Stone*, Cobain expressed a desire to "be erased from my association" with Pearl Jam. He also expressed an obligation to advise kids of "false music" that was claiming to be underground or alternative.

Asked for a response, Pearl Jam founder Jeff Ament suggested that Kurt must have had some deep-seated insecurities to think that his group was riding Nirvana's coattails. Ament, who had played with members of Mudhoney in proto-grunge band Green River before forming Pearl Jam, concluded, "We could turn around and say that Nirvana put out records on money we made for Sub Pop—if we were that stupid about it."

"Eighties"

When Nirvana's second single from *Nevermind* was announced, Cobain was apprehensive about it because of the song's similarity to Killing Joke's 1984 single "Eighties." A decade and a half after the fact, Dave Grohl told *Metal*

Hammer, "They were sort of pissed off about it and there was potential litigation, but it never came to that."

In 2002, Dave met up with Killing Joke front man Jaz Coleman in a New Zealand hotel bar. They hung out and got drunk together, talking about everything from UFOs to the World Bank. Later that evening, someone reminded Jaz—who happened to be dressed up like a priest that night—about how Nirvana kind of plagiarized his song.

"He just went for my throat," added Grohl—who went on to contribute drums to Killing Joke's eponymous 2003 comeback album. "I had to run off down the road. But someone calmed him down and we ended up laughing about it. Eventually."

"Nirvana" Settlement

In May 1992, a British band from the 1960s with the same name as the one used by Cobain, Novoselic, and Grohl came out of the woodwork, filing a lawsuit against the group and Geffen Records over rights to the moniker. Gold Mountain intervened and promptly settled with the aging British band—whose members included Patrick Campbell-Lyons and Alex Spyropoulos—paying them $100,000 for continued use of the name.

21

Married, Buried

Far East and Too Far Gone

North Spaulding

W hen Kurt Cobain and Courtney Love returned to Los Angeles in mid-January, they settled into a nice, $1,100-a-month apartment at 448 N. Spaulding in West Hollywood, between Melrose and Fairfax. At the time, Kurt—who didn't really care for Los Angeles but wanted to be with Courtney—was up to a $100-a-day heroin habit. When he wasn't nodding off, he would listen to and create music, draw, paint, and watch television.

Flipper Babies

With fatherhood at the forefront of his mind since Love had conceived in late 1991, Cobain couldn't help but thinking that his child might be born with defects. Some of his concern was valid—with their intravenous drug use, he and Courtney weren't exactly living an ideal lifestyle—but some of his fear could also be blamed on a teenage fixation with drawing deformed fetuses and "flipper babies" in his journals.

Cobain's apprehensions were assuaged the following month when Love visited a Beverly Hills gynecologist who specialized in birth defects, and who purportedly explained to the couple that using heroin in the first trimester of pregnancy posed few risks.

A subsequent ultrasound revealed the baby was healthy. After watching their unborn child on video, Kurt was entranced. He marveled how it looked like a "little bean." Courtney took this as a sign from God and decided to stop taking heroin.

Months later, having determined the baby's gender, the couple settled on Frances as her first name, in honor of Frances McKee from the Vaselines. Her middle name, Bean, came from the nickname Kurt had given her while watching the sonogram.

Detox

With Nirvana's tour of Australia and Japan less than two weeks away and Courtney committed to stop using heroin to preserve the health of her baby,

Kurt agreed to detox with her. Having already experienced withdrawal on the road the previous fall, he knew it would be a good time to try and get clean. As he acknowledged in his journal, there was no way he would be able to get heroin in the Far East, and he didn't want to have to go through withdrawal halfway around the world.

The couple checked into a Holiday Inn together for several days, where they experienced side effects including diarrhea, vomiting, chills, and insomnia. Nirvana's tour manager Alex MacLeod would check up on them daily and bring them food and cigarettes. Quitting heroin was hard enough, Love rationalized—even with sleeping pills and methadone—but even if she was pregnant, there was no way she was giving up smoking.

"Come as You Are"

Cobain still looked like a wreck when he left his self-imposed detox a week later, on January 19, to shoot the video for *Nevermind*'s second single. Kevin Kerslake directed the clip on location at Cobain's apartment in Wattles Garden Park in north Hollywood and inside a hangar at Van Nuys Airport.

According to Kerslake, Cobain picked him because he liked his work on Mazzy Star's "Fade Into You." At the band's insistence, their faces were obscured by water and cellophane, but any attempts to try to slow the momentum of the single, or *Nevermind*, were unsuccessful.

"[Kurt] was sick of himself and all the other guys ending up on all the magazine covers," the director told the website blankmaninc.com in 2013. "All the newsstands were filled with their pictures, and I think they were just over the publicity aspect of doing promotion." By the time the video debuted on MTV the following month, "Come as You Are" was already a radio hit.

Hippie-Crites

With the success of *Nevermind*, *Rolling Stone* avidly pursued Nirvana for a cover story throughout late 1991 and early 1992. At first, Cobain was against the idea, and adamantly refused the notion of an interview to his managers, who thought such exposure was essential.

Kurt went so far as to write a letter to the magazine in early 1992, although he never sent it. "At his point in our, uh, career, before hair loss and bad credit, I've decided I have no desire to do an interview," he explained in the letter, published in *Journals*, revealing that he failed to see the benefit of such coverage and dismissing the magazine's average reader as "a middle-aged ex-hippie turned hippie-crite."

Instead of sending the letter, however, Kurt relented to Gold Mountain's enthusiasm for a cover. By February, he was sitting down with Michael Azerrad.

Physeptone Down Under

The tour of Australia got underway on January 24 at Sydney's Phoenician Club. Gigs with revered US alternative-rock band the Violent Femmes followed over the next three days at the Big Day Out Festival in Sydney, Fisherman's Wharf in Gold Coast, and Brisbaine Festival Hall.

On the January 28, however, Nirvana were forced to cancel a series of shows because of Cobain's stomach pain. Cobain, who was down to just one hundred pounds, couldn't keep any food down and was vomiting blood. Despite his condition, according to his journal, he overheard an emergency-room nurse dismiss him as "just a junkie" and left the facility, refusing treatment, as a result.

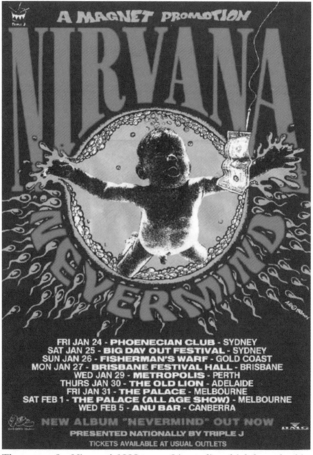

The poster for Nirvana's 1992 tour of Australia, which launched in Sydney on January 24 and was advertised to conclude on February 5 in Canberra. The trek actually wound down with a pair of gigs at Sydney's Coogee Bay Hotel on February 6 and 7.

Author's collection

Nirvana's handlers put him in contact with an Australian doctor who had worked with the likes of Keith Richards. He prescribed Physeptone—which contained methadone—and Cobain felt better.

Hormoaning

In support of Nirvana's tour dates in Australia, New Zealand, and Japan, DGC released a six-song EP called *Hormoaning* to those markets on February 5, 1992. Comprising the B-sides from the "Teen Spirit" single ("Even In His Youth" and "Aneurysm") plus the four cover songs from the band's October 1990 John Peel session, the disc became hotly sought after across the globe.

In Australia, just 15,000 copies were released—10,000 on CD, 1,000 on cassette and 4,000 on burgundy twelve-inch vinyl. Upon its release, it reached #2 on the Australian album charts. The Japanese pressing had a wider availability and different artwork, culled from the inside of the *Nevermind* booklet.

An advertisement for Nirvana's performance with the Violent Femmes at Fisherman's Wharf in Gold Coast, Australia, on January 26, 1992.
Author's collection

Riot Gear

The Nirvana tour continued onward to Brisbane, Adelaide, and Melbourne, where the band played four shows without incident. However, on February 5 at the Australian National University Union Bar in Canberra, an uprising broke out when close to a thousand fans couldn't get inside to see the band in the small venue. As the band played inside, Nirvana's Aussie disciples ripped off the venue's doors. Finally, when police arrived in riot gear, the crowd disbursed.

Lying to *Rolling Stone*

Despite all of the drama inside the Nirvana camp, *Rolling Stone* trailed the trio during their run of shows in the Far East for an article that would run that April. In the wake of the *BAM* piece and the recent suggestion in *HITS* that he "had been dancing with Mr. Brownstone," Cobain lied about not doing heroin (although at the time of the interview he was probably using prescription methadone instead).

Calling drugs "a waste of time," he told *Rolling Stone*, "They destroy your memory and your self-respect and everything that goes along with your self-esteem." He also said he had given up alcohol because his stomach condition made him feel so weak.

It was Kurt's contention that—after one hundred shows in five months—he just needed a break from the road to alleviate his stress. "I'm going to get healthy and start over," he insisted, adding, "This tour has definitely taken some years off of our lives."

Turning Japanese

After a one-off gig in Auckland, New Zealand, on February 9, Nirvana flew to Japan for a short, four-date, mid-month run of shows in Osaka, Nagoya, Kawasaki, and Tokyo. Before the tour got underway, Cobain caught up with the ladies in Shonen Knife, who took him to dinner at a bratwurst restaurant in Osaka and gave him gifts of toy swords plus a new motorized Chim Chim monkey.

The next night, while onstage at the Kokusai Koryu Center, Kurt told the crowd he was cutting the show short so that he could go see some of Shonen Knife's performance at a nearby venue. As the only blond-haired man at the club—and dressed in pajamas, no less—he was hard to miss.

Hitched in Hawaii

Love flew to Tokyo to be with Cobain for his twenty-fifth birthday, and she joined Nirvana in Hawaii for the last two shows of the tour at Pink's Garage in Honolulu. On the second night, after a cathartic set, Grohl was seen carrying Kurt from the stage. These would be the group's last gigs for four months.

On the flight to Honolulu, the couple decided they would stay on after the shows to get married and honeymoon in Hawaii. At the suggestion of John Silva, Kurt had a prenuptial agreement drawn up. Although he had yet to receive much money from the band yet—his gross income for 1991 was just under $30,000—the move would protect his future earnings. It

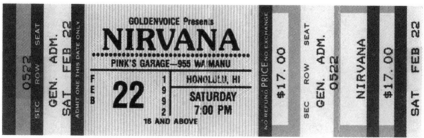

A ticket from Nirvana's show at Pink's Garage on February 22, 1992.   *Author's collection*

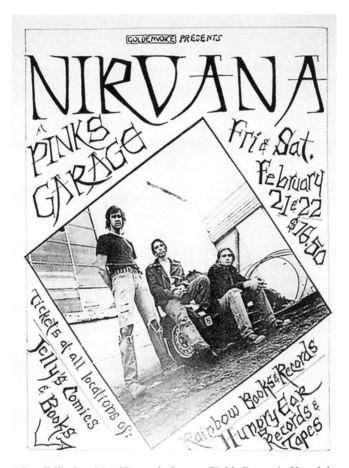

A handbill advertising Nirvana's shows at Pink's Garage in Honolulu
on February 21–22, 1992—the band's last performances for four
months.   *Author's collection*

wasn't a sticking point for Courtney, who had leveraged her fiancé's fame into
a $1 million record deal with DGC.

On Monday, February 24, 1992, at sundown, Kurt and Courtney were married on Waikiki Beach by a female non-denominational minister. Love wore a
silk dress that had once been worn by actress Frances Farmer, while Cobain
wore blue plaid pajamas. He confessed to writer Michael Azerrad the following
year that he took heroin beforehand so that he wouldn't get sick during the
ceremony.

Dylan Carlson flew in with his girlfriend for the wedding to be the best
man. As Kurt's best drug buddy, his presence served another purpose—he
brought Kurt enough heroin for the rest of his stay in paradise. It was the first
time Love and Carlson had met.

Dave Grohl, Alex MacLeod, and two members of the road crew rounded out the wedding party, which totaled just eight people.

When asked to explain the chemistry between him and Courtney, a love-struck Cobain told *Rolling Stone,* for its April 1992 article, "It's like Evian water and battery acid. And when you mix the two? You get love."

Not Invited

Despite the fact that Krist and Shelli Novoselic had been two of Cobain's biggest allies in the development and success of Nirvana, when it came time for the front man to marry Courtney Love, they were curiously absent. Kurt had uninvited them after finding out that Shelli had been talking to members of the group's inner circle, including Barrett Jones' girlfriend, about her concerns that Love had been doing drugs while she was pregnant.

After exchanging words with Kurt about the situation, Novoselic stood by his wife. He, like most sensible people, agreed that using drugs of any sort—let alone heroin—during pregnancy was inexcusable.

Instead of attending the Cobain wedding, Krist and Shelli packed for their February 25 return to Seattle. When all was said and done, the bassist assumed that the tensions between him and Kurt meant that Nirvana was no more. And, for the next eight weeks, the band was essentially over. After a cooling off period, however, Kurt and Krist began to talk on the telephone, and by April they were back in a room together.

Back to Los Angeles

When his supply of heroin was close to running out, Cobain pushed to return to Los Angeles. Although he disliked the City of Angels, heroin was in ample supply there.

Kurt and Courtney's apartment in the Fairfax district was extremely modest. According to journalist Michael Azerrad, the contents of Cobain's small living room were unspectacular: he had an unstrung electric guitar, a Fender Twin Reverb amp, a homemade Buddhist shrine, plus CDs and tapes by the likes of Calamity Jane, the Beatles, Cheap Trick, and the Cosmic Psychos. On the mantel sat a collection of naked plastic dolls that he and Love had collected.

Heroin Kit

By March, Cobain had resumed using heroin on a daily basis. He shot up at home but did his best to keep his habit from Love, who had so far managed to stay clean since their detox.

Kurt maintained a box (or heroin kit) where he kept his drugs, needles, rubbing alcohol, and spoons. It wasn't long before Courtney found out what he was up to and, in a fit of rage, broke every one of his unused syringes. She was trying to stay clean for their baby, and she didn't need the temptation, but Kurt would just go buy new ones.

I Hate Myself and Want to Die

That spring in L.A., Kurt wrote songs sparingly. He had already accumulated a number of tunes for Nirvana's next record, some which were songs the band had already been playing on their recent tours.

A spring tour of North American arenas, slated to start on April 10 in Chandler, Arizona, was scratched as Kurt delved deeper into drugs. Cobain's art from this era—undoubtedly fueled by his heroin addiction—included bizarre but imaginative depictions of skeletons and aliens.

Cobain was also obsessed with a bootleg VHS of R. Budd Dwyer, a Pennsylvania state official who had shot himself in the head on live television in 1987. It was around this time that he came up with a tentative title for Nirvana's third record: *I Hate Myself and Want to Die.*

This offbeat 1992 publicity photo of Nirvana, autographed by Cobain, features the front man in one of his cherished cardigans, wearing a shirt in support of the UK band Captain America and clutching a prized bottle of cough syrup. Meanwhile, Grohl and Novoselic seem to be mesmerized by a container full of rubber cement.   *Author's collection*

Exodus

Kurt's addiction had become so disgusting to Courtney that she insisted his handlers at Gold Mountain assist her in staging a formal intervention to get him some help. In late March, Kurt entered the Exodus treatment facility at the Cedars-Sinai Medical Center in Los Angeles at the suggestion of addiction specialist Bob Timmins.

Timmins felt that because of Cobain's medical issues, including his stomach condition, hospitalization was essential to him getting well. Although Kurt lasted just four days in the facility, the treatment helped. He began to take methadone, which stopped his withdrawal symptoms, but he refused to take part in the 12-step meetings.

Rolling Stone

Aside from the memorable cover, for which Kurt Cobain wore a homemade T-shirt emblazoned with the words "Corporate Magazines Still Suck," there were many key revelations in Michael Azerrad's article entitled "Inside the Heart and Mind of Kurt Cobain," which ran in *Rolling Stone* on April 16, 1992. Here are the five most interesting:

1. Kurt explained that he had no desire to be a representative for his generation ("I don't want to be a fucking spokesperson").
2. When *Rolling Stone* followed Novoselic to a cash machine, Krist was startled to discover that another $100,000 had just been deposited into his bank account.
3. Cobain revealed that he had spray-painted the line "Homosexual Sex Rules" on the wall of an Aberdeen bank in 1985 with Novoselic and Buzz Osborne in tow. When asked about it, Osborne denied this, swearing Kurt wrote "QUIET RIOT" in homage to the California metal band.
4. When Novoselic signed the contract on his five-bedroom Seattle home in December 1991, he had enough cash to buy the house outright. When a friend asked him about making his mortgage payments not long after Krist took occupancy, he replied, "What payments?"
5. When asked about what Nirvana's next album might sound like, Kurt suggested it would be a mix of acoustic music and raging catharsis. Cobain promised some "raw" songs and some "candy pop."

Flipside Lies

Perhaps as a means to counter Nirvana's mainstream exposure in *Rolling Stone*, Cobain agreed to talk to underground mainstay *Flipside* that March for the magazine's May/June 1992 issue. Yet when the revered punk rock 'zine asked tough questions of Kurt, he didn't always give straight answers.

Cobain lied about his heroin use, insisting he was off drugs. He was adamant that he wasn't a drug addict, and expressed frustration with journalists who reported otherwise, before conceding that he dabbled occasionally.

"I don't like to condone anyone using any kind of drugs," he said. When asked about the rumors that surfaced of him overdosing during Nirvana's tour of Australia, Kurt denied it, saying, "My body wouldn't allow me to take drugs on tour even if I wanted to. I'd die in a day."

Scaling Down

Cobain's unhappiness with Nirvana's level of fame had him thinking toward the future, and to ways he might be able to control the size of his audience. In the

Flipside interview, he imagined doing a club tour where the audience would be made up of diehard fans.

Kurt spoke of how kids might have to prove they were into Nirvana by wearing worn-out "Fudge packing" shirts to smaller venues, before dismissing the idea as unrealistic and impossible.

He also suggested that when Nirvana's next record came out and failed, he would lose the audience that "doesn't matter in the first place." He seemed excited by the notion of losing passive fans (those drawn to the commercial sounds of *Nevermind*).

Homeward Bound

Kurt and Courtney flew to Seattle in early April with plans to look for a house in Washington. Among the residences they considered purchasing was a Victorian mansion in Aberdeen.

Wendy's extended family took this as an opportunity to throw the couple a combined wedding reception and baby shower. Unfortunately, some members of the Fradenburg clan never got to meet Kurt's new wife, as in typical fashion the couple showed up several hours late for their own party. The event was slated for 2:00 p.m., but they didn't even show up until 7:00 p.m.

Bootleg Seizure

One night during their stay in Seattle, the couple went to Orpheum Records, where they were stunned by the number of Nirvana bootlegs being sold in the store.

Courtney took all the CDs, seizing them for being illegal, but not before she wrote a note to the store's absent proprietor for the clerk, who feared being fired. It read, "I need for you not to make money off my husband so I can feed my children. Love, Mrs. Cobain."

Kurt then took the pen from Courtney to write, "Macaroni and cheese for all."

Return of the Rat

On April 7, Nirvana came together at Barrett Jones' Laundry Room studios in Seattle for a quick one-day recording session. Grohl flew in for the session, having spent the time since Nirvana's Hawaiian gigs at home in Virginia with his mom while also writing and demoing his own solo material.

The band recorded "Return of the Rat" for an upcoming Wipers tribute album named *Eight Songs for Greg Sage and the Wipers*. Other songs recorded included "Oh, the Guilt"—which was eventually used on a 1993 split single with the Jesus Lizard—and "Curmudgeon," which would serve as one of the B-sides to "Lithium" later that year.

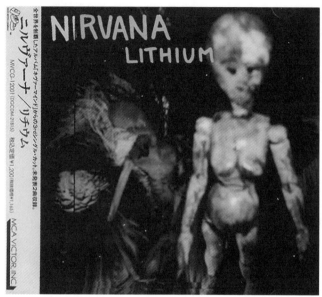

A Japanese promotional pressing of "Lithium," Nirvana's third proper single from *Nevermind*, which was officially released on July 13, 1992. The cover was a photo taken by Cobain of his original artwork.   *Author's collection*

According to Jones, the tracks were all done in one or two takes and came together quick and easy, despite the fact that his room and equipment were a far cry from what could be had Sound City. Curiously, the producer told Everett True that the trio hadn't even played the songs together before.

As for the atmosphere, Barrett would explain that things were obviously strained between Krist and Kurt, and they barely spoke during the session.

Reconnecting with Kim

The day after Nirvana's session, Cobain drove his trusty Valiant to Aberdeen, where he stayed for a couple of days before returning to Seattle to retrieve his sister. It was during these travels that that Kurt first learned his sister was a lesbian, and that she had become involved with a woman named Jennifer.

For a man who spoke so freely of his support of the homosexual world, Cobain found it hard to accept that his sister was gay. According to what Kim told Charles Cross, Kurt actually tried to talk her out of being a lesbian before he ultimately relented and gave her an accepting hug.

During a long chat on the swings at Sam Benn Park, Kurt shared a secret of his own with Kim, then twenty-two. First, he warned her of the perils of hard drugs, but she explained that she had no interest in such substances. Then he told her he had used heroin.

Although he didn't get into the specifics of his troubles with the drug, he was trying to come to terms with his problem in his own convoluted way. Coming clean about his addiction to Kim was harder than he thought, which explains why he lied and told her he had been drug free for eight months. In truth, it had been only a few weeks, and he was still taking methadone. Either way, she was stunned to find out her brother was a junkie.

Publishing Rift

Despite their recent reunion at the Laundry Room, Nirvana very nearly ceased to exist again when Cobain went back to Novoselic and Grohl to inform them that he was seeking a revision to the trio's publishing deal. Originally, Kurt had agreed to split the songwriting royalties evenly—despite the fact that he was the group's principal songwriter—in an arrangement crafted with lawyer Alan Mintz. But with millions of records sold since, he felt he deserved a bigger cut, and hired attorney Rosemary Carroll, who happened to be married to Nirvana's manager, Danny Goldberg.

Cobain's new proposal demanded a retroactive restructuring that would give him most of the money. Kurt wanted 100 percent of the publishing from his lyrics, with a 75/25 split on the music.

Even if Kurt's original arrangement was extremely generous, it was hard for Krist and Dave not to feel hurt by the notion of retroactivity. At the same time, the bassist and drummer very much wanted to continue as Nirvana. According to interviews given to Charles Cross by Rosemary Carroll, when Cobain implied he would break up the band if he didn't get his way, they were left with little choice.

"His focus was laser-like," Carroll explained, of Cobain's determination to get what he felt he deserved. From then on, Nirvana became more of a business than a band, and things between Kurt and Krist would never be the same.

Sayonara, Friends

Although Cobain was back in Washington, he made little time, if any, for his Olympia friends. He had essentially dropped the people he once held dear, including Ian Dickson, Calvin Johnson, Nikki McClure, Slim Moon, and Tobi Vail.

To most of them, it seemed Cobain had made his choice. He had chosen Courtney—who most of them disliked—and the very idea of him living in L.A. went against their values.

Of all the people he knew in Olympia, Kurt only remained close with Dylan Carlson. That association continued to be essential to Cobain, since Carlson had always been there to help him get drugs.

Back on Smack

In May, Cobain went back to Los Angeles, and by the end of the month, just six weeks after his detox, he was back on heroin. The timing was unfortunate, with a run of European dates—most of them rescheduled from December 1991—slated to begin in Dublin on June 21.

When Jesse Reed visited Kurt that month, Kurt spent most of the afternoon shooting up and waiting for a new heroin delivery. Once the drugs were delivered, the friends traveled to a nearby Circuit City store, where Reed watched Cobain plunk down close to $10,000 on new video equipment.

In a *Los Angeles Times* article that ran on May 17, Steve Hochman wondered why Nirvana—the most successful rock band in recent memory—were sitting out the lucrative summer touring market. "Nirvana's low profile has renewed public speculation that Kurt Cobain has a heroin problem."

Kurt acknowledged the difficulties of using heroin on tour in an interview with *Melody Maker* that July. He suggested it was an impossibility, "unless you're Keith Richards and you're being given blood transfusions every three days, and you have runners going out and scoring drugs for you."

Speaking to the UK music weekly on July 18, Cobain said, "If I'm going to take drugs that's my own fucking business." In interviews held in his L.A. apartment in the second week of June, right before the European tour, Cobain acknowledged that he still regularly used drugs but adamantly contended that he was "not a fucking heroin addict."

Cobain on Canvas

Despite Jesse Reed's concerns about his friend's deep spiral into addiction, he was surprised and pleased to see that Cobain's apartment was filled with art supplies and his unique, harrowing paintings. Kurt—who had acquired one hundred feet of canvas and was working with acrylic and oil paints—even spoke of quitting music and opening his own art gallery.

Kurt's work was mesmerizing. One painting with a vibrant orange tone was augmented by a diseased dogtooth, which hung on a string in the center of the canvas. A second displayed an alien with a small, shriveled penis on puppet strings. Elsewhere, he utilized photocopies of Love's sonogram as inspiration for a number of paintings. In others, he glued broken porcelain doll parts and newspaper clippings to his work.

European Tour Troubles

Bearing in mind Cobain's condition—and the fact that he and Krist were still barely talking during tour rehearsals—the band's European trek seemed doomed. Even with two of Kurt's favorite bands, Teenage Fanclub and the Breeders, in line to support Nirvana on most dates, his stomach problem and dependence on methadone made him irritable, and as a result the tour had its share of incidents.

During the second gig of the tour, at the King's Hall in Belfast on June 22, Cobain tried to break up a fight between a member of the venue's security staff and a fan. One of the guards took out his frustration on Kurt, punching him several times in the stomach. The following morning, Kurt collapsed during breakfast and had to hospitalized.

Cobain was forced to cancel several interviews as a result, and when a reporter witnessed the singer being carted out of the hotel on a stretcher—and taking into account his growing reputation—it led to speculation that Kurt had suffered a drug overdose. The media was later informed Cobain had been treated for acute stomach pains brought on by ulcers.

Two days later, Nirvana were in Paris for a show at Le Zenith. Much to Cobain's frustration, his management had hired a pair of private security men to stop him or Courtney leaving their hotel to buy heroin. The couple gave their security detail the slip and relocated to another hotel without notifying Nirvana's handlers. Kurt—who loved using hotel aliases—checked in under the name Simon Ritchie, the birth name of the late Sex Pistols bassist Sid Vicious.

"The Money Will Roll Right In"

By the time Nirvana arrived in Valencia, Spain, for a gig at Plaza de Toros on July 2, they had started playing a rendition of Fang's "The Money Will Roll Right In" as their set opener. Considering the

As evidenced by this ticket stub, Nirvana's first concert after a four-month break occurred at the Point in Dublin, Ireland. They were supported by Teenage Fanclub and the Breeders—fronted by Kim Deal from the Pixies—at this memorable gig.   *Author's collection*

This poster was designed to help publicize Nirvana's concert in Stockholm, Sweden, on June 30, 1992. Before the encore, Cobain pulled about fifty-dozen fans onstage to dance alongside the band during "Smells Like Teen Spirit."

Author's collection

A poster for Nirvana's concert at Plaza de Toros de Valencia in Valencia, Spain, on July 2, 1992.

Author's collection

disagreements they had been having over money in recent months, the timing seemed downright ironic.

The hard-stomping number found Cobain thumbing his nose at the very machine that made him a wealthy celebrity very quickly. Kurt wryly sang the lyrics about the joys of stardom and being "rich as shit." Perhaps the most memorable line in this song about conquering Hollywood in the 1980s—which the band played again in August during their headlining appearance at the Reading Festival, before it vanished from their set list—was "I'll get to fuck Brooke Shields."

Ready to Get Raw

During the band's overseas visit, Nirvana were interviewed for the July 25 issue of *Melody Maker*, and took the opportunity to talk about plans for their next album.

Cobain indicated that he was planning to move back to Seattle that year with the idea of heading back into Reciprocal Studios to record with Jack Endino at the eight-track facility. Later, he said he envisioned reworking the exact same material in a twenty-four-track studio with Big Black's Steve Albini, the veteran producer behind two of Kurt's all-time favorite records: the Pixies' *Surfer Rosa* and The Breeders' *Pod*.

Kurt, Krist, and Dave had unanimously agreed that they wanted to make a more raw-sounding album, with minimal resemblance to *Nevermind*. In fact, Cobain informed the music weekly that he had no intentions of writing another single as big as "Smells Like Teen Spirit."

Courtney's Contractions

After playing shows in Madrid and Bilbao on July 3 and 4, Cobain was forced to cut the tour short by two dates so that he could to return to Los Angeles with Love on the recommendation of her gynecologist. Courtney—who had just entered her seventh month of pregnancy—had begun having early contractions in Spain, which deeply worried the couple.

For the long return flight home on July 5, Kurt bought his wife a pair of first class seats so that she could lie down and be more comfortable. When they got off the airplane they went straight to Courtney's doctor, where they were advised that there were no concerns with her pregnancy.

Bathtub Flood

When Cobain returned home to his L.A. apartment, he discovered that a pipe had burst above their bathtub, causing the bathroom to flood. In most cases, this wouldn't have been a major issue, but for some reason Kurt decided it would be a good idea to store many of his prized possessions in the tub, believing it to be the last place thieves would look.

Kurt's blue Mosrite guitar, his precious journals and drawings, and two cassettes featuring his guitar ideas for Nirvana's third record were among the items ruined. The Cobains were thinking of moving soon anyway, because the very pregnant Courtney had grown tired of Kurt's heroin dealers showing up at their place at all hours. Still, the flood was the main motivation for them to ask John Silva to help them locate another home.

6881 Alta Loma Terrace

By late July, Kurt and Courtney had moved into 6881 Alta Loma Terrace in north Hollywood. The rent on the house, which sat in the Hollywood Hills on a bluff alongside several homes and ten apartments, ran to $1,500 per month. In order to get up to the bluff—which was remarkably private—residents would use a key to access an old crate elevator.

The house on Alta Loma Terrace had large windows with impressive views. And although Love would later describe it as "yucky" to Everett True, the house overlooked the Hollywood Bowl, and was unique enough to be used on location in films like Robert Altman's 1973 movie *The Long Goodbye* and the 1991 thriller *Dead Again.*

Cobain Ponders Suicide

That summer, Cobain's stomach woes had gotten so bad that he was considering taking his own life. The methadone he was trying to get by on wasn't cutting it. In his journal, he wrote of how he had "decided to kill myself or stop the pain," adding, "I bought a gun, but chose drugs instead." When he went back on heroin, however, it wasn't nearly as effective as it once had been in treating his ailment.

Producing the Melvins

Later that month, Kurt began working with the Melvins at Razor's Edge studios in San Francisco after being hired to produce the group's fifth album and major label debut, *Houdini*. The sessions were a disaster.

Osborne and Crover weren't willing to listen to Cobain's suggestions of ways to make their songs sound more alluring. Kurt threw his hands up in frustration and quit. Back in Los Angeles, he would later tell *Melody Maker* that the Melvins "don't understand anything."

Not surprisingly, Osborne remembered it differently in 2008, telling *Kerrang!* that his band was at odds with Cobain because they wanted to do a record that wouldn't alienate its fans. "It got to the point where Kurt was so out of control that we basically fired him and went our separate ways," Buzz said. As for Kurt's mental and physical state, Osborne added, "I don't have a whole lot of fond memories of that—it was an absolute tragedy."

More than a year later, when the Melvins' record was completed and released through Atlantic on September 21, 1993, Kurt wound up with a production credit for six tracks, including the song "Spread Eagle Beagle," for which he is credited as a percussionist. Another number, "Sky Pup," featured his guitar work.

Rehab Again

When he couldn't get any relief for his stomach pain through heroin use, Cobain agreed to try drug treatment again at the urging of Love and his management team. He went back to Cedars-Sinai on August 4, 1992, under the direction of a new physician, and consented to participate in a thorough sixty-day detoxification program at the hospital.

Days later, on August 7, Courtney checked into the same facility under an alias. Eight months pregnant, Love was suffering from exhaustion, exacerbated by a fax she had just received of an upcoming *Vanity Fair* cover story about her that was to hit shelves on August 11. In medical records that would be leaked later to the press, it was revealed that Love was being given methadone and prenatal vitamins.

During their respective hospitalizations, Hole guitarist Eric Erlandson became the couple's biggest ally. Eric, who was dating actress Drew Barrymore at the time, would visit them both and help to raise their spirits with discussions about music and other common interests, not to mention all they had to live for, with Courtney's due date just weeks away.

An ultra-rare US one-song promotional CD released to radio in the summer of 1992. "On a Plain" made it to # 25 on *Billboard*'s Modern Rock Tracks chart.   *Author's collection*

Appreciate Your Concern

Vanity Fair, Reading, and the VMAs

Frances Bean Is Born

At 7:48 a.m. on August 18, 1992, Frances Bean Cobain was born at Cedars-Sinai Medical Center. While Dr. Paul Crane was delivering Frances, her father was detoxing in the birthing room. She weighted seven pounds and one ounce.

Courtney had been in the hospital for the preceding week and a half on bed rest. When her contractions began that morning at 4:00 a.m. she went to retrieve Kurt from his room in the hospital's chemical-dependency wing. When Cobain resisted, because he was in serious drug withdrawal, Love ordered him to come down and help her through the delivery.

According to an interview Courtney later gave to Michael Azerrad, Kurt was vomiting and ultimately fainted during the final minutes of her labor. As a result, he missed the actual birth of his daughter.

Vanity Fair Hysteria

Frances Bean's birth was enough to cause a media circus. Coupled with the publication of the *Vanity Fair* article about the Cobains titled "Strange Love" and published on August 11, it sparked an onslaught of unwanted attention, with the focus on Love for using heroin during her pregnancy.

Lynn Hirschberg's depiction of the couple had them suddenly fearing they might lose custody of their baby, but the story was accurate, and was exacerbated by Courtney's own arrogance.

"We went on a binge," she told Hirschberg of the couple's time in New York for Nirvana's *Saturday Night Live* appearance in January. "We did a lot of drugs. We got pills, and then we went down to Alphabet City and we copped some dope. Then we got high and went to *SNL*. After that, I did heroin for a couple of months."

Elsewhere, a business associate who had been on the road with the couple told the magazine, "It was horrible. Courtney was pregnant and she was shooting up. Kurt was throwing up on people in the cab. They were both out of it."

That, observation, plus a close friend's report of the "sick scene" in the couple's apartment, would be enough to startle anyone. When the story broke, media hysteria was in full effect.

Although Love vehemently denied making the controversial comments, suggesting Hirschberg had made up the quotes, *Vanity Fair* stood by its story and its writer. The reality was that Love was far too trusting of Hirschberg, whom she had only just met. Lynn was a professional journalist who gave Courtney a false sense of security. Courtney had let her guard down and shot her mouth off. Simply put, she was too candid.

Within weeks, supermarket tabloid the *Globe* had picked up on the story, running a headline that proclaimed, "Rock Star's Baby Is Born a Junkie." Despite the fact that Frances had been born healthy, the publication ran a misleading picture of a deformed infant, implying it was "the Cobain baby."

Everyone had been talking about the subject, from syndicated radio host Howard Stern to Guns N' Roses front man Axl Rose. On tour in support of his band's *Use Your Illusion* albums, Rose—who was hardly a saint in his own right—told his audience, "Kurt Cobain is a fucking junkie with a junkie wife. And if the baby's born deformed, I think they both ought to go to prison."

A Loaded Gun

The day after his daughter was born, Cobain escaped his drug rehabilitation at Cedars-Sinai and went to buy some heroin. After shooting up, he returned with a loaded .38 pistol. Kurt reminded Courtney of a suicide pact they had made that promised they would kill themselves if they ever lost Frances.

Although both were deeply worried they might lose their baby in the wake of Hirschberg's article, Courtney knew she wanted to live for her daughter. She thought fast and tricked Kurt by telling him she wanted to go first. When he handed her the pistol, she talked him out of committing suicide. She gave the gun to Eric Erlandson, who got rid of it.

"I held this thing in my hand and I felt that thing that they said in *Schindler's List*. I'm never going to know what happens to me," she told *Rolling Stone* in 1994. "And what about Frances? 'Oh, your parents died the day after you were born.'"

"We were totally suicidal," Kurt told *Musician* a year earlier. "I just decided, 'Fuck it. I don't want to be in a band anymore.' I want to kill [Hirschberg]. As soon as I get out of this fucking hospital I'm going to kill this woman with my bare hands. I'm going to stab her to death."

Nearly Dead

Although Courtney had succeeded in keeping her husband from taking his own life, Kurt continued on a destructive path. The next day, he had heroin delivered to him at the hospital, found an empty room near Love's, and shot up. But he took too much and overdosed.

"He almost died," Love told David Fricke in 1994. "The dealer said she'd never seen someone so dead. I said, 'Why don't you get a nurse?'" A nurse was located, and Cobain was kept from death for the second time in two days.

Letter to MTV

From MTV News to daily newspapers, the media ran wild with the *Vanity Fair* story. Drug use aside, the article played Courtney out to be a money-grabber with a "train-wreck personality."

None of this sat well with Kurt, who was seriously bothered by the way MTV could make him famous and then embrace what he would describe in a letter to the network as "trash journalism." Taking aim at Hirschberg, he called her "an overweight, unpopular-in-high-school cow who severely needs her karma broken." He also vowed, "My life's dedication is now to do nothing but slag MTV and Lynn Hirschberg."

He signed the letter "Kurdt Kobain, professional rock musician. Fuck face," but never sent it.

Unfit Parents

On August 20, a Los Angeles County social worker showed up at Cedars-Sinai, allegedly clutching the *Vanity Fair* article and looking for an explanation. Love immediately went on the defensive—understandably—and began to square off with the Department of Children's Services employee.

Things didn't go well. The county launched a petition to have the Cobains deemed unfit parents. In the interim, their custody of Frances would be suspended, and the baby would be held in the hospital at a time when most newborns would go home with their mothers and fathers.

Only after a court-appointed guardian was arranged and approved by the county on August 24 was Kurt and Courtney's infant daughter released from the hospital. But the implications of Hirschberg's article were very serious in the eyes of the court, which insisted that the couple could only have supervised visitation with Frances Bean. Meanwhile, Kurt was ordered to undertake thirty days of drug rehabilitation, and both he and Courtney were subject to random urine tests until the matter was settled.

After much deliberation due to the lack of available, willing, and capable relatives at the time, and to satisfy the demands of the court, Courtney's estranged half-sister Jamie Rodriguez was recruited as the best option as guardian to Frances. Although she was hesitant at first, she went along with the Cobains' scheme after they bribed her—as Danny Goldberg would explain to Cross—with a sizable sum. As a result, Jamie requested and was granted temporary guardianship of the baby by the L.A. County courts.

At the same time Jackie Farry—a friend of Gold Mountain's Janet Billig who loved children and had been working in the promotion department of Epic Records—was hired as the baby's nanny. Despite having no formal experience, Farry was trustworthy, and she quickly became the one constant in Frances' life at a time of great turmoil.

Jamie, Jackie, and Frances were quickly set up in the Oakwood Apartments, where Nirvana had stayed during the creation of *Nevermind*. Sad and frustrated, but with little choice in the matter, Kurt and Courtney went back to the house on Alta Loma and—in between daily visits with their newborn daughter—focused hard on getting themselves together.

Reading

Despite the madness at home, Nirvana had been booked to headline the 1992 Reading Festival. On August 26, Cobain flew to the UK to play the event, which was slated for Sunday August 30 and boasted an audience of 60,000, plus an array of talent Kurt had helped select. The lineup consisted of Nick Cave, the Beastie Boys, Mudhoney, Screaming Trees, Pavement, L7, the Melvins, Eugenius (formerly Captain America), and the ABBA tribute band Bjorn Again.

Rumors shrouded the event throughout the afternoon. Some claimed Nirvana had broken up and were canceling their appearance. Others suggested that Cobain was dead. Kurt decided to play to the hype and arranged to have journalist Everett True push him onstage in a wheel chair. Sporting a white wig and a hospital gown, Nirvana's front man fell out of the wheel chair and collapsed center stage. The audience fell silent for a second.

"You're gonna make it, man," Novoselic told him encouragingly, looking downright odd as an outspoken vegetarian in leather jacket and pants. "With the support of his friends and family," he continued, "you, guy, are going to make it."

A few seconds later, Kurt—free of his disguise—strapped on a guitar and launched the band into a cathartic rendition of "Breed," affirming that he wasn't dead yet. Later in the set, Cobain dedicated "All Apologies" to his daughter, pledged his love to Love from the stage, and even incorporated a piece of Boston's 1976 classic "More Than a Feeling" into "Smells Like Teen Spirit." Despite all the drama in Kurt's personal life, Nirvana actually looked like they were having fun again.

Before they left the stage, the trio insisted that the Reading appearance wasn't the last that fans would hear of the band. In fact, they revealed plans to either make a new record or hit the road before the end of the year, and Kurt

A full-page magazine advertisement promoting the 1992 Reading Festival. Nirvana headlined the third day (August 30) as part of a bill that the group helped curate and which featured Nick Cave, Mudhoney, Teenage Fanclub, L7, Pavement, Screaming Trees, and the Melvins.   *Author's collection*

and Krist even bantered onstage about what their next steps might be. Then, following a frenzied rendering of "Territorial Pissings," they smashed their equipment to bits.

The final spectacle began when Cobain began trashing Grohl's drum kit. Dave, refusing to be outdone, ruined several of Kurt's guitars, pulling them from their rack and beating them into the stage while Hole's Eric Erlandson videotaped the chaos.

Novoselic stayed out of his bandmates' equipment wars only to find when he came offstage that one of his favorite basses had been stolen. The Gibson RD he had relied on for most of the prior year's *Nevermind* shows had somehow been snatched right out from under him.

In spite of the equipment that was sacrificed, many regarded this gig—the band's largest UK show to date—to be Nirvana's best appearance of 1992. At the time, few would have imagined it would be their last-ever performance in England.

More Exodus

On September 2, Cobain was back in Los Angeles, preparing to return yet again to drug rehab. For his next attempt to kick heroin, Kurt made plans to shift to a different drug-treatment facility, leaving Cedars-Sinai behind in favor of a stay at Exodus in Marina del Rey.

This time out, Cobain had everything to lose. He embraced his 12-step meetings and underwent intensive individual and group therapy in an effort to try to regain some control of his life, which was crazy enough—between fame, fatherhood, and marriage—without the heroin.

During the day, he would be allowed to leave treatment briefly for visits with Courtney and Frances. At night, he spilled his thoughts into his journals and imagined a day when he might be free from addiction and his stomach condition.

Once Cobain was able to kick his physical addiction to heroin, he finally stopped using his stomach condition an excuse for using drugs.

"I feel real sorry for anyone who thinks they can use heroin as a medicine because, uh, duh, it don't work," he wrote in his journal. Going on to describe his withdrawal symptoms, he added, "You puke, you flail around, you sweat, you shit your bed."

Dr. Robert Fremont

That September, both Cobain and Love began receiving treatment from a controversial chemical-dependency specialist. Dr. Robert Fremont—who had once lost his medical license for prescribing himself narcotics but had a strong, firsthand grasp on drug abuse and its complications—had worked successfully with a number of celebrities.

Fremont prescribed legal drugs to help his clients detox, in this case buprenorphine, a narcotic effective in cutting heroin cravings with no known side effects. It also helped reduce Kurt's stomach pain. As he marveled in his journal, "It acts as an opiate, but it doesn't get you high."

Kurt's Drug Buddy

It was around this time in 1992 that Kurt first became friends with jazz saxophonist Buddy Arnold when the former junkie, then the head of the Musicians Assistance Program, which helped players with substance abuse problems, assisted Cobain with a treatment referral. Upon their introduction, Kurt was stunned to find out that Arnold, then sixty-six years old, had suffered with heroin addiction for thirty-one years until he finally got clean in the 1980s during a prison sentence.

"He was really a nice kid," Arnold, who died in 2003, told the television show *Extra* in 2001. "He'd come over the house a few times after treatment and we'd talk. He was warm, came from another side of music I know nothing about."

Despite this bond, Arnold worried that he wasn't reaching Kurt, who seemed more interested in hearing stories about Buddy's friendships with Charlie Parker, Billie Holiday, and Buddy Rich.

"Rape Me" on MTV

Having enjoyed a massively successful twelve months in large part because of MTV's support, Nirvana now agreed to appear at the network's Video Music Awards. As such, regardless of Cobain's drug treatment, band business prevailed during the second week of September.

On September 8, Cobain was granted leave from Exodus for a day for rehearsals at the Pauley Pavilion on the campus of UCLA. When the band arrived for soundcheck, Cobain told his friend at the network, Amy Finnerty, that he was going to play a new song. And while Finnerty was thrilled to hear the trio rip through "Rape Me," the network's bosses were alarmed when Nirvana didn't start playing the familiar opening notes of "Smells Like Teen Spirit."

Producers pulled Finnerty aside and expressed worry that somehow the song was a criticism of the channel. She told her bosses that the song—which Kurt wrote in 1990—was nothing of the sort, although Kurt had since tweaked his lyrics to take aim at the media—specifically his "favorite inside source" from the *Vanity Fair* article.

Still, MTV wasn't having it, and insisted Nirvana play their enduring hit. The network warned that if Cobain pulled a fast one during the broadcast, the band's videos would be banned.

With Kurt holding firm as he returned to Exodus for the night, the network went one step further and threatened to pull all clips by Gold Mountain acts, which included big names like the Beastie Boys and Sonic Youth. It was only when Finnerty visited Kurt, Courtney, Frances, and Jackie Farry in Marina del Ray to explain that her job was on the line that Cobain agree to back down.

"The MTV people were upset," Novoselic wrote in his *Seattle Weekly* blog in November 2008. "We were being asked from all corners not to. I thought we should play something off *Nevermind*, do the gig, and leave. Easy, right? No. Kurt was very stubborn and refused to play another tune. There was quite a swirl around this issue."

Eventually, the band compromised and settled on "Lithium," which they played note-for-note during rehearsals on the day of the show. But out of spite, Kurt—sporting a Daniel Johnston T-shirt—convinced his bandmates to pull a prank on the network's bosses. When the band was called to the stage, they started playing the first few chords of "Rape Me." Just as producers were about to cut to commercial, the men in Nirvana cracked wry smiles and shifted into the single from *Nevermind*. It was Kurt's very own secret "fuck you" to MTV for paying attention to Hirschberg's damaging article.

Bass for Your Face

During Nirvana's rendition of "Lithium," Novoselic's bass rig began distorting, making it difficult to hear what he was playing. As a result, he gave up on his musicianship and found a different way to entertain the crowd.

"Fuck it—time for the bass-toss shtick," Novoselic wrote in his *Seattle Weekly* column in 2008. He threw his instrument twenty-five feet in the air, only for it to come back down and—with millions of people watching at home—smack him in the head. Embarrassed, Krist faked as if he had knocked himself out. Eventually he stumbled offstage with his hands on his bleeding forehead.

Backstage, paramedics treated Krist and put a bandage on his wound. Once the dust settled, he joined up with Dave Grohl and Queen guitarist Brian May, and together they celebrated the evening with a glass of chilled champagne.

Hi, Axl

Backstage in the food-service area at the Pauley Pavilion before the broadcast, the Cobain family and their nanny were sitting together having a quiet moment when Axl Rose walked past with his model girlfriend Stephanie Seymour. As Frances sat on Kurt's knee, Courtney—who was already angry at Rose for his onstage remarks about her husband—took the opportunity to sarcastically ask the Guns N' Roses singer if he would be their child's godfather.

An extremely annoyed Rose ignored Love and turned threateningly to Cobain. "You shut your bitch up," he warned, "or I'm taking you down to the pavement." Kurt looked at Courtney and sarcastically said, "OK, bitch. Shut up!" Axl, a hard-rock god not used to being mocked, walked off in a huff.

Ironically, Axl had started out a Nirvana fan, and had hoped to have the group play his thirtieth birthday party that year. Of course, Nirvana were having none of it. The same was the case when GNR asked Nirvana to open for them on their spring 1992 stadium tour. These rejections fostered resentment in the GNR camp, and led to Rose's onstage tirade about Kurt and his "junkie wife."

Back onstage for Nirvana's rendition of "Lithium," as Novoselic stumbled off bleeding, Grohl grabbed a microphone and attempted to humiliate Rose.

Nirvana's Best New Artist Award for "Smells Like Teen Spirit" from MTV's 1992 Video Music Awards. *Author's collection*

"Hi, Axl!" he barked teasingly. "Where's Axl? Hi, Axl!"

Meanwhile, Cobain had made his way toward two grand pianos that had been arranged for an upcoming duet between Rose and Elton John and proudly spat across the one he assumed had been designated for Axl. Later, as he watched the show in Nirvana's backstage trailer, he realized he had spat on Elton John's piano by accident.

Krist Meets Duff

Later in the evening, after Cobain had already left the building, Novoselic and Kurt's guitar tech, Earnie Bailey, were walking back to Nirvana's trailer when a drunken Duff McKagan, bassist in Guns N' Roses, approached Krist, looking to start some trouble. A slurring McKagan—trailed by bodyguards and a cameraman—asked Novoselic why he had been badmouthing his band.

Despite towering over McKagan, Novoselic refused to take the bait, denying having said anything about Guns N' Roses. While he was confident he could take Duff in a fight, Krist realized he was outnumbered, and refused to be provoked. Instead, he walked off to Nirvana's trailer.

Minutes later, McKagan and his bodyguards found Novoselic inside his trailer with Bailey, Courtney, and Frances. As Krist would remember in a November 2008 *Seattle Weekly* article, Duff and his goons unsuccessfully tried to flip over the trailer before eventually giving up.

Moon Men

Nirvana had been nominated for four MTV "Moonman" statues that night, and they ended up winning two. When "Smells Like Teen Spirit" won the Best Alternative Video prize, the band did the only sensible thing and sent a Michael Jackson impersonator to the stage to collect their first trophy. Although the audience seemed perplexed, it was later explained that the idea stemmed from the fact that *Nevermind* had knocked Jackson from his spot at the top of the *Billboard* album charts.

Later, when Nirvana were named Best New Artist, the trio gathered on the stage. When it was Cobain's turn to speak, the *Vanity Fair* article was clearly still very fresh in his mind. "You know, it's really hard to believe everything you read," he told the audience.

Toward the end of the night, before Kurt left to make it back in time for his Exodus curfew, Cobain and Eddie Vedder—his one-time whipping boy in the press—came together for a slow dance to Eric Clapton's moving ballad "Tears in Heaven." But the idea of mending fences with the Pearl Jam singer wasn't Kurt's—it was the shared work of Love and Amy Finnerty. According to various reports, Kurt took the opportunity to tell Eddie, "You're a respectable human, even if your band does suck."

23

All the Kids Will Eat It Up If It's Packaged Properly

The Tracks

Released on December 15, 1992, in the United States, and a day earlier in Europe, *Incesticide* was a compilation of Nirvana material that served two purposes. For DGC, it was a way to capitalize on the success of *Nevermind*; for fans, it was a way to glean some insight into the band's past through unreleased demos, outtakes, covers, and radio sessions.

Just the same, with four successive singles in just over a year, both band and label feared overexposure. As a result, there was little promotion of the new record, which was purposely given a controversial name.

According to the book *Cobain Unseen*, Kurt sanctioned the project once he was given full control of the packaging. He created the haunting cover art, which depicts a skeleton being tugged on by a devilish looking character; the back cover features a picture of his rubber duck.

Incesticide—complete with "Parental Advisory: Explicit Lyrics" sticker— entered the US charts at #51 and ultimately peaked at #39 on the *Billboard* 200, eventually selling one million copies. For Nirvana collectors, the project offered a chance to hear unreleased tracks like "Hairspray Queen," "Aero Zeppelin," "Big Long Now," "Downer," and a revved-up, punk-driven "(New Wave) Polly." The latter was, of course, a variation on *Nevermind*'s memorable acoustic number. "Aneurysm" and "Been a Son" differed from the versions heard on the "Teen Spirit" single and the *Blew* EP.

For more recent fans, the compilation provided easy access to the material from the *Hormoaning* EP—including versions of Devo's "Turnaround" and the Vaselines' "Molly's Lips" and "Son of a Gun"—that the band had tracked for BBC radio DJ John Peel. The project also included "Mexican Seafood," which had appeared on the 1989 *Teriyaki Asthma Volume 1* compilation; "Beeswax," which could be found on 1991's *Kill Rock Stars* compilation; and what many considered to be the disc's high points, the two sides of the 1990 Sub Pop single "Sliver" / "Dive."

Announcing plans for the compilation to *Flipside* for the magazine's May/June 1992 issue, Cobain called "Sliver" his "favorite song to play live." He explained how he wanted to include it on *Incesticide* "because a lot of people haven't heard that single and I'd like them to hear that song."

The Liner Notes

In some ways, the liner notes of *Incesticide* were just as entertaining as the music itself. Cobain—calling himself "Kurdt (the blonde one)"—wrote of searching back issues of *NME* in his pursuit of the Raincoats' long-out-of-print debut

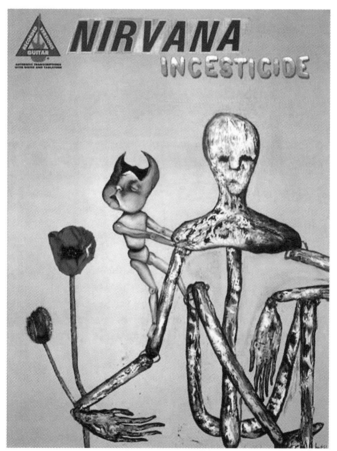

The cover of the guitar tablature book for 1992's *Incesticide*, complete with matching artwork, credited to Kurdt Cobain. The album was released on December 14, 1992, in Europe, and the following day in North America.   *Author's collection*

album, detailing the detective work necessary to track down that band's front woman/guitarist Ana da Silva at the London antique shop where she worked.

"Anna" promised to see if she had a copy lying around and said that if she did she would send it to him. Kurt wrote of the joy he felt when he went to the mailbox and found a pristine vinyl copy, signed by the band and boasting Xeroxed lyrics, pictures, and a personalized letter from da Silva.

"It made me happier than playing in front of thousands of people each night, rock-god idolization from fans, music industry plankton kissing my ass, and the million dollars I made last year," Cobain wrote. "It was one of the few really important things that I've been blessed with since becoming an untouchable boy genius."

Kurt expressed pride in paying tribute to the punk bands of his youth and wrote of the importance of Cheap Trick and the Knack. He went on to describe some of the other moments of happiness and excitement he had experienced during his ascent to fame, including kissing Novoselic and Grohl on *Saturday Night Live* ("just to spite the homophobes"), receiving drawings from eccentric singer/songwriter Daniel Johnston, and meeting heroes like Iggy Pop and the Wipers' Greg Sage.

Cobain revealed the pleasure he felt from bringing underground bands that he liked into the spotlight, including Shonen Knife, the Vaselines, and the Television Personalities. He also thanked Sonic Youth for mentoring Nirvana, and expressed gratitude at having shared the stage with the Breeders, Dinosaur Jr., Urge Overkill, and Hole.

Kurt spoke out against crimes against women—including a 1991 incident affected him deeply involving two "wastes of sperm and eggs" that raped a girl while singing the lyrics to "Polly." He also laid down the law with his fans, letting them know that those with any sort of biases against homosexuals, differing races, and women should "leave us the fuck alone." He didn't want them buying Nirvana records or coming to their concerts.

Perhaps most importantly, Kurt used his "open letter" as a way to support his wife and proclaim the mother of his child as "the supreme example of dignity, ethics, and honesty." Responding once again to the controversy brought about by the *Vanity Fair* article, he defended Courtney's unorthodox approaches and commended her unwillingness to be obedient, silent, and agreeable. He also took the opportunity to offer a big "fuck you" to those who suggested he was "so naïve and stupid" the he would allow himself to be "taken advantage of and manipulated."

24

Here in My Place of Recovery

Death Threats, Demos, and Calamity

Coming Clean

The morning after the MTV Awards, Kurt gave his first formal interview for a year when he sat down with *Los Angeles Times* staff writer Robert Hilburn in his Hollywood Hills home. In the piece, titled "Cobain to Fans: Just Say No," Kurt talked somewhat openly about his heroin use—while also explaining that he was now drug free—and discussed the future of Nirvana.

Kurt revealed fears that one day his daughter might get hassled by kids at school because his parents were junkies. Although he conceded that he once admired rock stars like Keith Richards who were associated with the glamorous side of heroin, he added that he was worried that he might have a hand in inciting drug use among his fans.

All the same, the article wasn't entirely truthful. Kurt made no mention of the fact that he was finishing up a court-ordered drug-treatment program at Exodus. Instead, he carefully acknowledged that he had been meditating, was going to a "pain-management clinic," and had been prescribed "some stomach medicine" to help ease his pain.

The piece also glossed over the complexities of Frances Bean's custody arrangements. Of course, Hilburn—and anyone outside of Nirvana's inner circle—would be none the wiser, as the couple put on a show in their efforts to depict their home life as downright normal.

As for the future of the band, Kurt reiterated his desire to make a raw-sounding record and revealed how he hoped to keep the band's tours manageable so that he might keep his stomach pain in check. "I would rather be healthy and alive," he insisted. "I don't want to sacrifice myself or my family."

"No on 9"

On September 10, Nirvana flew up to Portland to play a "No on 9" benefit that would help fight Initiative 9—a proposed bill by conservatives in the Oregon legislature to limit gay rights. It was important for Cobain, who had long been

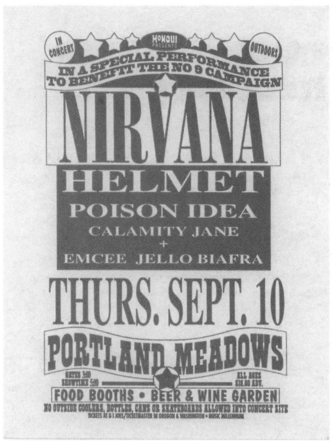

The day after Nirvana's legendary MTV Video Music Awards appearance, the band flew to Oregon to headline this No on 9 Benefit at Portland Meadows. Measure 9 took a homophobic stance on gay rights and public education, and the band's involvement in the cause helped raise national awareness and defeat the proposed amendment to the Oregon Constitution.   *Author's collection*

outspoken in his support of rights and equality for homosexuals, to play the show at Portland Meadows alongside Helmet, Nirvana's friends in Calamity Jane, and punk rockers Poison Idea.

Playing the show, he told the *Advocate* a few months later, was his way of "fighting homophobia in a real small way," adding that although he had fallen in love with Courtney, he was "definitely gay in spirit."

Death Threats at Seattle Center

Nirvana's ongoing public support of gay rights and pro-life initiatives made them a unique fixture in rock in 1992. Cobain's endorsement of such causes—

This ad promoted Nirvana's two Northwest shows in September 1992, including the aforementioned Portland Meadows performance and a concert booked at the Seattle Center Coliseum.   *Author's collection*

especially the latter—left him susceptible to another occupational hazard: death threats.

When Kurt and his family rolled into Seattle on September 11 for Nirvana's sold-out headlining gig at the Seattle Center Arena that night, an anonymous caller promised to shoot him the moment he walked onstage. To protect Kurt from armed right-to-life fanatics, Nirvana's management insisted the venue deploy metal detectors at the entryways.

Washington Music Industry Coalition Benefit

That evening's Washington Music Industry Coalition Benefit was tied to a cause close to Novoselic, Date House Bill 2554 (also known as the "Erotic Music Bill"). The bassist—who had previously protested with members of Soundgarden and Pearl Jam when Governor Booth Gardener signed it earlier in the year—had been working to raise awareness ever since, and even held a press conference in support of the Washington Music Industry Coalition the previous June.

In support of the WMIC, the members of Nirvana filed a complaint days after the press conference, asking for declaratory judgment and injunctive relief against the bill. For Novoselic, the idea of limiting free speech in record-ings—and holding record-store employees liable, and even subject to arrest, for selling music that was branded erotic or offensive to minors—took censorship too far. Working with the band and Nirvana's management, Krist organized a concert in Seattle for August 23 and petitioned diligently to spread information and understanding of how the passing of such a measure could have terrible consequences.

Although the show had to be postponed by several weeks because of the birth of Frances Bean, when it finally happened, the gig—which also featured Helmet and Nirvana's longtime friends in Fitz of Depression—did just what Novoselic had hoped. The show not only helped raise awareness about the bill's call to limit free speech on recordings but also raised $25,000 for the cause and led to the conservative measure's failure by funding the legal fight against the legislation.

Politics aside, the 16,000 fans in attendance were witness to what was argu-ably Nirvana's finest ever Seattle concert. During the performance, Novoselic was in celebratory mood as he spoke of how he had once been handed a life ban from the arena for getting drunk at a Neil Young concert. He also claimed that he found his picture on a wall alongside mug shots of some of the other troublemakers who were never to be given re-entry following similar infractions over the years.

Dad's Here

From the opening notes of "Breed" to the closing thumps of "Territorial Pissings," Cobain played the show as if he had something to prove—and he did. Not only had his family turned out for Nirvana's big homecoming but even his estranged father Don showed up backstage unexpectedly after showing security his driver's license. He had brought Kurt's half-brother Chad with him.

It had been seven years since Kurt and his father had spoken, and he couldn't help wonder why his dad had was turning up now. Was it because of his fame? His money? The reality was that Don had been trying to get in touch for months, but he didn't have Kurt's number. Messages to Nirvana's handlers went unanswered, but Don was persistent—he wanted to meet his granddaughter, and make sure Kurt knew how to reach him if he wanted.

As uncomfortable as the reunion made him feel, Cobain was still relieved to see Don and startled at how much older his father looked. "I was happy to see him because I always wanted him to know that I didn't hate him anymore," Kurt told Jon Savage in 1994.

Things were less amicable between Wendy and Don as they encountered one another backstage in the company of Kurt's sister Kim, his half-sister Breanne, Courtney, and Frances Bean. Courtney was taken aback at just how much her husband had resembled his father.

Eighteen years after their divorce, things were still incredibly strained between Don and Wendy. When Don started needling Wendy about her age and being a *grandma*, Kurt put his father in his place. He made it clear that he wasn't going to stand by and watch Don put his mother down.

A few minutes later, after his mother and sisters left the room, Cobain signed a poster for Chad and spoke with his dad. He promised to keep in touch, and the meeting ended on a positive note.

Secret Performances

Cobain surprised a California audience on September 26 when he took the stage during a Sonic Youth show. He played Lead Belly's "Where Did You Sleep Last Night" before joining his friends in Mudhoney (who were supporting alongside Pavement) on guitar for one of his favorite songs—a cover of Fang's "The Money Will Roll Right In."

Then, on October 3 and 4, Nirvana appeared as the opening act for a pair of Mudhoney gigs in their home state. The first, at Western Washington University, was a total surprise, with the band forgoing "Lithium" and "Teen Spirit" in favor of old material, much of which was pegged for their upcoming rarities compilation, *Incesticide*. Because a number of the songs hadn't been played in a couple of years, Kurt struggled to remember the words to certain tunes and ended up mumbling his way through them.

At the end of Nirvana's set, two seven-year-old fans were brought up onstage. After Kurt and Krist strapped their instruments the boys, the crowd began to chant, "Smash it! Smash it!" The kids followed the crowd's orders, to the delight of all in attendance.

Later, after Mudhoney's encore, Cobain returned to the stage to again play guitar on the aforementioned Fang number and a cover of Black Flag's "Fix Me."

A rare club appearance at the Crocodile Club followed the next night, with Nirvana booked to open for Mudhoney as "Pen Cap Chew." During the hour-long set, the trio again played lesser-known numbers like "Mexican Seafood," "Beeswax," and "Curmudgeon," plus the yet-to-be-recorded "Pennyroyal Tea." At the end of Mudhoney's show, Kurt joined in again on the same punk covers he'd played the night before.

Carnation

After spending a long time looking for a home, Kurt and Courtney settled on a rundown mansion on eleven acres in the rural town of Carnation, Washington. They paid $300,000 for the house, which was located thirty-seven miles from Seattle. It was in such a state of disrepair that it actually had a tree growing through it. As a result, Cobain commissioned the construction of a new home on the land. In the meantime, the Cobain clan—which also included Farry and

Rodriguez—bounced between four-star Seattle hotels like the Sorrento, the Four Seasons, and the Inn at the Market.

Discord Continues

Cobain and Novoselic continued to be in communication about band business, but the friendship they had shared prior to Kurt's wedding had evaporated. The days of them hanging out together socially—let alone as friends—were long over.

Yet even when they fought on the telephone about plans for Nirvana, they would still try to end things on an up note, recognizing that what they had built was bigger than their own egos. "At the end of the phone call he'd say, 'Well things are going to get better,'" Novoselic told Charles Cross. "That's what we'd agree upon, just to feel better about things."

As for Grohl, there is speculation in *Heavier Than Heaven* that Cobain had considered firing his one-time roommate whenever the drummer did something onstage or out from behind his kit that didn't meet with Kurt's approval.

Corporate Rock Whores

In October, Nirvana got wind that a biography being written about the band by UK journalists Victoria Clarke and Britt Collins was shaping up to be a sensational and controversial tome. News of the direction the book—to be titled *Nirvana: Flower Sniffin', Kitty Pettin', Baby Kissin' Corporate Rock Whores*—was taking, including interviews with the likes of Cobain enemy Lynn Hirschberg and Love's ex-husband Falling James, left Kurt and Courtney seething.

That month, Kurt and Courtney left a barrage of threatening messages on Clarke's answering machine. Some of the calls were made with Grohl and Kurt's aunt Jody—who had been interviewed for the book under the pretense that it was an authorized project—and were made from Jack Endino's studio, where the band had started demoing material in the final week of October.

Clarke turned over the recordings—some of which can be heard on YouTube—to the police. In one of them, Kurt calls her a "parasitic fucking cunt" and fumes, "If anything comes out in this book that hurts my wife, I'll fucking hurt you." Elsewhere, he promises, "I don't care if this is a recorded threat, I'm at the end of my rope. You'll understand when you see me in person. I've never been more serious in my life."

When the *New York Times* picked up on the story, Cobain—through Danny Goldberg—denied making the calls. Later, however, he conceded he had made them, and even vowed to get even with Clarke and Collins in an interview with Michael Azerrad in which he expressed a desire to kill the pair. "When people unnecessarily fuck with me, I just can't help but want to beat them to death."

A few months later, Love approached Clarke in a Los Angeles nightclub and allegedly threw a glass at the writer. Victoria filed a complaint with the police that night, claiming Love had doused her in beer and pulled her along the floor by her hair. Courtney countered with her own complaint the next day, insisting she had acted in self-defense.

After receiving copies of the answering machine messages, *Entertainment Weekly* scribe Tim Appelo ran a story on December 4 in which Love defended Kurt's threats and her own. "I don't think it's that bad," Love said of the messages. "I mean, I know we're right. We might have been mean to them, but they violated us and raped us, and it's just scary. I remember saying, like, 'I'll fucking haunt you till you fucking die,' and I meant it, because this kind of shit cannot go on."

Eventually, after obtaining parts of the working manuscript, Gold Mountain sued Clarke and Collins to prevent the book from being published.

Sessions with Endino

After a postponement in August, around the time of Frances Bean's birth, Nirvana began work on their next studio album with Jack Endino on October 24, 1992. But when Cobain didn't show up or call, the sessions didn't actually get started until the following day.

Endino—who had shut down Reciprocal Studios and was now running Word of Mouth Productions—was quick to observe the lack of communication between the band members, and especially the tension in the room between Novoselic and Courtney Love once she showed up. To Endino, the dynamic was far different from the experience he had had while working with Nirvana in the past.

During the making of *Bleach*, the musicians were unified in everything they did. Now, it seemed, the regularity of Kurt's tardiness and absences had become accepted by Nirvana's rhythm section. When Cobain finally showed up, he played with indifference. Or, as Jack observed in *Nirvana: The True Story*, "Kurt acted like he didn't even want to be there."

Endino worked with the same mixing console that had been used to make *Bleach* during the two-day session, which eventually took place on October 25–26. Phil Ek—who would become known for his work with Band of Horses, Built to Spill, and the Shins—served as assistant engineer for the session.

Basic tracks (sans vocals) were cut for "Dumb," "Frances Farmer Will Have Her Revenge on Seattle," "Tourette's," "Pennyroyal Tea," and "Radio Friendly Unit Shifter." A sixth song, "Rape Me," did feature Cobain's vocal, which was recorded with his daughter Frances crying in his lap. This material remained incomplete and untouched for twelve years until the latter song was eventually mixed and released on Nirvana's 2004 boxed set *With the Lights Out*.

At one point during recording, Jack received a noise complaint from a neighbor as a result of Dave Grohl's loud drumming. He told Seattle police that he had Nirvana—one of the biggest bands in the world—in his studio, but the officers were uninterested and told him to keep it down. Once Krist had completed his parts, he left. Dave followed soon after, leaving Kurt and Courtney to work with the engineers.

Albini Yes, Endino No

Aside from the dysfunction in the room, Cobain spent much of his time talking about working with Steve Albini, with the hopes of giving his next record a sound akin to *Surfer Rosa* or *Pod*. All the same, Endino's stark production on *Bleach*—which had since outsold the Pixies and Breeders albums in question—certainly qualified him for the job.

"Kurt was like, 'What do you think, do you think we should have Albini do the record?' Jack told Gillian G. Gaar in her 2006 book, *In Utero*. "And what am I going to say? 'No. You should have me do the record.' I just kept my mouth shut."

While Endino hoped for the assignment, he recognized the enormous pressure any producer accepting he project would be under. On the one hand, the record company would be looking for an album similar in sound to *Nevermind*, while on the other, Nirvana had already made it clear that they wanted to make a raw and aggressive-sounding record. As a result, the man who had sat behind the boards for *Bleach* balanced his disappointment with relief when Cobain sought out Albini instead.

"In Bloom"

Nirvana re-teamed with "Come as You Are" director Kevin Kerslake on October 15 to film a music video for "In Bloom," which was slated to be the fourth video and final UK single from *Nevermind*. Featuring former People's Court host Doug Llewelyn parodying 1960s variety television host Ed Sullivan and introducing Nirvana as "thoroughly all right and decent fellas," the clip shows the humorous side of the band—something that had become less and less apparent by the autumn of 1992.

Dressed in the sort of outfits that pop bands of the day like Herman's Hermits or the Dave Clark Five might wear—complete with Cobain's nerdy glasses, Novoselic's squeaky-clean haircut, and Grohl's hilarious blond wig—the band were an ideal match for the vintage footage of ecstatic screaming teen girls that was interspersed were their performance. Midway through the clip, Kerslake suddenly cut to footage of the trio playing in dresses and gyrating awkwardly before destroying their equipment.

Easily Nirvana's most enjoyable entry into the medium, "In Bloom" would go on to win an MTV Video Music Award for Best Alternative Video in 1993. When asked by *Melody Maker* in December about the subversive implications of wearing a dress in the film, Cobain explained, "There's no way you can be subversive in rock anymore, unless you ram a stick of dynamite up your ass. Queen dressed in drag. It just feels comfortable, sexy, and free wearing a dress. It's fun."

Calamity in Buenos Aires

When Nirvana took the stage at the Estadio Jose Amalfitani in Buenos Aires, Argentina, on October 30, the band's collective outlook was dour. Minutes earlier, the crowd of 50,000 had mistreated Cobain's handpicked, all-female opening act, Calamity Jane, going so far as to spit on them, throw rocks and clumps of mud at them, and boo them from the stage. The group—consisting of Gilly Ann Hanner, Megan Hanner, Joanna Bolme, and Marci Martinez—left the stage crying.

"They were calling us whores and bitches in Spanish, spitting, throwing dirt clods—did I mention the spitting? I couldn't believe how far they could spit," Martinez told *Annabelle* in 2005. Following this tragic appearance, Calamity Jane, who had formed in 1988, were left feeling so downhearted that they disbanded for good.

When Cobain realized what had happened, he wasn't just incensed—he was out of his mind. "It was terrible," he told *Request* the following year. "Just a mass of sexism all at once."

Cobain was so upset about the incident that he couldn't keep his frustration to himself and decided to punish the crowd by withholding "Smells Like Teen Spirit" from the set list. He also teased the crowd by playing play the opening few bars to his biggest hit at the start of "Breed" and "Drain You" and then stopping.

After "Polly," Novoselic and Grohl started jamming and Kurt joined in, playing a fifteen-minute-long, improvised, feedback-drenched instrumental. When it came time for "Come as You Are," Cobain altered the first verse for fans by singing "Hey" over and over instead of the words. It was his way of shaming those in the audience who had upset his friends.

Getting Guardianship

In mid-November, the Cobains were finally granted full custody of Frances Bean by the Los Angeles courts, although Children's Services still intended monitor the case. (By March 1993, Kurt and Courtney learned that the authorities had opted to take no further interest in Frances.)

Thanks in part to the hard work of the Cobains' lawyers and Nirvana's management, Courtney's half-sister Jamie Rodriguez was relieved from her guardianship duties, and Kurt and Courtney were finally granted custody of their daughter. Jackie Farry remained as nanny, and handled most of the principal care duties, from feeding and nap schedules to diaper changes. Although Kurt and Courtney relished their time with their daughter, they were both responsible enough to know that they were too irresponsible to raise a baby without adequate help.

Like Jamie before her, Jackie knew to shield the child from her parents when they were high or nodding off. The reality of the situation was that, just two months after telling the *Los Angeles Times* he was clean, Cobain was back on heroin.

Million Dollar Man

In a February 1993 cover story for the *Advocate*, Kurt disclosed that although he had earned more than one million dollars in 1992, he and Courtney were quickly burning through his income. According to the piece, he had spent $380,000 on taxes, put $300,000 toward his house in Carnation, and the rest— save for his personal living expenses of $80,000 for the year—on doctors and lawyers.

The Cobains' legal bills alone added up to $200,000, with the rest going toward an array of doctors. According to *Heavier Than Heaven*, the medical care costs included drug rehabilitation expenses for both Kurt and Courtney, costs related to the birth of Frances Bean, plus charges from an array of corrupt physicians who would prescribe narcotics to the couple for money.

25

It Was All Here Yesterday

Influences

Common Ground

The founding members of Nirvana solidified their lineup in September 1990 when they discovered that former Scream kit man Dave Grohl shared many of their musical interests. From Led Zeppelin to Fugazi, the Sex Pistols to the Rolling Stones, Kurt Cobain and Krist Novoselic stood on common ground with their new drummer.

"We all grew up listening to the same stuff," Grohl told *Metal Hammer* in 2005. "It was one of the first conversations that I had with Kurt. From Celtic Frost to Neil Young to Public Enemy, we all loved the same music."

Once, in his journal, Cobain compiled a list of his fifty favorite albums, among them the Stooges' *Raw Power* (1973), Fang's *Landshark* (1982), MDC's *Millions of Dead Cops* (1982), Saccharine Trust's *Paganicons* (1981), Gang of Four's *Entertainment!* (1979), the Frogs' *It's Only Right and Natural* (1989), P. J. Harvey's *Dry* (1992), the Knack's *Get the Knack* (1979), The Saints' *Eternally Yours* (1978, and incorrectly listed as *Know Your Product*), Kleenex's *Kleenex/LiLiput* (1982), the Slits' *Cut* (1982, and incorrectly listed as *Typical Girls*), the Clash's *Combat Rock* (1982), a split EP by Void and Faith (1982), Fear's *The Record* (1982), Public Image Ltd.'s *Flowers of Romance* (1981), Public Enemy's *It Takes a Nation of Millions to Hold Us Back* (1988), the Marine Girls *Beach Party* (1982), Swans' *Young God* EP (1984), Mazzy Star's *She Hangs Brightly* (1990), and self-titled records by Scratch Acid (1984), the Raincoats (1979), Rites of Spring (1985), and Tales of Terror (1984).

To be fair, the actual number of acts that influenced Nirvana could run to the hundreds. That said, the list below comprises the bands that had the most evident impact on Kurt, Krist, and Dave.

ABBA

By the time of Nirvana's first *Rolling Stone* cover story, all three members of Nirvana were proudly embracing the pop music of their 1970s childhoods. During the group's late-'91 European trek, the most popular CD on their tour bus was ABBA's *Greatest Hits*.

Of course, the Swedish foursome—Agnetha Fältskog, Björn Ulvaeus, Benny Andersson, and Anni-Frid "Frida" Lyngstad—had massive hits like "Dancing Queen," "Fernando," "Take a Chance on Me," and "SOS" during their 1974–80 chart reign. Nirvana's appreciation of he band prompted them to hire the tribute group Björn Again to perform on the bill with them at the 1992 Reading Festival.

Aerosmith

Kurt Cobain once listed 1976's *Rocks* as one of his fifty favorite records of all time, and listening to Aerosmith classics like "Back in the Saddle" and "Rats in the Cellar," it's easy to hear how the Boston hard-rock quintet would have made an impact not just on Nirvana's front man but on the band's other members too.

With enduring early singles like "Dream On" (1973), "Same Old Song and Dance," (1974), and the one-two punch of "Sweet Emotion" and "Walk This Way" from their revered third album *Toys in the Attic* (1975), the band's exciting brand of hard rock quickly appealed to a young teenage Novoselic. Grohl found the band in his mid-teens after gravitating toward blues-inspired hard-rock acts like Led Zeppelin.

B-52s

As a ten-year-old, Dave Grohl was instantly taken with the weirdness of the B-52s' eponymous 1979 album after seeing their *Saturday Night Live* debut. He was lured in by unconventional songs like the experimental "Planet Claire," the urgent "Rock Lobster," and keepers like "Dance This Mess Around" and "6060-842," and captivated by the band's kitschy clothes and unique arrangements, telling *Melody Maker* in 1997, "This was definitely the first thing after Kiss or Rush that totally absorbed me like that."

Bad Brains

In Cobain's list of his top fifty albums, he ranked *Rock for Light* at #12. The group also had a major impact on Dave Grohl in his formative years, as covered in detail elsewhere.

"They were connected in a way I'd never seen before," Nirvana's drummer told *Melody Maker*'s Rebellious Jukebox in 1997. "They made me absolutely determined to become a musician, they basically changed my life, and changed the lives of everyone who saw them."

Beginning as a D.C.-area jazz-fusion band called Mind Power in 1975, the group became obsessed with punk rock when a friend turned them on to it in 1977. Taking their name from the Ramones number "Bad Brain," they released the single "Pay to Cum" in 1979 and a subsequent self-titled cassette-only release on New York's ROIR Records in 1982. The group's heralded 1983 LP *Rock for Light* was followed by the 1986 hardcore classic *I Against I*, released on SST Records.

Beat Happening

Formed at Evergreen State College in 1982, Beat Happening were Olympia's original indie-rock band. The group, which consisted of Calvin Johnson, Heather Lewis, and Bret Lunsford, began recording the following year, releasing their first cassette, *Three Tea Breakfast*, in 1984 on Johnson's own K Records label. A proper eponymous album followed in 1985, with the acclaimed lo-fi LP *Jamboree*—one of Cobain's favorites—seeing release in 1988, while *Black Candy* dropped in 1989.

Not only was Kurt a fan—as he revealed in numerous interviews—he and Johnson had become friendly after Cobain settled in Olympia, with Calvin turning him on to records he never would have heard in Aberdeen via mixtapes. As a result, Nirvana's front man became an outspoken fan of eccentric singer/songwriter Daniel Johnston, plus underground pop bands like the Raincoats and the Vaselines, among dozens of other national and international underground acts. And of course Cobain went so far as to get the K Records logo tattooed on his forearm in tribute to Johnson's label.

The Beatles

The Fab Four had a major impact on the young Cobain, Novoselic, and Grohl. Like many kids of their generation, they found it impossible not to be impacted by the Lennon/McCartney songbook. But unlike a lot of the hip, punk-inspired bands of the mid- and late 1980s who dismissed the Beatles, Nirvana actually owned up to the quartet's influence.

Just prior to the release of *Nevermind*, Kurt told *Kerrang!* that the Beatles were as important to him as Black Sabbath, and would later list *Meet the Beatles* as the album by John, Paul, George, and Ringo that impacted him most. Five months later, when Nirvana had become stars, Grohl explained to *Rolling Stone* that when it came to pop, there was only one word: Beatles.

Novoselic praised the pop geniuses in a January 2008 *Seattle Weekly* column, explaining that the Beatles "were masters of melodic hooks" and remarking on how "all roads lead to Liverpool." He also cited McCartney as one of his favorite bass players, and insisted that Paul's "bass riff owns 'Come Together' off *Abbey Road*."

Black Flag

SST Records' flagship band may be the most important American hardcore band that ever existed. That was certainly the case for Dave Grohl, as evidenced by the homemade four-bar tattoo he gave himself with a pen as a teen. The band—steered by Greg Ginn and fronted by Henry Rollins—also had a major impact on Cobain and Novoselic during their tenure as Melvins hangers-on. Kurt even cited 1981's *Damaged* and 1984's *My War* as two of his all-time favorite records. In interviews to promote *Nevermind*, he would famously describe Nirvana's sound as a cross between Black Flag, Black Sabbath, the Knack, and the Bay City Rollers.

Black Sabbath

The crushing proto-metal sounds of Ozzy Osbourne, Toni Iommi, Geezer Butler, and Bill Ward had a major influence on Nirvana. On more than one occasion, Cobain and Novoselic spoke of the heavy impact Black Sabbath had on them, specifically citing albums like 1971's *Master of Reality* and 1972's *Volume 4*.

Speaking to *Kerrang!* in 1997, Grohl explained his love for the band. "They were great, they were dark and they made an amazing contribution to music. They taught everyone that you could tune your guitars down to a D or C or A, and that's a big deal."

"We were totally into them in Nirvana," Dave continued. "When you're sitting around in the practice room and someone breaks in on a Sabbath riff, everyone joins in—they're just classic riffs."

David Bowie

Although Dave Grohl's sister had fed him a steady diet of Bowie growing up, Cobain and Novoselic weren't familiar with his records—save for his hits like "Let's Dance"—when drummer Chad Channing educated them about an album called *The Man Who Sold the World* during the Boston stop of Nirvana's 1989 tour.

When the band stayed over at a fan's house during that tour, Channing copied the acclaimed 1970 recording onto cassette and played it as they traveled. Kurt immediately loved it and was receptive when Chad suggested that Cobain dig deeper, recommending Bowie's classic album *Hunky Dory*, among others.

Nirvana subsequently recorded a version of "The Man Who Sold the World" for *MTV Unplugged*. Although it was not one of Bowie's best-known songs, he would resuscitate it for his live shows after Nirvana popularized it. When asked about Nirvana's version by *USA Today*'s Edna Gundersen in September 1995, Bowie described it as "heartfelt," adding, "Until this version it hadn't occurred to me that I was a part of America's musical landscape. I always felt my weight in Europe, but not in the US."

The Breeders

In late 1991, Cobain told *Spin* that his favorite album of the year was the Breeders' *Pod* (which in fact had originally surfaced on May 28, 1990). Talking to *Melody Maker*'s Rebellious Jukebox column in August of the following year, he called the disc "an epic" and cited the appeal of the group's "unique" and "atmospheric" song structure.

Originally formed as the Boston-based side-project of 4AD labelmates Kim Deal (of the Pixies) and Tanya Donnelly (of Throwing Muses), *Pod* was recorded in Edinburgh, Scotland, with the Perfect Disaster's Josephine Wiggs on bass and Slint's Britt Walford on drums. Walford, who came by recommendation of the album's producer, Steve Albini, was credited on the record as Shannon Doughton.

Kurt had been a major Pixies fan, but upon hearing *Pod* he knew it was magical. "I wish Kim was allowed to write more songs for the Pixies," he told Rebellious Jukebox, "because 'Gigantic' is the best Pixies song, and Kim wrote it."

The Breeders became Deal's full-time pursuit when the Pixies acrimoniously disbanded in 1993. After the release of their second album, *Last Splash*, that August, Cobain tapped the group to appear as a support act on their *In Utero* tour.

Butthole Surfers

Formed in San Antonio, Texas, in 1981 by Gibby Haynes and Paul Leary, the Butthole Surfers appealed to the members of Nirvana in their formative years because of their musical ingenuity, punk attitude, and crude sense of humor. In his top fifty list, Kurt placed the band's 1983 EP *Pee Pee The Sailor* at #10 and 1987's *Locust Abortion Technician* at #39.

During Nirvana's tenure at Sub Pop, the trio began running into the Surfers on the road, and the two bands shared bills from time to time. While in Los Angeles during the making of *Nevermind*, Kurt, Krist, and Dave socialized with the Buttholes, whose members also included King Coffey and Jeff Pinkus.

In early 1994, Nirvana tapped the Butthole Surfers—who had since jumped from stints with Touch and Go and Rough Trade to Capitol Records—to support them on what would prove to be their final run of North American dates. Ironically, Gibby Haynes had wound up as Cobain's roommate two months later, during Kurt's final stint in drug rehab that March.

Celtic Frost

Zurich's Celtic Frost were equally inspired by metal bands like Black Sabbath and Judas Priest, the hardcore punk group Discharge, and goth outfits like

Bauhaus and Siouxsie & the Banshees. Uncharacteristic of the heavy-metal genre, the group's brand of doom metal resonated with Novoselic and Cobain at the outset of Nirvana.

In 1990, when they teamed with Grohl, Nirvana's founders discovered that the Swiss band was yet another of the many artists they had a common appreciation of. "Kurt and Krist loved Celtic Frost as much as me," Dave told *Metal Hammer* in 2005, not long after he had teamed with the group's original front man Tom Gabriel Fischer for the making of his 2004 solo project *Probot.*

Devo

While Novoselic was mocked at school for liking Devo after he moved to Aberdeen in 1979, Cobain was allowed to appreciate the Ohio band in the same community without ridicule. The band's use of synthesizers, video, and multimedia made a lasting impression on Kurt, who—according to the *Guardian*—once said, "Of all the bands who came from the underground and made in the mainstream, Devo were the most challenging and subversive of all."

A look at the video for the band's chart topping single "Whip It" confirms that the Mark Mothersbaugh–fronted outfit was a big fat anomaly in 1980. Grohl, meanwhile, was mesmerized by the band's far-out presentation—including their flower-pot helmets—in the sixth grade. As he told *Melody Maker* in 1997, "They were these aliens you really wanted to know."

Flipper

It took three listens to *Generic Flipper*—on loan from Buzz Osbourne in the mid-1980s—for Krist Novoselic to truly appreciate the band's dark, loose, lo-fi approach. He deemed the San Francisco–based avant-punk band "too weird and too dangerous for the world" in a December 2008 column for *Seattle Weekly.* "Flipper were proto-grungers," he explained.

Speaking to the Washington State Legacy Project the following year, Krist relayed how the Will Shatter–fronted outfit had a significant impact on Cobain. "Kurt took *Generic Flipper* and he mixed it with his knack for a mean pop hook, and for melodies," Novoselic said. "And then you have a record like *In Utero.* So *Generic Flipper* is such a monument."

Half Japanese

Cobain had been introduced to Half Japanese—the punk band formed by Jad Fair—via Calvin Johnson, and he became a quick study of the group's experimental, un-tuned guitar approach. In 1992, Kurt spoke of listening to Jad Fair with headphones on while carousing through shopping malls. He imagined that if the strangers around him could hear what he was hearing, they would lose complete control of themselves.

Cobain had such an appreciation of records like *Sing No Evil*, *Music to Strip By*, and *Charmed Life* that he asked Fair and his band to open for Nirvana during their *In Utero* trek in 1993. He was wearing a Half Japanese T-shirt when he died.

Hüsker Dü

Minneapolis punk trio Hüsker Dü held a strong musical sway over each member of Nirvana. In fact, reports suggest that Cobain had sought out the band's guitarist/singer Bob Mould to produce *Nevermind* based on the sounds he'd achieved on the trio's final three studio records, *Flip Your Wig* (1985), *Candy Apple Grey* (1986), and *Warehouse: Songs and Stories* (1987). Mould was working on a comeback with his new band Sugar at the time, however, and declined the offer.

Grohl was equally influenced by the band and once cited *Zen Arcade*, the group's acclaimed 1984 double-album, as his favorite. "When it comes to guitar playing and song structure, I think that Hüsker Dü might be my biggest songwriting influence," he told *Classic Rock* in May 2011. Although Mould never collaborated with Nirvana, Grohl did successfully recruit his guitar hero to appear on the track "Dear Rosemary," from the Foo Fighters 2011 album *Wasting Light*.

Daniel Johnston

Kurt Cobain cherished his copy of Daniel Johnston's 1983 cassette release *Yip/Jump Music* and often touted the eccentric singer/songwriter in interviews during 1992. In September of that year, Kurt famously wore a T-shirt promoting Johnston's subsequent cassette *Hi, How Are You?*

From 1989 on, parts of Daniel's catalog were reissued by indie label Homestead Records, broadening his audience enough so that Olympia's hipsters might discover him. Of course, Cobain's endorsement three years later made the unthinkable happen—Johnston was signed to major label Atlantic Records for 1994's *Fun*, which was produced by the Butthole Surfers' Paul Leary. Unfortunately, that record—issued while Johnston was in a mental institution—was a critical and commercial flop.

Prior to the Atlantic deal, Johnston had been offered a deal with Elektra Records. He declined the offer because he believed his potential labelmates in Metallica were possessed by Satan.

Lead Belly

Cobain first learned about black folksinger Lead Belly, born Huddie William Ledbetter, when he read an article about him by William S. Burroughs soon after he moved to Olympia. And after Kurt discussed the article with his friend Slim Moon, his neighbor lent him a copy of *Lead Belly's Last Session*.

Kurt was drawn to the record's raw presentation and heartfelt delivery, not to mention Lead Belly's backstory. The singer taught himself guitar in prison after being caught in a liquor-bootlegging bust during Prohibition. After escaping from prison, he was caught again after killing a relative in 1918 in a fight over a woman. Through his music, he eventually earned the appreciation of Texas Governor Pat Morris Neff and was released after serving seven years of his sentence. While serving further time on a subsequent attempted murder charge relating to the death of a white man at Louisiana's Angola Prison Farm, he was discovered by John and Alan Lomax, who recorded him in 1934 for the Library of Congress. He was released later that year by governor Oscar K. Allen.

In homage to Lead Belly, Cobain began playing the Southern Appalachian traditional "Where Did You Sleep Last Night," which Lead Belly had popularized in 1944, during Nirvana shows in 1989 and 1990. Nirvana revisited the song again during their legendary 1993 performance for *MTV Unplugged.*

Led Zeppelin

As noted earlier, Krist Novoselic first discovered Led Zeppelin while he was living in the Los Angeles area in his early teens. Cobain became a student of the band around the same time. The pair's appreciation for 1970s hard rock surfaced in "Aero Zeppelin," which eventually saw release on *Incesticide.*

For Grohl, who caught the punk bug early, an appreciation of albums like *Led Zeppelin IV* and *Houses of the Holy* came later, when he was sixteen and balancing his hardcore roots with the bombastic drum fills of John Bonham and the mystical guitar work of Jimmy Page. Of course, Zeppelin went hand in hand at the time with his regular use of marijuana.

The Meat Puppets

Formed in 1980 in Arizona by Curt and Cris Kirkwood, the Meet Puppets soon aligned with Greg Ginn's SST Records and released seven albums for the label between 1982 and 1989. Following the Kirkwood brothers' appearance with Nirvana on *MTV Unplugged* in 1993, few could deny that Kurt Cobain held the band close to his heart. Nirvana performed three songs from 1984's *Meat Puppets II* during their set: "Plateau," "Oh Me," and "Lake of Fire."

Novoselic's relationship with Curt Kirkwood didn't end there. The two briefly played with Sublime drummer Bud Gaugh as Eyes Adrift in 2002. Then, in March 2013, the Meat Puppets supported Dave Grohl's Sound City Players—whose members included Stevie Nicks, Rick Springfield, John Fogerty, Cheap Trick's Rick Nielsen, and Fear's Lee Ving—when they played at Stubb's. The Puppets were promoting their fourteenth album as part of that year's SXSW festival.

The Melvins

Before Kurt and Krist were in a band of their own, the Melvins taught them the ropes of life in an underground touring band. But aside from the mentorship and the friendship that Buzz Osborne, Dale Crover, and their assorted co-conspirators offered Cobain and Novoselic, that *other* trio from Grays Harbor also made an important sonic impact on the world. How else would Dave Grohl have uncovered their *Glue Porch Treatments* in Amsterdam while on tour with Scream in 1987?

For Grohl, the allure of the Melvins stemmed from the pacing of the music. Osborne's songs asserted that heavy numbers could be powerful and slow, but it was Crover's fascinating drumming that really caught Dave's ear. It began to impact his playing as much as John Bonham's had a few years earlier.

Summing up the Melvins' effect on Nirvana and the world in 2009, Novoselic told John Hughes:

> I think at the end of the day when you look at rock 'n' roll music and the pantheon of rock 'n' roll, the Melvins are going to get their due because it's very sophisticated, well crafted, hard rock music. And we all come from somewhere. We come from Black Sabbath or The Who, or we come from punk rock music—Sex Pistols. But in the lineage of rock 'n' roll, the Melvins have a place there because they've added something to it. They've just not regurgitated this idea, or rehashed that idea . . . Buzz and Dale have been true artists. They are taking this form and they're making it their own.

Mission of Burma

Formed in Boston in 1979, Mission of Burma were a thought-provoking post-punk band that released sonic missives like "Academy Fight Song" and "That's When I Reach for My Revolver" during their four-year run. The band called it a day in 1983, in part because of singer guitarist Roger Miller's worsening tinnitus. A posthumous live album—*The Horrible Truth About Burma*, culled from their final tour—was released in 1985, and found its way into the hands of Dave Grohl.

Grohl went on to champion the loud, powerful band—also featuring Clint Conley, Peter Prescott, and Martin Swope—by putting them in the same company as Rites of Spring. In a 1997 *Melody Maker* interview, he marveled how the "really inspirational" foursome "just totally changed the template" of punk music in the 1980s. Eventually, the music world caught up with Mission of Burma, and in 2002 the band reunited for a tour, with Shellac kit man Bob Weston taking over for Swope. They went on to release the albums *ONoffON* (2004), *The Obliterati* (2006), and *Unsound* (2012).

Mudhoney

Although Nirvana would go on to surpass Mudhoney in a commercial sense, the two Seattle-area groups spent so much time in each other's company that they couldn't help but have an impact on one another. Krist Novoselic was first introduced to the band's front man Mark Arm in 1983 by Melvins members Buzz Osborne and Matt Lukin, who brought him to witness Arm's first band, Mr. Epp & the Calculations. Arm would go on to form Green River with Steve Turner in the mid-'80s before launching Mudhoney in 1988. He was also the first person to use the term "grunge" (to describe his new group).

Drawing on the Sonics, the Stooges, and the hardcore scene they once occupied, Mudhoney put the Seattle music on the map with "Touch Me I'm Sick" and helped to establish the Sub Pop brand. "The new Mudhoney started playing shows and were a sensation right from the start," Novoselic wrote in a July 2008 *Seattle Weekly* column, congratulating the band on its twentieth anniversary. Explaining the formula that elevated the band—which also featured drummer Dan Peters and bassist Lukin—above their peers, Krist cited the combination of Arm's wry wit and songs with strong hooks.

In 2013, Mudhoney celebrated a quarter-century together (albeit having since replaced Lukin with bassist Guy Maddison) with the April 4 release of *Vanishing Point*, the band's ninth album overall and sixth for Sub Pop.

Pixies

Kurt once spoke of how 1988's *Surfer Rosa* changed his outlook on music and helped to phase out some of the nihilism that had been rampant in his mind and in his music. As much as he worshipped Steve Albini's production, he was captivated by the Pixies' songs, which included numbers like "Bone Machine," "Broken Face" "Gigantic," and "Where Is My Mind?" Through repeated listening, Kurt began to acknowledge his love of pop-inflected rock music following several years as a punk elitist.

Meanwhile, Grohl had an appreciation for the Pixies more polished work on 1989's *Doolittle*, 1990's *Bossanova*, and 1991's *Trompe Le Monde*, and eventually hired the producer of those records to helm the Foo Fighters' 1997 album *The Colour and the Shape*. When forced to pick, Dave would ultimately cite the quartet's final LP—*Trompe Le Monde*, recorded while the Pixies were falling apart—as his favorite, heralding the diversity of the disc, which veered from punkish noise to blatant pop without warning.

The Raincoats

This British, female post-punk band made such an impression on Cobain, that he—along with members of Sonic Youth—was instrumental in having Geffen reissue their three albums—1979's self-titled set, 1981's *Odyshape*, and 1984's *Moving*—in 1993.

Kurt was first drawn to the group's honest, raw debut—and their finest moment, "Fairytale in the Supermarket." Or, as he told *Spin* in February 1994, "When I listen to the Raincoats, I feel as if I'm a stowaway in an attic. We're together in the same old house and I have to be completely still or they will hear me spying."

R.E.M.

Cobain listed R.E.M.'s *Green* (1988) as one of his fifty favorite albums. Like the records before it—which Cobain and Novoselic would also devour—the Athens, Georgia, group's sixth album proved rock could be contagious and yet have a conscience, as evidenced by the disc's lead single, "Orange Crush," which made reference to the effects of chemical defoliant Agent Orange on young American soldiers back from Vietnam.

As Novoselic would later note, Nirvana recruited Scott Litt to work on *In Utero* because of his work with R.E.M. In a September 2010 *Seattle Weekly* piece, Krist acknowledged that he discovered the band later than most—around the time of 1987's *Document*—because the quartet weren't part of the American punk revolution.

"I liked their sound right away," he explained, citing "About a Girl" when adding that singer Michael Stipe, guitarist Peter Buck, bassist Mike Mills, and drummer Bill Berry "made an impact on what Nirvana was working on at the time."

Sex Pistols

Driven by anger, attitude, and noise, the Sex Pistols were a giant middle finger to the UK rock establishment when they first emerged in late 1976. A year later, *Never Mind the Bollocks* emerged and over time would come to be considered one of the most influential records ever made.

For Kurt Cobain, songs like "Anarchy in the UK," "God Save the Queen," "Pretty Vacant," and "Holidays in the Sun" were exhilarating, but it was the sound of the record that amazed him. "[It] has the best production of any rock record I've ever heard," he told *Melody Maker* in August 1992. "It's totally in-your-face and compressed."

Shonen Knife

Upon hearing *Burning Farm*, Shonen Knife's cassette-only release on K Records, Cobain said it affected him so deeply that he began to cry. Stunned to discover that a band from Japan could write such amazing songs, Kurt was actually nervous to meet them when they played together for the first time on a UK tour. He was concerned that his unshaven and unkempt appearance might frighten them—which it did.

Cobain was drawn to the group's sincerity, lack of pretention, and endearing qualities. Formed in Osaka in 1981, the trio found their own inspiration from the Ramones, the Beach Boys, and early girl groups. According to a 2003 *Rolling Stone* feature on Shonen Knife, upon seeing the band live in Los Angeles in 1991, Kurt explained, "When I finally got to see them, I was transformed into a hysterical nine-year-old girl at a Beatles concert."

Sonic Youth

Sonic Youth's impact on Nirvana is well documented in this book. In addition to their musical influence (perhaps most obviously 1988's *Daydream Nation*), the members of the band, most notably the husband-wife duo of Thurston Moore and Kim Gordon, nurtured Cobain, Novoselic, and Grohl into the mainstream, connecting them to management and record label people that launched the band.

This relationship is clearly evident to anyone who has seen the documentary *1991: The Year Punk Broke*, which chronicles Sonic Youth's European tour that year with Nirvana as the opening act. Unfortunately, within a year, the relationship between the bands had become more distant as Kurt spiraled into addiction.

The Vaselines

"Nirvana loved to play Vaselines tunes," Krist Novoselic explained in *Seattle Weekly* in May 2009. "We played them every chance we got." A simple look at the band's set lists between 1991 and 1993 confirms this—not to mention the band's renditions of "Son of a Gun" and "Molly's Lips" on *Incesticide* and "Jesus Wants Me for a Sunbeam" on *MTV Unplugged in New York*.

Original Nirvana drummer Chad Channing had first turned Krist on to the band, comprised of Eugene Kelly and Frances McKee, in 1988, when he played Novoselic the duo's *Dying for It* EP in his Bainbridge Island apartment. Cobain was already hip to the pair, having learned that Calvin Johnson's band, Beat Happening, had collaborated with them. Once he became famous, Kurt did everything he could to spread the word about Kelly and McKee, proudly announcing them as his favorite songwriters in the world.

The Who

The sheer power of the Who—perhaps best exemplified on *Live at Leeds*—caught the attention of Nirvana's members. Although Cobain once wrote, "I hope I die before I become Pete Townshend" in one of his journal rants, he was clearly took his destructive cues from the guitarist.

Novoselic meanwhile was charmed by John Entwistle's dexterous but heavy bass work. Krist was an ardent student of "The Ox," from his lead parts on "My Generation" and "Boris the Spider" to his flexible playing throughout 1971's classic *Who's Next*.

In a *Seattle Weekly* article, Nirvana's bassist once marveled at how the Who's four-string maestro could run up and down the neck of his instrument while still keeping the melody of a song in his sights.

Young Marble Giants

Cobain loved *Colossal Youth*, the lone 1980 album by Young Marble Giants, and ranked it among his all-time favorites. Despite the cheesy drum machine heard on the record, Cobain became mesmerized when he was introduced to it in 1988.

Kurt later told Everett True that he had a crush on the group's singer, Alison Statton, who delivered aloof, melodic lyrics on subjects like painting her nails. Considering Cobain uncovered this record during his time spent in Olympia, likely on the recommendation of Calvin Johnson, it seems only fitting that the band's one-time guitarist Stuart Moxham wound up producing Beat Happening's final album, 1992's *You Turn Me On*.

26

We Spoke of Was and When

True Stories

Fingering Ozzy

During a two-hour SiriusXM radio special hosted by Jon Stewart to celebrate the twentieth anniversary of *Nevermind* in September 2011, Grohl spoke of how he and Cobain tried to gain weight drinking protein shakes. Funny as that might sound, perhaps the funniest story in Nirvana history concerns the band's interaction with legendary Black Sabbath front man Ozzy Osbourne.

While Nirvana were working on *Nevermind* in May 1991, Osbourne was recording his album *No More Tears* (which included the hit "Mama, I'm Coming Home") in an adjacent studio. At one point, Osbourne walked into the studio lounge where Dave and Kurt were playing pool. He gave them a curious look.

Later, after the heavy-metal icon left the room, Grohl and Cobain looked down at their hands and burst out laughing, realizing that the look was because they had both jokingly written "OZZY" on their fingers in Sharpie during a drunken binge the night before.

Greasy Flag

When MTV arranged for a pre-show game of Twister in Boston with the members of Nirvana, Smashing Pumpkins, and Bullet Lavolta, Novoselic had Cobain grease up his nearly nude body with Crisco shortening. After the event, Krist used an American Flag hanging on a wall inside the club to wipe off the oil. It didn't sit well with the New England patriots at the show.

"These jocks came up and were really bad-vibing me," Novoselic told *Spin* in January 1992. "Like, 'hey, you don't do that to our American flag.'" As a result, a bodyguard was arranged to escort Krist around the venue for the rest of the evening.

Trashing TAMA

During Nirvana's first tour of Japan in early 1992, Dave Grohl managed to upset the president of TAMA, his Aichi-based drum sponsors. Because the head of the company was unfamiliar with the group's destructive ways, when Grohl started trashing his drum kit—with help from Cobain and Novoselic—during their Nagoya gig, the executive worried it was because he didn't like his instruments.

Backstage, Barrett Jones—who served as Dave's drum tech for the tour—assured TAMA's president that the drums were fine. He explained how destruction was often part of a Nirvana show—just as Krist shot off a fire extinguisher.

Forget *Rolling Stone*

Cobain once explained that he had completely forgotten his promise to speak to *Rolling Stone* during Nirvana's early 1992 tour of the Far East. He had been pressured into doing the piece by his bandmates and the band's managers, and reluctantly agreed to do the interviews while they were in Australia, despite feeling overexposed.

When a subsequent photo shoot was arranged, he thought he might be able to sabotage the cover story if the pictures were unacceptable. "On my way there I just decided, 'I'm going to write something on my shirt that's offensive enough to stop getting our picture on the cover,'" Kurt later told the *Advocate*, explaining his decision to write "Corporate Magazines Still Suck" on his T-shirt.

In doing so, he could say that he went along with the shoot, but that somehow the group didn't get picked to be on the cover. "I wasn't necessarily challenging *Rolling Stone*, saying, 'You suck' and 'We don't want to have anything to do with you,' but we'll still use you for our exposure."

Despite Kurt's attempts to thwart the cover shoot, however, *Rolling Stone* was happy to put Nirvana on the front of the magazine any way it could. In fact, the shot—taken in the hot Australian landscape—has since become one of the publication's most enduring covers.

Waxed

While walking through London in August 1992 prior to Nirvana's headlining appearance at the Reading Festival, Kurt found himself in need of a restroom as he stood in front of the city's Rock Circus wax museum. When he entered the building to see if he could use their facilities, he was refused and instructed that the bathrooms were for patrons only. Ironically, the business was thriving on his likeness—there was a waxwork statue of Cobain holding a guitar in the window of the museum.

Tall Tales

Interviewed by travel magazine *Monk* in his suite at the Hotel Sorrento after the band's Seattle Center Arena show in September 1992, Kurt seemed completely animated. He was also full of fabrications, weaving a farcical tale to writer James Crotty of how he had been run out of his hometown.

"They chased me to the Castle of Aberdeen with torches, just like the Frankenstein monster," Cobain explained. "And I got away in a hot-air balloon. And I came here to Seattle."

He next told the unbelievable tale of how the towering, Paul Bunyan–esque Novoselic was beaten up after returning one night to the local Denny's. "Some locals were giving him the eye, and I don't think it was sexual," Cobain said deadpan. "They started beating him up in the men's room, saying 'some local hero you are.' Next thing he remembers, he was dancing on a table."

Elsewhere, the one-time junk-food addict claimed his favorite foods were water and rice. When probed about the subject of reincarnation, Kurt theorized, "If you're a really mean person you're going to come back as a fly and eat poop. You'll come back as a fly or Matt Lukin." Asked what he might one day name his autobiography, he offered the title *I Was Not Thinking*.

Pants on Fire

By the time final mixes of the *In Utero* album were completed on February 26, 1993, the members of Nirvana were in the mood to celebrate. In addition to alcohol, the band took things up a notch while hanging on the grounds at Pachyderm Studios, lighting their pants on fire.

According to Pat Whalen, a friend of the band, they all poured solvent on their jeans and lit themselves on fire. Passing the flame from one person to the next, pant leg by pant leg, they prevented actual physical harm by pouring beer on each other.

Heart-Shaped Burn

In Los Angeles during the late summer of 1993 for the video shoot for "Heart-Shaped Box," Love and Cobain had a protracted argument while they were holed up at the Four Seasons Hotel. Courtney had been nagging Kurt about the importance of how he looked in the video.

Cobain eventually grew sick of his wife's complaints, and after he had reached his limit he decided to extinguish his cigarette in the middle of his own forehead. As a result, during filming, Kurt required extensive makeup to cover the nasty, self-inflicted burn on his face. For close-ups, a piece of his hair was glued down above his brow to cover the scab.

Spitting at Fans

In November 1993, just days before Nirvana filmed their memorable *MTV Unplugged* episode, Kurt Cobain was in a foul mood, which led him to react negatively when he was approached by three fans in front of the St. Regis Hotel in Manhattan. Instead of obliging them in their requests for autographs and photos—or simply ignoring them—he turned nasty as he climbed into his van, which was to take him to SST Rehearsal Studios in Weehawken, New Jersey.

Responding to his followers' claims of love and worship, Kurt got out of the van, stood on its running board, and spat on the fans. Then, as the van drove away toward the band's rehearsal across the Lincoln Tunnel, he looked back to see said fans had been left astonished by his despicable behavior.

27

One More at the Door of My Heart

In Utero

Train Wreck in Sao Paulo

On January 16, 1993, Nirvana took the stage at the Hollywood Rock Festival in Sao Paulo, Brazil, before their biggest-ever audience of 110,000 people. Although the gig was notable for Flea from the Red Hot Chili Peppers playing trumpet on "Teen Spirit" and Cobain diving into the massive audience and smashing his guitar to pieces, many consider the gigantic stadium show to have been the worst performance of the trio's career.

According to Charles Cross's Cobain biography, Kurt was nervous about playing before such a large crowd and mixed pills and alcohol before the gig in the hope of relaxing. It worked so well that he was having trouble playing his guitar. And, to worsen matters, Nirvana hadn't rehearsed.

The show began with a series of Nirvana staples, but the performances were iffy. Things spiraled downward after about thirty minutes, with Kurt dragging the band through an onstage medley/jam of Iron Maiden's "Run to the Hills" and Led Zeppelin's "Heartbreaker."

Nirvana's karaoke-inspired set continued with covers of Queen's "We Will Rock You" (sung as "We Will Fuck You"), Terry Jacks' '70s pop number "Seasons in the Sun," Kim Wilde's "Kids in America," the Clash's "Should I Stay Or Should I Go," Tommy Tutone's "867-5309/Jenny," and Duran Duran's "Rio." Novoselic failed to see the humor in Cobain's impromptu madness. When Kurt wouldn't stop his covers routine, Krist threw his bass at him to let him know he was done. After watching the bass land in Kurt's vicinity, Krist walked offstage to have what he would describe to MTV later that year as a "mental breakdown."

Realizing that, contractually, the band had to play for a minimum of forty-five minutes in order to get paid, members of the band's crew went to retrieve Nirvana's bassist. When Novoselic came back onstage he picked his bass up from where it had been thrown and, without tuning it, joined the group for their final three numbers, "Lounge Act," "Heart-Shaped Box," and "Scentless Apprentice." At one point during these final numbers, Cobain picked up a cantaloupe that had been rolled onstage by his guitar tech Earnie Bailey and began smashing it on his six-string.

Suicidal in Rio de Janeiro

Following the show in Sao Paolo, and with a week until their next gig at the Hollywood Rock Festival in Rio de Janeiro, Nirvana checked into a luxury high-rise hotel in Brazil's second largest city. It was early into this stay that Cobain—depressed and downhearted as a result of drug withdrawal—threatened to jump from his balcony after he and Courtney got into a fight (presumably about arranging to buy heroin).

Kurt was afraid to buy the drug himself, fearing that he might be arrested, which would then force him to be completely honest to reporters about his usage. With no one else in Nirvana's entourage willing to help him, and most of them keeping a keen watch over him, he was in a very fragile and irritable state.

In an order to keep Kurt from jumping from any heights, Courtney insisted they stay in a first-floor hotel room. Because there were few—if any—three- or four-star hotels with ground-level rooms in Rio, Cobain was forced to stay in an economy motel for the rest of his time in Rio.

BMG Ariola

During the week between gigs, Nirvana booked three days of studio time at BMG Ariola Ltda. Studios in Rio, beginning on January 19. With soundman Craig Montgomery serving as the producer and engineer, the band ran through versions of several new songs, including their first attempt at "Heart-Shaped Box," a song that Cobain had worked on with Love.

With engineer Ian Beveridge and his assistant Dalmo Beloti, the group worked on twenty-four-track demo versions of "Scentless Apprentice" "Milk It," "Very Ape," "The Other Improv," "I Hate Myself and Want to Die," "Moist Vagina," and "Gallons of Rubbing Alcohol Flow Through the Strip." They also cut a version of "Seasons in the Sun" with Kurt singing and playing drums, Novoselic on guitar, and Grohl on bass.

Grohl also recorded and played all the instruments on his song "Onward into Countless Battles," with backing vocals from Cobain. Some Hole songs were also attempted, including "The Only Rape I Know" "I Think That I Would Die," "It's Closing Soon," and "Miss World." Kurt played bass and provided backing vocals on some of these songs, which were tracked with Courtney and new Hole drummer Patty Schemel.

Back in Form

When Nirvana took the stage for their next show, at the Hollywood Rock Festival in Rio on January 23, the band seemed in good spirits. Despite the lack of available heroin, Kurt had managed to keep himself preoccupied with the recording sessions. When the group took the stage at Apoetose Stadium, they emerged triumphant. The performance served as redemption after the previous week's unfortunate spectacle.

Novoselic sang the opening lyrics to Electric Light Orchestra's "Telephone Line" as the group started up with a jam of "L'Amour Est Un Oiseau Rebelle," the habanera from Georges Bizet's 1875 opera *Carmen*. This gave way to "School" and a run through various Nirvana favorites, plus the newly perfected "Heart-Shaped Box." Late in the set, the trio jammed on Aerosmith's "Sweet Emotion," but this time the members of Nirvana were in alignment about the song choices.

Surprisingly, during "Scentless Apprentice," Cobain stood before one of the video cameramen filming the show and performed a lewd act. According to attendees, he could be seen exposing and touching his genitals. This was transmitted on the jumbo screen above the stage. Music aside, Kurt had given Rio something to remember him by.

Jag-Stang

Back in the early days of Nirvana, out of poverty, Kurt Cobain would fuse guitar parts together to create "Frankenstein" instruments as a means to salvage the equipment he had destroyed in his onstage rages. Then, in February 1993, Fender Guitars came to him to offer him the opportunity to design his own custom electric guitar. Two left-handed Jag-Stang guitars—a cross between Fender's Jaguar and Mustang models, which took their names from popular sports cars in the 1960s—were crafted for Kurt's own use by one-time Custom Shop Master Builder Larry L. Brooks.

In a 1994 interview, Kurt explained that he took Polaroids of both models, cut the photos in half, and joined them together. He also sketched out the guitar in his journals. Plans to sell a version of Cobain's design were in the works at the time, although the guitar wasn't formally released until the fall of 1995. It was then made available in "Fiesta Red" and "Sonic Blue."

"Oh, the Guilt"

On February 15, Nirvana released a split single with the Jesus Lizard through the latter's label, Touch and Go Records. Nirvana's offering, tracked ten months earlier during a session at Laundry Room with Barrett Jones, was supposedly inspired by the guilt and uneasiness Cobain felt after making a difficult decision.

The Jesus Lizard—David Yow, Duane Denison, David Wm. Sims, and Mac McNeilly—were granted the A-side of the release for their song, "Puss," making them benefactors of Nirvana's popularity. That month the single peaked at #12 in the UK.

If the notion of a split-single was curious for a band of Nirvana's stature, the teaming with a significant underground like the Jesus Lizard was a reminder to the music community that, despite the multi-platinum success of *Nevermind*, Nirvana intended to stay true to their punk roots.

Raw Concept

Because of their discontent over the polished sound of *Nevermind*, Nirvana aspired to make a multi-dimensional album that balanced the raw, unrefined sounds of their debut while retaining some of the pop sensibility that helped make them a household name. Kurt felt that Steve Albini's work with the Pixies and the Breeders, two of his favorite bands, made the Big Black veteran the perfect candidate for the job of producing the new album.

Kurt loved the way Albini made *Surfer Rosa* and *Pod* sound. He was impressed with the way Albini placed microphones around the studio to capture the natural ambience of the room and wanted Nirvana's third record to have a similarly visceral vibe.

When Cobain expressed his interest in working with Albini to the UK press in the summer of 1992, long before Nirvana approached the Chicago-based producer, Albini denied he was involved in the project. Days later, Gold Mountain contacted Steve to ask him if he would want to work with Nirvana.

According to Michael Azerrad, Albini had once dismissed Nirvana as "R.E.M. with a Fuzzbox," trashed *Nevermind* as "a standard hack recording," and suggested they were an unexceptional version of the Seattle sound. Despite this, he agreed to work with them, although he later claimed he only did so because he felt sorry for them and equated them to "the same sort of people as all the small-fry bands I deal with."

Kurt sent Steve their Brazil demos and, in turn, the producer sent Cobain a copy of *Rid of Me*, the P. J. Harvey album he had just produced at Pachyderm in December 1992. He did this in order to help the Nirvana front man get a sense of how a recording made in Cannon Falls might sound.

Pachyderm

The making of Nirvana's third album, tentatively titled *I Hate Myself and Want to Die*, got underway on February 13, 1993, at Pachyderm Studios in Cannon Falls, Minnesota. Due to delays in the arrival of the band's instruments, the sessions began three days later than planned.

With Albini at the helm, the trio was booked for the sessions under the alias "The Simon Ritchie Bluegrass Ensemble." Cobain, who often checked into hotels under the name "Simon Ritchie," had once again secretly honored the late Sex Pistols bassist Sid Vicious by using his birth name.

In addition to Albini, studio maintenance technician Bob Weston IV (who played in the acclaimed 1980s indie band Volcano Suns before teaming with Albini in Shellac in 1991), studio engineer Brent Sigmeth, and the members of Nirvana were accompanied by a macrobiotic chef who happened to be Weston's girlfriend. Aside from Albini's commission, the total cost to make the album at Pachyderm—including recording, mixing, and lodging at a house on the studio grounds—was $24,000.

Flat Fee

Unlike most producer-artist agreements, Albini declined royalty points in his arrangement with Gold Mountain to produce Nirvana. Instead, he insisted on a flat fee of $100,000, despite the fact that—based on sales predictions—a standard royalty contract would have earned him a half-million dollars. For Albini, it was about principle. As he would explain in *Come as You Are*, he felt that taking "points" from the artists he worked with—even an act as popular as Nirvana—was immoral. Furthermore, he suggested the band pay for the sessions themselves to mitigate record company meddling. He set a two-week deadline to complete the album.

No Intrusions

In accordance with the agreement between Nirvana and Albini, there were to be no intrusions from the band's record company or management during the production of the album.

In addition to the project's engineer and technician, Steve spoke only to with Kurt, Krist, and Dave, and purposely avoided the others in the group's entourage, telling Jim DeRogatis, in his 2003 book *Milk It: Collected Musings on the Alternative Music Explosion of the '90s*, that the band's associates were "the biggest pieces of shit I ever met."

In spite of the hiccup with their equipment, Nirvana worked efficiently during their two weeks at Pachyderm. They would usually get started around noon, break for lunch and dinner, and work through until around midnight.

The rural, snow-covered setting was ideal in keeping Cobain from distractions, and allowed the trio to put down the basic tracks for the album in just five days, recording most of them together at once. Albini's focus on the drums was notable—he placed thirty microphones around Grohl's kit. When it came time to put down the drums to "Very Ape" and "Tourette's," he moved Grohl's set to the kitchen because of the room's natural reverb.

Two days of overdubs followed, during which time Kurt added extra guitar tracks, guitar solos, and vocal parts. As with *Nevermind*, Kurt continued to tweak the lyrics to certain songs while others were being tracked. Just the same, he explained to Darcy Steinke in *Spin* that year that the lyrics were "more focused, they're almost built on themes."

Cobain's vocals—which the producer refused to double-track—were supposedly recorded in just six hours. From there, Albini began to mix the material, which took five days. The album was completed on February 26. Sort of.

Cranking Eddie

During Nirvana's two-week stay at Pachyderm, which coincided with Kurt's twenty-sixth birthday, he only left the facility twice. Once, he traveled to a Minneapolis gig by the local punk-blues band Cows, and on another occasion, he went to the sprawling Mall of America in Bloomington, where he shopped for plastic anatomical models of the Visible Man for his collection.

Sometime during their stay in Cannon Falls, the members of Nirvana and Albini made crank calls to people they knew, including Pearl Jam singer Eddie Vedder. When Steve was frustrated with how things were going in the studio, he would also set things on fire, much to the band's amusement.

No Love for Love

About a week into the work at Pachyderm, Courtney Love and Frances Bean arrived in Cannon Falls to see Cobain. Immediately, the dynamic changed and the atmosphere shifted from upbeat to tense.

Although members of the band, Albini, and Love herself have never spoken publicly about the matter, the studio's chef witnessed Courtney being critical of Kurt's work on the basic tracks and overdubs and confrontational with the others present. Another account says she was specifically critical of Grohl.

Track by Track

It wasn't until several months after the sessions were finished that Nirvana settled on a title for their third record. Kurt's provisional, troubling name of *I Hate Myself and Want to Die* didn't sit well with Novoselic. The phrase first surfaced in Cobain's journals in the middle of 1992 and served as his answer whenever people would ask him how he was feeling.

Although Kurt thought it was humorous—a way of letting everyone know not to take Nirvana so seriously—others didn't get the joke. Krist was successful in talking Cobain out of using the title by explaining that it could somehow leave the band susceptible to lawsuits were any listeners to act on the suggestion.

For a short time, the group considered the title *Verse Chorus Verse*, from their song of the same name, which was later retitled "Sappy." Eventually, they settled on *In Utero*, which was culled from a poem written by Courtney Love.

"Serve the Servants"

The first song on *In Utero* is also Cobain's most lyrically direct. The track's opening lines acknowledge the "teenage angst" payday of *Nevermind*, but Kurt also lashed out at his critics—whom he branded "self-appointed judges"—and belittled the media for its witch hunt against Courtney and its branding of her as a drug addict, bad mother, and a cancer to Nirvana. Perhaps more importantly, he sung of his parents' divorce and the disappointment he felt toward his dad.

In liner notes that he wrote but decided not to use that eventually surfaced in *Journals*, Cobain acknowledged that he wrote the song, in part, to voice his frustration at his father Don's lack of communication, absence from his life, and inability to show affection to him. "I don't need a father/son relationship with a person whom I don't want to spend a boring Christmas with," Kurt wrote. "In other words: I love you; I don't hate you; I don't want to talk to you."

"Serve the Servants" is a contagious pop arrangement wrapped in brutal, forceful rock instrumentation. Its keen balance of hooks, distortion, and fury—the three key ingredients in Nirvana's sound—made it an ideal choice to launch the record.

"Scentless Apprentice"

Cobain based the lyrics to the album's second number on the Patrick Süskind horror novel *Perfume: The Story of a Murderer*. The book told the tale of a perfume-shop apprentice with a great ability to smell but no body odor of his own who began killing virgin women so that he could create the ideal fragrance.

The song was credited to Cobain, Grohl, and Novoselic, but its origins were actually Dave's. He brought the guitar riff and drum arrangement to his bandmates, and collectively they honed the music.

If this was the rare songwriting collaboration at this point in the trio's existence, when *In Utero* was released, Kurt admitted that he was actually open to songwriting collaborations again. He explained that by letting Novoselic and Grohl bring their ideas forward, it alleviated the pressure he was feeling to come up with all of the songs.

Looking back on the roaring, walloping song in January 2010, Grohl told *Mojo*, "One of my favorite lines in a Nirvana song is where Kurt sings, 'You can't fire me because I quit.' If there's one line in any song that gives me the chills it's that one. Maybe all those things that people wrote about him painted him into a corner that he couldn't get out of."

"Heart-Shaped Box"

Although the chorus to Nirvana's first single from *In Utero* sounds sarcastic in its delivery, "Heart-Shaped Box" is Cobain's ultimate love song to Courtney. The line "forever in debt to your priceless advice" was even recycled from a sincere letter he once sent to Love. The title, of course, stems from the box Love apparently gave Kurt when she was courting him.

In the song, Cobain mentions both his and Courtney's astrological signs—Pisces and Cancer—while chronicling their volatile relationship and the way he was lured into her "magnet tar-pit trap." But, like many of Kurt's compositions, "Heart-Shaped Box" has multiple meanings, and Kurt would soon enough acknowledge that parts of the song were inspired by the sadness he felt after watching television documentaries about children suffering from cancer. The song was originally titled "Heart-Shaped Coffin," until Love suggested he rethink its morose implications.

The origins of "Heart-Shaped Box" date back to early 1992. Several months then passed before Kurt revisited his ideas for the song during the summer, around the time the couple moved into their Hollywood Hills home. According to a 1994 interview with *Rolling Stone* to promote Hole's *Live Through This*, Courtney revealed that Kurt wrote the main riff to the song inside a closet in their house. When she asked if she could have it for one of her songs, her dear husband told her to "Fuck off," closed the door, and got back to work.

When he brought the song to the band, it was in rough shape structurally, but after repeated attempts to get the music right, the trio locked down the arrangement. Kurt's vocal melody followed.

In the UK, the tune preceded its parent album by several weeks when it was released as a single on August 23, 1993. Backed with the melodic, Grohl-sung "Marigold"—a hint at what he might be capable of, fronting his own band—"Heart-Shaped Box" reached #5. Although a commercial single was not released in the US, where Geffen was focused entirely on album sales, a promotional radio single was serviced to college and album-rock stations. As the label expected, the track took off at alternative radio and quickly topped the *Billboard* Modern Rock Tracks listings, driving CD sales just as the label had hoped.

"Rape Me"

Written on an acoustic guitar in Los Angeles in May 1991 while *Nevermind* was being mixed, "Rape Me" is an anti-rape song sung from the perspective of the victim. "It's like she's saying, 'Rape me, go ahead, rape me, beat me. You'll never kill me. I'll survive this and I'm gonna fucking rape you one of these days and you won't even know it,'" Cobain told *Spin*'s Darcy Steinke in October 1993.

Although some have suggested that the song was written in response to the media's outlook on his personal life, Cobain's success and public battle with drugs emerged months after. In December 1993, "Rape Me" was released as a double-A-side with "All Apologies" in the UK, where it reached #32. Not long after, Kurt agreed to let his record company list the song as "Waif Me" on copies of *In Utero* sold in the Wal-Mart and Kmart retail chains.

"Frances Farmer Will Have Her Revenge on Seattle"

As the fifth song on *In Utero* suggests, Cobain was well aware that he was becoming harder and harder for his management, his record label, and even his bandmates to deal with. With this track, he effectively describes himself as the Frances Farmer of alternative rock music.

Like Cobain, Farmer had her demons. She was a movie star in the 1930s and '40s but fell from grace and spiraled into alcoholism. Arrested for drink-driving, the actress was released but was subsequently sent to a mental hospital after she violated her parole by traveling to Mexico. After being institutionalized, she was given shock treatments and, ultimately, a lobotomy.

As Kurt learned when he read the 1978 novel *Shadowland*, a fictionalized account of Farmer's life by William Arnold, the Seattle native was actually given another shot at stardom and wound up having her own television show in the late 1950s before alcoholism, and ultimately cancer, led to her death in 1970.

The parallels between the actress—who once listed her occupation as "cocksucker" when she was arrested—and the rocker are remarkable. Both were strong-willed and rebellious, and defiant for the sake of their art.

"Dumb"

Over time, "Dumb"—one of Nirvana's most accessible songs—has become a favorite on American alternative radio. Cobain once suggested the song was informed by the marijuana he regularly smoked as a teenager. In his unused liner notes about the song, he would blame pot for affecting his memory, damaging his nerves, strengthening his destructive tendencies, and prompting him to seek out stronger drugs like heroin, hence the line that refers to floating around and hanging out on clouds before succumbing to a hangover.

Despite this explanation, when Kurt spoke to *Melody Maker* about the song in August 1992, he claimed that the track was about people who were easily amused and television fed. Not unlike the many people he knew in Montesano and Aberdeen, these "Dumb" people had crummy, mundane jobs, yet somehow seemed happy.

"Very Ape"

The aggressive approach of "Very Ape" is fitting considering its lyrical slant, which seems to take aim at the macho mentality that exists inside many men. With its overdriven guitar lines, pulverizing rhythms, and lack of melody, the song depicts an inconsistent character who—at first—comes off as "very nice" and respectful to women before revealing a dark side.

"Milk It"

A strong indication to fans that Cobain was still Love-sick and drowning in drug addiction, "Milk It" finds Nirvana's front man singing of being his "own parasite" while smelling the scent of Courtney on his clothes while in recovery. Lyrical themes aside, the song is a showcase for Grohl's drumming abilities and ranks among one of his most inventive performances with the band.

"Pennyroyal Tea"

In part a lyrical collaboration with Love about an unreliable herbal abortive, "Pennyroyal Tea" finds Kurt confessing to having "very bad posture" while also singing about living life on his own schedule and taking warm milk and laxatives to fight his opiate-driven constipation. It has also been suggested that the song's title was an intentionally self-deprecating play on the phrase "Penny Royalty."

However, in 1993 Kurt told *Impact* that the song was about someone suffering from deep despair, without fully admitting it was autobiographical. "The song is about a person who's beyond depressed," he explained. "They're in their death bed, pretty much."

Cobain did concede that his own stomach pain informed the song. He went on to explain his line about a "Leonard Cohen afterworld," saying that, along with Samuel Beckett's novel *Malloy*, Cohen's records were his "therapy" when he was "depressed and sick."

The music for the song dates back to the fall of 1990, when Cobain and Grohl worked on it on a four-track when they were living together in Olympia. Cobain claimed to Michael Azerrad that he wrote the music "in about thirty seconds."

Although Nirvana had planned to release the song as a UK single in April 1994, the unexpected end of the band prompted its cancelation. German copies of the CD single did hit the market, but they were recalled and destroyed. Just the same, the song remains a favorite among Nirvana fans. In 2004, *NME* ranked it as #8 among the "Top 20 Nirvana Songs of All Time."

"Radio Friendly Unit Shifter"

Call it an antidote to the slick, radio-ready Nirvana heard on "Teen Spirit," this guitar-driven, feedback-laden track was originally titled "Four Month Media Blackout" in response to the massive reception the former song was given between October 1991 to January 1992.

The term "radio-friendly" refers to a song with commercial appeal, while a "unit-shifter" is a song that helps sell albums. Yet Cobain was being intentionally ironic, as this was perhaps one of the most discordant numbers on the record. The lyrics were something of an afterthought, with Kurt even deeming it a throwaway song, and indicating that he had written the various lines separately before linking them together.

"Tourette's"

At just ninety-two seconds, this sonic eruption is aptly named, as it is indeed the musical equivalent of a Tourette's sufferer's outburst. Nirvana's furious but memorable performance is driven by Grohl's drum assault, Novoselic's hypnotic bass, and Cobain's roaring guitar and cathartic vocals.

"All Apologies"

Originally titled "La, La, La . . . La," the idea for Nirvana's third *Billboard* Modern Rock #1 first surfaced in 1990, and the song was initially recorded during studio demo sessions with Craig Montgomery in Seattle on January 1, 1991.

The trio's first attempt at the music took place in acoustic form, with Novoselic playing a second guitar in lieu of his bass while Grohl augmented his drumming with tambourine. A full-on electric version of the song was eventually tracked with Steve Albini on February 14, 1993, and featured the cello work of guest player Kera Schaley, the only outside musician to play on Nirvana's third studio disc.

When it came time for Cobain to deliver his vocals, he had decided to title the track "All Apologies" and dedicate it to his wife and daughter. Although he insisted it wasn't actually about his family, Kurt would convey to Michael Azerrad that the upbeat and peaceful tone of the recording—one of the more accessible numbers on *In Utero*—and its lyrics about being at ease in the sunshine made it a good choice to honor his loved ones.

All the same, the song wasn't entirely positive. Kurt's uncertain and unhappy outlook is hard to ignore. Based on his prose, the guilt and sadness he felt about the kind of drug-addled husband and father he had become was impossible to ignore.

Bonus Material

At various points in 1993, Nirvana had tracked extra material that was deemed good enough for release but not suitable for *In Utero*. Of the four leftover songs, three were to augment planned singles, while one was chosen as a hidden track for overseas CD buyers.

"Gallons of Rubbing Alcohol Flowing Through the Strip"

This bonus song was exclusive to European pressings of *In Utero* and was placed as a hidden track, twenty minutes after the completion of "All Apologies." Touching lyrically on themes of writer's block and bad relationships, the track's loose, jam-oriented vibe—tracked during Nirvana's January 1993 travels to Brazil—doesn't exactly add much to *In Utero*, and was wisely buried.

"Marigold"

Dave Grohl's first and only solo songwriting credit and lead vocal performance with Nirvana, this song was penned when the band's drummer lived with Cobain in Olympia, soon after he joined the band. Originally called "Color Pictures of a Marigold," it's a solid indication of the kind of music he might make as a solo performer.

The song first surfaced on *Pocketwatch*, an album Grohl made under the pseudonym Late! Produced by Barrett Jones and Geoff Turner, it was recorded on December 23, 1990, at Upland Studios in Arlington, Virginia, and released on the label Simple Machines in 1992.

Recorded again at Pachyderm by Grohl—who played all the parts, save for a little bass assistance from Novoselic—it is the only song issued in the history of Nirvana that had no input from Cobain. Despite this, Kurt agreed to use the song as the B-side to "Heart-Shaped Box."

"I Hate Myself and Want to Die"

Although it was tracked with Albini, this song was kept off of *In Utero* because the band agreed they already had enough abrasive material. "It was just a typical, boring song," Cobain told *Guitar World*. "We could write that song in our sleep. There was no point to putting it on the record."

Initially known as "2 Bass Kid," the song's dour title was a joke, according to Cobain, and not meant to be taken literally. Although Cobain would never know it, Oasis guitarist Noel Gallagher would later explain that he penned that band's classic "Live Forever" as an uplifting response to Nirvana's negative message.

In October 1993, Nirvana gave the track to the compilation album *The Beavis and Butthead Experience*. Cobain was an enormous fan of the cartoon, and although he worried about how such a commercial move might be perceived, he went forward with it anyway. Geffen records paid Nirvana $60,000 for their trouble.

"Moist Vagina"

A great musical moment from the *In Utero* sessions, "Moist Vagina"—also known as "MV," and originally titled "Moist Vagina and Then She Blew Him Like He's Never Been Blown, Brains Stuck All Over the Wall"—was relegated to B-side status thanks to its controversial lyrics. Some sources would later indicate that the song was left off the record because the band's camp feared that there was already enough controversy surrounding "Rape Me." In fact, Cobain once denied that "Moist Vagina" was even about oral sex, as many assumed, suggesting instead that it was about marijuana.

The song was eventually released as the B-side to the band's double-A-side single "All Apologies" / "Rape Me" in December 1993.

Subpar Sound

When an un-mastered but otherwise complete version of the Albini-produced album made its way into the hands of Nirvana's managers and key people at DGC—including Geffen head Ed Rosenblatt—the reactions were negative. The album's lack of commercial appeal worried just about everyone with a decision-making role in the group—except, of course, the band. A week after mixing was completed at Pachyderm, Cobain called Albini to explain that his A&R man, Gary Gersh, hated the disc.

In 1993, radio play meant significant record sales, and—as it stood—Nirvana's third album seemed doomed. But the coarse sound of the record wasn't the only concern, as Kurt relayed to Michael Azerrad in *Come as You Are*. He was told his songs on the new album were inferior to the material on *Nevermind*.

That response was discouraging to Cobain, who began to see himself as a conduit to cash for the label. He started to realize that if he were to buckle to that kind of logic, Nirvana could forget about ever being able to create the kind of art they wanted. Thankfully, the band received encouragement from their friends, who were closer to the indie-rock community and appreciated the fact that the band had made the kind of record they would want to play in their own homes.

Albini Declines to Remix the Album

The more Cobain listened to the un-mastered version of his new studio album, however, the more he hated how it sounded. Unlike Nirvana's previous records, *In Utero* didn't sound the way he had imagined it would. "I got no emotion from it," he told the *Melody Maker*'s Stud Brothers that summer. "I was just numb."

Unhappy mostly with the sound of the bass and the vocals, Kurt called Albini in early March to explain that he was having second thoughts, and that he wanted the producer to remix some of the tracks. Novoselic also relayed to Steve in a separate conversation that he didn't think the album sounded as good now as he had first thought.

After some consideration, Albini phoned Cobain to explain that he was declining the request to remix the songs, advising Kurt that he didn't believe he could improve on the recordings they made the month before.

With Albini out of the picture, Kurt and Krist hoped they would be able to remedy their concerns during the mastering process. But when Bob Ludwig—an iconic engineer who had mastered everyone from Led Zeppelin and Jimi Hendrix to the Who and the Rolling Stones—turned out his finished product, only Novoselic approved of it. Kurt was supposedly still unhappy with the sound. In a 2002 interview with NirvanaClub.com's Rasmus Holmen, Ludwig disputed this, saying, "There were no mistakes or omissions. All the original masters were approved by the group and/or producers and met with their expectations."

Albini Makes Waves

On April 19, Albini spoke out about his work with Nirvana, telling Greg Kot of the *Chicago Tribune* that he doubted Geffen Records would release the album he had recorded with the band. In an article titled "Record Label Finds Little Bliss in Nirvana's Latest," he blasted the group's label and handlers.

"Geffen and the band's management hate the record," Steve said bluntly. "They considered it an indulgence when Nirvana asked to record with me. I have no faith this record will be released."

"I got a call from Kurt and he was confused and distressed, and wanted my opinion," the producer continued. "I told him to stop listening to those fools and to put out the record. He seemed buoyed by that, and told me he was going to stick to his guns."

"It's not a record for wimps," he concluded—but that was exactly what worried the label and Gold Mountain. A source close to the band confirmed that Geffen executives were unhappy with the lack of palatable radio-ready songs.

You Call This Nirvana?

The May 16 issue of *Newsweek* magazine included a story about Nirvana's "unreleasable" and "stridently anti-commercial" album. It explained that Nirvana had decided to allow engineer Andy Wallace—famous for his work on *Nevermind*—to tinker with their latest recordings and give them a more accessible touch.

The piece cited a Gold Mountain press release that explained how Nirvana was considering doing some additional recording, adding that the band had "not yet decided on the final composition of the album."

Meanwhile, Albini was quick to point out a clause in his contract with Nirvana that stated no one could tamper with his tapes, while making Geffen out to be the "evil faceless record company" and reminding readers that the label once sued Neil Young and released an album by pop duo Nelson.

When asked for his opinion, Jesus Lizard front man David Yow said, "They shouldn't compromise. As far as I can tell, they're happy with the record, and they should make the record company release it as it is."

Not long after the *Newsweek* piece ran, Cobain came out publicly to refute the claims. "There has been no pressure from our record label to change the tracks we did with Albini," Kurt said in a prepared statement. "We have 100 percent control of our music." The statement also ran as a full-page ad titled "Nirvana's Kurt Cobain Debunks Rumors of Geffen Interference" in *Billboard* magazine on May 17, 1993.

Cobain went on to condemn *Newsweek* for ridiculing the group's relationship with Geffen on the basis of "totally erroneous information." If that wasn't enough, the label's founder and namesake, David Geffen, called the magazine to complain, while Rosenblatt issued his own statement, insisting that DGC would release "whatever record the band delivers to us" once the group had finished the album to their satisfaction.

Not surprisingly, Novoselic added some levity to the band's statement, saying, "All this press is great. I'm just waiting for a right-wing Christian group to deem the record satanic. That would really move some units."

Litt

Despite being considered for the project, Andy Wallace was never actually used. Instead, veteran R.E.M. producer Scott Litt was hired to remix two of the key tracks on *In Utero* at Seattle's Bad Animals studio that May. But getting Albini to hand over the master tapes took some convincing. Novoselic had to call Steve and reason with him before he would release the tapes to Gold Mountain.

Even though Cobain had hoped to deliver raw music to his fans, he recognized the importance of MTV and radio in sustaining his band's success. He also knew that Nirvana needed some hit-worthy material if he was going to successfully lure in record buyers.

As a result, he elected to rework the vocals for "Heart-Shaped Box" and "All Apologies" with Litt. For the former, Kurt even added an acoustic guitar part and harmony vocals.

During the session with Litt, the band also tasked the producer with recording a new take on "Sappy." The revised version of the song appeared on *No Alternative*, a 1993 compilation album released to raise awareness about AIDS.

Media Stink

A month after the *Newsweek* article, *Rolling Stone* ran its own version of the Nirvana saga. If Fred Goodman's piece seemed like old news, it did at least offer fans some new and interesting details.

First, A&R executive Gary Gersh called "bullshit" on Albini for making the label out to be "some big corporate conglomerate glopped onto Nirvana's legs." Gersh explained that he and Cobain had developed something of a father-son relationship over the previous two years and made it known that all sides—except Albini—had concluded that the album needed more work. When Steve declined to continue working on the album, the band had no choice but to seek outside help.

Although Albini wound up putting Nirvana on the spot, by the time Goodman had gotten to him, the outspoken producer seemed downright reticent. "I enjoyed working on the record and admire the band," he said. "I've thought from the beginning that the band should just make their feelings known, and I'm glad that they have."

Still, Danny Goldberg—who had moved from Gold Mountain to become the President of Atlantic Records but still served as a consultant to Nirvana—took exception to the trouble Albini had caused. Comparing the producer to Branch Davidian leader David Koresh, Goldberg snapped, "Steve Albini takes the position that anything he thinks is good is good. He is God. And if the artist doesn't like it, then the artist is somehow selling out because they don't agree with his personal vision."

A copy of *In Utero*—Nirvana's third and final studio album—autographed by Cobain, Novoselic, and Grohl. *Author's collection*

Packaging

Robert Fisher, who had served as the art director on both *Nevermind* and *Incesticide,* worked again with Cobain on *In Utero.* Kurt—who had been the ideas man behind the artwork on all of Nirvana's releases—came to Fisher with a unique concept for the album jacket: a transparent anatomical manikin imposed with angel wings.

For the back cover, Kurt created a collage that placed model fetuses and body parts atop a bed of flowers. After he had arranged it to his liking, he called photographer Charles Peterson over to his Seattle living room to take a picture of his creation. Kurt then arranged the song's titles and cuttings from Barbara G. Walker's book *The Woman's Dictionary of Symbols and Objects* around the edge of the back jacket.

According to Gillian G. Gaar's 2006 book about the album, when Kurt was asked what the collage represented, he replied, "Sex and woman and *In Utero* and vaginas and birth and death."

Critical Reaction

When advance copies of Nirvana's third record found their way into the hands of music critics in the late summer of 1993, the response was mostly positive. *Rolling Stone*'s David Fricke gave it four and a half stars and summed his view up by announcing, "*In Utero* is a lot of things—brilliant, corrosive, enraged, and thoughtful, most of them all at once. But more than anything it's a triumph of the will."

NME was also impressed, giving the album a score of eight out of ten and explaining, "Kurt should be proud of it. As a follow-up to one of the best records of the past ten years it just isn't quite there. Perhaps it was dumb to expect anything more."

Elsewhere, Robert Christgau of the *Village Voice* gave the album an A-grade, while *Entertainment Weekly*'s David Browne rated it a B+. In *Time*, Christopher John Farley wrote, "Despite the fears of some alternative-music fans, Nirvana hasn't gone mainstream, though this potent new album may again force the mainstream to go Nirvana."

Commercial Response

In the week following its September 14 release in the US, *In Utero* sold well. Debuting at #1 on the *Billboard* 200, the disc sold a respectable 180,000 copies. Considering that Kmart and Wal-Mart—two of the biggest CD retailers of the day—refused to stock the album because of its artwork, the numbers were impressive.

Both chains objected to the potentially offensive packaging, fearing that Cobain's art would upset their shoppers. Four months later, in January 1994, Cobain agreed to have the cover art altered so that *In Utero* could be sold in the stores. He also conceded to another change in order for the ban to be lifted when the title "Rape Me" was changed to "Waif Me."

Although the disc would eventually rack up sales of five million copies glob- ally, Nirvana's position as the best-selling rock band in North America was about to change. When Pearl Jam released their sophomore album *Vs.* on October 19, it set the record for the most copies of an album sold in its first week on sale in the US. After ten days, it had sold a remarkable 1.3 million copies, on its way to total sales of more than seven million.

Legacy

There's little disputing that *In Utero* was a significant commercial success, but next to *Nevermind* some perceived it to be a failure. As *Guitar World* proclaimed in 2003, "If it is possible for an album that sold four million copies to be over- looked, or underappreciated, then *In Utero* is that lost pearl."

The album has continued to be praised in the years since its release. Most notably, Pitchfork.com ranked it at #13 on its list of the one hundred best albums of the 1990s, and *Rolling Stone* placed the disc at #439 in its survey of the "500 Greatest Albums of All Time."

Krist's Assessment

Looking back on *In Utero*, Krist Novoselic would eventually deem it to be his favorite Nirvana album. Relaying his opinion to Charles Cross, he took pride as he declared it his band's creative and artistic triumph.

According to Krist, during the quick and efficient recording of the record, the trio thrived by leaving all of their personal issues at the door, and in doing so crafted an album that would be heralded by fans and critics alike.

Upon completion, Novoselic and his bandmates left the sessions proud of what they had done and optimistic about the future of the band. As Krist told the *Heavier Than Heaven* author, "things were on the upswing."

28

All in All, the Clock Is Slow

Dysfunction at Home

11301 Lakeside Avenue

In February, not long after the Cobains supposedly recorded the songs "Hello Kitty," "Lemonade Nation," and "Twister" and sent the demos to Dischord Records and *Maximumrocknroll* under the premise that they were two musical sisters, the couple moved into their home at 11301 Lakeside Avenue, in close proximity to Lake Washington.

With view of the Cascade Mountains and Mount Rainer, the $2,000-per-month rental home represented Kurt's first official residence in the city he had been most closely associated with. At 5,000 square feet, the house had more space than Kurt, Courtney, and their six-month-old daughter would ever need.

"Sliver" Clip

Although *Incesticide* had fallen off the charts by the spring of 1993, Nirvana hoped to sustain some interest in the compilation and took to the Cobains' new garage in February to shoot a new clip for "Sliver" on Super-8 film.

Directed by Kevin Kerslake, the "Sliver" video includes footage of Kurt's piercing blue eyes, shots of him making an infant Frances Bean dance, and images of his prized Chim Chim monkey doll interspersed with visions of Novoselic and Grohl rocking out in the room, which was adorned with dolls and a poster of one of their favorite bands, Mudhoney. The clip debuted on MTV that April.

Cali

In April, Jackie Farry announced that after eight months of loyal service, she was exhausted and resigning as Frances Bean's nanny. Because neither Kurt nor Courtney had the wherewithal to hire a replacement, Farry took the lead in interviewing candidates for the position. Unfortunately, she had little luck with professional nannies, who expected structure when it came to caring for a child. At the Cobain house, life was unpredictable.

Courtney Love's unorthodox choice for the role was Michael "Cali" DeWitt, a one-time roadie for Hole. Yet somehow, Love and Cobain felt that Cali, aged just twenty, was an ideal caregiver who bonded well with Frances. Ingrid Bernstein, the mother of Sub Pop publicist Nils, was also hired to help with the child on a part-time basis.

Bosnian Benefit

On April 9, 1993, Nirvana performed a rare, one-off show—their first in the US in six months—at the Cow Palace in San Francisco. The gig—a benefit for the Tresnjevka Women's Centre in Zagreb that also featured L7, the Breeders, and the Disposable Heroes of Hiphoprisy— was arranged by Novoselic to help raise awareness and money for rape survivors in Bosnia-Herzegovina.

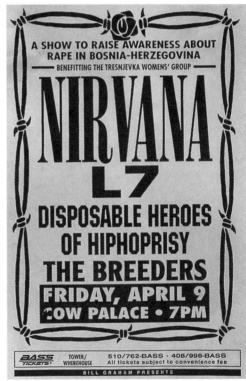

"I was really pissed off by everything I'd been reading and nobody was doing anything about it," Krist told Azerrad. The event, in front of 11,000 fans, raised $50,000 for the cause. Serbia, of course, had once been part of Yugoslavia, the country from which Novoselic's family had emigrated.

As for the show itself, Nirvana's set included eight new tunes, including "Milk It," "Dumb," and "Frances Farmer." Portions of the show were filmed, with footage of "School," "Blew," and "Something in the Way," surfacing on MTV.

Heroin and *Hamlet*

On the early evening of May 2, 1993, Cobain returned home after injecting $30–40 worth of heroin at a friend's house. After listening to Courtney lecture him about driving while he was loaded, he went upstairs and locked himself in a bedroom. She threatened to call the police and his family if he

A poster promoting Nirvana's San Francisco show from April 9, 1993, which featured special guests L7, Disposable Heroes of Hiphoprisy, and the Breeders. The benefit show was designed to raise awareness about rape in Bosnia-Herzegovina, a cause close to the heart of bassist Krist Novoselic, who had lived in the former Yugoslavia as a teenager and still had family ties to the area.

Author's collection

didn't open the door. When he didn't answer her, she phoned Kurt's mother and sister, who were nearly two hours away in Aberdeen.

By the time Wendy and Kim arrived, Kurt had come out from behind the locked door. Courtney had injected him with the anti-opioid Narcan to counteract the heroin, and gave him several other pills—including four Tylenol with codeine, three Benadryl, and one Valium—to induce vomiting. When he began to turn blue, the three most important women in his life called the paramedics.

Responding to a King County 911 emergency call from the Cobain home, police and responders arrived to discover Kurt awake and sitting on a living-room couch. Emergency workers found him conscious but impaired, babbling about Shakespeare's *Hamlet*. Sadly, as the police report would reveal, "This type of incident had happened before to Victim Cobain."

Kurt was transported to the city's Harborview Medical Center by ambulance, while his sister followed behind and stayed with him for several hours while he was given additional treatments of Narcan until he could be released. Meanwhile, Courtney stayed behind to flush away Kurt's stash, which she found in the pocket of his bathrobe.

Intervention

Not long after Cobain's latest scare, his wife elected to get herself sober through the use of a psychic. Courtney tried to stop smoking, started juicing, and went to Narcotics Anonymous meetings, while Kurt returned to his heroin habit, using Dylan Carlson and Cali DeWitt to get his drugs.

With Love out of the house, Kurt had ample time to shoot up and nod off. But he wasn't fooling anyone, and on June 1, 1993, Courtney held an intervention at the couple's Seattle residence.

Novoselic, Cobain's mother and stepfather, publicist Nils Bernstein, and Gold Mountain's Janet Billig were gathered downstairs, but Kurt locked himself in a bedroom on the second floor of the home. After refusing to come out for some time, he eventually came downstairs to face everyone and listen to the reasons he should get clean. Before long, however, he became argumentative and went back upstairs, refusing to heed their pleas to get help.

Guns and Crack

On June 4, following lengthy arguments with Kurt about him keeping guns in the house, Love called 911. When the police arrived, Kurt was arrested for domestic assault.

Matters had first escalated when Cobain bragged about his drug use in front of Love and her psychic. After he suggested to his wife that he might try crack cocaine and baited his wife with phone calls to his dealer, Love became angry and threw her juicer at Kurt. He responded by shoving her to the floor and started to choke her, leaving a scratch.

When officers arrived, they seized three of Kurt's guns—a Colt AR-15 semi-automatic assault rifle and two .38 pistols—at Courtney's insistence. To resolve the dispute, and in accordance with Washington State law—which calls for at least one of the parties in any domestic violence incident to be arrested—officers took Kurt into custody at the North Precinct. After three hours in King County Jail, he was released on $950 bail.

The assault charges were eventually dropped, and when news of the incident finally made the *Seattle Times* nearly a month later, Love denied that she had ever been a victim of domestic violence. "It's not a true story," Courtney told a Hole audience at Seattle's Off-Ramp club on July 1. "I'd just like to stick up for my husband."

By then, the couple had reconciled. Weeks after the dispute, Courtney had written, "You better love me, you fucker" on their bedroom wall. The Cobains' marriage was as it always was—as emotionally unpredictable, volatile, and chaotic as ever.

Scream Reunion

While Cobain continued to take heroin and mulled over whether to pay $50,000 to own one of Lead Belly's guitars, Grohl kept busy in early July on the road with his old band, Scream, for a two-week tour in support of their new album, *Fumble*, which had actually been recorded in December 1989.

The band's itinerary launched with a July 4 gig outdoors near the Lincoln Memorial and, after eleven dates, wrapped with a sell-out show at the Whisky a Go Go in Los Angeles.

A 1993 press photo of the reunited Scream members, including Grohl (center), who by then had already gone on to success with Nirvana.

Author's collection

29

I'm So Tired, I Can't Sleep

Back to the Push and the Pull

New Music Seminar

On July 23, 1993, Nirvana played an unannounced gig at New York's Roseland Ballroom as part of the city's annual New Music Seminar. The show, with support from the Jesus Lizard, was memorable in that it marked the first the band had played with cellist Lori Goldston. It was also the only time Kurt's guitar tech "Big" John Duncan—once of UK punk group the Exploited—played with Nirvana, lending second guitar on "Drain You," "Tourette's," "Aneurysm," and "Very Ape."

Despite the gig being a "secret" performance, word had spread quickly, and 4,000 people turned out for set that mixed new and old material. With Cobain out in front, sporting his red-and-black-striped sweater and bug-eyed sunglasses, the mood was frantic during the loud, fast opening part of the show. But before long, Kurt took the band in a softer direction, utilizing Goldston—a veteran of Seattle's Black Cat Orchestra—on "Heart-Shaped Box" and "All Apologies" before taking Nirvana into a full-on acoustic mini-set.

Not knowing what to expect, the crowd grew impatient during stripped down renditions of "Polly," "Dumb," "Something in the Way," and Lead Belly's "Where Did You Sleep Last Night." As Nirvana left the stage, the audience—which included VIPs like Beck, the Beastie Boys, Sonic Youth, Urge Overkill, and the Melvins—waited to see what would happen next. Moments later, the band gave their fans what they wanted when they came back out as a trio and roared through "Smells Like Teen Spirit."

Kurt Dies

Although no one in the crowd that night knew it, early that same evening, Kurt Cobain had died. After taking a lethal dose of "China white" heroin, Nirvana's front man was found unresponsive by his wife on a rug in their hotel room.

When Cali DeWitt heard Love screaming for him, he ran down the hallway from his room to find Cobain on the floor in his underwear with a needle in his arm. His eyes were frozen open, and he wasn't breathing.

Cali pulled the needle from Cobain's arm, picked him up, and started slapping him in an effort to wake him up. Eventually, the couple's nanny—who had no formal CPR training—punched Kurt in the sternum. On the third try, Cobain started coughing, and ultimately began breathing again.

While Kurt was in a daze, Cali got him dressed. Love was still in shock at the idea that her husband had been dead, if only for a moment. Courtney and her nanny kept the incident secret from the rest of the Nirvana camp while DeWitt took Cobain down to Times Square for some air and some food.

Four hours later, Kurt took the stage with Nirvana. Save for Love and DeWitt, no one at the Roseland Ballroom had any idea that it had very nearly been Cobain's last night on earth.

Mia Zapata Benefit

Back in Seattle, two weeks later, Nirvana played another surprise show, turning up at the King Performance Center in Seattle on August 6 to help raise money for the Mia Zapata Investigation Fund. The show—which also included TAD and Kill Sybil—was orchestrated to help solve the vicious rape and murder of the Gits' front woman in Seattle's Central District on July 7.

According to witnesses, Nirvana—who were booked only as "special guests"— played parts of Led Zeppelin's "No Quarter," Terry Jacks' "Seasons in the Sun," and Men Without Hats' 1983 novelty "Safety Dance" during the August 6 show. The Zapata benefit marked the last time Nirvana would ever perform as a trio.

Pat Smear Joins

On August 9, 1993, guitarist Pat Smear joined Nirvana in rehearsals in Seattle, with Lori Goldston also in tow. The changes to the group's touring lineup were designed to flesh out Nirvana's sound and give them some added musical capabilities onstage.

Were it not for Courtney Love—who had first befriended Smear in the 1980s, when they both appeared as extras in the 1984 film *Breakin'*—the Germs' guitarist may have never joined Nirvana. For Smear, who counted the band among one of his favorites of the era, it was the opportunity of a lifetime.

Love had actually tipped off Smear that Cobain would be calling to extend an invitation for him to join the band. Smear didn't take any time to mull the offer—he accepted the job immediately. But when he flew up to play with the group, it wasn't without apprehension.

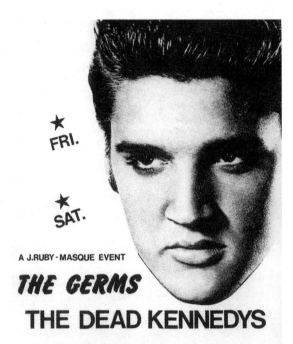

★
FRI.

★
SAT.

A J.RUBY-MASQUE EVENT

THE GERMS

THE DEAD KENNEDYS

6314 SANTA MONICA BLVD
SANTA MONICA & VINE

A flyer promoting an early-1980s hardcore-punk gig starring the Germs—the Los Angeles band co-founded by future Nirvana guitarist Pat Smear—and the Dead Kennedys.   *Author's collection*

"It was pretty intimidating," he told the Internet Nirvana Fan Club in 2002. "It took a while to get over the feeling that I didn't deserve it. But Kurt and Courtney invited me into their home and treated me like family and we sounded great at rehearsal, so I got comfortable real fast."

Georg Ruthenberg

Born Georg Ruthenberg on August 5, 1959, Nirvana's new second guitarist was already an underground icon by the time he joined forces with Cobain, Novoselic, and Grohl in time for the group's touring and promotional efforts in support of *In Utero*.

Born and raised in West Los Angeles to an African-American and Native American mother and a German immigrant father, Smear was the youngest child and only son among six children. His parents forced him to take piano lessons as a child, and the instrument came easily to him, as did the guitar, when he picked it up at the age of twelve and learned to play songs by Alice Cooper, David Bowie, and T. Rex. Cooper's 1971 album *Love It To Death* was the impetus for Smear to pick up the instrument.

Before long, Bowie's guitarist Mick Ronson and Yes's Steve Howe also made an impact, but it was Queen's Brian May who blew Smear away when he first heard the group's eponymous 1973 debut. Later, when punk music made it to L.A., Pat was taken with the riff work of the Sex Pistols' Steve Jones, the Runaways' Joan Jett, and the Damned's Brian James. Listening to these players gave him the confidence to start his own band.

While Pat was attending the Innovative Program School (part of Los Angeles' University High School), he befriended Jan Paul Beahm, who would adopt the onstage persona Darby Crash when they formed the Germs together in 1977.

Prior to settling on that moniker, the pair considered the names Sophistifuck and the Revlon Spam Queens.

By the time the group were ready to play out—with bassist Lorna Doom (a.k.a. Teresa Ryan) and drummer Donna Rhia (born Becky Barton)—they were plotting their first single. Rhia had been a last minute replacement for her friend Dottie Danger (best known as future Go-Go's singer Belinda Carlisle), who had come down with mononucleosis.

That spring, following their debut at the Orpheum Theater, the band recorded their first single "Forming" on a two-track machine in Smear's parents' garage. Backed with a crude, live recording of "Sexboy," the 45 was pressed on the What? Label that July. Clearly, employees at the manufacturing plant didn't quite grasp the Germs' punk stylings, as they sent finished copies back to the band with a note printed on the sleeve: "Warning: This record causes ear cancer."

In 1978, as the Germs' notoriety rose in Los Angeles, local magazine *Slash* offered to release a mail-order single by the band through its record label. The result was a three-song seven-inch called Lexicon Devil that was produced by scene fixture Geza X. Weirdos drummer Nicky Beat filled in on drums for the session, although Don Bolles had by then been named as a permanent replacement for Barton.

The band entered Golden Age Recording in Hollywood with producer Joan Jett in October 1978. The resulting album, *GI*—arguably the first US hardcore record ever released—was released in January 1979. The *All Music Guide* would later give the album five stars, calling it a "blast of self-lacerating L.A. punk in its original glory," with critic Ned Raggett naming it "simply classic: a commanding, rampaging sneer at everyone and everything."

Unfortunately, Crash was plagued by drugs—especially heroin—and was often incoherent onstage. By 1980, the Germs had called it a day, with the singer moving on to the Darby Crash Band, but that outfit was short-lived. On December 3, 1980, the Germs reunited for a performance at the Starwood in L.A., but came to an abrupt end four days later when Crash committed suicide by drug overdose.

Smear briefly played with 45 Grave and another Hollywood punk band, the Adolescents, before teaming with former Screamers keyboardist and future Black Flag bassist Kira Roessler in Twisted Roots. From there, he played with Nina Hagen, Vagina Dentata, Celebrity Skin, and Tater Tots. He also recorded the solo albums *Ruthensmear* (1987) and *So You Fell in Love with a Musician* (1992), and played on two albums by Deathfolk.

In between his musical pursuits, Smear began picking up money in the 1980s by playing a punk-rock extra on NBC's *Quincy, M.E.* and *CHiPs*. He also appeared in the films *Blade Runner, Howard the Duck*, and the aforementioned *Breakin'*, and in the music video for Prince's 1985 hit "Raspberry Beret."

"Heart-Shaped" Video

In the late summer of 1993, Nirvana filmed the music video for "Heart-Shaped Box" with acclaimed director/photographer Anton Corbijn, who by then had worked with everyone from U2 to Depeche Mode. Featuring images of birth, death, addiction, disease, and sexuality, the clip alarmed director Kevin Kerslake, who had already storyboarded very similar ideas with Cobain before being dropped from the project.

In the official video, an aging Jesus figure is seen dressed as the pope. Elsewhere, the men of Nirvana are shown waiting in a hospital room while "Jesus" is fed from an IV connected to a bottle containing a fetus. A crow-covered Christian cross, a young Aryan-looking girl in a Ku Klux Klan costume, and shots of Kurt lying on his back in a poppy field were also incorporated. The video premiered on MTV on September 19.

Although Cobain would tell friends these were images from his dreams, Kerslake objected, alleging copyright infringement, and sued the band. The matter was settled out of court.

Corbijn also created an alternate version of the video, with different footage appearing during the song's final verse. This take on the clip is featured on the DVD *The Work of Director Anton Corbijn*.

No Singles

Although a commercial single for "Heart-Shaped Box" had been released in some countries, DGC's stateside marketing plan was to focus strictly on album sales. A promotional radio single was sent to rock outlets, but there was no major push toward Top 40, and that was Cobain's preference.

"We're certain that we won't sell a quarter as much [as *Nevermind*]," Kurt told Chicago journalist Jim DeRogatis. "And we're totally comfortable with that because we like this record so much."

A Rare Duet

On September 8, Kurt and Courtney appeared together at Club Lingerie in Los Angeles as part of a Rock Against Rape benefit. It marked the first and only time that the couple collaborated together onstage.

At the end of a set in which Courtney performed solo, Kurt took the stage, to the surprise of many, with the couple performing "Where Did You Sleep Last Night" and "Pennyroyal Tea." The show also featured sets by 7 Year Bitch, X's Exene Cervenka, and Concrete Blonde's Johnette Napolitano.

The performance helped raise money for the L.A.-based First Strike Rape Prevention organization, which assisted victims and potential victims by offering education and teaching self-defense techniques.

SNL with Smear

Nirvana's second performance on *Saturday Night Live* took place on September 25, 1993. In addition to marking the live television debuts of "Heart-Shaped Box" and "Rape Me," the show was Pat Smear's first live appearance with the band. Propelled by two guitars and the cello work of Lori Goldston, the band's sound was noticeably richer.

The group also appeared more animated than they had been in some time, thanks to the nervous energy of Smear. In turn, Pat's new bandmates seemed thrilled to be in the company of one of their punk heroes.

As was the case nearly every time Cobain had been in New York since 1992, he overdosed on heroin. This time, however, when Courtney called for DeWitt, he was nowhere to be found. According to Everett True's *Nirvana: The Biography*, Cali and another Nirvana staffer, Rene Navarette—who had been serving as the Cobains' assistant—had gone off to score their own drugs and vacation in the notorious bowels of St. Marks Place.

Helping Hole

In the second week of October, just days before Nirvana were slated to hit the road in North America in support of *In Utero*, Kurt flew to Atlanta to join Courtney and her band Hole—guitarist Eric Erlandson, bassist Kristen Pfaff, and drummer Patty Schemel—who had been booked to work on their DGC debut, *Live Through This*, from October 8 to 30 with the production team of Paul Q. Koderie and Sean Slade (Lemonheads, Buffalo Tom, Radiohead) at Triclops Sound Studios in Marietta.

Although Kurt was there for moral support, Courtney pushed for him to sing backing vocals. Instead, he spent most of his time jamming with Erlandson in the rental house they were staying in—and, of course, getting high.

In Utero Tour

On October 18, Nirvana launched a forty-five-date tour in Phoenix, Arizona, at Veterans Memorial Stadium on the Arizona State Fairgrounds. Backed by two large reproductions of the angel-winged woman seen on the cover of the album, the band tapped Mudhoney and Santa Monica punk band Jawbreaker to open gigs in places like Albuquerque, Kansas City, Davenport, and Milwaukee.

On opening night, the Arizona crowd got an earful from Cobain after they booed his friends in Mudhoney and chanted for Nirvana during the support band's performance. Novoselic, however, was happy to be back in such an environment. "I felt like the bass player from Aerosmith when they brought out all the lighters," he told *MTV News* that month about the vibe before the encore, before breaking into a version of the Boston band's "Dream On."

NIRVANA

Special Guest: MUDHONEY & WIPERS

THURSDAY, OCTOBER 21 • 7:30 PM
MEMORIAL HALL

O N   S A L E   N O W

Reserved & General Admission tickets available at Memorial Hall Box Office and all TICKETMASTER
locations including Hy-Vee Sound Warehouse
and Gomers. Or Charge-By-Phone: (816)931-3330

P R O D U C E D   B Y   C O N T E M P O R A R Y

A poster advertising Nirvana's show at Memorial Hall in Kansas City, October 21, 1993. The band was supported by their good friends in Mudhoney and up-and-coming punks Jawbreaker. Despite being listed on the bill, the Wipers did not perform.   *Author's collection*

Performing sets that balanced material from their three records, the band seemed more playful in the company of Smear. At several shows, Kurt sang a line from the current 4 Non Blondes hit "What's Up?" as a joke.

Still, some jokes just aren't funny, and you could have heard a pin drop on October 23, when opening comedian Bobcat Goldthwaite poked fun in Chicago at the murder of the father of the Bulls' beloved Michael Jordan. And if that wasn't bad enough, the band skipped the obligatory "Teen Spirit" when they took the stage that night at the Aragon Ballroom. These shows did, however, mark the unveiling of a new song, "You Know You're Right."

Sans Courtney

During these early weeks of the tour, Nirvana were caravanning without Courtney, who was still in Atlanta recording with Hole. Free from the tense dynamic she often created, the band's members seemed happy in her absence—even Kurt, who was willing to take in a Treepeople gig with Smear during a night off in Kansas City.

At times, things felt like they had before Love had entered the picture. Such was the case in November, when Novoselic, Grohl, and tour manager Alex MacLeod came together on Cobain's tour bus to watch Cheech and Chong's classic marijuana-themed movie *Up in Smoke* en route to a gig in Springfield, Massachusetts.

There was minimal open partying during the tour. Novoselic was trying not to drink before shows, while Kurt got "well" in private. Krist's wife Shelli was often present, and Grohl's fiancé, photographer Jennifer Youngblood, was also around for many of the dates.

Meeting Burroughs

On the afternoon of the Kansas City show on October 21, MacLeod drove Cobain to Lawrence, where he finally got to meet revered beat writer William S. Burroughs, author of the cult classic *Naked Lunch*. Although the pair had recently collaborated on a ten-inch record entitled "The 'Priest' They Called Him"—released on Tim/Kerr Records in 1993—they had worked in different studios to create this musical piece about a heroin addict looking to score drugs on Christmas Eve.

After completing the collaboration, Cobain wrote Burroughs on August 2, 1993, to ask him to appear in the "Heart-Shaped Box" video. "As a fan and student of your work," he explained, "I would cherish the opportunity to work directly with you."

Although Burroughs declined the request to appear in the video, he agreed to a short visit from Cobain, where they spoke mostly about their mutual appreciation of Lead Belly. Despite their shared history with heroin addiction, however, they never discussed the drug.

Surprisingly, according to *Nirvana: The True Story*, the eccentric Burroughs found Kurt was even odder. "There's something wrong with that boy," he said of their meeting. "He frowns for no good reason."

Released on one-sided ten-inch vinyl by Tim/Kerr on July 1, 1993, "The 'Priest' They Called Him" was a collaboration between Cobain and novelist William S. Burroughs.   *Author's collection*

Pissy Halloween

On October 27, Nirvana and their new openers, the Boredoms and the Meat Puppets, rolled into Detroit for a gig at the Michigan Fairgrounds Coliseum. During "Scentless Apprentice," Cobain was hit in the head by a shoe thrown from the crowd. Visibly irritated, he slammed down his guitar and left the stage.

Four nights later, during a gig at the University of Akron, the band performed in costume. Cobain dressed as a Jack Daniel's–slugging Barney the Dinosaur, Smear pretended he was Slash from Guns N' Roses (complete with top hat), Grohl was a mummy, and Krist dressed as a white-faced Ted Danson in tribute to the actor's controversial decision to appear in public in blackface at a roast for his then-girlfriend, actress/comedian Whoopi Goldberg.

Although the night was a fun one for the band, things went downhill when Cobain was hit by another shoe. This time he took the shoe, peed in it, and considered throwing it back into the crowd until the shoe's owner explained that someone else had thrown it onstage. Kurt then apologized and offered to buy the fan a new pair of shoes.

Nirvana were supported by the Meat Puppets and Boredoms at this show at the Hara Arena in Dayton, Ohio, on October 30, 1993.   *Author's collection*

Puppets Unplug

Cobain first befriended the Meat Puppets' Curt Kirkwood when they were introduced by telephone through a Seattle booking agent named Jeff Holmes during a 1992 New Year's Eve party. Holmes and Kurt had been talking about bands they admired, and when the revered SST band came up, Holmes rang Kirkwood at home in Arizona.

Fast-forward ten months, and Kirkwood's band were supporting Nirvana for part of the *In Utero* tour, including a sold-out gig at Toronto's Maple Leaf Gardens on November 4. Backstage that night, Novoselic joined the Meat Puppets for a late-night party, and the celebration turned musical when Krist joined the Kirkwood brothers in a jam on acoustic guitars.

Novoselic wound up having so much fun playing with the band that it gave him an idea about how Nirvana might properly execute the *MTV Unplugged* episode they had been approached to tape later that month.

Rolling Along

When the Nirvana caravan rolled southward into Virginia on November 7, the Breeders and Half Japanese took over as openers, appearing first at a show at the College of William and Mary in Williamsburg. More university arena gigs followed at Drexel in Philadelphia and Lehigh in Bethlehem. The band's sets remained strong, and the hijinks were frequent.

On November 10 in Springfield, Maryland, Novoselic dumped a bottle of Evian water over Cobain's head. Two nights later, at the George Wallace Civic Center in Fitchburg, Cobain threw his guitar repeatedly at the disco ball the band had suspended over the stage, smashing it to pieces. He then followed up by wrecking his guitar.

Two nights later, at Washington's American University, Cobain had hoped to repeat the feat, but he was unsuccessful. Eventually—after a rendition of "Do Nuts" with journalist-turned-vocalist Everett True— Kurt gave up and Krist carried him off the stage.

New York

Nirvana kicked off back-to-back shows in Manhattan on November 14 at the Javits Center Coliseum. Once again, True joined the band for the encore. But the real excitement occurred backstage, where Alex McLeod tossed supermodel Kate Moss—who was not on the guest list—from the VIP backstage area.

The next night, at Roseland Ballroom, the group kept things loose and wrapped the "intimate" show in front of just 5,000 in a

A flyer promoting Nirvana's concert in Springfield, Massachusetts, on November 10, 1993. The Breeders and Half Japanese were the support acts for this show, which concluded with Novoselic dumping a bottle of Evian water over Cobain. *Author's collection*

memorable way. Late in the set, following "On a Plain," Grohl paid homage to Kiss by playing part of the Gene Simmons number "Living In Sin." Then, after renditions of "Scentless Apprentice" and "Blew," Cobain led the group and the members of Half Japanese through Iggy Pop's classic "I Wanna Be Your Dog."

At the end of the latter song, the young stepson of Half Japanese's Jad Fair was asked onstage, and with the encouragement of Pat Smear, the boy smashed a guitar—much to the crowd's delight.

30

What Else Should I Be?

Unplugged and Unraveling

MTV Unplugged

As noted already, Novoselic's post-gig acoustic jam with Cris and Curt Kirkwood in Toronto on November 4 helped solidify Nirvana's plans to appear on *MTV Unplugged*. Although the network had been pursuing the band to appear on its hit acoustic-based show for some time, it wasn't until Krist came up with the idea of adding the Meat Puppets to the mix that he was able to convince his front man that doing the show would be a good idea if they could put their own unique stamp on it.

Kurt also took inspiration from Mark Lanegan's 1990 album *The Winding Sheet*, which he had been involved in the making of. By agreeing to do the show, Nirvana aimed to go beyond what most acts were doing—playing acoustic renditions of the hits—to create something lasting and memorable.

Using the first three days of an eleven-day break in touring, Nirvana gathered with Smear and Goldston for a pair of rehearsals at the SST Rehearsal Facility in Weehawken. But experiment with new approaches came with difficulties, as the group struggled to translate some of their songs—including "Molly's Lips" and "Been a Son"—into acoustic form during their practices on November 16 and 17.

Meanwhile, the network was hoping for stars like Eddie Vedder and Tori Amos to make guest appearances during the set, and balked at the suggestion of the Meat Puppets. But Nirvana held their ground, and the band ultimately won out. There would be no Pearl Jam warbling or quirky, piano-led duets of "Teen Spirit" during Cobain's performance.

If the notion of the group sidestepping their hits for six obscure covers—David Bowie's "The Man Who Sold the World," Lead Belly's "Where Did You Sleep Last Night," the Vaselines' "Jesus Wants Me for a Sunbeam," and three Meat Puppets tracks—did not sit well with executives, Cobain—who was between heroin binges, in withdrawal, and completely irritable—didn't care. In fact, he would actually refuse to play the show for a period of time during the day before the taping.

Kurt ultimately had a change of heart, but the gig—which was preceded by a three-hour rehearsal on the day of the event—was serious business to him. There were no smiles or jokes during the taping.

During rehearsals in advance of the show, it was decided that it might be best to let the Kirkwood brothers play the main instrumentation on the three Meat Puppets originals, "Plateau," "Lake Of Fire," and "Oh Me." It seemed that Kurt, Pat, and Krist were having trouble perfecting their parts due to the unusual tunings the Kirkwood brothers used, so it just made more sense have the Puppets play along with them.

In rehearsals, the band even worked up a version of Lynyrd Skynyrd's "Sweet Home Alabama," which was attempted but ultimately left off the set list when Nirvana taped their performance on November 18, 1993 at Sony Studios in New York City.

For the show, Cobain wasn't entirely unplugged—he ran his acoustic guitar through an amplifier and effects pedals. Because of this, producer Alex Coletti wound up building a fake box and placing in front of Kurt's amplifier to hide it from view.

Unlike most episodes of the show, which tended to pick the best of several performances of each song, Nirvana filmed their entire fourteen-song set in one take. As for the décor, Kurt asked that the stage be decorated with black candles, stargazer lilies, and a crystal chandelier, to give the performance a funeral vibe.

Following the show's finale—a rendition of the aforementioned Lead Belly number—Nirvana were asked to play an encore. Cobain refused, explaining that there was no way he could improve upon his performance.

ALL ACCESS

An "All Access" backstage pass from Nirvana's 1993 North American Tour.   *Author's collection*

Keep Your Shoes On

When Nirvana's tour resumed on November 26 in Jacksonville, Florida, things were running relatively smoothly. The lone hiccup came from Novoselic's repeated jumping onstage, which caused his bass cord to come loose and affected the group's timing on a couple of songs.

During that night's gig at the Morocco Shrine, Cobain borrowed a hunting cap from a kid in the audience and wore it for the rest of the show. During "Blew," the finale, he pulled the fan back onstage and showed him how to smash a guitar.

One trend that continued to bother Cobain during the tour was the throwing of shoes. When the Breeders' Kelly Deal got hit in the chest with a shoe, Kurt lectured the audience. From then on, he usually took a minute at the outset of their shows to warn his audiences, in places like Miami and Lakeland, that he would stop playing if anyone was hit by a flying shoe.

Staying with Stipe

After their Florida shows, Nirvana arrived in Atlanta, Georgia, on November 29 for a gig at the Omni. Following the performance, Kurt, Cali, and Frances went to stay with R.E.M. singer Michael Stipe at his home in nearby Athens. Cobain had been an enormous R.E.M. fan for a number of years, and he was thrilled to be able to call Stipe a friend.

During Kurt's two-day visit with Stipe, they socialized, toured the famous college town, and visited Michael's friend, well-known local singer/songwriter Vic Chestnutt. Although Cobain and DeWitt's accommodations weren't of the four-star variety to which they had become accustomed, neither seemed to mind sleeping on the floor in the small, unfurnished house owned by the R.E.M. front man.

Bored

While the Breeders stayed on the tour until the Christmas break, scuzzy New York rockers Come were switched out with Shonen Knife—one of Kurt's all time favorites—after shows in Birmingham and Tallahassee. But the company of the all-female Japanese pop/punk act did little to improve morale, and the groups barely spoke to one another, onstage or off, at shows in New Orleans, Dallas, and Houston.

On December 5 at the Fair Park Coliseum in Dallas, Nirvana played a lengthy twenty-five song set. Unfortunately, short-lived superstar Vanilla Ice—the man behind the 1990 hit "Ice Ice Baby"—wound up missing the show after being turned away by Nirvana's handlers. When the band found out, they tried to have someone retrieve him, but Ice had already left.

The tour continued in Oklahoma City, Omaha, and St. Paul, but by now the shows had become virtually interchangeable. Life on the road in Nirvana had become as predictable as Cobain's drug habit. More and more, Nirvana was a job to him.

Pier 48

On December 13, Nirvana appeared alongside the Breeders and popular rap outfit Cypress Hill at Seattle's Pier 48 for a concert filmed for TV broadcast and slated to be shown on New Year's Eve 1993 as *MTV Live and Loud*. Reaction to the show was mixed. Many fans loved it, but longtime Nirvana photographer Charles Peterson felt the opposite, later describing it to Everett True as an "abortion."

Pearl Jam had originally been scheduled to appear, but when they backed out, Nirvana's headlining set was extended. Following "Endless, Nameless," the group closed out the performance with a fit of destruction. Nothing was left unmolested—including monitors, amplifiers, and chunks of the stage.

With the band's instruments in splinters, Novoselic returned to his dressing room to find that someone had stolen his and Shelli's wallets. Although it was never proven, they believed the thief to be someone close to the band who needed money to get heroin.

Courtney and Corgan

The MTV show marked Kurt's reunion with Courtney after several weeks apart. But things were reportedly tense as Cobain began to suspect that his wife was having an affair with her ex-boyfriend, Smashing Pumpkins leader Billy Corgan. According to *Nirvana: The True Story*, Corgan had even offered to take Love with him on vacation.

Whether there was any basis to Kurt's suspicions or not, it made the tension very thick. Kurt retreated to heroin to ease his heartache. Courtney, in turn, took her pills. Each hid their drugs from the other the best they could, and their relationship grew more and more dysfunctional.

No Groping

The night after the Seattle show, Nirvana and the Breeders moved on to Oregon for a gig at the Salem Armory Auditorium, with the Melvins also in support for the first of four dates.

At the Pavilion on the campus of Idaho's Boise State University on December 15, Cobain told the crowd to fold up the chairs that he had set out so they could move freely around the floor. Instead, the audience left the chairs scattered about chaotically.

The next night, at the Golden Spike Arena in Ogden, Utah, Novoselic witnessed a fan grab the breast of a female attendee. He jumped into the crowd to handle the situation. Upon the bassist's return to the stage, Kurt told the audience, "If anyone sees anybody groping a girl, beat the shit out of him."

The last show before Nirvana's Christmas break occurred in Denver on December 18. During the Melvins' final number, Grohl came out to play alongside his friend and drumming idol Dale Crover on "Night Goat."

Crazy Eddie

After a break of a week and a half, Nirvana headed back out on tour, beginning with a date at the San Diego Sports Arena on December 29. The gig included new tour openers Chokebore—an Amphetamine Reptile act—plus comedian Bobcat Goldthwaite and the Butthole Surfers.

At the Great Western Forum in Inglewood, during the group's post-"Blew" destruction sequence, Cobain took one of the angel arms from the statues onstage and used it to strum his guitar. Later, as Novoselic started singing the Kinks' "You Really Got Me"—also popularized by Van Halen—Cobain took a drill to his guitar and spun it above his head before smashing it to pieces.

Those moves were also an homage to the legendary hard-rock guitarist Eddie Van Halen, who had showed up drunk backstage. Van Halen begged Novoselic and Cobain to let him join them onstage, but they declined his offer by explaining that they didn't have any extra guitars.

According to witnesses, Eddie then pointed in Pat Smear's direction and ordered them to let him use "the Mexican's guitar," before asking if Smear was Mexican or black. Kurt took offense to this and told Eddie that he could go onstage after their encore and play with himself, but Smear wasn't so offended. Van Halen had been one of his personal heroes, and he could play amazingly well—even if he was a disappointment in person.

Hit with a Coin

The tour arrived in Oakland on New Year's Eve before moving on to shows in Central Point, Oregon, and Spokane, Washington, which sandwiched a pair of gigs at the Pacific National Exhibition Forum in Vancouver, Canada. At the first of these British Columbia gigs, on January 3, someone threw a coin at Kurt's head.

According to NirvanaGuide.com, Kurt stopped mid-song to laugh about it. "Somebody just hit me in the head with a Canadian quarter," he giggled, before advising the audience that it didn't hurt. Later, however, after someone up front kept yelling for "Tourette's," he snapped, "What am I, a fucking jukebox?"

The West Coast leg of the tour wrapped up close to home with back-to-back gigs at the Seattle Center Arena. These performances—the band's last with cellist Lori Goldston—would also be their final North American concerts. According to Goldston, most of the band members had to play on despite suffering from the flu.

A Lexus and a Mansion

On January 2, 1994, Kurt bought a Lexus at Courtney's insistence. But after three days, he returned the vehicle because he thought it was too ostentatious.

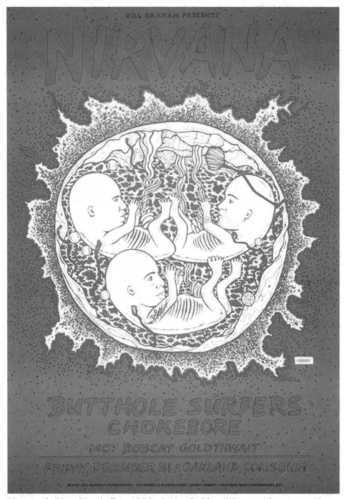

Nirvana's New Year's Eve 1993 gig in Oakland featured support from the pioneering and controversial Butthole Surfers—who had signed to Capitol Records amid the rise of alternative music—and Chokebore. Stand-up comedian and actor Bobcat Goldthwait was the evening's MC.

Author's collection

Clearly uneasy with what the car represented, the couple reverted back to their 1986 Volvo sedan.

Despite the tension in their unusual marriage, which was plagued with suspicion, distrust, and drugs, the Cobains bought a mansion on January 19, 1994. Built in 1902, the three-story home in Seattle's ritzy Denny-Blaine district cost the couple $1,130,000.

The property was adjacent to Viretta Park and had a huge, beautifully landscaped yard, a greenhouse, and a two-story garage. R.E.M. guitarist Peter

Buck was one of the neighbors. In an executive neighborhood full of brand new BMWs, Cobain's aging Plymouth Valiant certainly stuck out.

Cobain's nanny-turned–house sitter/drug buddy Cali DeWitt ran most of the errands, taking care of grocery shopping and drug deliveries while still looking after Frances from time to time. DeWitt also served as the go-between for Courtney and Kurt when things got volatile. As a result, he usually had plenty of cash, and a credit card with a rumored limit of $50,000.

Advocate for Fagdom

On January 24, the *Advocate* released its February 1994 issue. Inside was a letter from Cobain, who wrote, "Of all the gut-spilling and, uh, whining I did in 1993, I never felt more relaxed than with the *Advocate*. What can I say?"

Kurt went on to thank the publication's editors, and announce, "I'll always be an advocate for fagdom."

The Butthole Surfers and TAD opened for Nirvana at this concert held at the Pacific National Exhibition Forum in Vancouver, British Columbia, on January 4, 1994. The date was added in response to the high demand for tickets for the previous night's show at the same venue. *Author's collection*

Robert Lang's

Nirvana planned to return to the recording studio on Friday, January 28, for a three-day session at Robert Lang's in North Seattle. However, while Novoselic and Grohl turned up on the first day ready to work, Cobain didn't make it until the third day, when he showed up without a guitar or an amp. Luckily, guitar tech Earnie Bailey had a modified Univox guitar and a pedal board in his car that Cobain used with an amp that belonged to the facility.

After setting up and breaking together to go get a pizza dinner, the trio worked for ten hours straight, cutting eleven basic tracks and completing the vocals to just one other, "You Know You're Right." Eleven months after the *In Utero* sessions, it marked the last studio work the band would do together.

Officially released in 2004 as part of the boxed set *With the Lights Out*, "You Know You're Right" was a classic, biting Nirvana number that incorporated their trademark loud/soft approach. The lyrics of the track—which became a posthumous hit—offered a direct reflection of the frustration Cobain felt in his marriage, specifically the line, "She just wants to love herself."

Elsewhere, he expressed a desire to "crawl away for good," while injecting sarcasm into depictions of his mental and physical state. Although it wound up being his unplanned farewell, with "You Know You're Right" Cobain actually sounded like a man who was thinking of taking back control of his troubled life.

31

End It Someday

Checking Out

Europe

When Nirvana flew out to Europe on Tuesday, February 2, to embark on a lengthy run of television appearances and concert dates, Cobain was without the company of his spouse. Love was needed stateside, where she was gearing up for the April release of *Live Through This*, Hole's DGC debut, by taking label meetings and doing long-lead press to promote the record.

So while Novoselic was joined by his wife, and Grohl had the companionship of his fiancée, Jennifer Youngblood, Kurt was accompanied by the Cobains' assistant, Rene Navarette. Cali DeWitt remained in Seattle, and later Los Angeles, with Courtney to help with Frances.

The dates were different from the US tour in that Lori Goldston was supplanted by Melora Creager, one of three cellists in the New York–based band Rasputina. Cobain had decided to shift backing-vocal duties away from Grohl, reassigning them, without explanation, to Smear.

Emulating the Knack

February 4, 1994, found the band performing in a Paris television studio, where the foursome dressed in black jackets in homage to 1970s new-wave heroes the Knack. Appearing on the French television variety show *Nulle Part Ailleurs* on the Canal+ network, Cobain, Grohl, Novoselic, and Smear delivered versions of "Rape Me" and "Pennyroyal Tea," to the delight of fans.

However, when it came time for the final number, "Drain You," Cobain appeared to lose his cool. He slammed his guitar to the floor, caterwauling into the microphone until the song's conclusion. In spite of his tantrum, the performance is now regarded as one of Nirvana's best-ever TV appearances.

Coke with the Buzzcocks

The band's official tour launch occurred in Cascais, Portugal, on February 6, with support from Manchester, England's iconic and influential Buzzcocks, who were staging a comeback. The Pete Shelley–fronted band stayed on with Nirvana for twelve days, playing gigs with them in the Spanish cities of Barcelona and Madrid, and in Toulouse, Toulon, Paris, Rennes, and Grenoble in France.

In Madrid, Cobain was especially bothered when he observed fans smoking heroin from tinfoil and looking to him with cheers and thumbs up. He had, it seemed, become a sad junkie idol to his fans.

Still, this didn't keep Cobain from changing his behavior, as Buzzcocks guitarist Steve Diggle explained to *Spinner* in 2011. In the first few days of the trek, Diggle was on Cobain's bus when he asked tour manager Alex MacLeod for some cocaine. "He took out the coke and he went upstairs on the bus, and I offered the coke to the other guys. So we did the [two grams], and when Kurt comes downstairs he says, 'Where's the coke, Steve?' I said, 'Fuck, the coke! I offered it to everybody else.'"

Diggle found Kurt—who loved the Buzzcocks—pretty amiable despite his underlying sadness. "There were obviously a lot of things that he wasn't happy about," Steve added, explaining that although Cobain was a little isolated from the others, "he didn't seem out of order."

Not Canceled

After a week away from home, Kurt called Love from Madrid in tears, telling her that he wanted to cancel the tour. Courtney put the pressure on him, reminding him that the money he earned now would solidify his daughter's future.

When he asked the band's production manager about the ramifications might of calling off the tour, Cobain was informed that the group would be culpable for all costs, which would have amounted to at least several hundred thousand of dollars.

That news, coupled with pressure from Love to stick it out, kept him soldiering on the best way he

A poster for Nirvana's concert at Palacio de Los Deportes in Madrid, Spain, on February 9, 1994, featuring support from influential UK punk band the Buzzcocks.

Author's collection

could. Courtney reiterated to Kurt that he had many commitments to Gold Mountain, the band, and the road crew.

Love also reminded Kurt that he was on the hook for most of the year—something he didn't want to think about. Although a $7 million payday was promised for the band's planned participation in that summer's 1994 Lollapalooza package tour, he just wanted to be home.

Suspicions About Courtney

As the tour progressed, Kurt's outlook grew bleaker. He was lonely, thousands of miles away from his daughter, his wife, and the comforts of his mansion. Touring wasn't just grueling for him; it was hell much of the time, as he was once again withdrawing from heroin. In order to try and keep it together, he began taking morphine when he could arrange to get hold of it.

Several weeks into the dates, he learned that Love had been hanging out with friends like Evan Dando and her former boyfriend Billy Corgan in L.A., where she was holed up at the Chateau Marmont, running up a $37,000 tab. Cobain had become suspicious of Courtney—and especially her relationship with Billy—in recent months. Later, he even asked DeWitt—an eyewitness to the relationship in Cobain's absence—whether he thought Courtney was cheating on him. Despite suspecting that she might be, Cali told Kurt he hadn't seen anything, mindful of what he had heard from Rene Navarette about his boss's extremely fragile state. Deep depression aside, Kurt looked ghastly.

When Cobain eventually challenged Love on the phone with his suspicions that she had been cheating on him, Courtney adamantly denied it. She blamed his paranoia on his drug problem, and insisted that Billy and Evan were just her friends.

At the same time, his insecurity continued to grow as Love repeatedly broke promises to him that she would fly out to Europe with Frances. With each successive postponement, Kurt got closer and closer to the end of his rope.

Rifle Mouth

In Paris on February 13, Cobain posed for French photographer Youri Lenquette with a sports pistol and, later, a rifle. At one point Kurt—who was on drugs during the photo shoot—posed with the rifle in his mouth.

It wasn't just a disturbing image; it was a bad sign. Yet it was not the only time he had been photographed in this way. Another photograph exists of him posing with the nose of an AIR-17 BB gun in his mouth, leaning on the hood of a vintage car, with Novoselic and Grohl smiling along in an image that undoubtedly haunts them to this day.

Throat Troubles

With his drug and alcohol use, his cigarette smoking, and his nightly screaming ritual, it was unsurprising that Kurt's voice began to fail during the 1994
European tour. With the assorted throat sprays Kurt was using only temporarily
easing the discomfort, Alex MacLeod took the singer to see doctors in several
of the cities they visited.

Physicians told Cobain to take a two-month hiatus from performing and
learn to sing professionally to cure his ailment. Of course, Kurt knew that wasn't
realistic, and despite his attempts to treat it with herbal remedies and other
concoctions, the problem persisted.

Falling Apart

By the time Nirvana arrived in Modena, Italy, on February 21, the Melvins had
returned as openers. Yet even with Buzz Osborne and Dale Crover in tow, Cobain
was miserable and uninspired. Nirvana's shows reflected his mood.

Two days later, during an appearance on *Tunnel*, an Italian television show
filmed in Rome, his voice sounded like it was breaking down, and from a physical standpoint he looked like he was at an all-time low. It was Nirvana's last-ever
television appearance.

"It was weird," Melora Creager told author Carrie Borzillo-Vrenna, "The
band didn't talk much. I felt like Krist cared a lot about Kurt, but whatever
happened over the years that I wasn't privy to . . . he just seemed sad about
Kurt's state."

Crappy Anniversary

The Cobains were apart when their second anniversary rolled around on
February 24. Courtney was still in Los Angeles, while Cobain was alone in Milan,
missing his wife and daughter. Following a second gig in the city the next night,
Cobain again expressed interest in canceling the tour.

Novoselic pleaded with Kurt to hang on in there. The band's next gig, on
February 27, was set for Ljubljana, Slovenia—part of the former Yugoslavia where
Krist had once lived. The gig, which provided an opportunity for Novoselic's
relatives to see the band, was extremely important to him.

The show was one of several during the European tour to feature the Cars'
"Best Friend's Girl" as part of the set. After playing "About a Girl," the group
jammed on "Standing on the Corner" ("Stojim Na Kantunu") by the Croatian
band Davoli.

Bronchitis in Munich

Nirvana's concert at Terminal Einz, a 3,000-capacity airplane hanger in Munich, on March 1, 1994 wound up being their last-ever show. Before the gig, Cobain—who had taken an advance on his per diem, presumably to buy drugs—was in an extremely dark place.

According to his attorney Rosemary Carroll, Kurt had called her before the gig after an argument with Love. He told his lawyer he wanted a divorce. Whether he truly intended to go through with the split is unknown, but he was lonely, emotional, and high on drugs when he dialed Carroll's number in Los Angeles.

He was also terribly sick. When he was diagnosed with severe laryngitis and bronchitis, a second night at the venue had to be postponed until April 28, 1994.

Suicidal in Rome

When doctors ordered Cobain to rest, Nirvana were forced to take a nine-day break. On March 3, the Novoselics flew home to Seattle, where their home was undergoing a renovation. Grohl remained in Germany, where he filmed a music video for the Beatles song "Money" with Soul Asylum's Dave Pirner, the Afghan Whigs' Greg Dulli, Sonic Youth's Thurston Moore, Gumball's Don Fleming, and R.E.M.'s Mike Mills to promote their participation in the soundtrack to *Backbeat*, an upcoming movie about the Beatles' early days in Hamburg.

Alongside Pat, who was also sick with bronchitis, Kurt traveled to Rome, where he checked into the Hotel Excelsior. Inside Suite 541, Kurt awaited the arrival of Courtney—who had stopped in London for two days of shopping and promotional interviews with *Select* and *Melody Maker*—and Frances. Unable to

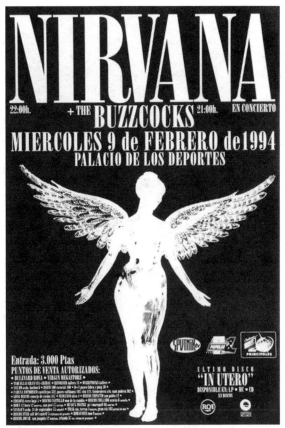

A ticket to Nirvana's concert at Flughafen Riem Terminal 1 in Munich, Germany, on March 1, 1994. This was to be the band's final performance.   *Author's collection*

arrange for a heroin delivery, he recruited a bellboy from the five-star hotel to fill a prescription for the tranquilizer Rohypnol—a drug ten times more potent than Valium.

Hoping for a romantic evening after more than a month apart from Love, Kurt ordered red roses, two bottles of champagne, a number of large, expensive candlesticks, and a pair of three-carat diamond earrings. When Love arrived, however, she was exhausted, and not in the mood for romance. Much to Cobain's frustration, Courtney took some pills and went to sleep.

At some point later that evening, Kurt sat down to compose a suicide note on Hotel Excelsior stationery. In it, he wrote of the advice he had received from Dr. Baker, one of the numerous addiction specialists he had seen in his attempts to get clean. He needed to choose between life and death, and he was choosing the latter. He again expressed how he was tired of touring, and how despondent he was over fears Courtney was or would soon be cheating on him with Corgan. He also wrote about how, after the pain of his parents' split, he would rather die than go through another divorce.

Sometime before 6 a.m. on March 4, 1994, Courtney woke up to find Kurt on the floor, still in his clothes but unconscious. In his pocket she found the three-page suicide note and $1,000 in cash. Love called the front desk, and an ambulance was quickly summoned to transport Kurt's lifeless body to Rome's Umberto I Polyclinic Hospital. Cobain had fallen into a coma and was placed on life-support. After doctors pumped his stomach, they determined that Kurt had ingested fifty or sixty individually unwrapped Rohypnol pills, which he washed down with champagne.

"I reached for him, and he had blood coming out of his nose," Love told *Select* of the scene in a subsequent interview, adding, "I have seen him get really fucked up before, but I have never seen him almost eat it."

Death Report

Kurt's pulse had returned by the time CNN reported that he had died of a drug overdose. Novoselic heard the same news—which originated from David Geffen's office—shortly after arriving back in Seattle. A caller named Courtney (who later turned out to be an impersonator) had left a message with the label boss, informing him that Kurt was gone.

As word reached America that Cobain had died, he was actually showing signs of life. When he eventually woke up, he asked for a strawberry milkshake.

Damage Control

On March 6, Cobain was moved to the Rome American Hospital, where Love felt he would get better care. Love, Gold Mountain's Janet Billig, and Geffen's publicists then began to spin the story to the media, explaining that Kurt had not attempted suicide but had instead overdosed accidentally.

In a press conference held on March 7, Cobain's doctor, Osvaldo Galletta, announced, "Kurt Cobain is clearly and dramatically improving. Yesterday he was hospitalized in a state of coma and respiratory failure. Today he is recovering from a pharmacological coma, due not to narcotics, but the combined effect of alcohol and tranquilizers that he had been medically prescribed by a doctor."

Flying Home

Despite the surreal experience of having been briefly declared dead, Kurt's main concern upon his release from the hospital and return to the US was to arrange for a gram of heroin to be delivered to the bushes outside of his house. Arriving at Sea-Tac airport, he looked terrible as he was pushed to an awaiting car in a wheelchair.

Although he had attempted suicide, nobody outside of Kurt's immediate circle—not even Krist, Dave, or Dylan Carson—knew any different than Gold Mountain's statement about his "accidental overdose." When reporters came to his mom's door, looking for her perspective, she tearfully explained to reporter Claude Iosso of Aberdeen's *Daily World* that her son was "in a profession that he doesn't have the stamina to be in."

Guilt and Guns

The postponed European shows were eventually canceled, but plans for Lollapalooza were still in place. In the eyes of Gold Mountain and Courtney Love, Nirvana had confirmed their appearances, even though Kurt was against the festival and hadn't actually signed a contract to do it. At home, Love continued to try to persuade Kurt to play the traveling festival, which would have earned him several million dollars.

In Cobain's mind, however, Nirvana no longer existed. He was planning instead to collaborate with R.E.M.'s Michael Stipe in Atlanta, but the idea fell through in mid-March.

On March 12, 911 dispatchers received a call from the Cobain home, but the caller hung up. Love told the responding officer that they had been fighting, but that the issue had now been resolved. According to the police report, officers suggested therapy to Cobain when he revealed that "there was a lot of stress" between the couple.

Six days later, after Kurt locked himself in an upstairs room with a gun where he had threatened to kill himself with a .38 revolver, Courtney again called the police. At Love's request, three pistols, a Colt AR-15 semi-automatic rifle, and twenty-five boxes of ammunition were seized. Police also took away a large, illegally obtained bottle of Klonopin, an anti-seizure medication that Kurt was using to fight heroin withdrawal. Unfortunately, these pills made him fearful, agitated, and delusional. Seattle police arrested Cobain and took him downtown to the station, but he wasn't formally arrested.

Shooting

Kurt spent much of the month of March hanging out at the home of Cali's girl-friend Jennifer Adamson at the Granada Apartments complex in the city, doing drugs and killing time away from the house. The close proximity of a dealer named Caitlin Moore—whose clients also included a number of other Seattle rockers—made her apartment on Denny Way a convenient place to escape and shoot up when he was pressed for time.

Kurt spent so much time at Adamson's apartment and took drugs in such abundance that she feared he might die there. When she confronted him about this, Cobain promised her that drugs wouldn't be the thing that killed him. "He told me he was going to shoot himself in the head," Adamson told Cross. She assumed he was—at least in part—joking.

No Powders

Love had long since established a "no drugs" policy in the house, which applied to powders like cocaine, speed, and heroin. But her pills were deemed an exception.

The couple continued to argue incessantly over guns, exorbitant purchases, and drugs. To taunt her, Kurt would tell his wife he was planning to try crack, which made her extremely angry.

At one point, during the middle of the month, Cobain walked away from an argument with Love and took off with Navarette. They wound up heading down to the Marco Polo Motel on Aurora.

In an attempt to thwart Cobain's ability to acquire drug, Love had his bank-cards canceled. Regardless, Kurt and Rene managed to get drugs, and Kurt ended up taking so much heroin that he overdosed in the motel room. Rene managed to revive him, but it took him twenty minutes to get Kurt on his feet.

Chatoff

That month, Danny Goldberg contacted Steven Chatoff from the Steps Recovery Center. Cobain agreed to talk with Chatoff, and he was unexpectedly oblig-ing. Their telephone conversations covered Kurt's stomach pain as well as his addictions and his need to self-medicate with opiates. They also delved into his unresolved childhood and family issues, as well as his frustration with his fame and his marriage.

Chatoff hoped that by attempting to deal with the underlying problems in Cobain's life they might eventually get him to a point where he could embrace sobriety. Still, Chatoff was not told about Cobain's suicide attempt earlier in the month, and he would later say that he believed this hindered his ability to help guide Kurt successfully.

Failed Intervention

On March 21, Chatoff and Love planned an intervention with Cobain, but it was canceled. Novoselic had told Kurt what was coming after visiting his bandmate at one of his favorite drug haunts, the Marco Polo, where he could see how out of it Kurt was. Cobain was delusional; he spoke about buying a motorcycle but refused to talk about the real issues.

Krist had showed up with his van full of sleeping bags and guitars and told Kurt he wanted to take him out to a cabin in the wilderness so that he could withdraw from drugs. Kurt considered it for a moment, but eventually declined Krist's offer.

Speaking later to Cross, Krist explained how Kurt only wanted to "get fucked up into oblivion." He also admitted that he told Kurt about the planned intervention because he was worried that staging such a confrontation might merely prompt his front man to vanish.

Dart

On March 24, Kurt went to Seattle's American Dream car lot, where he plunked down $2,500 for a light blue 1965 Dodge Dart. Despite his vast wealth, he had decided to get rid of his classic Valiant, but although he parked it on a street in the residential Madrona neighborhood with a "For Sale" sign on it, he didn't get any offers.

Another Intervention

By now, another counselor named David Burr had been hired, and another intervention was planned for Friday, March 25. This time, Cobain was caught off guard when Love gathered Novoselic, Smear, Erlandson, John Silva, Danny Goldberg, Janet Billig, Gary Gersh, Mark Kates, and others at their house on Washington Boulevard. In order to keep Kurt from leaving, she slashed the tires on their cars.

Cobain was not in the best frame of mind. After partying all night with Dylan Carlson, he woke up, shot up again, and came downstairs to find a room full of guests. Kurt was taken aback and at first thought Carlson had been in on the whole thing. After Cobain went into a rage and threw a recycling container at his friend, Carlson denied having anything to do with it and suggested they both leave.

Instead, Kurt decided to stay and listen to what his friends and business associates had to say. Gold Mountain threatened to stop representing him; Geffen's executives said they would drop the band; Pat said Nirvana would break up for good. When Love spoke, she told him she wanted him to get clean for Frances (who was staying with Kurt's mom at the time), and vowed that if they got divorced because of his drug use, his visitation would be minimal.

Kurt retaliated against Courtney, telling her that although she had shifted from heroin to pills, she was as much of an addict as he was. But when she informed him of her own plan to get clean—she was leaving for a controversial doctor-supervised rehab at the Peninsula Hotel in Los Angeles that day—there wasn't much else he could say. He agreed to accompany her, but mostly just to keep her from nagging him.

Basement Bound

That afternoon, Kurt escaped to the basement with his guitar for a while. Most of the intervention participants began to make their way home (many of them to L.A.), but Pat Smear and Eric Erlandson stayed behind and joined Kurt in recording songs like "Clean Up Before She Comes," "Dough Ray and Me" (also referred to by some as "Me and My IV"), "Opinion," "Talk to Me," and Bowie's "The Man Who Sold the World."

Later, after everyone had left, Courtney flew down to L.A. with Janet Billig. By now, Cobain had declined to go to rehab. He wound up spending the evening at Caitlin Moore's apartment getting high, but when he overdosed, he had been moved to the backseat of his car by her other clients—the logic being that if he died in her apartment, it would be bad for business.

Although everyone who was with him that night had expected him to die, Kurt woke up the next morning and drove home.

Goodbye Punch

On Saturday, March 26, 1994, Jackie Farry resumed her role as the Cobains' nanny (taking over from Cali DeWitt) after collecting Frances from Wendy O'Connor and taking the child down to Los Angeles. DeWitt's own drug use had gotten so far out of hand that he knew he was in no shape to look after a toddler. Plus he now had other obligations, with Courtney insisting he shadow Kurt's every move and report back.

Kurt's mother and sister Kim tried to talk some sense into him, but he was still out of it. When they left him they were heartbroken and disgusted with him. Perhaps their parting tears had an effect. Kurt still felt awful, following his overdose the night before, and knew he needed help.

On Monday, Kurt called Rosemary Carroll in desperation and once again agreed to try treatment. Rosemary booked him a flight and arranged to have Krist take him to Sea-Tac Airport.

However, as Novoselic drove him along Interstate 5 to the airport the next day, Kurt had a change of heart and began crying and screaming. Near the Tukwila exit, he tried to jump out of the moving car. Then, minutes later, after they arrived at the airport, where Novoselic forced Cobain from the car, Kurt made it clear that the band was over before punching his old friend right in the face (or smacking him with a guitar, depending on whose recollection is believed) and running off.

Novoselic went back to his car and drove away, bawling. He knew he had lost his dear friend and that there was nothing he could do. His sadness turned to rage as he stopped in to see guitar tech Earnie Bailey. According to Bailey (via Everett True), Krist said, "Fuck him, I'm done with that guy."

Bailey figured it would all blow over. Instead, it was the last time Kurt and Krist ever saw one another.

Remington

On March 30, after talking on the phone the night before with Love and her psychiatrist, Dr. Steve Scappa, Cobain finally agreed to go to Los Angeles for treatment. Prior to his departure, however, he had two personal matters to take care of.

The first was to take as much heroin as he could; the second involved a shotgun. Kurt drove to Dylan Carlson's condominium and asked him to buy a gun, explaining that he needed it for protection, adding that the police had seized all of his other guns. Carlson agreed, and together he and Kurt drove to Stan Baker Sports at 10000 Lake City Way.

Dylan—who had lent Cobain guns before—did not suspect Kurt was suicidal when he picked out the Remington M-11 twenty-gauge rifle. On his friend's orders, Carlson also selected a box of ammunition and paid the shop attendant $308.37 in cash.

Exodus Again

Cobain returned home to pack for his trip to Los Angeles, where he would once again enter Exodus. After keeping Washington Limousine Service driver Harvey Ottinger waiting for an hour, Kurt came out of the Lake Washington house with a small backpack. Then, en route to Sea-Tac, he realized he still had the box of ammunition in his bag and asked the driver to get rid of it for him.

That evening, Pat Smear and Gold Mountain's Michael Meisel picked Cobain up at LAX and took him to the Exodus Recovery Center at Daniel Freeman Marina Hospital in Marina del Rey. His roommate in room 206 happened to be Gibby Haynes, front man for the Butthole Surfers, a one-time hero and later friend of Kurt's.

On Thursday, March 31, Cobain began his treatment. Substance abuse counselor Nial Stimson observed that Kurt was in complete denial about his problem and downplayed the fact that it had nearly killed him in Italy. If only Stimson had known that the Italian incident was in fact a suicide attempt, Cobain would have been moved to the hospital's psychiatric unit.

According to Cross' biography, Kurt hardly touched on his marital problems and instead spoke largely to Stimson about his fears that he might end up on the losing end of Kevin Kerslake's lawsuit over the "Heart-Shaped Box" video. Were the video director to be victorious, the ensuing damages would drastically cut into Cobain's fortune.

That afternoon, Farry brought Frances to visit with Cobain, but Courtney did not join them as it was too soon in his recovery. Kurt seemed out of it as he spoke to Jackie about his battle with Love over Lollapalooza.

A second, short visit occurred the following morning. Cobain seemed upbeat, more lucid, and unusually happy as he played with his infant daughter, throwing her in the air as she giggled. He held Frances close and whispered in her ear.

Farry attributed his change in mood to the withdrawal medications Kurt had been given, including Valium and benzodiazepine. As Kurt kissed his daughter goodbye, there was no way Farry could know it would be the child's final encounter with her father.

Exodus from Exodus

On Friday afternoon, Cobain—just out of detox—was out in the smoking area with Haynes, visitor Pat Smear, and his friend Joe "Mama" Nitzburg, a recent graduate of the treatment center. Nitzburg was a friend of Courtney Love's who had endeared himself to Kurt the year before, and when Mama's financial aid for art school fell through, Cobain had kindly picked up the tab.

Although Love had been unable to reach Kurt by phone, she sent Nitzburg over to the treatment center with a letter, a music fanzine, and some candy for him. As they lit up on the patio, where they talked and joked between cigarettes, Haynes—who was a week ahead of Kurt in the program—told the story of a friend who went over the wall at Exodus to break free.

"I was talking to him about a friend of mine who was in the same position we both were who had climbed over the wall," Haynes told CaughtintheCrossfire. com. "He had decided to leave rehab and climbed over the wall and broke out! You know, he didn't have to break out; he could have just walked down the hallway and walked out the doors! We were laughing!"

Smear and Nitzburg left at around 5:00 p.m. Then, after trying to reach Kurt by phone all day, Love finally got hold of him on the facility's pay phone. "No matter what happens, I want you to know that you made a really good record," Love later told the *Seattle Times* in 1994 he had told her. When she asked him what he meant, he added, "Just remember, no matter what, I love you." It was the last time they ever spoke.

At approximately 7:25 p.m., Cobain told staffers at the clinic that he was going out to the patio to smoke. Outside, he scaled the six-foot brick wall, and he was gone. He left behind a pair of shirts and a spiral notebook containing the beginnings of a few songs.

Delta 788

Late on Friday evening, Cobain boarded Delta flight 788 bound for Seattle at LAX after using his credit card to buy a first-class ticket. He also called ahead to arrange a car service from the airport and phoned his wife, but she wasn't in.

In the hours since he had left rehab, Love had left her own detox program and was out searching for him. Worried that Kurt had left to score drugs in L.A., she enlisted friends like Joe Nitzburg to take her to visit various dealers, hoping to find Kurt.

Instead, Cobain was flying north in first class, sitting next to Guns N' Roses bassist and Seattle native Duff McKagan. The bad blood of the 1992 MTV Awards was long gone as Kurt told Duff how he had just left Exodus. McKagan—a recovering heroin addict—understood Kurt's struggles perhaps better than any of the Nirvana front man's own associates.

"We were both fucked-up," McKagan remembered in a *Seattle Weekly* blog post in February 2010. "We talked, but not in depth. I was in my hell, and he in his, and this we both seemed to understand."

Sensing something was wrong, McKagan thought of inviting Cobain over to his new house—it turned out they were neighbors—as they went to claim their baggage after the plane's landing at 1:45 a.m.

"I had a real sense that he was lonely and alone that night," Duff wrote. "I felt the same way. There was a mad rush of people there in public. I was in a big rock band, and he was in a big rock band. We were standing next to each other. Lots of people stopped to gawk. I lost my train of thought for a minute, and Kurt said goodbye and left to his waiting town car."

April 2

It's unclear if Cobain went to sleep that night. At 6:00 p.m. he went into the bedroom where Cali DeWitt and his girlfriend Jessica Hopper had been sleeping. As Cali slept off a cocaine bender, Hopper explained that Courtney had been calling all night and was freaking out. Cobain picked up the phone and called the Peninsula Hotel, only to be told that Love wasn't taking any calls. When he told them who he was, the operator insisted he provide the code name needed to reach her. But in typical Cobain fashion, Kurt had forgotten her alias.

At around 6:30 a.m., Cobain called Graytop Cab Co., and upon being picked up told the driver that he had "recently been burgled and needed bullets." It was at least two hours before any Sporting Goods stores would be open, so he got a ride to 145th and Aurora, near Caitlin Moore's house, where it is believed he checked into the Crest or Quest Motel. That morning, he also bought a box of twenty-gauge shotgun shells at Seattle Guns. Later that day, Love canceled Cobain's credit cards, hoping it might help her track him down.

April 3

On Sunday, April 3, Love hired private investigators Tom Grant and Ben Klugman after finding their names in the Los Angeles phonebook. They reported to her hotel room at the Peninsula, where she explained that her husband had escaped from rehab, and that she was worried about his health and mental state. Grant arranged for a Seattle area P.I. to set up surveillance on Caitlin Moore's house and the condo belonging to Dylan Carlson.

No one bothered to check the Lake Washington house because Courtney figured Cali would have told her if he had seen Kurt. But DeWitt was so out of it himself (he was using $400 to $500 of cocaine and other drugs a day by this point, according to *Nirvana: The True Story*) that he failed to answer the house phone that entire weekend.

That evening, Cobain was seen at the Cactus Restaurant with a man and a woman believed to be Moore. When his credit card was refused, Kurt was embarrassed at having to write a check to pay for dinner.

April 4

It wasn't until early on Monday that Hopper relayed to Cali during an argument about his drug abuse that she had seen Kurt on Saturday morning. DeWitt picked up the phone to call Courtney and share this information.

Love tried to keep it together enough to conduct an interview with *Los Angeles Times* music critic Robert Hilburn, but she broke down in tears about Kurt's disappearance. Later that day, she reached Carlson by phone. He swore that he hadn't seen Kurt since the week before, when they went shopping for his new shotgun. This news alarmed Love, who called the Seattle Police impersonating her mother-in-law, Wendy, to file a missing person's report.

"Mr. Cobain ran away from a California facility and flew back to Seattle," the report read. "He also bought a shotgun and may be suicidal. Mr. Cobain may be at [Moore's] location for narcotics." Cops were asked to check Moore's Capitol Hill apartment and the Cobains' Lake Washington home but saw no sign of Kurt, while the private investigators Tom Grant had contacted in Seattle were unable to find Cobain during surveillance or at the drug hotels Love knew he frequented.

Police would later deduce that Cobain had probably spent the night nearly forty miles away at the house in Carnation with a friend. Neighbors also claimed to have seen him in the park adjacent to his home at some point on Monday. Hopper—who was in DeWitt's room—claimed that she heard footsteps in the hallway and upstairs in the Lake Washington house Monday night. When she called out "Hello?" there was no answer, but she believed it might have been Kurt.

April 5

On Tuesday afternoon, Hole guitarist Eric Erlandson showed up at the house at Courtney's request, looking for Cobain and his gun. When he was unable to find Kurt there, he went to the Carnation property. Hours earlier, Cali had needed to retrieve something from the basement; because Cobain had been missing, he feared that Kurt might be down there and insisted Hopper go with him. Nobody thought to check inside the garage or the greenhouse.

Earlier that morning, as the sun rose while DeWitt and Hopper slept downstairs, Cobain had awoken in his own bed, where he slept without their knowledge. The night before, he had slept in his clothes—somehow, in all the madness of the previous week, no one had thought to arrange a delivery of heating oil.

In a trusty pair of worn Levi's, his beloved Half Japanese shirt, his green Converse One Star sneakers, and his favorite brown corduroy jacket, Cobain turned on MTV, but left the sound turned off. He put on R.E.M.'s acclaimed 1992 album *Automatic for the People*, injected himself with heroin, and wrote a one-page suicide note in red ink. He addressed the note to his imaginary childhood friend Boddah.

"This note should be pretty easy to understand," Cobain wrote to his family, friends and fans. "I haven't felt the excitement of listening to as well as creating music along with reading and writing for too many years now."

He went on to explain how the roar of the crowd backstage as the lights went down didn't mean as much to him as it should, citing the adoration in which someone like Queen's Freddie Mercury once basked.

"The worst crime I can think of would be to rip people off by faking and pretending as if I'm having 100 percent fun," Kurt added. He expressed worry that his daughter might become the same unhappy, self-destructive person he was, and praised his "goddess of a wife who sweats ambition and empathy."

He closed out the note by expressing gratitude to his fans for their letters and concern during his struggles with fame and addiction. "Thank you all from the pit of my burning nauseous stomach," he wrote. "I'm too much of an erratic, moody baby! I don't have the passion anymore and so remember, it's better to burn out than to fade away."

Cobain had previously written a long letter to Love during his short stay at Exodus, which he carried with him on the plane back to Seattle. He left it for her under a pillow in their bedroom. In it, he repeatedly told his wife he was sorry and pledged his love to her and Frances.

"I don't know where I'm going," he admitted. "I just can't be here anymore."

At some point during the day of April 5, Cobain barricaded himself in the greenhouse above the garage by propping a stool against the French doors. He smoked five Camel Light cigarettes, drank a can of Barq's Root Beer, and removed the hunter's cap he often wore to keep from being recognized. He took out the note he had written and added one more line:

"Please keep going Courtney, for Frances, for her life which will be so much happier without me. I love you. I love you."

Kurt took his wallet out and threw it on the floor. It opened to reveal his driver's license, which Seattle police would later use to identify him. Then he took one large, final dose of "black tar" heroin and pulled a chair up to a window that looked out toward Puget Sound. He pushed the barrel of the Remington to his head and used his thumb to pull the trigger. He was gone.

32

Never Speak a Word Again

The Aftermath

Canceling Lollapalooza

On April 6, Ted Gardner, the organizer and co-founder (with Jane's Addiction vocalist Perry Farrell) of Lollapalooza, issued a press release, explaining that Nirvana would no longer be headlining the traveling festival "due to the ill health of Kurt Cobain."

Although Kurt was missing, and it looked like the band was in fact over, no one knew yet that he had taken his life. Ironically, Billy Corgan's band the Smashing Pumpkins would take Nirvana's place as headliners.

Courtney's Overdose

Back in Beverly Hills, Love wasn't handling the stress of Kurt's disappearance well. She relapsed, and on April 7 police received a 911 call about a possible overdose victim at the Peninsula Hotel. When an ambulance and law enforcement officials arrived at the hotel, they found Love with Erlandson, who had since flown back from Seattle to be with her. Frances and Jackie Farry had been staying in the room next door.

Love was admitted to Century City Hospital at 9:30 a.m. that morning and released at noon. Upon her departure, Courtney was arrested by Beverly Hills Police for "possession of a controlled substance, possession of drug paraphernalia, possession of a hypodermic syringe, and receiving stolen property."

Her lawyer, Barry Tarlow, later argued that she wasn't under the influence of heroin, nor did she overdose. Instead, he told *Rolling Stone* that June, she had had an allergic reaction to the tranquilizer Xanax. Tarlow also claimed that the blank prescription pad found in the room wasn't stolen, as cops alleged, but had been left there by Love's doctor. As for the controlled substance, it was actually Hindu good-luck ashes that Rosemary Carroll had given her as a gift.

Three hours after her arrest, Love posted $10,000 and was freed on bail. No longer welcome at the Peninsula, she checked into the same Exodus facility in

Marina del Rey that Cobain had left six days earlier. She would check out the following day.

Kurt Is Found

On the morning of Friday April 8, an electrician named Gary Smith showed up at 171 Lake Washington Boulevard to complete the job of installing a new alarm system, which he had begun a day earlier. The previous day, police had come by to put workers on alert that the home's owner, Kurt Cobain, was missing but had been seen in the area.

Around 8:40 a.m., Smith was working near the greenhouse when he looked in through a window and noticed a body lying on the floor. "I thought it was a mannequin," he told the *Seattle Times*. "Then I noticed it had blood in the right ear. I saw a shotgun laying across his chest, pointing up at his chin." He called the police and then his bosses at the alarm company.

Word quickly spread after the alarm company dispatcher told one of his friends, who called and broke the news to local rock station KXRX. Upon hearing the news, Cobain's sister Kim called the on-air DJ, Marty Riemer, in disbelief.

Soon after that, police confirmed that the body of a young male had been found at Cobain's house but added they had yet to identify the victim. But when *Seattle Times* photographer Tom Reese saw Kurt's green sneakers, he knew.

The news quickly reached Los Angeles. Carroll went to Exodus to break it to Courtney. They then flew back up to Seattle by Learjet with Frances, Farry, and Eric Erlandson. Waiting for them in Seattle that afternoon was a doctor who had been hired to stay with Love at all times. Hole quickly canceled their imminent spring tour.

By midday, an Aberdeen *Daily World* writer rang the doorbell at Wendy O'Connor's home. "Now he's gone and joined that stupid club," she told the reporter. "I told him not to join that stupid club." The implication was that Cobain was now among the many famous musicians who had died tragically at age twenty-seven, including Jimi Hendrix, Janis Joplin, and Jim Morrison.

By Friday afternoon, Cobain's typically private Lake Washington residence and its surrounding neighborhood were crawling with reporters and police. Inside, friends like Screaming Trees front man Mark Lanegan, *Melody Maker* writer Everett True, Erlandson, DeWitt, Farry, Novoselic, and Grohl, plus record label and management personnel, gathered awkwardly around Courtney, Frances, Wendy, and Kim.

Meanwhile, the King County medical examiner rushed to complete a preliminary autopsy. Dr. Nikolas Hartshorne—a Nirvana fan who had promoted a gig by the band as a college student several years earlier—confirmed that Kurt had died of a shotgun wound to the head that appeared to be self-inflicted. There was also evidence of benzodiazepine and deadly levels of heroin in Cobain's system.

That evening, while police concluded their investigation of the crime scene, Pearl Jam's Eddie Vedder—visibly grief-stricken—told a Washington D.C. crowd, "I don't think any of us would be in this room tonight if it weren't for Kurt Cobain. Don't die. Swear to God."

Back at the house, Love refused to take off Cobain's blood-splattered corduroy jacket, which she insisted investigators leave for her. Later, a private security guard witnessed her following Cobain's final footsteps up to the greenhouse, which had yet to be professionally cleaned. She rubbed the palms of her hands in her late husband's blood and recovered a small piece of his scalp before retreating to their bedroom. There, alongside Cobain's grieving mom, she slept in his clothes.

Last Goodbyes

On Saturday, April 9, Love traveled to the funeral home where Kurt Cobain's body was to be cremated. Courtney—who had been swallowing the various pills that her friends had been giving her for comfort—visited quietly with her husband's corpse and made sure that arrangements had been made to first make plaster casts of his hands. She took locks of hair from his head and his pubic region.

The other core members of Nirvana had also been invited to say goodbye. Novoselic came to have a few final minutes with Kurt, and understandably broke down in tears. Grohl declined the invitation. Meanwhile, Cobain's death was reported on throughout the weekend by CNN and even made the front page of the *New York Times*.

Novoselic told the Associated Press that he supposed Cobain's death was the result of many different things. "Just blaming it on smack is stupid," Krist said. "Smack was just a small part of his life."

It took Dave some time to be able to speak publicly about Kurt's death. In 2009, speaking to Jo Whiley on BBC Radio 1, he called it "a terrible surprise," revealing that Cobain's suicide left him "heartbroken," and that the experience was "the worst thing that has happened to me in my life."

The Vigil

On Sunday, April 10, a private memorial service and a candlelight vigil took place simultaneously. The two events were arranged with the help of Soundgarden manager Susan Silver.

The emotional vigil took place in front of some 7,000 fans at the Seattle Center's Flag Pavilion, near the Space Needle. Fans came to the event clutching candles and flowers. Local radio personalities spoke alongside a suicide counselor, and a pre-recorded message from Novoselic was broadcast.

"We remember Kurt for what he was: caring, generous, and sweet," Krist said. "Just catch a groove and let it flow out of your heart. That's the level that Kurt spoke to us on: in our hearts. And that's where the music will always be, forever."

A lengthier message from Courtney followed. In it, she admitted to being uneasy and sad, and explained that although Kurt had left a note, she wasn't going to read it aloud. Moments later, however, she contradicted herself and did just that, adding her own opinions and frustrations with her late husband in between his lines.

Early on in her recording, Love called her husband an "asshole" for killing himself and asked the crowd to repeat the word. Later, when she read aloud as he cited the Neil Young line "It's better to burn out than to fade away," she stopped to criticize him again.

Finally, Courtney expressed regret that she hadn't been there for Kurt in his final days, wishing she had put him first and revealing her remorse over trying to stop him from using heroin.

"We all should have let him have his numbness," she said. "We should have let him have the thing that made him feel better, that made his stomach feel better." In parting, she called him a "fucker" before expressing her everlasting love for him.

Private Service

As the vigil got underway, Cobain's family attended a private memorial service at the Seattle Unity Church. Guests included everyone from Kurt's old art teacher Bob Hunter and former girlfriends Tracey Marander and Mary Lou Lord to his stepmother Jenny and his grandfather Leland. As they entered the church, they were each greeted with pictures of Kurt aged just six, which had been placed upon the pews.

According to Gillian G. Gaar, the Reverend Stephen Towles began the service by reading the 23rd Psalm and telling the one hundred or so invited guests, "A suicide is no different than having our finger in a vise. The pain becomes so great that you can't bear it any longer." Towles ended his remarks by reading a poem entitled "The Traveler" before asking Kurt's friends to share their thoughts.

Sub Pop's Bruce Pavitt came to the podium and expressed his love and sadness. Novoselic gave a short eulogy similar to what he had recorded for the candlelight vigil. Dylan Carlson read a Buddhist poem.

Next, Courtney read aloud from the Book of Job and recited some of Cobain's favorite poems from Arthur Rimbaud's *Illuminations*. She told stories from Kurt's childhood and read lines from his suicide note.

After Gary Gersh read a faxed eulogy by Michael Stipe, Danny Goldberg took the podium to speak fondly of Kurt and confess that he believed Kurt would have "left this world several years ago if he hadn't met Courtney." Reverend Towles concluded the ceremony with a reading from Matthew 5:43.

While many attendees returned to the Lake Washington house to continue mourning, Love made her way over to the Seattle Center, where the vigil had by now ended. She showed some of the fans who still remained in the park Kurt's actual suicide note, much to the shock of witnesses, and gave a few of them pieces of her late husband's clothing.

Ashes

Upon receipt of Cobain's ashes in mid-April, Love took some from the urn and buried them next to a willow tree in the front yard of their house. The following month, she took more to be buried at the Namgyal Buddhist monastery near Ithaca, New York.

Then, in May 1999, the remainder of Kurt's ashes were scattered in a creek behind Wendy O'Connor's house outside of Olympia, which Courtney had bought for her mother-in-law. Tracy Marander and Kurt's father Don were among the guests invited to the final ceremony, which included a prayer recital by a Buddhist monk.

33

Find Your Place

Life Beyond Nirvana

N irvana altered rock music forever. Perhaps *Rolling Stone*'s Even Serpick put it best when he claimed, "few bands in rock history have had a more immediate and tangible impact on their contemporary pop musical landscape than Nirvana did in the early nineties." As a result, in the months and years that followed, the band's business and legacy continued to grow, just as the surviving members continued to evolve creatively and build new identities for themselves.

Krist and Dave: Music and More

Krist Novoselic and Dave Grohl made their first post-Nirvana appearance together at the Yo-Yo a Go-Go indie rock festival in Olympia in the fall of 1994, backing the Stinky Puffs, the group helmed by Jad Fair's ten-year-old stepson Simon Fair Timony and Cody Linn Ranaldo, the young son of Sonic Youth guitarist Lee Ranaldo. The final song of the Stinky Puffs' set, "I Love You Anyways," was an emotional number about Cobain penned by Timony, whom Kurt had befriended during Nirvana's last tour.

Shortly after the Stinky Puffs show, Krist and Dave formed bands of their own. They would both also collaborate with other artists and pursue projects outside of music with varying degrees of success.

Sweet 75

Sweet 75 took shape when Krist Novoselic met Yva Las Vegas, a Venezuelan street busker his then-wife Shelli had hired to sing at his thirtieth birthday party. Although Krist first envisioned producing an album for Yva, they evolved into a band as they began to write songs together, with the addition (initially) of drummer Bobi Lore. Taking their name from a poem by Theodore Roethke, they played a few Northwestern shows and—on the strength of Krist's Nirvana pedigree—signed to Geffen.

The group's eponymous, Paul Fox–produced album was recorded with ex-Ministry drummer Bill Rieflin, and included guest appearances by R.E.M.'s Peter Buck, Anisa Romero of Sky Cries Mary, and jazz great Herb Alpert. But by the time the album was released, on August 26, 1997, Rieflin had been replaced by former Shudder to Think drummer Adam Wade.

Perhaps because of Krist's stature, critics were polite about the record. Allmusic.com's Stephen Thomas Erlewine wrote, "Novoselic attempts to bring adventure and experimentation back to guitar-oriented alternative rock with Sweet 75's eponymous debut, with mixed results. It's admirable that the duo blends indie-rock with heavy rock, Mexican music, lunge, and country, but the intentions are often better than the final product." Sales were miniscule, however, and the band disbanded in early 1998. Sweet 75 regrouped with Rieflin a few months later, but plans for a second album were soon scrapped.

Sunshine Cake and the No WTO Combo

By mid-1999, Novoselic had begun focusing his attention on Sunshine Cake, a band he and Rieflin had been working on with Romero. Concurrently, Krist directed his first movie, *L7: The Beauty Process*, a low budget, tongue-in-cheek documentary about Nirvana's former touring partners assembled from footage that he shot on tour in 1997.

By the fourth quarter of 1999, Novoselic had launched a one-off punk band called the No WTO Combo with former Dead Kennedy's front man Jello Biafra, Soundgarden guitarist Kim Thayil, and drummer Gina Mainwal. They booked a gig at the Showbox for the night before the World Trade Organization summit in Seattle, but it was postponed because of "curfew zone" issues and rescheduled for the following evening.

A recording of the gig would ultimately see release via Biafra's Alternative Tentacles label as *Live from the Battle in Seattle*. The anti-globalization punk outfit cut four songs, including the DK classic "Let's Lynch the Landlord," D.O.A.'s "Full Metal Jackoff," and two originals, "New Feudalism" and "Electronic Plantation." Jack Endino mixed the EP, which also included a fifteen-minute speech by Biafra.

Eyes Adrift

Novoselic next formed Eyes Adrift with Meat Puppets front man Curt Kirkwood and former Sublime drummer Bud Gaugh. "It's been fun for us to get back to playing music," Krist told me on August 27, 2002, in an interview for *Rolling Stone*. "After all, we're musicians, we should be playing and creating music."

Speaking just a few weeks ahead of the trio's debut via the now defunct New York indie label SpinART Records on September 24, 2002, Krist was hesitant to accept Eyes Adrift being labeled a "super-group." Citing the likes of eighties bands Asia and Mike & the Mechanics, he joked, "That term has a bad connotation. We've all got our pasts, which we're really proud of, but our future is Eyes Adrift."

"People have it in their heads that we got together because we all had tragic situations in our previous bands," he added, referencing Cobain's suicide, Sublime singer Brad Nowell's 1996 death from a heroin overdose in 1996, and Meat Puppets bassist Cris Kirkwood's battle with drug addiction after his wife Michelle Tardif died of an overdose in 1998. "But it was purely coincidental. That would be like saying that we all got together because we all come from trios."

Novoselic explained how the trio came together after he dropped in on a solo gig that Curt was playing in Seattle in the fall of 2001. "I was like, 'Wow, Curt's still got it.' Afterwards, I approached him about getting together to jam. Ironically, Bud—who I' never met, but was a fan of Curt's guitar style—was thinking the same thing after he saw Curt was playing solo down in California. So he called Curt up to see if he'd be interested in jamming. Once we all got together, I had some songs and Curt had some songs, and we made up some more, and it was really comfortable."

Honing that new material in Kirkwood's hometown of Austin, Texas, Eyes Adrift road-tested the songs during a club tour in January and February 2002. Those gigs, at venues like I-Spy in Seattle, the Troubadour in L.A., and Emo's in Austin—in front of fans in old Nirvana, Sublime, and Meat Puppets T-shirts— were quite reassuring to Krist and the others.

"How could we not feel confident in that environment?" he explained. "No one who showed up really knew what to expect from us—I hope they weren't expecting 'Teen Spirit' or 'Backwater.' But by the end of each show, people were into it. We didn't see anyone walk out of those shows. And for ten or twelve bucks, we gave 'em some real entertainment."

After that preliminary tour, Eyes Adrift spent three weeks in an Austin studio and came away with a diverse twelve-song rock 'n' roll debut. The melodic "Inquiring Minds" was one of three songs that Novoselic sang, lashing out about the media circus that exploited the 1996 death of Jon Benet Ramsey.

"I was in a supermarket in Austin, when we were in the early stages of the group, just working out the material," he added. "And I saw one of the tabloids, and it had one of those computer-enhanced photos of Jon Benet with a headline about what she would have looked like now, had she lived. I found the whole thing quite sickening. I also kind of identified with it because of what I personally experienced back in '94, with the death of Kurt."

Despite Krist's positive outlook, *Eyes Adrift* failed to light a spark at radio or retail—according to Billboard.com, it sold just 9,000 copies in its first year. Not long after wrapping a three-month tour at San Antonio's White Rabbit on December 8, 2002, Eyes Adrift split up. In a post to the band's official website on August 5, 2003, Novoselic wrote, "I quit. I can't deal," expressing his frustration with the music business. "Every band I've ever been in just falls apart. That hurts but I've got a thick hide from years of conditioning."

Novoselic, aged thirty-eight at the time, went on to say that he wasn't quitting making music altogether, but revealed he was thinking about a run for political office. "I'm relatively young," he wrote, "and I want to follow my compulsions."

Novoselic's Political Pursuits

Krist's political side first became apparent as he spoke to reporters when Nirvana broke in 1991, and it blossomed through the humanitarian benefits it played at the height of the group's popularity. In January 1995, after the Erotic Music Law was reintroduced to the Washington State Legislature as the Matters Harmful to Minors bill, he formed JAMPAC (the Joint Artists and Music Promotions Political Action Committee) with the intention of protecting musical artists' freedom of expression and the freedom of choice for music buyers. It was Novoselic's belief that all forms of music—regardless of its content—warranted First Amendment protection.

JAMPAC was initially formed to lobby against censorship, and Novoselic traveled to Washington on several occasions as the organization's founder and president to speak before Congress on related issues. JAMPAC was instrumental in eliminating the 1985 Seattle Teen Dance Ordinance, which prevented those under twenty-one years of age from attending late night concerts.

In 1998, Krist participated in the Spitfire tour of college campuses, which was organized by Rage Against the Machine front man and human rights advocate Zack de la Rocha and featured a range of artists, actors, and activists. It found Novoselic discussing civil liberties, social issues, and environmental justice.

In October 2004, Novoselic released his first book, *Of Grunge and Government: Let's Fix This Broken Democracy*, which explored his music career and focused on his longstanding interest in politics, his belief in electoral reform, and his support of grassroots movements to rid politics of corruption and waste. In tandem with the book's publication, Krist joined the board of (and toured with) FairVote, which according to its website aspires to "transform our elections to achieve universal access to participation, a full spectrum of meaningful ballot choices and majority rule with fair representation for all."

That same year, Novoselic had considered running for Lieutenant Governor of Washington as a democrat, and he briefly considered challenging an incumbent from the same party until he concluded it would be inappropriate to do so.

In 2008, Novoselic replaced former republican congressman and 1980 presidential hopeful John B. Anderson as FairVote's chairman. Novoselic—who supported the election of democratic senator Barack Obama in 2008—became an elected state committeeman advocating universal voter registration, a national popular vote for president, and instant run-off voting.

In 2009, Novoselic ran for county clerk of Wahkiakum County Washington under the Grange Party, but ultimately withdrew from the race. Although a member of the National Grange of the Order of Patrons of Husbandry, the Grange is not a political party, and Krist was only running for the office in order to protest his home state's system, which allows a candidate to claim any party as their own without support of the party.

Flipper and Beyond

In between all of this political activity, Krist returned to music for a time, joining Flipper on bass in November 2006 for touring and recording purposes. In 2008, a studio album titled *Love* was recorded at Novoselic's Murky Slough Studios on his farm near Deep River with singer Bruce Loose, guitarist Ted Falconi, and drummer Steve DePace. It was produced by Jack Endino.

Novoselic left the band in September 2009 to focus on his responsibilities at home. From November 2007 to September 2010, he maintained a regular column in the *Seattle Weekly*, where he most often wrote about music and politics. He also appeared as a newspaper vendor in the 2009 Robin Williams movie *World's Greatest Dad*. And on a personal note, having divorced his first wife Shelli Dilley in late 1999, he married Darbury Stenderu, an acclaimed textile artist, in early 2004.

Foo Fighters

After appearing on *Saturday Night Live* with Tom Petty & the Heartbreakers in the fall of 1994 and being offered a job as their drummer after the exit of longtime member Stan Lynch, Dave Grohl instead decided to pursue his own music. Building on the experience of making his *Pocketwatch* cassette, Dave started anew as a guitarist and singer, launching Foo Fighters—named for the "UFO" sightings of Allied aircraft pilots in World War II—as a one-man band.

Grohl entered Robert Lang Studios in Shoreline, Washington on October 17, 1994, with plans to record fifteen songs. Save for one guitar part on the song "X-static," which was played by Afghan Whigs front man Greg Dulli, he crafted the entire record by himself in a single week.

With the album finished, Grohl approached Novoselic about playing in his band, but after weighing up the pros and cons of reuniting, they decided against it. Dave instead recruited bassist Nate Mendel and drummer William Goldsmith from the newly defunct Sunny Day Real Estate, and asked Pat Smear to play guitar.

The band played their first show on February 23, 1995, and soon after, Grohl licensed the album to Capitol Records through his own Roswell Records imprint, named in homage to the alleged July 1947 New Mexico UFO crash. *Foo Fighters* was released on July 4, 1995. Although Dave had modest expectations, four singles ("This Is a Call," "I'll Stick Around," "For All the Cows," and "Big Me") were released during the next year as the band toured the world. The eponymous album went on to sell 1.5 million copies in the United States.

Grohl hired producer Gil Norton (the Pixies, Catherine Wheel, Counting Crows) for Foo Fighters' second album, *The Colour and the Shape,* their first studio effort as a complete band. But early attempts at the material—much of which was influenced by Grohl's 1996 divorce from photographer Jennifer Youngblood—were not to Dave's liking. Grohl re-recorded the drum parts for the record without Goldsmith's knowledge. Goldsmith felt insulted when he found out and quit the group.

In May 1997, the album and first single "Monkey Wrench" were released, but soon after that—during a live MTV broadcast from Radio City Music Hall—Smear announced he was leaving the Foos (on friendly terms). Drummer Taylor Hawkins, a veteran of Alanis Morissette's band, was already in place when guitarist Franz Stahl supplanted Smear. The success of additional singles "Everlong" and "My Hero" saw *The Colour and the Shape* sell slightly better than its predecessor.

After Stahl was fired from the group, Foo Fighters recorded 1999's *There Is Nothing Left to Lose* as a trio at Grohl's home studio in Alexandria, Virginia, before Dave hired lead guitarist Chris Shifflet, a veteran of punk bands No Use for a Name and Me First & the Gimme Gimmes. The album was licensed to RCA and released on November 2, 1999. As with previous Foo Fighters albums, and on the strength of "Learn to Fly" and "Breakout," it was certified platinum by the Recording Industry Association of America for one million sales. It earned a 2001 Grammy Award for "Best Rock Album."

The follow-up, 2002's *One by One*, repeated the feat, landing a "Best Rock Album" Grammy in 2004 and spawning singles like "All My Life" and "Times Like These." A double album entitled *In Your Honor* followed in 2005, selling 1.4 million copies in the United States. The disc was nominated for four Grammy Awards and featured guest appearances by Norah Jones, Queens of the Stone Age's Josh Homme, Led Zeppelin's John Paul Jones, and Wallflowers keyboardist Rami Jaffe. It included the single "Best of You."

The Foo Fighters' sixth album, *Echoes, Silence, Patience, and Grace*, was their least commercially successful offering. Although it failed to reach a million in US sales, the half-rock, half-acoustic album earned the band a third "Best Rock Album" Grammy and spawned the singles "The Pretender," "Long Road to Ruin," and "Let It Die."

Foo Fighters' *Greatest Hits* emerged two years later, and included the new songs "Wheels" and "Word Forward." Grohl later revealed he had written the latter after the drug-related passing of his lifelong friend Jimmy Swanson in 2008.

Grohl's trophy shelf scored another Grammy for "Best Rock Album" with 2011's *Wasting Light*. Recorded in his California garage on analog equipment with *Nevermind* producer Butch Vig, the disc marked the official return of Pat Smear to the band on rhythm guitar and featured the singles "Rope," "Walk," and "These Days." Special guests included Krist Novoselic, who played bass and accordion on "I Should of Known," plus Bob Mould, Tubes singer Fee Waybill, and keyboardist Rami Jaffee, who toured with the band in support of the set.

Grohl's Side

Aside from his efforts with his band, Grohl has kept extremely busy playing with an endless list of rock, punk, metal, and pop artists. In 1994, he played drums on former Minutemen/fIREHOSE bassist Mike Watt's solo album *Ball-Hog or Tugboat?*, and the following year he played on the Ringspiel tour with Watt, Goldsmith, Smear, and Pearl Jam's Eddie Vedder. Foo Fighters opened the shows.

During downtime from the band in the early 2000s, Grohl worked on a metal album he called Probot, for which he recruited veteran singers like Lemmy Kilmister of Motörhead, King Diamond, Voivoid front man Snake, Mike Dean from Corrosion of Conformity, and Sepultura's Max Cavalera. The album was released in February 2004 and also featured guest guitarist Kim Thayil of Soundgarden and a hidden track sung by Tenacious D's Jack Black.

Grohl had first collaborated with Black and comedian Kyle Gass on Tenacious D's 2001 debut album, and appeared as a demon in the group's video for "Tribute." He reprised the role for the joke/metal duo's 2006 movie *Tenacious D in the Pick of Destiny*, and played with Black and Gas on the duo's 2012 disc *Rize of the Fenix*. In 2000, he played drums and sang on "Goodbye Lament," from Black Sabbath singer Tony Iommi's album *Iommi*.

In 2002, Grohl played drums on Cat Power's *You Are Free* and guitar on David Bowie's *Heathen*. He also teamed up with his friend Josh Homme on *Songs for the Deaf*, the acclaimed third album by Queens of the Stone Age, and toured with the band in support of the disc. He again joined the Queens in the studio to play drums on some of the songs for 2013's . . . *Like Clockwork*.

Grohl's extracurricular efforts continued the following year as he worked in the studio with Killing Joke and paid tribute to the Clash's Joe Strummer at the 2003 Grammy Awards, trading verses of "London Calling" with Bruce Springsteen and Elvis Costello. Between 2004 and 2010 he drummed on sessions with Nine Inch Nails, Garbage, Pete Yorn, Juliette & the Licks, the Prodigy, and former Guns N' Roses guitarist Slash.

In July 2009, Dave announced his participation in the super-group Them Crooked Vultures with Homme and Led Zeppelin's John Paul Jones. Live shows that summer in Chicago and in London preceded the release of a self-titled debut that November.

Grohl had previously jammed with another childhood hero in June 2008, when Paul McCartney asked him onstage at Liverpool's Anfield football stadium. Grohl played guitar and sang "Band on the Run" before drumming on "Back in the U.S.S.R." and "I Saw Her Standing There." Twenty months later, he rejoined Sir Paul for a 2010 Grammy performance of the latter before paying tribute to his legendary friend by singing a duet of McCartney's "Maybe I'm Amazed" with Norah Jones at the 2010 Kennedy Center Honors that December.

Foos on Film

An officially sanctioned documentary about the history of the Foo Fighters directed by James Moll and titled *Back and Forth* saw theatrical release in March 2011. Around that time, Grohl began thinking about directing his own film. The resulting *Sound City* told the story of the Van Nuys recording studio of the same name where Nirvana made *Nevermind*. The film, which features interviews with artists who had recorded at the studio during its heyday like Fleetwood Mac, Tom Petty, and Rick Springfield, premiered at the Sundance Film Festival on January 18, 2013.

On a personal note, Grohl's first marriage to Jennifer Youngblood began in 1994 and ended in 1997. In 2001, Dave met Jordyn Blum in the bar at the Sunset Marquis Hotel in Los Angeles. They were married on August 2, 2003, and have two daughters, Violet Maye (born in 2006) and Harper Willow (born in 2009).

Nirvana Business

When Kurt Cobain died without a will in 1994, his net worth was unclear. But by October 2011, CBS News was reporting that Kurt's estate was worth an estimated $450 million, with over 75 million records sold worldwide—including more than 25 million RIAA-certified units in the US alone. Here are some of the most noteworthy Nirvana-related business happenings since his passing.

Courtney Love vs. Novoselic and Grohl

Following the release of *MTV Unplugged in New York* and *From the Muddy Banks of the Wishkah*, Dave Grohl and Krist Novoselic began to make plans for a boxed set of unreleased Nirvana material. When Love refused to move ahead with the project (which she had previously been in agreement with them about, and which fans had been clamoring for) and instead pushed for the release of a "best of" compilation that would feature "You Know You're Right" as its lead single, Dave and Krist took the battle public.

Novoselic, Grohl, and Love had formed Nirvana LLC in September 1997 to handle Nirvana-related business and nourish the band's assets and legacy. When communication between the two sides broke down following their disagreements over the boxed set, Love filed a suit to dissolve the LLC on May 9, 2001. In doing so, she obtained an injunction to halt the release of any future Nirvana projects until the case could be resolved.

Courtney claimed that she had signed the Nirvana LLC partnership agreement on bad advice and argued that Kurt Cobain *was* Nirvana—and that Krist and Dave were merely his sidemen. Novoselic and Grohl, who were understandably insulted, countersued on December 12, 2001. They claimed that Love had sanctioned the release of the boxed set in 1998, and that her change of heart had forced the corporation to breach its agreements with Geffen Records. In their suit, Krist and Dave asked the Superior Court of Washington for King County to supplant Love in the LLC with another member of Cobain's estate.

In an open letter to Nirvana fans released the day of the countersuit, Novoselic and Grohl explained how they believed Love's actions were less about "proper management and revitalization of Kurt's legacy" and more about "the revitalization of her career motivated solely by her blind self-interest," adding, "She couldn't care less about Nirvana fans." The letter claimed that Love was using Nirvana's music as a "bargaining chip" in her own lawsuit with Geffen, which she had filed in February 2001 over the terms of her recording contract with Hole. They claimed her actions were a means to increase publicity and attention for her "waning recording and acting career."

The following day, Love responded with her own statement, suggesting that the partnership had become unworkable, and that she wanted to make sure that future Nirvana releases were of the quality the fans deserve. "Krist and Dave have distorted the real issues with unwarranted and spurious personal attacks. Under United States law, Kurt's interests pass to his heirs who then have the responsibility for overseeing his interests."

In a letter signed "The Family of Kurt Cobain," Courtney closed by saying, "We wish Krist and Dave great success in their current careers and hope they will soon leave control of Kurt's legacy to his rightful heirs."

While Love and her handlers took the high road, matters behind the scenes had Novoselic and Grohl contending that she was too "incapacitated" to manage her end of the partnership. In the spring of 2002, she was asked by Krist and Dave's attorney to submit to a psychiatric examination, but Superior Court Judge Robert Alsdorf ruled against the request.

Settling for the Hits

On September 29, 2002, Novoselic and Grohl announced a settlement with Love over Nirvana's music and plans for *Nirvana*, the retrospective set released on November 12, 2002. "We are pleased that these issues have been resolved positively and we can move on," Krist, Dave, and Courtney said in a joint statement issued on the day that the case had been scheduled to go to trial in Seattle.

Love had first hinted to radio host Howard Stern a month prior that the members of Nirvana LLC had reached a settlement involving "lots and lots of money." Details of the settlement were not made public, although Love's attorney O. Yale Lewis told *Seattle Post-Intelligencer* pop music critic Gene Stout, "Basically, the parties have agreed to a new way of doing business, which should be beneficial to everyone."

The new agreement made provisions for Frances Bean Cobain in relation to the long-term management and preservation of her father's music, and paved the way for the *Nirvana* hits compilation Love had wanted, while finally allowing for the boxed set Krist and Dave had long hoped for to hit the market in 2004.

Journals

According to a January 2003 article by Chris Nelson in the *New York Times*, Riverhead Books, a division of Penguin Putnam, reportedly paid Courtney Love a $4 million advance for the material that appears in *Journals*. The book offers an extraordinary look at Kurt Cobain through his letters, drawings, lists, Nirvana-related observations, and personal confessions, reproducing actual-size pages from his notebooks.

The 280-page book collects material from twenty spiral-bound notebooks left by Kurt, with some entries dating back to his teenage years. It was published in hardcover in November 2002, retailing at $29.95, and was successful, debuting at #1 on the *New York Times* Best Seller list and selling out its initial print run of 360,500. A paperback edition followed a year later.

Journals opens with a letter that Cobain wrote to Dale Crover in 1988 and concludes with a rant about a Larry King interview with Sylvester Stallone that was penned on "Hotel Excelsior—Roma" notepaper in 1994. The bestseller was welcomed by many Nirvana fans who sought to learn more about Kurt and get a glimpse at his private writings. Others felt it was an invasion of his privacy, and that Love was wrong to exploit her deceased husband's innermost thoughts.

The book also includes drafts and unsent letters to Dave Foster, Tobi Vail, Eugene Kelly, Love, Jad Fair's stepson Simon Fair Timony, *MTV*, *Rolling Stone*, and the *Advocate*, plus Kurt's lists of his favorite bands and albums, an early draft of "Smells Like Teen Spirit," and unused liner notes for *In Utero*. There are also sketches of Iron Maiden's mascot "Eddie," a preliminary drawing of Nirvana's "Elvis Cooper" backdrop, and dark, violent illustrations—including one of a rooftop sniper shooting a Ku Klux Klan member.

Because of its dark content, a self-portrait/collage of Cobain featured on page 204 was banned from use in articles about or in reviews of *Journals*, according to a 2002 article by *Seattle Weekly* scribe Tim Appelo. Surrounded by the lyrics to the chorus of "Smells Like Teen Spirit," Kurt revealed his own skeletal frame and painful expression. Above his head were six lines he had cut and glued from the optimistic Alicia Ostriker poem, "A Young Woman, a Tree" and the handwritten word "Swingers." The artwork appeared to be a reflection of Cobain's belief that he had lost much of his creativity, and a presentation of just how conflicted he felt about his public and private images.

$50 Million for Courtney

On April 13, 2006, Courtney Love officially finalized a deal to sell 25 percent of her share of Nirvana's publishing rights to Primary Wave Music Publishing for more than $50 million. As the owner of her late husband's songwriting copyrights, Love had made it no secret that she had been seeking an investor "as a partner in the proper development and exploitation of the catalog," as her then-spokesperson Alan Nierob told MTV.com.

Primary Wave was founded by Larry Mestel, an executive at one of Love's former labels, Virgin Records. Through the deal, Love and Mestel had planned to create more awareness and value for the Nirvana catalogue. As a result of the deal, Primary Wave now held a greater percentage of Nirvana's rights than Krist Novoselic and Dave Grohl's shares combined.

Love was evidently in need of an influx of cash. The previous October, while undergoing a drug rehabilitation program following a widely publicized oxycontin overdose (which led to her losing custody of eleven-year-old Frances Bean, who was placed in the care of Cobain's mother, Wendy O'Connor), she had been hit with a lawsuit from the Seattle law firm that had helped her win control of the publishing rights to Nirvana's songs. Hendricks & Lewis claimed she owed more than $340,000 for their efforts, which included getting her a $4 million advance on *Nirvana* in 2002 and a similar sum for *Journals*.

In a statement announcing the Primary Wave deal—which would allow Love to settle those debts—Love promised fans that she would not misuse Nirvana's songs when licensing them. "We are going to remain very tasteful and true to the spirit of Nirvana while taking the music to places it has never been before," she said. But by 2012, the BMI catalog revealed that Larry Mestel now owned 100 percent of the administrative rights over Nirvan's music, meaning that only he and Primary Wave had the power to decide how Cobain's music could be used. This might explain how "Smells Like Teen Spirit" was used in the 2011 Disney movie *The Muppets*.

That year, an inside source told the *Washington Post* blog the Fix that Primary Wave had since acquired another 25 percent of Cobain's publishing rights. When asked for comment, Larry Mestel would neither confirm nor deny owning 50 percent of Kurt's publishing.

Kurt's Avatar

When an "unlocked" Kurt Cobain avatar appeared in the *Guitar Hero 5* video game in September 2009—allowing for the Nirvana guitarist to perform any song in the *Guitar Hero* catalogue—Dave Grohl and Krist Novoselic took aim at Activision, the game's manufacturer.

"We want people to know that we are dismayed and very disappointed in the way a facsimile of Kurt is used in the *Guitar Hero* game," Nirvana's rhythm section said in a press release issued on September 10 that year. "The name and likeness of Kurt Cobain are the sole property of his estate—we have no control whatsoever in that area."

Krist and Dave went on to acknowledge that they knew Cobain's image would be used alongside two Nirvana songs in the game, but they were unaware that players could "unlock" the character to perform other artists' music in the company of *Guitar Hero*'s other cartoon characters. In the statement, they urged

Activision to "do the right thing in 're-locking' Kurt's character so that this won't continue in the future."

Earlier the same day, Love had revealed that she was planning to sue Activision, announcing on Twitter: "wait to you see what MY lovely lawyer has cooked up. I never ever signed off on this . . . BTW we get NO money for this, travesty, Frances gets No money for the rape."

Activision responded in its own press release. "*Guitar Hero* secured the necessary licensing rights from the Cobain estate in a written agreement signed by Courtney Love to use Kurt Cobain's likeness as a fully playable character in *Guitar Hero 5*."

Through her lawyers, Love argued that the contract didn't allow for Activision to denigrate Cobain's image. While the legal outcome has never been revealed, it is an equally frightening and amusing sight to watch Kurt rapping Public Enemy's "Bring the Noise" in his Daniel Johnston T-shirt, or perform songs by Bush—a band that clearly aped Nirvana's sound—and Bon Jovi.

Control of Kurt's Name, Likeness, and Appearance

In December 2010, Frances Bean Cobain was given control of the right to her late father Kurt's estate in exchange for a loan of $2.75 million to her mother Courtney Love from her $75 million trust fund. Documents obtained in May 2012 by the Fix revealed that in exchange for the loan, Love agreed to step down as acting manager of End of Music LLC, the corporation that generates money from Cobain's publicity rights. Until Love pays the loan back, she will be unable to receive profits made from Kurt's name or likeness.

Frances had become estranged from Courtney in 2009, when she was granted a restraining order against her mother as a result of Love's drug addiction, violence, and the deaths of two pets, including a dog that passed away after swallowing a pile of pills. Love then lost control of her daughter's trust fund.

Posthumous Honors

Nirvana have reaped their fair share of posthumous acclaim, including being inducted into the UK Music Hall of Fame in 2004 as the "Greatest Artist of the 1990s" and being named among *Rolling Stone*'s "100 Greatest Artists of All Time" at #30 in 2011. *Nevermind*—which has sold 30 million copies worldwide since 1991—has been praised by the Rock and Roll Hall of Fame, which ranked it at #10 on a list of "The Definitive 200 Albums of All Time" in 2007, while *Rolling Stone* listed Nirvana's breakthrough album at #1 on its list of "The 100 Best Albums of the Nineties." "All Apologies" and "Smells Like Teen Spirit" appear on The Rock Hall's list of "The Songs That Shaped Rock and Roll." And on October 16, 2013, Nirvana were nominated for the Rock and Roll Hall of Fame in their first year of eligibility.

Parting Thoughts

"Nirvana were miles in front of the rest, and they kicked the door open again. It was some of the most incredible music I've heard in decades."

—Tom Petty

"I think [Kurt] had a connection to his audience that was very, very deep. His music is powerful, very intense. That kind of power is rare."

—Bruce Springsteen

"[Kurt] was an amazing guy. He was a complete gentleman. I still believe to this day that [Nirvana] are the best fucking band I've ever seen. And I miss the guy more than I could ever express."

—Mark Lanegan

"Remember Kurt for what he was: caring, generous, and sweet."

—Krist Novoselic

34

We Can Have Some More

Posthumous Releases

MTV Unplugged in New York

Released on November 1, 1994, *MTV Unplugged in New York* assembled the acoustic material recorded by Nirvana for broadcast a year earlier. As the group's first album release since Cobain's death, it was an immediate success, debuting at #1 on the *Billboard* 200. Selling 310,500 copies in its first week, it went on to earn RIAA certification for US sales in excess of five million.

The album was produced by Scott Litt, who had overseen the performance, and the idea to release it in the fourth quarter of 1994 came after Geffen initially announced a live double album, *Verse Chorus Verse*. But when that project seemed too much of a challenge for Grohl and Novoselic—who were still emotionally raw from the loss of their front man—to assemble, *Unplugged* took its place.

In advance of the album's release, "About a Girl" was released as a single in Australia and Europe that October. In the US, it was serviced as a radio single, and it wound up becoming Nirvana's fourth #1 on *Billboard*'s Modern Rock Tracks chart. Promotional singles for "The Man Who Sold the World," "Polly," "Lake of Fire," and "Where Did You Sleep Last Night" kept interest in the album high through 1995.

The album was praised by critics like *Entertainment Weekly*'s David Browne and

The cover of the guitar tablature book for the songs found on Nirvana's *MTV Unplugged in New York*, taped on November 18, 1993, and released on November 1 the following year.

Courtesy of eil.com

Released as a single on October 24, 1994, a week ahead of *MTV Unplugged in New York*, "About a Girl" (which appears here in its French Promotional Version) would go on to top *Billboard*'s Hot Modern Rock Tracks survey, and reach #29 on the US Top 40.   *Courtesy of eil.com*

the *Village Voice*'s Robert Christgau, who both gave it an A rating, and went on to earn a Grammy award for Best Alternative Music Album in 1996. *Rolling Stone* ranked it at #313 in its 2003 listing of "The 500 Greatest Albums of All Time."

A DVD of the classic MTV performance (chronicled elsewhere in this book) was released in 2007.

Live! Tonight!! Sold Out!!!

The idea for this long-form video originated with Cobain, who wanted to document his own band's ascent, but the project was not completed until after Kurt's death, when Grohl and Novoselic came together to finish it.

Released on VHS and laserdisc on November 15, 1994, *Live! Tonight!! Sold Out!!!* combines footage from live performances from 1991 onward—shot at shows in locations including London, Seattle, Honolulu, Osaka, and Rio de Janeiro—with home video dating back to late 1990. The high point is arguably Kurt's Morrissey-esque rendition of "Smells Like Teen Spirit" from *Top of the Pops.*

Rounded out with band interviews, the DVD reissue—which dropped on November 7, 2006—appends five extra tracks that were shot live in Amsterdam in November 1991. A hidden "Easter egg" bonus clip of "On a Plain" from early '91 is also included.

Singles

Released before Christmas 1995 for the European market, this boxed set collects all six of Nirvana's CD singles from their second and third studio albums: "Smells Like Teen Spirit," "Come as You Are," "In Bloom," "Lithium," "Heart-Shaped Box," and "All Apologies" / "Rape Me" plus their respective B-sides. The third *In Utero* single for "Pennyroyal Tea," deleted after Cobain's suicide, is not replicated here.

From the Muddy Banks of the Wishkah

Nirvana's long-awaited electric live album hit stores on October 1, 1996, and culled performances from concerts between 1989 and 1994. Compiled largely by Novoselic, who also wrote the liner notes, the disc debuted at #1 on the *Billboard* 200 and went on to sell more than one million copies in the United States. The album's title references the river that went under the Young Street Bridge near Cobain's childhood home.

Lorraine Ali praised the album in *Rolling Stone*, calling it the "emotional, visceral flip-side" of *Unplugged* in a four-and-a-half-star review. Her colleagues agreed it was one of 1996's better records, placing it

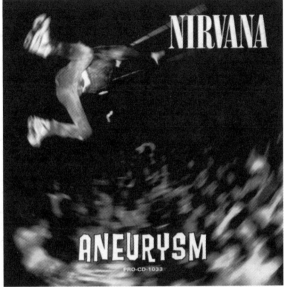

The sleeve of a rare promotional single serviced to select radio stations to promote Nirvana's 1996 live album *From the Muddy Banks of the Wishkah*. This version of "Aneurysm" was taped live by Westwood One at the Del Mar Fairgrounds on December 28, 1991.   *Courtesy of eil.com*

at #9 in the magazine's ranking of the year's ten best albums.

Nirvana

Released on October 29, 2002, this "best-of" compilation was the result of a settlement between Cobain's widow and Nirvana's surviving members. At the heart of the long-running legal dispute was the song "You Know You're Right," which was tracked in January 1994.

Novoselic and Grohl had hoped to release the song on a proposed rarities boxed set, but Love was against the idea and sued Cobain's one-time bandmates to block the song's release as part of that project. In Courtney's eyes, the song had hit potential, and she worried it would be lost among a multi-disc set of rarities. Instead, she pushed for a single CD hits compilation.

Eventually, Love won out, the suit was settled, and the single topped the charts at Modern Rock and Mainstream Rock radio, leading the album onto the charts, where it also debuted at #1.

With liner notes from *Rolling Stone* writer David Fricke, *Nirvana* debuted at #3 and sold 234,000 copies in its first week. It has since sold 7 million copies worldwide.

Krist Novoselic   Dave Grohl   Kurt Cobain

NIRVANA

S-U-B
P-O-P

GEFFEN RECORDS, INC.   ©2002 Geffen Records, Inc. Permission to reproduce limited to editorial uses in newspapers and other regularly published periodicals and television news programming.

A publicity photo used to promote *Nirvana*, the band's October 2002 compilation album, featuring the lost recording of "You Know You're Right," which topped *Billboard*'s Mainstream and Modern Rock Tracks charts that year.   *Author's collection*

With the Lights Out

Nirvana's long-awaited three-CD and DVD boxed set was finally issued on November 23, 2004. Comprised of rarities and unreleased material, the project includes B-sides, demos, live recordings, and rehearsal tapes. The project sold 105,760 copies in a single week and went on to sell one million copies, setting a record for sales of a boxed set.

Each of the three discs was designed to cover the period surrounding one of Nirvana's three studio albums, with the DVD featuring rare live footage. The accompanying sixty-page booklet contains liner notes by Sonic Youth's Thurston Moore and music journalist Neil Strauss.

The first disc goes back as far as Nirvana's first show, which is represented by the band's cover of Led Zeppelin's "Heartbreaker." Other early numbers are culled from its May 1987 KAOS radio session, band rehearsals, Cobain's solo four-track recordings from the era, and the group's January 1988 session with Jack Endino.

The second disc begins with Kurt's September 1990 solo performance on Calvin Johnson's KAOS radio show and then covers the Smart Studios sessions with Butch Vig before wrapping with material from the April 1992 Laundry Room sessions with Barrett Jones. The final CD includes boom-box demos of songs from *In Utero*, including "Rape Me"; a band version with Jack Endino of the same song; and an acoustic home demo of "You Know You're Right" from late 1993.

Sliver: The Best of the Box

Nearly a year after the boxed set was released, it was followed by this compilation of highlights. In order to lure in the Nirvana completists who had already picked up *With the Lights Out*, Geffen added three previously unreleased recordings: a 1985 demo of "Spank Thru" from Cobain's *Fecal Matter* cassette, a 1990 studio rendition of "Sappy," and a 1991 boom-box recording of "Come as You Are."

Compared with Nirvana's other posthumous releases, *Sliver* was a sales disappointment. Only 300,000 copies were sold in the United States, where it stalled at #19 on the *Billboard* 200.

Live at Reading

Issued on November 2, 2009, this live album and its companion DVD were culled from Nirvana's triumphant 1992 performance at England's Reading Festival. While the CD stalled at #37 on the *Billboard* 200, the DVD debuted at #1 on the same publication's Top Music Video listings.

The project received overwhelmingly positive reviews upon its release. Pitchfork.com rated it a 9.5 out of 10, *Spin* gave it four and half stars, and *Entertainment Weekly* gave it an A grade.

Bleach (20th Anniversary Deluxe Edition)

Sub Pop reissued Nirvana's debut on November 3, 2009, complete with a forty-eight-page booklet featuring never-before-seen photos and a previously unreleased, complete live audio performance of the group's gig at the Pine Street Theater in Portland on February 9, 1990. The bonus concert material was remixed by Jack Endino, who also oversaw the remastering of the entire set. Surprisingly, *Bleach*-era rarities—like the group's four-song John Peel session from 1990, the original seven-inch mix of "Love Buzz," and their contribution to the *Sub Pop 200* compilation—were left off of the reissue.

Icon

A second "greatest hits" compilation appeared in 2001 as part of Universal Music's Icon series. This eleven-track CD opens with "You Know You're Right" and includes the four singles from *Nevermind*, four of the most popular tracks from *In Utero*, and two acoustic numbers from *MTV Unplugged in New York*.

Nevermind (20th Anniversary Deluxe Edition)

Nirvana's best known album was expanded in two variations for a twentieth-anniversary reissue that dropped on September 27, 2011. Both versions feature the entire 1991 album and its respective studio and live B-sides on the first disc, with a second disc of early takes tracked with Butch Vig (and Chad Channing) at Smart Studios. They also include boom-box recordings of the material from band rehearsals and a pair of BBC sessions from the era. The *Super Deluxe* edition adds a disc of "Devonshire Mixes" by Vig of songs from the album, as well as the CD and DVD versions of *Live at the Paramount*.

Live at the Paramount

Issued in conjunction with the twentieth anniversary of *Nevermind*, and as a standalone product, this DVD and Blu-ray release, shot on 16-millimeter film, captures the band live in concert in Seattle on Halloween 1991.

In Utero (20th Anniversary Deluxe Edition)

Released in multiple editions, the twentieth-anniversary reissues of *In Utero* celebrates Nirvana's final song-cycle in proper fashion. Dusting off non-LP numbers like "I Hate Myself and Want to Die" and the Grohl-sung keeper "Marigold," the September 2013 edition of the album offers an updated mix overseen by producer Steve Albini at Abbey Road Studios. While the two-disc version offered plenty to most fans—including primitive demo instrumentals—obsessive collectors had the option of a straight CD remaster, a three-LP vinyl pressing, and a $149.98 three-CD box with more than seventy remastered, remixed, and rare recordings, plus a DVD of the complete *Live and Loud* show from December 13, 1993, at Seattle's Pier 48. The latter was also issued as a standalone home video offering.

35

Steamed Hot Towel on My Face

Twenty-One Random Nirvana Facts

Smells Like . . . Trivia!

A stound guests at your next flannel party with these twenty additional Nirvana-related facts.

1. Cobain always wrote "NIRVANA" in all capital letters.
2. When Kurt lived in Olympia, his phone number was (206) 352-0992.
3. In the "Smells Like Teen Spirit" video, Dave Grohl is wearing a Scream T-shirt.
4. Cobain and Grohl's mothers were introduced in New York in January 1992, before Nirvana's *Saturday Night Live* performance.
5. The liner notes of the "Lithium" CD single feature an ultrasound picture of Frances Bean.
6. The initial storyboard for the "Lithium" video was for a cartoon about a girl named "Prego."
7. The first time Kurt and Courtney Love slept together, she was mortified to discover that he wore zebra-print briefs. She told him if she wanted to continue sleeping with her, he needed to start wearing boxers. Kurt complied.
8. Kurt and Krist voted for Bill Clinton in the 1992 presidential election.
9. The woman on the cover of *In Utero* is actually Frances Bean's nanny/Cobain's personal assistant, Michael "Cali" DeWitt, dressed in drag.
10. At the time Pat Smear was hired as Nirvana's second guitarist, he was working at SST Records' retail store in Los Angeles.
11. During the filming of Nirvana's *MTV Unplugged*, Smear performed without shoes.
12. In December 1993, Kurt revealed he smoked Benson & Hedges Deluxe Ultra Light Menthols. By the time of his death, however, he was smoking Camel Lights.
13. In the music video for Hole's "Doll Parts," guitarist Eric Erlandson plays one of Kurt's guitars.

14. In R.E.M.'s 1994 tribute to Cobain, "Let Me In," the band utilizes one of his Jag-Stang guitars. The instrument is also seen in the video for one of the band's singles from the same era, "What's the Frequency Kenneth?"

15. "Love Buzz" can be heard in the opening scene of the 1995 Drew Barrymore movie *Mad Love*.

16. In August 2005, two of Cobain's early drawings sold for $14,400 and $8,400 respectively. The first was a cartoonish pencil sketch of Ronald Reagan done during a high school art class that belonged to his sister Kim. The second was a Christmas card he drew for his grandparents, Leland and Iris, when he was only six years old.

17. Because Cobain has no grave, a park bench in Viretta Park adjacent to his former home has become the de facto gathering place for fans. Kurt actually sat on these park benches from time to time.

18. Novoselic plays bass on a cover of "Sliver" featured on the 2010 album *This Is Fun!* by children's performer Caspar Babypants, a.k.a. Chris Ballew of the Presidents of the United States of America.

19. On July 19, 2013, the surviving members of Nirvana—Grohl, Novoselic, and Smear—performed together at Seattle's Safeco Field with rock pioneer and founding Beatle Paul McCartney. When Sir Paul proposed the idea to Dave a few weeks earlier, Grohl called Krist and Pat, and they joined him onstage for Beatles classics like "Get Back," "Helter Skelter," and "The End." The four musicians had first joined forces on an original song, "Cut Me Some Slack," which they recorded for Grohl's 2012 *Sound City* documentary. McCartney had first performed the song with Nirvana's surviving members at the "12.12.12" Hurricane Sandy Relief Concert at Madison Square Garden seven months earlier.

20. In December 2013, Cobain, Novoselic, and Grohl were nominated for a 2014 Best Rap Song Grammy as songwriters on Jay Z's "Holy Grail." The rap superstar had sampled parts of "Smells Like Teen Spirit." Simultaneously, Novoselic, Grohl, and Pat Smear also earned a nomination alongside Paul McCartney for the aforementioned "Cut Me Some Slack."

21. As *Nirvana FAQ* was being finalized, Nirvana's induction into the Rock and Roll Hall of Fame was announced on December 16, 2013. Not long after, Hoquiam—the Washington town where Cobain lived as an infant—announced it would devote an official day to Kurt. April 10, 2014, would be declared "Nirvana Day" to celebrate the band's induction into the Rock and Roll Hall of Fame on that same day. "They bring great honor, I think as I say, to our entire community. And I think that it's good Kurt Cobain lived in Hoquiam for a little while, but he and Krist Novoselic are part of our community, and I think it's good to honor our sons and their great accomplishments," Hoquiam mayor Jack Dunrey told local radio station KXRO. At the time of this writing, Nirvana, nominated at the first opportunity twenty-five years after their first recording was released, are slated to be inaugurated in tandem with Kiss, Peter Gabriel, and Cat Stevens in a planned ceremony at Brooklyn's Barclays Center.

Selected Bibliography

Books

Azerrad, Michael. *Come as You Are: The Story of Nirvana*. Three Rivers Press, 1993.

Branigan, Paul. *This is a Call: The Life and Times of Dave Grohl*. Da Capo Press, 2011.

Cobain, Kurt. *Journals*. Riverhead Trade, 2003.

Cross, Charles R. *Cobain Unseen*. Little, Brown and Company, 2008.

Cross, Charles R. *Heavier Than Heaven: A Biography of Kurt Cobain*. Hyperion, 2002.

Editors of Rolling Stone. *Cobain*. Rolling Stone Press, Little, Brown and Company, 1997.

Gaar, Gillian, G. *Nirvana's In Utero*. Continuum, September 1, 2006.

Gaar, Gillian, G. *Treasures of Nirvana*. Sterling, 2011.

Heatly, Michael. *Dave Grohl: Nothing Left to Lose*. Titan Books, 2011.

Hughes, John, and Novoselic, Krist. *Of Grunge & Grange: An Oral History eBook*. Washington State Legacy Project, 2009.

Novoselic, Krist. *Of Grunge & Government: Let's Fix This Broken Democracy!* RDV Books, 2004.

Sandford, Christopher. *Kurt Cobain*. Orion Paperbacks, 1995.

True, Everett. *Nirvana: The True Story*. Omnibus Press, 2009.

True, Everett. *Nirvana: The Biography*. Da Capo Press, 2007.

Websites

Nirvana.com
Nirvanaclub.com
Nirvanaguide.com
Nirvanamusic.com
LiveNirvana.com
SubPop.com

Periodicals

Al (The Big Cheese). "Flipside: Nirvana," *Flipside*, June 1989.

Al and Cake. "Just Like Heaven: An interview with . . . Kurt Cobain," *Flipside*, May/June 1992.

Allman, Kevin. "Nirvana's front man shoots from the hip," the *Advocate*, February 1993.

Anderson, Dawn. "It may be the Devil and it may be the Lord . . . But it sure as hell ain't human," *Backlash*, September 1988.

Anderson, Dawn. "Signing on the Dotted Line and Other Tales of Terror," *Backlash*, March 1991.

Appelo, Tim. "Memories of Nirvana . . ." *Hollywood Reporter*, September 23, 2011.

Appelo, Tim. "The Nerve," *Entertainment Weekly*, December 4, 1992.

Arnold, Gina. "Spontaneous Combustion: Better Dead Than Cool," *Option*, Jan/Feb 1992.

Azerrad, Michael. "Inside the Heart and Mind of Nirvana," *Rolling Stone*, April 16, 1992.

Azerrad, Michael. "Nirvana: New Noise for '93," *Rolling Stone*, January 7, 1993.

Azerrad, Michael, "Kurt Cobain: The Rolling Stone Interview," *Rolling Stone*, October 25, 1993.

Bernstein, Nils. "Berlin Is Just a State of Mind," the *Rocket*, December 1989.

Bliss, Karen. "Metal on the Rise," *M.E.A.T.*, September 1991.

Boddy, Jennie, "Nirvana Bio," Sub Pop Records, Fall 1989.

Cameron, Keith "Nirvana," *Sounds*, October 1990.

Cameron, Keith. "Nirvana, Be in My Gang?" *NME*, August, 1991.

Cameron, Keith. "Love Will Tear Us Apart," *New Musical Express*, August 29, 1992.

Chapel, Jon. "Guitar in the '90s," *Guitar*, June 1993.

Chirazi, Steffen. "Smells Like . . . Bullshit," *Kerrang!*, February 8, 1992.

Chirazi, Steffen. "Nirvana: The Year of Living Famously," *RIP*, June 1992.

Chirazi, Steffan. "Lounge Act," *Kerrang!*, November 29, 1993.

Corr Cronin LLP. "The Legacy of the Music of Nirvana at Stake in Washington Court Case: Musicians Grohl and Novoselic Answer Courtney Love's Claims in December 12 Filing," Presspass press release, December 12, 2001.

Crazy Chris. "Interview with Nirvana," *Rockview*, August 22, 1991.

Cross, Charles R. "A Heart Shaped Box" the *Rocket*, April 27, 1994.

Crotty, James, "Go for the Grunge," *Monk Magazine*, October 1992.

Darzin, Daina. "Wearing a Dress to Headbanger's Ball," *Village Voice*, November 26, 1991.

di Perna, Alan. "The Making of *Nevermind*" *Guitar World*, Fall 1996.

Edwards, Gavin. "Just Like Heaven/Nirvana Adjust to the Smell of Success," *Details*, February 1992.

Filson, Anne, and Begley, Laura. "Radio Interview with Kurdt Kobain," 91.9 WOZQ-FM, Hampshire College, April 27, 1990.

Fricke, David. "Krist Novoselic," *Rolling Stone*, September 13, 2001.

Fricke, David. "Kurt Cobain," *Rolling Stone*, January 27, 1994.

Gaar, Gillian G. "Verse Chorus Verse: The Recording History of Nirvana," *Goldmine*, February 14, 1997.

Gardner, Elysa. "Grunge Redux," *USA Today*, September 1993.

Gehman, Pleasant. "Artist of the Year: Nirvana," *Spin*, December 1992.

Gehman, Pleasane. "Womb! There it is." *RIP*, February, 1994.

Giles, Jeff. "The Poet of Alienation," *Newsweek*, April 18, 1994.

Gitter, Mike. "Revenge of the Nerds," *Kerrang!*, August 24, 1991.

Goodman, Fred. "Nirvana to 'Newsweek': Drop Dead," *Rolling Stone*, June 24, 1993.

Greenblatt, Leah, "Kurt Cobain in 'Guitar Hero 5': Former Nirvana Bandmates Are 'Dismayed and Very Disappointed," EntertainmentWeekly.com, September 10, 2009.

Handy, Bruce. "Never Mind," *Time*, April 18, 1994.

Hedges, Dan. "Nirvana Smells Life At The Top," *Circus*, May 31, 1992.

Hilburn, Robert. "Cobain to Fans: Just Say No; Nirvana's New Father Addresses Drug Use," *Los Angeles Times*, September 21, 1992.

Hilburn, Robert. "Nirvana's Kurt Cobain Swaps Alienation for Optimism," *Atlanta Journal*, September 19, 1993.

Hirschberg, Lynn. "Strange Love," *Vanity Fair*, September 1992.

Hobbs, Mary Anne. "'Vana Be Adored," *NME*, November 23, 1991.

Kanter, L.A. "Kurt Cobain's Well-Tempered Tantrums," *Guitar Player*, February 1992.

Kelly, Carmella, "Courtney Love Loses Rights to Kurt's Image," TheFix.com, May 2, 2012

Kelly, Christina. "Kurt and Courtney Sitting in a Tree," *Sassy*, April 1992.

Kot, Greg. "It's the Jesus and Nirvana Chain!" *Rolling Stone*, April 1, 1993.

Marcus, Greil. "Kurt Cobain: Artist of the Decade," *Rolling Stone*, May 1999.

Matheson, Whitney. "Making *Nevermind*," *USA Today*, September 27, 2011.

McCulley, Jerry. "Nirvana's Impact," *BAM*, January 19, 1992.

Morris, Chris. "The Year's Hottest New Band Can't Stand Still," *Musician*, January 1992.

Mothersole, Ben. "Nirvana's Kurt Cobain: Getting to Know *Utero*," *Circus*, November 30, 1993.

Mundy, Chris. "NIRVANA," *Rolling Stone*, January 23, 1992.

Mundy, Chris. "Random Notes, Nirvana at the VMAs," *Rolling Stone*, October 29, 1992.

Nelson, Chris. "Nine Years After Kurt Cobain's Death, Big Sales for All Things Nirvana, *New York Times*, January 13, 2003.

Overton, Frank. "Nirvana: Mind Over Matter," *Hit Parader*, May 1992.

Pareles, Jon. "Nirvana. The Band That Hates to Be Loved," *New York Times*, November 14, 1993.

Poneman, Jonathon. "Family Values," *Spin*, January 1992.

Pouncey, Edwin. "Bleach Review," *NME*, July 8, 1989.

Price, David J. "Nirvana's *Bleach* Turns 20, New Live Recording Coming," *Billboard*, August 4, 2009.

Punter, Jennie. "In Womb," *Impact*, October 1993.

Push. "Heaven Can't Wait," *Melody Maker*, December 15, 1990.

Robb, John. "White Heat," *Sounds*, October 21, 1989.

Roshan, Maer. "Inside the Mind of Courtney Love," TheFix.com, February 1, 2012

Savage, Jon. "A Lengthy Kurt Cobain Interview," *Howl*, July 22, 1993.

Savage, Jon. "The Lost Interview with Kurt Cobain," *Guitar World*, October 1993.

Scanlon, Ann. "Heaven Can Wait," *Melody Maker*, September 14, 1991.

Spencer, Jim, "Nirvana Makin' Their Own Rules," *Hit Parader*, March 1994.

Steinke, Darcy. "Smashing Their Heads on the Punk Rock," *Spin*, October, 1993.

Stout, Gene. "Courtney Love, former members of Nirvana settle suit," *Seattle Post-Intelligencer*, September 30, 2002.

Sutcliffe, Phil. "King of Pain," *Q*, October 1993.

Thompson, Dave. "The Boys Are Back in Town," *Alternative Press*, October 1993.

True, Everett. "All Dressed Up," *Melody Maker*, December 12, 1992.

True, Everett. "Crucified by Success," *Melody Maker*, July 25, 1992.

True, Everett. "Dark Side of the Womb: Parts 1 and 2," *Melody Maker*, August 21–28, 1993

True, Everett. "In My Head, I'm So Ugly," *Melody Maker*, July 18, 1992.

True, Everett. "Interview with Kurt Cobain," *Melody Maker*, April 9, 1993.

True, Everett. "Kurt Cobain of Nirvana talks about the records that changed his life," *Melody Maker*, March 18, 1989.

True, Everett. "Rebellious Jukebox," *Melody Maker*, August 29, 1992.

True, Everett. "Latest Wizards from Sub Pop," *Melody Maker*, October 21, 1989.

True, Everett. "Pine Street Theatre—Portland," *Melody Maker*, March 3, 1990.

True, Everett. "Station to Devastation," *Melody Maker*, November 2, 1991.

True, Everett. "TAD and Nirvana: The Larder They Come," *Melody Maker*, March 17, 1990.

True, Everett. "Kurt: 'The Biggest Fuck You Of My Life,'" *Melody Maker*, January 30, 1993.

Turman, Katherine. "Smells Like . . . Nirvana," *RIP*, February 1992.

Unknown author. Sub Pop Records, Nirvana Artist Bio, spring 1989.

Unknown author. "Bleach Bums," uncredited interview from June 1991, Nirvanaclub.com

Unknown author. "Nirvana Achieves Chart Perfection!" *Billboard*, January 25, 1992.

Unknown author. "Kurt OD In Belfast," *Melody Maker*, July 4, 1992.

Unknown author. "Here We Are Now . . . Entertain Us!" *Kerrang!*, August 7, 1993.

Unknown author. "One of the last interviews Kurt Cobain did: The Fender Frontline Interview," *Fender Frontline Magazine*, fall 1994.

Vig, Butch. "Mix It Raw," *EQ*, April 1992.

Vineyard, Jennifer. "Courtney Love Sued by Law Firm That Helped Her Win Rights to Cobain Material," MTV.com, October 26, 2005.

Vineyard, Jennifer. "Courtney Love Sells Substantial Share of Nirvana Publishing Rights," MTV.com, April 13, 2006.

Wallace, Ray. "Here We Are Now, Entertain Us—Interview from 1990," *Peace*, April 1992.

Walls, Seth Colter. "The *Nevermind* You've Never Heard," *Slate*, September 27, 2011.

West, Phil. "Hair Swinging Neanderthals," the *Daily* (University of Washington), May 5, 1989.

Wice, Nathaniel. "How Nirvana Made It," *Spin*, April 1993.

Williams, Carl. "America's Latest Import: Nirvana," *Metal Forces*, January 1990.

Willis, Brian. "Domicile on Cobain St.," *NME*, July 24, 1993.

Young, Charles, and O'Donnell, Kevin. "Nirvana: Album Guide," *Rolling Stone*, April 11, 2010.

Index

THE FAQ SERIES

Armageddon Films FAQ
by Dale Sherman
Applause Books
978-1-61713-119-6.........$24.99

Lucille Ball FAQ
*by James Sheridan
and Barry Monush*
Applause Books
978-1-61774-082-4......$19.99

The Beach Boys FAQ
by Jon Stebbins
Backbeat Books
978-0-87930-987-9...$19.99

Black Sabbath FAQ
by Martin Popoff
Backbeat Books
978-0-87930-957-2....$19.99

James Bond FAQ
by Tom DeMichael
Applause Books
978-1-55783-856-8....$22.99

Jimmy Buffett FAQ
by Jackson Quigley
Backbeat Books
978-1-61713-455-5.......$24.99

Eric Clapton FAQ
by David Bowling
Backbeat Books
978-1-61713-454-8......$22.99

Doctor Who FAQ
by Dave Thompson
Applause Books
978-1-55783-854-4....$22.99

The Doors FAQ
by Rich Weidman
Backbeat Books
978-1-61713-017-5.........$19.99

Fab Four FAQ
*by Stuart Shea and
Robert Rodriguez*
Hal Leonard Books
978-1-4234-2138-2.......$19.99

Fab Four FAQ 2.0
by Robert Rodriguez
Hal Leonard Books
978-0-87930-968-8..$19.99

Film Noir FAQ
by David J. Hogan
Applause Books
978-1-55783-855-1......$22.99

Grateful Dead FAQ
by Tony Sclafani
Backbeat Books
978-1-61713-086-1.......$24.99

Jimi Hendrix FAQ
by Gary J. Jucha
Backbeat Books
978-1-61713-095-3......$22.99

Horror Films FAQ
by John Kenneth Muir
Applause Books
978-1-55783-950-3....$22.99

Stephen King Films FAQ
by Scott Von Doviak
Applause Books
978-1-4803-5551-4.....$24.99

KISS FAQ
by Dale Sherman
Backbeat Books
978-1-61713-091-5.......$22.99

Led Zeppelin FAQ
by George Case
Backbeat Books
978-1-61713-025-0.......$19.99

Nirvana FAQ
by John D. Luerssen
Backbeat Books
978-1-61713-450-0.....$24.99

Pink Floyd FAQ
by Stuart Shea
Backbeat Books
978-0-87930-950-3..$19.99

Elvis Films FAQ
by Paul Simpson
Applause Books
978-1-55783-858-2.....$24.99

Elvis Music FAQ
by Mike Eder
Backbeat Books
978-1-61713-049-6.....$24.99

Rush FAQ
by Max Mobley
Backbeat Books
978-1-61713-451-7........$24.99

Saturday Night Live FAQ
by Stephen Tropiano
Applause Books
978-1-55783-951-0.....$24.99

Sherlock Holmes FAQ
by Dave Thompson
Applause Books
978-1-4803-3149-5.....$24.99

Bruce Springsteen FAQ
by John D. Luerssen
Backbeat Books
978-1-61713-093-9......$22.99

Star Trek FAQ
(Unofficial and Unauthorized)
by Mark Clark
Applause Books
978-1-55783-792-9......$19.99

Star Trek FAQ 2.0
(Unofficial and Unauthorized)
by Mark Clark
Applause Books
978-1-55783-793-6.....$22.99

Three Stooges FAQ
by David J. Hogan
Applause Books
978-1-55783-788-2......$19.99

U2 FAQ
by John D. Luerssen
Backbeat Books
978-0-87930-997-8...$19.99

The Who FAQ
by Mike Segretto
Backbeat Books
978-1-4803-6103-4....$24.99

Neil Young FAQ
by Glen Boyd
Backbeat Books
978-1-61713-037-3........$19.99

Prices, contents, and availability
subject to change without notice.

FAQ.halleonardbooks.com